# What is
# Medieval History?

# What is History?

Peter Burke, *What is Cultural History?*
John C. Burnham, *What is Medical History?*
Stephen Morillo & Michael Pavkovic, *What is Military History?*
J. Donald Hughes, *What is Environmental History?*
Pamela Kyle Crossley, *What is Global History?*

# What is
# Medieval History?

JOHN H. ARNOLD

polity

First published in 2008 by Polity Press
Reprinted 2009

Polity Press
65 Bridge Street
Cambridge CB2 1UR, UK

Polity Press
350 Main Street
Malden, MA 02148, USA

ISBN-13: 978-07456-3932-1
ISBN-13: 978-07456-3933-8 (pb)

A catalogue record for this book is available from the British Library.

Typeset in 10.5 on 12 pt Sabon
by SNP Best-set Typesetter Ltd., Hong Kong
Printed and bound in Great Britain
by the MPG Books Group

For further information on Polity, visit our website: www.polity.co.uk

# Contents

List of Illustrations                                    vii

Preface and Acknowledgements                            viii

1  *Framing the Middle Ages*                               1
   A Medieval Tale                                         1
   Medievalisms and Historiographies                       8
   The Politics of Framing                                16

2  *Tracing the Middle Ages*                              23
   Polyphony or Cacophony?                                23
   Editions and Archives                                  26
   Using Documents                                        30
   Chronicles                                             36
   Charters                                               40
   Images                                                 46
   Legal Records                                          51

3  *Reading the Middle Ages*                              57
   Anthropology                                           58
   Numbers and Statistics                                 65
   Archaeology and Material Culture                       72
   Texts and Cultural Theory                              79

4 *Debating the Middle Ages*                    86
    Ritual                                      88
    Social Structures                           95
    Cultural Identities                        104
    Power                                      109

5 *Making and Remaking the Middle Ages*        119

Notes                                          128

Further Reading                                143

Index                                          148

# Illustrations

Map of Europe, *c*.900                                          x
Map of Europe, *c*.1360                                         xii

Figure 2.1
(a)  Early medieval handwriting, from a late
     eighth-century manuscript of biblical extracts            32
(b)  High medieval handwriting, from a
     twelfth-century manuscript of canon law                   32
(c)  Late medieval handwriting, from a
     mid-fourteenth century manor court roll                   33

Figure 2.2   Les Très Riches Heures du Duc de
Berry, month of February                                       49

# Preface and Acknowledgements

This is a book about what historians of the middle ages do, rather than a history of the middle ages itself, though it will also provide a sense of that period. Each chapter focuses on a different aspect of the historian's task, and the conditions of its possibility: chapter 1 discusses the idea of 'the middle ages' and its associations, and the foundational contours of academic medievalism. Chapter 2 looks at sources, the possibilities and problems that they present to the historian. Chapter 3 examines intellectual tools which medievalists have borrowed from other subject areas, and the insights they provide. Chapter 4 tries to indicate the shape of some key and broad-ranging discussions in current historiography. The final chapter addresses the very purpose of medieval history – its present and potential roles, in academic debate and society more broadly. The book is written neither as a blankly 'objective' report on the field, nor as a polemical call to arms, but as an engaged survey which seeks to both explain and comment upon the wider discipline. In what follows, I assume some knowledge of, and interest in, history on the reader's part, but little prior sense of the medieval period (roughly the years 500–1500). Rather than always listing particular centuries, I have sometimes made use of the loose division of the medieval period into 'early', 'high' and 'late'. All that is meant by this is c.500–c.1050, c.1050–c.1300 and c.1300–c.1500. My coverage tends towards western Europe, but I have tried to indicate the greater breadth of medievalism that exists beyond; to do more would take a much bigger book.

I am indebted to various people in my attempt to chart, in so few pages, so large an area. Rob Bartlett, Mark Ormrod and Richard Kieckhefer all kindly answered particular queries at key moments. Rob Liddiard and Caroline Goodson helped me understand aspects of archaeology, Sophie Page did similarly with regard to magic and David Wells assisted my grasp of Wolfram von Eschenbach. Major thanks are due to those who very generously read and commented on individual chapters or indeed the whole book: two anonymous readers for Polity, Cordelia Beattie, Caroline Goodson, Victoria Howell, Matt Innes, Geoff Koziol and Christian Liddy; Matt and Geoff also kindly shared unpublished material with me. Any errors are entirely my own fault. Thanks are owed also to Andrea Drugan at Polity, for prompting me to write the book and for being an understanding editor during the process. As ever, I am grateful to Victoria and Zoë for giving me the support and the space in which to write.

Lastly, this book is dedicated to all those who have taught me how to teach, from my parents, Henry and Hazel Arnold, to my students past and present.

Map of Europe, c.900

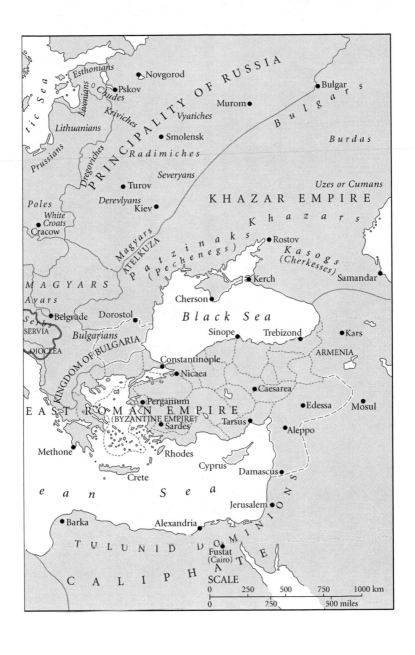

Baltic Sea
Esthonians
Novgorod
Chudes
Livonians
Pskov
Krichives
Vyatiches
Murom
PRINCIPALITY OF RUSSIA
Bulgar
B u l g a r s
Lithuanians
Smolensk
B u r d a s
Prussians
Dregovitches
Radimiches
Severyans
Turov
Magyars
ATELKUZA
Derevlyans
Kiev
KHAZAR EMPIRE
Uzes or Cumans
K h a z a r s
Poles
White Croats
Cracow
P a t z i n a k s
(P e c h e n e g s)
Rostov
K a s o g s
(Cherkesses)
M A G Y A R S
Kerch
Samandar
A v a r s
Cherson
B l a c k   S e a
Serb.
Belgrade
Dorostol
SERVIA
Sinope
Trebizond
Kars
Bulgarians
KINGDOM OF BULGARIA
ARMENIA
DIOCLEA
Constantinople
Caesarea
E A S T   R O M A N   E M P I R E
(BYZANTINE EMPIRE)
Nicaea
Pergamum
Edessa
Mosul
Sardes
Tarsus
Aleppo
Methone
Rhodes
Cyprus
Damascus
Crete
e a n   S e a
Jerusalem
Barka
Alexandria
T U L U N I D   D O M I N I O N S
Fustat
(Cairo)
C A L I P H A T E

SCALE
0        250       500       750      1000 km
0                  250              500 miles

Map of Europe, *c.*1360

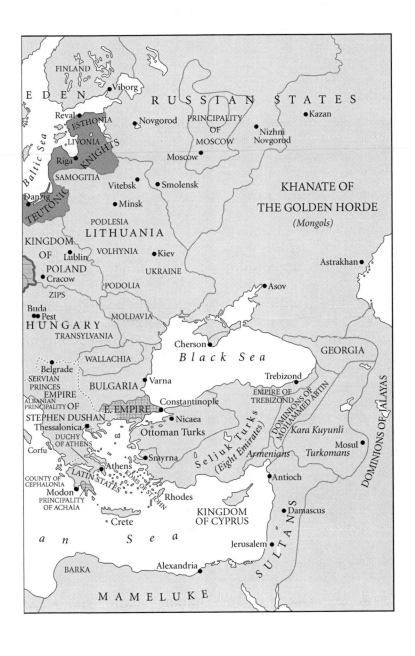

# 1
# Framing the Middle Ages

## A Medieval Tale

The first time Bartolomeo the priest talked to them was on 9 February 1320, in the papal palace at Avignon, and his interrogation probably took up most of one day. A notary, Gerard, wrote down his words; thus they survive for us today. Three very powerful men – a cardinal, an abbot from Toulouse, and the pope's legate for northern Italy – questioned, listened and re-questioned.

Matters had begun, Bartolomeo explained, the previous year, in October. A letter had arrived from Matteo Visconti, duke of Milan, summoning the priest to his presence. And so Bartolomeo had obeyed.

He met with the Visconti conspirators (he explained to his interrogators) in a room in Matteo's palace. Scoto de San Gemignano, a judge, was there, as was a physician, Antonio Pelacane. Initially Matteo drew him to one side. He told the priest that 'he wished to do Bartolomeo a great service, benefit and honour, and that he wished that Bartolomeo would do Matteo a great service, indeed the greatest, namely the greatest that anyone living could do for him; and Matteo added that he knew for certain that Bartolomeo knew well how to do the aforesaid service of which Matteo was thinking.' He would do whatever he could, Bartolomeo protested.

Immediately Matteo called to Scoto, the judge, telling him to show Bartolomeo what he had with him. 'Then the said lord Scoto drew out from his robe and held out and showed to Bartholomeo and Matteo a certain silver image, longer than the palm of a hand, in the figure of a man: members, head, face, arms, hands, belly, thighs, legs, feet and natural organs.' Written on the front of the statue were these words: *Jacobus papa Johannes*. The present pope, John XXII, had been called Jacques d'Euze before taking the pontifical title.

This was not the only thing written on the image. There was a sign, like a reversed 'N', and a name: *Amaymo*. The name of a demon.

'Bartolomeo, behold this image,' said Matteo, 'which I have made to bring destruction to the pope who persecutes me.' What Matteo wanted of Bartolomeo was for the priest to help finish the magical object, by suffusing the image with incense from *zuccum de mapello* ('What is *zuccum de mapello?*' asked Bartolomeo's interrogators in Avignon, some months later. A kind of poison, he explained. But, he emphasized, he did not want to go along with Matteo's plan).[1]

Bartolomeo told Matteo that he had no *zuccum de mapello*, and was unable to help. He then left, threatened by the duke to keep silent. But some time later Scoto came to see him, to ask his advice on the details of some books of sorcery. Prompted by Bartolomeo, Scoto again showed him the statue. It had been finished by a different sorceror from Verona, and was inscribed with a new word, *Meruyn*. All that now need happen, Scoto explained, was to hang the statue up for seventy-two nights, placing it night after night in a fire. As, little by little, the fire consumed the image, so would its target, little by little, be destroyed.

And that was all he knew, Bartolomeo explained to the cardinal, the abbot, the legate and the scribe. He had come to Avignon to warn Pope John XXII that his life was in danger.

But that was not the end of it, because some months later, on 11 September 1320, Bartolomeo was once again before this gathering of interrogators, explaining what had happened to him in the intervening period. When he had returned to Milan the previous March, he said, he had immediately been arrested and brought before Scoto. The Milanese knew that he had been to Avignon, and suspected that he had revealed the plot concerning the statue. He was imprisoned, in chains, for weeks. Scoto came to interrogate him many times. Bartolomeo told him that he'd gone to Avignon to treat a sick man, a knight who was under a magical curse. Scoto did not believe him. Matteo was very angry with him, Scoto explained; it would be better to confess now. 'Come, Bartolomeo, tell the truth, why you went to the Curia', Scoto said one time. 'Because you know absolutely that in the end it will happen that you tell the truth; and if you will not speak courteously, you will end up speaking under torture. Although I want you to know that I do not want to place you in torment, however in the end it will have to be, that you are tortured, unless you spontaneously wish to say the truth.' Bartolomeo stuck with his story.

And he was tortured. Stripped, his hands tied behind him to a stick, a heavy stone was placed on his legs, whilst Scoto's assistants yanked his arms back. They pulled him up, then released him, pulled him up, then released him. He was then untied, and led back to his cell. Look, said Scoto, we can do this to you every night. Every night until you die. Just confess.

But Bartolomeo did not confess. What saved him eventually was the intervention of another powerful northern duke, Galeazzo Visconti, Matteo's son. Galeazzo had him freed, apologized for what had happened, hoped that he was all right. But Galeazzo was also in on the plot, and inveigled Bartolomeo into helping once again: the statue must be freshly suffused, and Bartolomeo was the man to do it – by implication, a proof of Bartolomeo's loyalties. And by implication, prison, torture and death the alternative. Let me think about it, Bartolomeo pleads. Very well, says Galeazzo; but 'you should know that I have had Master Dante Alighieri come to me regarding this matter that I'm asking of you.' Good, says Bartolomeo: I would be very pleased if he did what you are asking. But no: Galeazzo really doesn't want to ask Dante to do it – because he knows that Bartolomeo can do it, *will* do it.

Two days later Bartolomeo agreed, set about finding more *zuccum de mapello*, and retrieved the statue from Galeazzo. He returned with it to his home town – and then he fled to Avignon once more.

And where is the statue?, asked his interrogators. I brought it with me, Bartolomeo replied. He produced a bundle tied with twine, unwrapped it, and drew out a silver figure in the shape of a man. And it was just exactly as he had described it, as the interrogators attested for the written record.[2]

There the story ends, Bartolomeo's story at any rate. The struggles between John XXII and the Visconti continued for some time, and other witnesses raised against them describe their impiety, their heresy, their usury and other crimes. The pope believed himself subject to further magical attacks, and encouraged inquisitors to be on the lookout for sorcery. The Visconti themselves survived as a family for a long time, ruling Milan late into the fifteenth century without break. But of Bartolomeo the priest we know nothing more.

At first sight this is what one might call a very medieval tale. It involves tyrants, a pope, intrigue, torture, and magical practices of a kind now usually described as 'superstitious'. We may have a fairly vivid mental image of some of the more lurid parts of the story, not least because this kind of middle ages has inspired (directly or indirectly) various aspects of modern culture. Film, television, novels and comics have pictured a dark, grubby, bloody middle ages: *The Name of the Rose*, *The Navigator*, *Braveheart* or the various films entitled *Joan of Arc* for example. There is a similar template for future barbarism: *Mad Max*, *Robocop*, *Waterworld* and others all bear the imprint of a certain kind of medievalism. 'I'm gonna get medieval on yo' ass,' as Marcellus Wallace threatens his erstwhile torturers in *Pulp Fiction*. So, in one sense, Bartolomeo's experiences are familiar.

But there is more here than immediately meets the eye. Matteo Visconti's plot against the pope may look typically 'medieval', but it contains elements that, on reflection, may surprise us. And it sits at an intersection of themes, lives, geographies and forces that are far more complex – and interesting – than those stereotyped depictions, which Umberto Eco once called 'the shaggy middle ages', would suggest.[3] Take magic. Everyone 'knows' that the middle ages was a superstitious age, full of witches, demons, spells, and the suppression of the same by the Inquisition. But the magic in this story is located not where we might expect to find it: not in the simple hut stuck at the end of the village, inhabited by a poor widow and her cat, but in learned Latin books, read and owned by clerics, right at the heart of the city and intellectual culture. This was not in fact unusual: whilst there were healers and soothsayers found in rural medieval parishes, the kind of magic described here was very much a *clerical* subculture, available only to those with Latin education. The roots of this magic were not 'pagan' in the sense of pre-Christian primitivism, nor was it, within medieval terms, a set of irrational ideas. Learned magic derived in part from classical scholarship, in part from ideas about hidden ('occult') natural forces, and in part from a long tradition of Christian theology, that saw demons as constantly present – and, in certain circumstances, harnessable to good or bad ends. Learned magic and science were intimately connected, and would continue to be for several centuries to come.

Nor were ecclesiastical attitudes to this magic always quite what one might expect. The Inquisition did not automatically pursue its practitioners, not least because there was no such thing as the 'Inquisition' in the sense of a permanent and central tribunal until the mid-sixteenth century (with the exception of Spain, where the Spanish Inquisition began under secular direction in 1480). Whilst inquisitors into heretical depravity were appointed directly by the papacy, their practical powers were largely dependent upon the co-operation of secular authorities in any particular area. Furthermore, local bishops, parochial priests and monastic orders could have different ideas from inquisitors and the papacy about desirable orthodox practice and the demands of the faith. The 'Church' was a complex and in some ways wildly heterogeneous edifice. The procedures that were used when interrogating Bartolomeo were inquisitorial in the sense of being a legal technique, and one could describe the cardinal, abbot and legate as 'inquisitors' only whilst they were engaged in interviewing the priest. Torture was involved in our story, but whilst it had indeed been permitted since 1252 in heresy trials, in this case, as we saw, it was the secular authorities in Milan that tortured poor Bartolomeo.

In any case, Bartolomeo's tale is not a story about magic at all. It is really about politics and communication. Despite all the evidence alleged against them, nothing happened to Matteo or Galeazzo Visconti, because the pope simply didn't have the power to touch them. The very reason that John XXII was in Avignon rather than Rome was that northern Italy had become too politically fraught for him to stay there (the papacy had moved to Avignon in 1309, through a combination of pressure from the French monarchy and factional political fighting in Rome; there it remained until 1377). If the Visconti were attempting to assassinate the pope, it was because of political matters: a few years before Bartolomeo's reports, John XXII had been attempting to stop conflict between Milan, Brescia and Sicily. Matteo Visconti had agreed to the terms of a peace treaty, but the pope had then, in March 1317, declared that Ludwig of Bavaria held the title of Holy Roman Emperor illegally. Since the Visconti based their right to rule Milan upon claims of a past imperial appointment, this threw them back into conflict with the papacy and Milan's neighbours; and in 1318 Matteo was excommunicated. In theory, excommunication was a very serious matter: one was removed from the community of the Christian faithful, denied the sacraments, and unless reconciled before death, denied entry into heaven. But John XXII had been a little too lavish in his use of excommunication as a political weapon, and contemporary commentators were quite clear that the political struggles going on were nothing to do with matters of faith.

So much for the politics (the complexities of which, if further explicated, could easily fill this entire book and a shelf-ful more). What of communication? Several forms and facets were apparent in Bartolomeo's tale, not least the very document in which it was recorded. Inquisition was a highly textual form of inquiry, and the rich details given above – all of which are drawn directly from the evidence – demonstrate in themselves the development of a particular kind of written technology. The magic being discussed was *written* magic, and although this was innately arcane and specialized, the existence of books and written documents in general was far from rare. A north Italian city such as Milan was by this period a highly literate society: some estimates suggest that the majority of adults in this kind of milieu could read and write in the vernacular. This was admittedly the likely pinnacle of medieval literacy; in other countries, in rural areas and in earlier centuries, access to texts could be much more limited. But mechanisms of communication were always more complex than a stereotyped picture of the middle ages would suggest. As we have already seen, matters of local, national and international politics involved the flow of information across Europe. Even in the countryside, villages might well have a notary who could act as the conduit for written information. And it was not only documents that could bring news, but also people. Bartolomeo travelled with relative ease between Milan and Avignon; the Visconti were capable (presumably through spies) of discovering where he had been in advance of his return. Trade routes linked together various European centres, and indeed connected Europe to the Middle East and North Africa. Letters, reports, recorded interrogations, archives, sermons, songs, stories and images all circulated across European kingdoms. It was not as information-rich an age as the twenty-first century; but neither was it as isolated or ignorant as often assumed.

For much of the middle ages, writing was seen as an artisanal skill, something which highly intellectual authors would not stoop to perform themselves; they would, rather, dictate their works to a scribe. Someone like Bartolomeo would have thought of himself as 'literate' (*litteratus*), but by this he would have meant particularly that he could read *Latin* rather than the vernacular, and that through reading Latin he was steeped in the wisdom and traditions of Christian intellectual thought. One could be fluent in writing a vernacular language – as for example many merchants would have been – and yet still be seen as *illitteratus*, lacking in Latin. However, at this very time and place, such conceptions were being challenged, by a marginal figure in Bartolomeo's story: Dante Alighieri. He appears within the tale as an alternative expert upon whom the Visconti could allegedly call. Dante was indeed connected to the northern Italian aristocracy – dependent upon them for his livelihood – and we know from other sources that he had knowledge of learned magic; but there is no direct evidence that he had any connection to magical plots against the papacy. Where Dante really matters is in his own writing, perhaps most famously *The Inferno*, a vision of Hell which also commented upon the society and politics of his time. The key thing about the poet was that he wrote, proudly, in Italian. He was not the first medieval writer to do such a thing, but he was perhaps the first to make a virtue of it, and to claim the ascendancy of the vernacular, as a poetical language, over Latin. And this made him famous, sufficiently famous that he could be invoked by Galeazzo as a credible, albeit veiled, threat to Bartolomeo. This was a world in motion, some of its essential elements changing in this very moment.

Thus if one scratches the surface of 'the medieval' something more complex appears. In introducing the study of medieval history, my first task has been to demonstrate that things are not quite as they initially seem. Yes, it was an age when religion loomed much larger than in many modern European countries. Yes, it contained knights and ladies and monks and saints and inquisitors and all the other inhabitants of a thousand lurid historical novels. But it was neither simple nor unchanging. It was not even 'one' thing, in part because when studying the middle ages one may be engaged with over a thousand years of history and thousands of square miles of geography. But also because if one asked John XXII and Dante Alighieri about the nature of papal power, one would receive two radically different answers. That is, to put the point more broadly, every element of 'medievalness' is situated within a certain perspective, differing between different times, places and people, rather than one universal and univocal feature of the period.

## Medievalisms and Historiographies

Over a couple of decades at the end of the seventeenth century, a classical scholar at the University of Halle in Germany, Christopher Cellarius (1638–1707), published a book under the title *Universal History Divided into an Ancient, Medieval and New Period*. Cellarius was far from the first person to subdivide western history into three periods: in his self-conscious links back to a classical tradition, the Italian poet Petrarch (1304–74) had inferred a difference – a darkness – about the period intervening between his own time and the antique past. The lawyer and classicist Pierre Pithou (1539–96) had talked of 'un moyen age', and the antiquarian William

Camden (1551–1625) similarly of 'a middle time'. The passing notion of a 'middle ages' was not new, but what Cellarius did was to build a complete framework for historical time around the notion. And his book was a textbook, imparted as foundational knowledge. Then and ever after, western historians have talked of 'antiquity', 'the middle ages' and 'modernity'.

The important thing to note here is that, from the first moments of its inception, 'medieval' has been a term of denigration. For Petrarch and later humanists, for the antiquarians, for Pithou, and for later Enlightenment philosophers, what mattered was the classical past, and the ways in which it informed and was renewed by the 'modern' world around them. Both the ancient 'then' and the contemporary 'now' were thrown into stark relief by the darkness in between: a darkness of ignorance, decay, chaos, confusion, anarchy and unreason. As the early modern period 'rediscovered' (largely via the very middle ages it disparaged) texts and artefacts from the Greek and Roman past, using them as models for its own cultural productions, the middle ages came to stand for a gross barbarity of style and language. Medieval historians were disparaged for their failure to conform to classical modes of rhetoric. Its art was seen as hopelessly unsophisticated, its literature as clumsy, its music similarly lacking. The judgements passed upon medieval politics were of a similar, almost aesthetic, vein. As the economist Anne-Robert-Jacques Turgot (1727–81) characterized the period:

> The kings without any authority, the nobles without any constraint, the peoples enslaved, the countryside covered with fortresses and ceaselessly ravaged, wars kindled between city and city, village and village [. . .] all commerce and all communications cut off [. . .] the grossest ignorance extending over all nations and all occupations! An unhappy picture – but one which was only too true of Europe for several centuries.[4]

As the last century of study has amply demonstrated, Turgot's caricature of the middle ages is grossly distorted. But its spirit continues to reside: we, no less than Enlightenment *philosophes*, tend to look *down* as we look back, feeling at a gut level that something from the middle ages must be basic, crude, and probably nasty. They believed the earth was flat, didn't they? (No, that's a later myth.) They burnt witches, didn't they? (No, that's mostly the seventeenth century.) They were all ignorant, weren't they? (No, there were universities across Europe from the thirteenth century, and the beginnings of experimental science, among other things.) They never left home, hardly knew the world around them, right? (No, there were trade networks connecting Scandinavia, Central Europe, the Middle East and North Africa.) But, surely, they behaved barbarically: constant local violence, waging wars against people they didn't like, torturing people, executing criminals? (And none of this happens today, even in developed western democracies?)

This initial, vast accretion of grime is the first veil that must be removed in order to do medieval history seriously. Put aside preconceptions about the period: some *may* have elements of truth to them, but they must be treated as a matter for investigation, rather than a foundation. The middle ages were what *they* were – the many things they were – rather than only the summed 'failures' of future ages' expectations. The medieval was not simply the opposite of what is deemed 'modern'; it was something much more complex, and, as we will see, something still interwoven with how we are today.

The second veil to be penetrated is bestowed by the politics of medievalism. The middle ages have frequently been an object of ideological struggle, even when being disavowed. Thus, for those fifteenth- and sixteenth-century Italian humanists who condemned the preceding centuries to 'darkness', a major consideration was the desire to deny any continuity between the old Roman Empire, and the medieval Holy Roman Empire – because of the legitimacy this would confer on the existing Holy Roman Emperor. For the Enlightenment *philosophes*, a major factor in denigrating the middle ages was its apparent religiosity, in thrall to the command of the Catholic Church: something against which the defenders of Reason, in the eighteenth century, continued to struggle. The nineteenth century brought, in several European countries, a more positive attitude towards the medieval: France, for example, fell in love once again with chivalry, whilst Germany looked back to a powerful combination of law and empire, and England glowed with quiet pride over its long history of parliamentary constitutionalism. But these reinventions of the medieval were also political, informed particularly by different strands of Romantic nationalism. Because of events in the twentieth century, we tend to see this as most poisonous in Germany, and certainly German historiography in the nineteenth century sought the roots of its *Volksgeist* in the medieval past, and looked back to the 'glory days' of the Empire. But it was a weakness to which every European country was prone, and whilst the medievalisms that it fostered varied according to nationality, they shared the tendency to romanticize, mythologize, and simplify the medieval past.

This is not to say that this reappropriation is all that the nineteenth century gave us. General histories of modern historiography tend to talk of a 'revolution' in historical method in the nineteenth century, associated particularly with Leopold von Ranke (1795–1886) and German historiography more broadly. Whilst there are reasons for being suspicious of some of the claims made by and about Ranke with regard to how revolutionary the use of primary archival sources actually was,[5] it is definitely the case that the foundations of modern, academic history were laid by Germany in the nineteenth century, and that a focus upon archives and source analysis was a primary part of this. Some version of Rankean historiography informed the creation of academic history teaching, and subsequently postgraduate training, in France, Italy, England, the US and elsewhere. As various writers have shown, it was rare that the adopters of von Ranke's ideas understood them quite in the way he intended: they tended to reify the notion of a 'scientific method' in an unwarranted fashion, and failed to see the abstract, spiritual element in Ranke's call for the historian *wie es eigentlich gewesen ist* ('only to show what actually [or, more accurately, 'essentially'] happened').[6] Moreover, whilst Ranke had broad interests in the Renaissance and Reformation periods, his followers tended to restrict their focus to high political history, based upon study of governmental archives, which meant that preexisting interests in social and cultural history were sidelined as rather 'amateurish' pursuits.

In England, in particular, the professionalization of history over the course of the late nineteenth and early twentieth centuries was played out in the study of the middle ages. This partly followed the German example – in both countries, it had been medieval records that formed the basis for the great series of edited sources, the *Monumenta Germaniae Historica* (begun 1826) and the Rolls Series (begun 1857) – but also reflected both an English pride in its long constitutional history, and an English abhorrence for current political argument. The middle ages, it was felt, was a suitably distant period for university study, unlikely to lead to unseemly debate and dissension among modern undergraduates. For Oxford and Cambridge, in the pre-war years, medieval history was political precisely by dint of being apolitical: no current religious debates or party political issues to cause upset, and hence a suitable arena of study for the developing minds of the Empire's future administrators. A succession of Grand Old Men of English medievalism are associated with both universities in the late nineteenth century, but none are read now for any present insight. They excluded from their middle ages anything that unbalanced the smooth progress of the ship of state; assumed rather than analysed the case for English 'exceptionalism', thus furthering England's tendency to look inward rather than outward; and a thick blanket of social and political complacency slumps suffocatingly over their prose. The interesting research and teaching was being done in London and Manchester, by figures such as A. F. Pollard and T. F. Tout; and the most exciting work was by a scholar of law, rather than history, F. W. Maitland.[7] Maitland is still worth reading today, for whilst later research has corrected some of the details of his work, his sensitive understanding of law's structural relationship to society continues to inspire.[8]

The next 'revolution' in historiography also had a strong medieval element, this time in France. Lucien Febvre and Marc Bloch, two graduates of the École Normale Supérieure, had a new vision for what history could become. The perspectives associated with the pair have become known by the title of the journal they founded: the *Annales* school. Febvre's work concerned the early modern period, but Bloch was a medievalist. They wanted to broaden the horizon of historiography, free it from the pursuit of factual political narrative and explore instead the fields of geography, society, culture, even the psyche. Strongly influenced by sociology and anthropology, Bloch's vision of the middle ages was complex and panoramic. His two-volume *Feudal Society* attempted to construct an analysis of the period, changing over time, that emphasized structural connections that ran vertically through all of society. Scholarship has moved on here in various ways, and (as we shall see in chapter 4) arguments about the nature of feudalism have altered considerably since Bloch's day; but his attempt at writing a complete history, sensitive to all parts of the medieval landscape, remains a solitary beacon. Bloch's other great legacy was his book on historiography, *Apologie pour l'histoire, ou Métier d'historien* (translated into English as *The Historian's Craft*). Despite being unfinished – Bloch, a member of the French resistance, was still writing it when murdered by the Gestapo in 1944 – it continues to provide a brilliant introduction to doing history.

The *Annales* mode of historiography continued strongly, never following a strict orthodoxy, but rather a broad perspective and set of complementary inclinations. Georges Duby and Jacques Le Goff developed the legacy of Bloch, the former pursuing in particular the important shifts in socioeconomic structures, the latter more interested in the cultural *mentalité* of the period. For all the French medievalists, Marxism provided a useful set of intellectual tools, and in the case of Duby in particular, encouraged the careful study of economic relations in understanding social structures. There had been earlier Marxist works of medieval history – Gaetano Salvemini had published a book on late thirteenth-century Florence in 1899 that considered its society in terms of class structures – but it was the *Annales* that brought theory sustainedly to bear on the period. This is not to say that Bloch, Duby, Le Goff and others were all Marxists in a personal sense; indeed, in a broader perspective, the *Annales* group were distanced from the more explicitly Marxist traditions. It was, rather, that the French educational system, then as today, saw the insights of Marxism as part of the intellectual landscape. In the latter half of the twentieth century, there were some medievalists writing within Communist societies: a number of East German scholars, and the Russian Aron Gurevich. The work of the former was deleteriously affected by their political context, restricted to following the Party line on topics such as medieval heresy (where one had to parrot the perspectives of Friedrich Engels's brief comments in his *Peasant War in Germany*) and the reflexive conflation of ecclesiastical and secular powers. Gurevich, inspired by the *Annales* tradition, but with a helpfully critical distance from it, is quite a different case. His work was hampered by his relative lack of access to archival source materials, but this handicap inspired deep reflection upon medieval society and culture, with a particular pursuit of the cultural fissures between medieval social classes. Marxism also provided a particular boost for historiography in England: the influential Historians' Group of the British Communist Party, which existed from 1946 to 1956, established a new historiographical tradition not dissimilar to that of the *Annales*, but with a more clearly political intent. Its medieval element resided particularly with Rodney Hilton, whose work pursued the theme of class conflict in medieval English society.[9] *Past and Present*, the journal that the Historians' Group founded, though itself now no longer wedded to Marxism, continues to provide a strong platform for medieval enquiry, among other periods.

Work in America has in part followed European tides – as in other countries, many American medievalists of the early twentieth century did their training in Germany, and brought Rankean models of historiographical pedagogy back to their own universities – but has also developed its own foci and interests.[10] The particularly American revolution in historiography, the 'New History' associated with Carl Becker and Charles Beard post-World War I, was notably unpopular with medievalists, who remained staunch defenders of 'scientific objectivity' against this perceived relativism. The biggest influence on medieval history in the first half of the twentieth century was an underlying commitment to modernizing 'Progressive' politics, associated with President Woodrow Wilson. Indeed, one of the formative figures in medieval studies, Charles Homer Haskins (1870–1937), was a friend and advisor to Wilson; and through Haskins's student Joseph Strayer, and Strayer's many graduate students, one can trace a continued line of interest in the growth of the medieval state, the modernizing elements within medieval society, and so forth.

Overall, the shifts within medieval history in the twentieth century largely followed broader currents in historiography. The Rankean period of professionalization focused its energy particularly on studies of high politics, with accompanying interests in the history of the law and the development of national constitutions. Over time, historiography came to admit medieval society and economics as legitimate areas that expanded the possibilities of the discipline; religion, for example, could be analysed as a sociocultural phenomenon rather than simply ecclesiastical governance. Women became a topic for study particularly in the 1970s (though pioneering work in this area dates back to the late nineteenth century), and the presence and treatment of minorities – Jews, lepers, heretics, homosexuals, slaves and 'Saracens' – in the 1980s (though excellent work on Jews and heretics had appeared some decades earlier), and in both cases American scholars largely led the way. New philosophies of history, often rather loosely and not very helpfully termed 'postmodernism', have occasioned medievalist engagement, most explicitly (both pro- and anti-) in the US and France.[11] The shifts had many causes, some stretching out into academia far beyond the particular field of medievalism, but all were facilitated by the entry into academe of people from more diverse backgrounds than the overwhelmingly white, male, and strongly patrician founding fathers of the early twentieth century.

Developments in historiography, of which the preceding paragraphs offer but a crude summary, did not of course end in the 1980s, and the movement from politics to culture has not been a linear path; indeed, a particular move in recent times has been the looping back of culture to politics. To this, and other topics of recent interest, we shall turn in later chapters. Nor does the preceding sketch mention a host of individually important figures for the development of the discipline, such as the nineteenth-century American scholar of inquisition Henry Charles Lea, or the Oxford don Richard Southern whose mixture of intellectual and cultural history inspired a generation, or many other more recent figures such as Caroline Walker Bynum, Barbara Hanawalt, Jinty Nelson, or Miri Rubin (to correct the earlier gender imbalance somewhat).

But, given the constraints of brevity, what should we take from the brief introduction above? I want to suggest that there are four problems of which any student of medieval history should be aware, and one overarching issue. The last I shall turn to at the end of this chapter; let us look first at the problems.

## The Politics of Framing

First is the lurking presence of nationalism, that key element in nineteenth-century Romantic ideology. The degree to which issues of race and nation informed the creation of modern medieval studies cannot be underplayed. Ranke and his disciples searched for the 'essence' in history, and that essence was quickly identified first with a *Volksgeist* (a 'spirit of the people') and then with a national and racial destiny. The medieval past provided an essential ballast to national unity and strength: when the Prussian army defeated Napoleon III in 1870, Georges Monod (founder of the *Revue Historique* and an historian of early medieval France) ascribed the German victory to the strength of national unity fostered by that country's historians, and shortly thereafter French schools introduced classes in 'civic instruction' based upon the study of French history.[12] Ernst Kantorowicz's populist biography of Frederich II, the thirteenth-century Holy Roman Emperor, was a great success in his native Germany in the 1930s, and this was due at least in part to the attraction of the past 'German' empire to the audience of that time, and possibly also the vision of a strong, charismatic leader for the German people, at just the moment that Adolf Hitler was elected as Chancellor.[13] This is not to suggest that medievalism, past or present, is fatally tainted by the later horrors of Nazi Europe; most historiography of the nineteenth century was affected by nationalism to some extent or other, and one should not abandon all elements of nineteenth-century Romanticism or philosophy because of later uses to which it was put.[14] But medieval history did play a particular role here, having been at the vanguard of historiographic developments over the period 1830–1930, and the link must be recognized, for its legacy if nothing else.

That legacy, the second problem, is the extent to which study of the middle ages continues to be framed, often unwittingly, by the attitudes, interests and concepts of the nineteenth century. First amongst those is the very idea of 'nation': we live in modern nation-states, our mother tongues tend to lead us to identify ourselves along national lines, and we correspondingly find it convenient to think of the world, both past and present, in terms of national boundaries. Indeed, I talked of 'Italy' in the first paragraph of this book, and mentioned 'France' and 'Spain' soon thereafter; in each case, to help the reader locate the action geographically. But these modern geographies fit awkwardly with changing medieval realities. There was no unified 'Italy' at any point after the late sixth century – rather, the Italian peninsula was continually carved up in different ways between the Holy Roman Emperor, the Papacy, and whichever monarch held the throne of Sicily (this being the very context for the Visconti's plot against John XXII). The strongest allegiances felt by people in what we now call north Italy were frequently to a particular city state – Milan, Venice, Florence – and not to a nation. Spain similarly did not exist in its modern form: for centuries much of the Iberian peninsula was under Muslim rule, and the Christian portions (expanding south in spasms of conquest, particularly in the eleventh, early thirteenth and fifteenth centuries) were divided into several separate kingdoms until the end of the middle ages. France is perhaps a slightly clearer entity, but the French kingdom in the period I mentioned – the early thirteenth century – had expanded much beyond the Île-de-France (into Flanders and lands previously held by kings of England) only in the preceding two decades, with Aquitaine still in English hands, Burgundy essentially separate, and Languedoc only coming into French possession in 1271. Even England, with arguably the most centralized kingship of any country from soon after the Norman Conquest, could be seen as a rather loose entity, with uncertain borders to the north and west, and a questionable sense of relationship to its holdings in what is now France. None of these labels – English, French, Spanish, Italian, German – is terribly helpful when applied to the early middle ages; and can, indeed, be deeply misleading even for later periods.

So nations are something medievalists now need to think about critically rather than unproblematically celebrate. Other hand-me-down concepts from the founders of medieval history have also been questioned in recent years: the coherence, in their contemporary settings, of different 'bodies' of law (Roman law and canon law in particular); the sense in which the Catholic Church was a singular, unitary entity; and the notion that there is a kind of 'hierarchy' of sources, moving initially from the official histories to governmental archives, and thence to 'lesser' materials. Anglophone medievalism has had a particular trait of Victorian (and later) scholarship to deal with: its tendency to ignore or even suppress 'vulgar' elements of the past that it found unseemly or which did not fit with its picture of the period. Thus, for example, Eileen Power's 1928 translation of the late fourteenth-century advice manual *Le Menagier de Paris* omits most discussion of sexual sins, out of deference for its modern readership.[15] And all modernist histories, whilst frequently focused on 'national' wars and struggles, have tended to homogenize and homeostatize the society of the middle ages, emphasizing its simplicity and organic changelessness rather than seeking out elements of social conflict, cultural friction, or gendered struggle.

Of course, the last half century or so of historiography has revised opinions in many of these areas. But traces of them still lurk, at their most distorting when not immediately obvious to modern practitioners. All forms of academic study periodically grapple with the conditions of their existence, and the legacies of their founders; such wrestling is informative, useful, necessary, but should not be the whole story nor lead us into analytical paralysis. Nonetheless, the second caveat stands: remember where we came from.

The third problem is of a different order. The differences in national historiographical trends sketched above (focused particularly on Germany, France, the UK and the US) have persisted. The historical study of the middle ages is conducted, in each of those places today, under differing conditions, within differing traditions, with differing expectations, and to some degree in pursuit of different ends. How history itself is periodized can vary from country to country and area to area: Italian historiography, for example, tends to relinquish 'medieval' for 'Renaissance' at some point in the fourteenth century, whilst some strands of French research treat 'l'Ancien Régime' as an entity which stretched from medieval times up to the Revolution without a significant break.

In broad terms the academic pursuits of each country have tended to have their individual timbre. France has long delighted in intellectual superstructures, more willing to sacrifice detail to the larger analysis, and examine *la longue durée* in an attempt to divine the structural essence of a period. French efforts, in this as much else, often disgruntle the English who are more frequently empiricist in method, focused upon the particular and the local, insistent on the importance of details and exceptions. Germany is perhaps also more wedded to large-scale intellectual tools than England, but tools rather different from France's: more usually a key, defining concept such as 'symbolic communication' which is used heuristically to provoke specific questions in a methodical way. The US – its academic community larger by far – has taken elements from all of these traditions, but has also perhaps tended to fetishize the (admittedly important) technical skills that medievalists deploy when studying original manuscripts, possibly paradoxically because of American scholars' geographical dislocation from the archives they study. At the same time, that distance has also perhaps encouraged more structurally comparative and theoretical work in the US.

Also important are the different material conditions under which scholars work. Germany and France have extremely centralized systems of training and subsequent recruitment, and one outcome from this is a very strong patronage system (as is also the case in Italy), which tends to lead research either into patrilineal currents of development, or else spasms of Oedipal rebellion. Elements of this are present elsewhere, but much less institutionally inevitable. Funding for study in Germany largely operates through the collaborative model of the sciences, building 'research institutes' focused on a particular issue over a period of years, whereas, until recently at any rate, funding and research in the US and UK have been very individualistic. In both the US and particularly the UK, young scholars live under a 'publish or perish' regime, which means that first books tend to come swiftly and noisily, as someone tries to gain their first job or tenure. Another difference is the location and nature of archives. England has long had both a centralized national archive, and (from the mid-twentieth century) local record offices; in recent decades these, like other important libraries such as the British Library and the Warburg Institute, have had a very 'customer-orientated' policy of access. France, whilst possessing several national libraries and many local archives, is rather more bureaucratically bound; negotiating access to a manuscript in the Bibliothèque Nationale in Paris, for example, involves the complex transference of three separate pieces of plastic card and several slips of paper between the researcher and the archivist. This does have an effect on the speed of the research one can undertake, if nothing else. Both Germany's and Italy's archives have always been regional, which thus affects the shape of the scholarship done there: very few Italian medievalists work comparatively across different city-states for example.

None of these national differences are absolute or insuperable, and the entrance of further players into the game – Spain, Poland, Japan, Hungary – helps to foster better communication across borders. All countries complain that their scholarship is insufficiently read abroad: at a recent conference, I had identical conversations along this line with two distinguished scholars, one English and one French, each bewailing the tendency of the other's country to ignore their compatriots' work. But conversations *do* happen, books get read, translated, discussed, ideas pass across borders, are reshaped in the process, then handed back to their progenitors in new forms. Medieval history is an international conversation, which is part of its pleasure; nonetheless, any student of the period must be aware of its national inflections.

The fourth and final problem is whether there is a 'middle ages' at all. As we have seen above, the notion of a different (and lesser) period separating the classical past from the 'modern' age was the invention of Renaissance humanists, and became a solidified periodization in the seventeenth century. We have got into the habit, over the course of the last few centuries, of talking about 'medieval' this and 'the

middle ages' that. For those of us working in academe, 'medievalist' often tends to be a source of professional identity
(which, if nothing else, excuses us from knowing about things
outside our period). But none of this is an essence drawn from
the past. We could attempt to periodize differently – or not
at all. The notional boundaries between 'late antiquity',
'medieval', and 'early modern' (or indeed 'Renaissance') are
all deeply problematic, and can obscure as much as they
reveal. At the earlier end for example, historians have increasingly seen continuities between some Roman structures and
practices and later 'barbarian' principalities; at the later junc-
ture, there has been great debate over the degree to which
intellectual, cultural and political developments of the
Renaissance were prefigured in twelfth- and thirteenth-century
Europe.

However, most who work on some aspect of the period
500–1500 do tend to feel, whether consciously or not, that
it has some features that distinguish it (or parts of it – we
usually specialize within that 1000 year span) from earlier or
particularly later eras. A crude but perhaps useful way of
reflecting on this is to think critically about the alterity, the
'otherness', of the middle ages – as I suggested that we do at
the beginning of this chapter. We may have certain expectations of medieval 'otherness' drawn from popular culture;
these can be put to one side, albeit perhaps with some effort.
But there is a more profound question which historians must
confront: were medieval people like us, or were they fundamentally different? Or, to put it with greater nuance, at what
points must one entertain the possibility of fundamental difference between then and now, and at what points might one
consider essential continuities? This is a theme to which we
shall return throughout the book.

Whilst some historians do attempt to chase themes over a
very *longue durée* – pursuing a history of death from antiquity to modernity for example – the majority specialize in
particular periods, and the depth of knowledge that this
facilitates is undoubtedly useful. But it should perhaps be best
remembered as a professional and intellectual *choice* rather
than something that the past somehow foists upon us; and,
as I will suggest later in this book, medievalists must also try
to think about how they might speak beyond their own

period, to join in even larger conversations than those they hold between themselves. Because framing the middle ages – placing it into some meaningful context or narrative – has always been and will always be a *political* act, as well as an historiographical one. This is the overarching issue mentioned above, and it informs, wittingly or unwittingly, all that we do as medieval historians. 'The middle ages', however they are understood, have always been part of a wider argument, even if only tacitly, about 'progress', 'government', 'human nature', 'civilization' and so forth. They currently play a particular role in arguments about the perceived 'clash of civilizations' between West and East, in the denunciation by some commentators of particular Islamic practices as 'medieval', in the use of the term 'crusade' by both an American president and anti-western Islamic radicals, and in the very sense in which 'West' is assumed to be geopolitically opposed to 'East'. Doing history is political, and doing medieval history no less so than other, more recent, periods.

# 2
# Tracing the Middle Ages

## Polyphony or Cacophony?

The rising began on 30 May 1381 at Brentwood in Essex, as arrows were fired at some justices of the peace. They were attempting to collect the third poll tax that, under the leadership of John of Gaunt, had been levied by the young Richard II's government. The peasantry of England were no longer willing to accede to such demands however, and within a few days the country was in rebellion, with commoners from Kent and Essex marching on London, and separate risings occurring in East Anglia, Yorkshire and elsewhere. In London, the rebels destroyed buildings and property, burnt documents, and beheaded several royal officials including the archbishop of Canterbury. Under the leadership of Wat Tyler they demanded an end to serfdom and lordship, the disendowment of the Church, and that the lands of lords and bishops be divided between the common folk. Tyler, however, was killed at Smithfield for insulting behaviour in the king's presence, and Richard II managed to convince the mob to leave the city peacefully. Thereafter many were hanged and fined; 'and thus ended this evil war'.[1]

So, at any rate, one important source tells it. Another fails to mention the tax collectors at the beginning of events, and depicts instead an organized and armed bid for liberty arising in Essex, copied then in Kent, and initially directed against lawyers and ancient customs. A third source does talk about tax collectors, but suggests that they had been harassing women in the villages, this being the original cause of dissension. The Peasants' Revolt of 1381 – or the English Rising, or Rebellion, or Revolution, or Insurrection, depending upon how one wishes to label and thus interpret it – is one of the most famous events in medieval English history. It has been a topic of investigation and debate ever since it occurred. But that does not mean that all is known or settled about the matter; indeed, quite radical reappraisals of the events of 1381 have been presented in recent years. In part this is because of the different conceptual tools that have inspired each generation of historians (a topic to be discussed in the next chapter). But a large measure of what permits historians to argue and reinterpret is the nature of the evidence. The surviving textual traces for 1381 are rich and copious. They do not, however, cover every possible detail, they agree on neither all specifics nor generalities, and they do not speak with one voice. The evidence is therefore not simply something one reads but something that one must *work* with – in order to find different ways of interpreting, viewing and understanding.

What materials remain extant for 1381? The three sources mentioned above were all chronicle accounts, specifically the *Anonimalle Chronicle*, Thomas Walsingham's *Chronica Maiora* and Henry Knighton's *Chronicon*. Late fourteenth-century England was a particularly rich period for chronicle writing, and a variety of other accounts survive in addition to these three. But these narrative sources are not the only things available. The suppression of the revolt generated quite a large amount of documentary evidence in the form of various regional inquiries, where local jurors made presentments about specific deeds committed by their neighbours during the uprising. Various trial records from the royal courts also survive, detailing the charges and sentences for particular individuals. Other government documents exist: records of Parliament's decisions before and after the revolt, orders given by the king for the suppression of the rising, royal letters of pardon to particular rebels, petitions to the king from other areas affected by the rising, and records relating to the poll tax itself. Transcribed within two of the chronicle accounts are six 'rebel letters', fascinating but frustratingly opaque documents that appear to record rather general or coded rallying cries circulated among the rebels, possibly originally in the form of broadsides (small documents posted up publicly, on church doors for example). The revolt left its mark in other literary places too, from sermons delivered in its aftermath, to brief verses on its suppression, to strands within lengthy poems such as Chaucer's *Canterbury Tales*, Gower's *Vox Clamantis* and Langland's *Piers Plowman*, the latter apparently revised in the aftermath of the revolt lest its call for social and spiritual reform be seen as too sympathetic to the Rising.

It is immediately apparent, from this brief list, that to write a history of 1381 involves more than reading the narrative accounts and repeating what they say. For a start, the various sources do not agree. At points they sing together in complex polyphony, but on some issues (the composition and aims of the rebels, for example) produce a discordant clamour. An attempt to synthesize one version of events from all of the evidence inevitably means that one must make selections and take interpretative decisions – silence some voices, in other words. For a long time, the main chronicles were given precedence, and this led historians in certain directions, in particular a tendency to see the rebels through those chroniclers' eyes, as largely uncoordinated scum, drawn from the bottom ranks of society, wild and vicious and ignorant. But research using a different set of sources, the trial records generated in the aftermath of the revolt, has produced a rather different picture. A large proportion of the rebels were from the upper end of village society, the kind of people who held local offices such as bailiffs and jurors. This suggests that their actions were of a rather different order and nature.[2] Moreover, the history one writes is affected not only by what sources one uses but *how* one uses them. In order to see the pattern of social composition of the revolt, the trial documents needed to be subjected to statistical analysis, calculating the numbers of people mentioned by their varied socioeconomic levels. To see how Langland revised his poem in the aftermath of revolt, some very careful comparative work on various surviving manuscripts needed to be done.

Even the best-known chronicle sources have been opened up to new perspectives in recent analysis, by reading them 'against the grain': that is, by looking for confusions, contradictions, elisions or other indications of tension within the texts that might allow one to see what the author was *not* saying, or saying between the lines, whether deliberately or subconsciously.

But in discussing interpretative techniques, we are getting ahead of ourselves. Let us begin with a more basic question: where do we find medieval sources?

## Editions and Archives

The simple response is, we find the sources in libraries and archives (and, increasingly, on-line). However, this hides further complexities. As nascent historians, we usually first meet primary sources in modern printed editions (and in translation), and indeed most historians continue to use at least some printed sources in their later research. They are invaluable, because of their relative ease of availability, and because part of the hard initial work has often been done by the editor: creating an index, explaining the immediate context, ascertaining the author and so forth. One of the main foundations of modern, academic history was the creation of grand, collaborative series of printed documents: Ludovico Muratori's *Rerum Italicarum Scriptores* begun in the early eighteenth century, the German *Monumenta Germaniae Historica*, the English Rolls Series, and Abbé Migne's *Patrologia Latina* to mention the most extensive four. Without these efforts, modern historiography would look very different.

But such series are not without their problems. There is the question of editorial selection, informed by certain historiographical and nationalist (or in Migne's case, religious) assumptions. In every case the series present a preponderance of chronicle or other narratives, establishing a 'canon' of important works. Certain kinds of document, such as the copious records of local manors, were rarely seen as sufficiently important to be edited, because they did not concern the deeds of 'great men', and were not of 'national' importance (although the various local record series, published particularly in England, have gone some way to remedying this bias). The classic print editions thus tended to direct attention towards certain areas, and occlude others: the role of women in medieval society, for example, is hardly visible in narrative sources like monastic chronicles, but has become much more so when other forms of documentation such as religious writings or local records are examined. Secondly, a print edition fixes in aspic what were originally more fluid texts. For example, the original editors of the Rolls Series, dealing with a series of manuscript chronicles from the abbey of St Albans, published them under four separate titles, assuming no overall author. Later work argued that all four were in fact different stages in the development of one chronicle written by Thomas Walsingham; or, perhaps, a major chronicle (*Chronica Maiora*) and a shorter version. Recently, however, a close examination of original manuscripts, rather than the print editions, has suggested a yet more complex picture of multi-authored compositions in various stages of production.[3] Conversely, the creation of an edited text often demands that one condense the slightly differing contents of several manuscript versions into one 'authoritative' amalgam. The means by which one does this, and the possibilities of demonstrating divergent readings, continue to be explored and debated by modern editors.[4] Nineteenth-century editions are often now seen to be flawed in this respect, either dependent upon a notion of textual 'purity' that modern scholars no longer find useful or convincing, or (particularly in the case of the *Patrologia Latina*) prey to poor and opportunistic editorial decisions.[5] Later historians have been as interested in manuscript variations as in the 'original' texts themselves (if an 'original' can actually be located): that Langland altered his poem is at least as important a fact as determining either the first or final versions of *Piers Plowman*, and changes that Walsingham made in later recensions of his chronicle tell us as much about the political vicissitudes in late medieval England as the details contained within any one 'best' or 'final' version.

None of this means that historians shun printed editions. They are terribly convenient: a good university library will hold at least some, and national research libraries will likely have the lot. But for in-depth research, historians often want to check the manuscripts of even well-known sources. And, of course, *many* more things survive in manuscript and document form than have been put into print. For these, one must usually turn to modern archives of medieval documents.

Where records reside today depends in large part on how and why they were originally created and kept. There are a few fantastic finds in unorthodox locations: the American medievalist Robert Brentano discovered some very rich local ecclesiastical records in the bell tower of a small Italian church, and quite a number of important medieval documents have been found used as bindings for later books.[6] Manuscripts deemed precious by later ages – works by famous authors, such as Chaucer or Dante, or beautiful books of hours and illuminated bibles – are often now found where the money to buy them is (or once was): in national libraries (such as the Bibliothèque Nationale in Paris, or the Royal Library in Stockholm), in Oxford and Cambridge colleges, or in elite American universities or private research libraries (the Huntington Library in California for instance). But most run-of-the-mill written sources survive because they were the product of an authority that wished to preserve them for possible future use. The authority with the largest European reach was the papacy, and the Vatican archives contain a wealth of documentation about ecclesiastical government and administration, as well as more spiritual works – although it was difficult for historians to gain access to this until relatively recent times. In France and England in particular the national archives were largely the product of increased and centralized bureaucracy from the twelfth and thirteenth centuries. The records they contain are thus predominantly the creations of royal government and justice: national tax assessments (such as one in England in 1377, presaging the revolt four years later), courts of royal justice, governmental letters, parliamentary decisions, and so forth. In other countries, such as Italy and Germany, this kind of centralization never happened during the medieval period, and archives continue to be much more dispersed. Cities such as Florence and Orvieto have 'state archives' which contain documents relating to mechanisms of medieval government, but the geographical scope of these are limited to the lands controlled by the particular city-state – admittedly extensive in some cases (such as Venice) but not corresponding to the modern nation.[7]

In addition to the central archives, both England and France also have regional record offices, which tend to hold different kinds of documents: particularly local administrative records (charters of land transactions, the proceedings of manor and leet courts for example), but often also ecclesiastical documents (parochial visitations, wills, tithe records). In France even small villages may still have some records going back to the middle ages under the care of the local mayor. As discussed in the previous chapter, the greater availability of these kinds of materials had a considerable impact on the kind of history one could pursue in the second half of the twentieth century. Prior to high-medieval developments in secular bureaucracy, the majority of western European archives were the creation of monasteries, which acted as repositories for not only records of a religious nature, but also charters of land transfers or other important decisions. The nature of record preservation is therefore evidence itself for how particular medieval societies acted: what kinds of information they deemed important, what they thought of as authoritative, how much the written record mattered for future consultation.[8] A fantastically rich archive of Jewish sources from the early middle ages survives because of a practice common to all religions in Egypt of that time: any document that might have written on it the name of God could not be thrown away lest it be desecrated, even if the contents had no practical importance. Such documents were stored in a room known as a Geniza, and in the Cairo Geniza the historian S. D. Goitein discovered hundreds of thousands of pages of material.[9] In the West, much more has been lost, principally because some documents were perceived as being of no further use and were discarded, but also because of later events. In France, for example, the aftermath of the Revolution of 1789 saw large-scale destruction of medieval documents and artefacts, as symbols of the *ancien régime* that had been overthrown. In England, during iconoclastic phases of the Reformation, many stained glass windows, sculptures, paintings, rood screens and even manuscript illuminations were defaced or destroyed.

## Using Documents

Knowing what one wants to do (in the sense of knowing what area one wants to investigate) is not always straightforward, and does not always precede the encounter with the source material. It is possible to bump into an interesting source whilst searching for something quite different, and it is frequently the case that the sources cannot answer one's initial question, but prompt the reformulation of the enquiry in a new and more productive direction. When first looking for materials, one usually begins with the assistance of various 'finding-aids' for archival sources, from brief catalogue entries which describe manuscripts, to detailed 'calendars' that summarize, item by item, their contents. Many are printed and increasingly some are available electronically, though most local archives will also have handwritten finding-aids, compiled by generations of archivists, only available to those who actually visit. Even then, much is uncatalogued, or poorly catalogued, and it is possible to find material previously missed or little noted.

Having located one's material, there are, of course, a number of questions that any historian asks: what type of document is it, what or who was it for? Who wrote this, under what conditions? When was it written and when was it read? Why was it created? And so on and so forth. But there are some matters that are more particular to medieval documents. The first and most obvious is actually reading the document in the first place. The vast majority of medieval sources are written in Latin, and often a form of Latin inflected by the vernacular language of the scribe. The style of Latin, and to some degree the vocabulary used, thus vary over time, place, and context. Some chronicles and some verbose papal bulls are particularly demanding, because of their ornate style of writing. On the other hand, many types of document are deeply repetitive and draw on a limited lexicon: sessions of a manor court, for example, are not tremendously taxing once one has grasped their particular vocabulary.

So some degree of Latin is usually a *sine qua non* ('that without which one cannot do') for medievalists. Documents do exist in the vernacular, either from regions that were never particularly subject to Latinate culture, such as northern Scandinavia, or those where a high level of lay literacy entered the documentary record at a relatively early stage, such as north Italy. But the vernacular languages were not identical to their modern equivalents, nor were they regularized across regions: Middle High German would be hard for a modern German national to understand, and Occitan, the romance language spoken and written in southern France, differs considerably from both modern French and medieval northern French. Both Old English and Middle English employ letter forms that have subsequently disappeared, although the latter is often quite comprehensible when read out loud if you know that thorn (þ) is pronounced 'th', and yogh (ʒ) as usually either the 'y' of 'yoghurt' or the 'i' of 'imp'.[10] An historian of medieval England may also want to read Anglo-Norman French which was used in Arthurian romances, some chronicles and letters, and for late-medieval legal records and parliamentary legislation. Some medievalists are particularly gifted at languages, and have expertise not only in the modern literature of several European countries but a reading knowledge of many medieval vernaculars. But most have abilities focused in particular areas: a knowledge of Latin plus reading knowledge in the medieval form of their native language for example.

There is also the question of handwriting. Some skill in palaeography is useful: even where handwriting is regular (as is usually the case with documents from earlier centuries) one must decode the system of compressions and elisions that scribes used, as written medieval Latin was somewhat like the kind of abbreviated English used in modern text messaging, with various letters and word endings often indicated only by technical marks. Whilst the handwriting in early medieval documents was often fairly regular – because not many people knew how to write, and those who did had been taught in a fairly standardized way – there was often no separation between words and no punctuation. In documents from the later middle ages, whilst word separation and some punctuation do make an appearance, the orthographic challenge is harder, as the numbers of people who could write – but write idiosyncratically and sometimes in a hurry – increased.

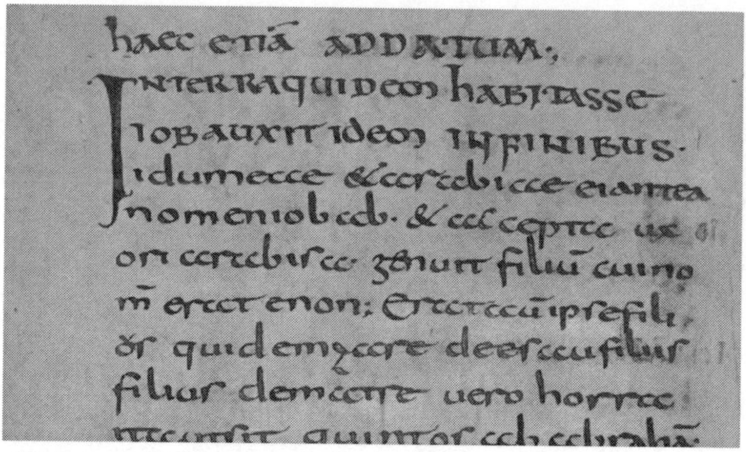

Figure 2.1(a)   Early medieval handwriting, from a late eighth-century manuscript of biblical extracts (Cod. Sang. 11, fo. 20, CESG by permission of the Stiftsbibliothek St Gallen)

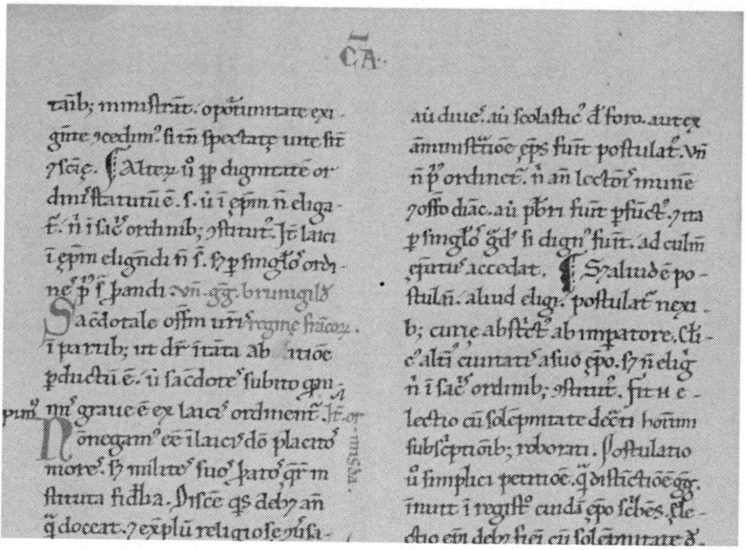

Figure 2.1(b)   High medieval handwriting, from a twelfth-century manuscript of canon law (Cod. Sang. 673, fo. 22, CESG by permission of the Stiftsbibliothek St Gallen)

Figure 2.1(c)   Late medieval handwriting, from a mid-fourteenth-century manor court roll (Conisbrough Court Roll, 1349–50, by permission of Lady Diana Miller)


The biggest help in working out what a document, written in an archaic language in squiggly handwriting and missing many letters, actually says, is to know what it's *likely* to say even before you begin to look at it. Many forms of medieval document are extremely formulaic: knowing *how* a genre of document works – the order in which it will mention certain things, the phrases that are likely to appear, the basic function of the document – is a major step towards understanding what a specific document means. To turn to a clear, albeit non-European, example, many official Japanese documents from the middle ages are presented in a few basic variations on the same formula, and this formula extends not only to particular words and phrases but to the orthographic layout of the page. Thus the date will appear in the same place, the addressee similarly, and in some forms of document, the name of the scribe at the end of the text. The opening lines will identify what kind of document it is. So even before attempting to work out the specific information contained in a document, a scholar of medieval Japan is able fairly swiftly to see what kind of document she or he is dealing with, when it was written, to whom and from whom, and therefore what it is likely to be about.[11] European medieval documents are not usually quite as structured on the page, but there are some similarities. Any document beginning *Sciant presentes et futuri* . . . ('All those present and future should know that . . .') is immediately identifiable as a charter, whereas something that, within the first few lines, contains the phrase *In primis lego* [or *commendo*] *animam meam deo* . . . ('Firstly I leave/ commend my soul to God') is a late medieval will. In practice the historian often already knows what kind of document he or she is looking at, because it's what he or she has just requested from the archivist. The formulaic nature of the evidence principally assists with decoding the handwriting and compressions. Thus someone working on an inquisitorial register, confronted with the terse *I. t. j. d. q.* knows that these should expand to *Item testis juratus dixit quod* . . . ('Item, the sworn witness said that . . .') because that is what a thousand other entries have similarly said.

The formulaic nature of medieval documents is not only helpful in working out the handwriting, it's also an important element in understanding how the document functions as a whole, and in turn seeing something of how medieval people thought about texts and writing. Take letters, for example. We tend to think of letters as very personal and intimate forms of communication, but this is rarely the case with medieval examples. There were rules of composition, drawn from classical rhetoric, which divided the letter into five parts: a formalized greeting, a quotation designed to put the recipient in a receptive frame of mind, the main narrative or exposition, the request being made by the sender, and the conclusion. Letters were very often public documents, intended for wide circulation beyond the specific recipient, or to set down in quasi-legal fashion a particular decision or instruction for later consultation. Moreover, many letters survive as exemplars of formulaic style, collated in ways foreign to their original compositional contexts.

Another fairly codified text was the sermon, which had notional rules of considerable complexity, and employed a sophisticated chain of ideas about biblical exegesis. This was so, at least, in written form: an essential, but usually unanswerable, question concerning sermons is the relationship between the written text and the presumed oral performance. Occasionally there are transcripts of actual sermons which may correspond fairly closely to what was said. We have, for example, extensive records in the vernacular for sermons given by Bernardino da Siena in fourteenth-century Tuscany, and the rhetorical power of his very individual performance leaps off the page. At the other extreme, some writers used the form of a sermon as a convenient way of structuring a text, without any intention that it actually be preached: Adam of Dryburgh makes this explicit in his work on the way of life of the Premonstratensian canons, which he explains he wrote in the form of fourteen sermons 'so that the understanding of those reading may be enlightened, and their feelings stirred as if it were a present address'.[12] Sermons often employed moral stories known as *exempla* ('examples'), and collections of these survive in considerable numbers, the assumption being that the preacher would make use of those appropriate to his theme at a particular point in the annual sermon cycle. Many *exempla* were intended to be taken as true stories from authentic contemporary or past sources, but others were drawn from classical literature, and yet more were recognized to be useful inventions. An *exemplum* about impious dancers who were cursed by a priest to dance continuously for a year (the dance continuing even beyond death) appears in a fourteenth-century English devotional manual called *Handlyng Synne* written by Robert Mannyng of Brunne.[13] Tales like this have sometimes been taken as indicative of the grotesque credulity of the period, but a careful reading of the text indicates that Mannyng knew that it was a tall story, and knew that his audience would know. As an *exemplum* it did not even originate in fourteenth-century England, and therefore how one decides to interpret it in this setting is far from straightforward.

In each of these cases, and others, it is therefore important to understand the form that a medieval text takes, the structure to which it is beholden, and the wider compositional assumptions that lie behind it, about intent, meaning, audience and usage. There are many different genres of textual evidence, and it would take a number of large books to cover all of these questions in detail. Nonetheless, as a way into the material, let us look at four particular types of source in greater detail: chronicles, charters, images and legal records. These are not categories of equal size or shape – chronicles are a fairly specific kind of text, whilst images encompass vast variations of size and type – but they help to illustrate some of the different ways in which sources can be used, and the challenges involved in bringing them to life in our histories.

## Chronicles

When we think of the medieval chronicle, popular perception might conjure up the image of a tonsured scribe in a remote monastery, at laborious work on a great manuscript that both recounts and denounces the wayward path of the secular world. This is misleading. There certainly were particular monastic centres of chronicle production, such as the abbey of St Denis, which under Abbot Suger began a series of histories in the service of the French kings, and St Albans, home to Roger Wendover, Matthew Paris, Thomas Walsingham and others. But in fact chronicles often sprang from places other than the monastery: most notably from cities, for which we have chronicle evidence from quite an early period (such as the Pisan annals of *c.*1119), royal courts (many Carolingian histories written in the ninth century were linked in some way to the court), and cathedral chapters (Anselm of Liège's eleventh-century continuation of the *Deeds of the Bishops of Liège*). Much chronicle writing was in Latin, but some vernacular examples appear by the twelfth century, and developed particularly in France and Italy.

Chronicles were thus produced for different purposes, and for different readers, albeit within a fairly limited set of contexts, usually relating to authority. This is true also of how they were *re*-produced: various manuscripts survive which compile key works of Frankish historiography, working to build a markedly uniform message of Carolingian triumph and legitimacy.[14] A monastic chronicler, such as Rodolphus Glaber ('Ralph the Bald'), could indeed intend the overarching message of his history writing to be a revelation of God's divine plan. Glaber, writing in the early eleventh century, structured his text around a complex system of four-fold divisions, linking (not just symbolically but at a spiritual level) the four corners of the earth, the four ages of the world, the senses of man (sight and hearing conjoined to reduce the number), the four gospels, the four elements, and so on.[15] Glaber's chronicle was dedicated to the abbot of Cluny, and his immediate audience was clearly monastic; yet politics is present here too, as Glaber first describes various troubling events which marked the turn of the millennium – heretics, volcanoes, the deaths of many nobles – in order to then emphasize the restoration of political stability under 'two most Christian kings', Henry of the Saxons and Robert of the Franks.[16] Dino Compagni, a successful merchant and politician, wrote a chronicle of his home city of Florence in the early fourteenth century. His intended audience would have been citizens of his own class – although in fact, due to the shifting political conflicts of the period in which he wrote, his work had to be concealed from his contemporaries, and was not reproduced at all until the late fifteenth century. Compagni's main concern was precisely the factional strife that beset his city, and his sense of how religion inflected history was rather different from Glaber's: his account of discord and strife was a warning against the consequences of the sin of backbiting, and the spiritual consequences of enmity. What caused such troubles, according to the medieval medical theory Compagni followed, were the physical traits that produced men's characters, such as their tendency towards inflamed passion.[17]

Chronicles were often direct repositories of certain kinds of power, as kings, princes, popes and bishops ensured that important documents were circulated to chronicle-writing centres in order that they be copied into the narrative, and thus preserved and disseminated. The chronicle written by the twelfth-century English monk William of Newburgh contains within it, to give just three examples, the canons of the Third Lateran Council (1179), an important letter from Pope Lucius III to Henry II concerning Saladin's capture of Jerusalem in 1187, and a set of legal statutes from the kings of England and France establishing financial support for the subsequent Third Crusade (1189–92). And the writing of history was frequently the product of trauma, as both Richard Southern and Gabrielle Spiegel have noted: an attempt by one part of the political landscape to deal with changing events by recounting a reassuring version of the past, and to explain change. Thus, the west Frankish chronicler Flodoard of Reims wrote in the wake of the deposition of Charles the Simple in 923; similarly, in the aftermath of the Norman Conquest, twelfth-century England saw a great outpouring of chronicles, that sought to find a coherent way to narrate, and hence stabilize, the apparently discontinuous history of the realm. In explaining the past to the present, the chronicle is an innately ideological form; yet, as Gabrielle Spiegel puts it, 'all the while dissimulating its status *as* ideology under the guise of a mere accounting of "what was"'.[18] That dissimulation is, of course, the precise source of its power. *The Chronicle of San Juan de la Peña* (*c*.1370), commissioned by Pedro IV of Aragon as an official history of his kingdom, was quickly circulated as such throughout the realm, in Latin, Catalan and Aragonese editions.[19] An official history was, in this context, not simply a pleasing ornament to royal power: it asserted the historic basis of that power, laid the ground for Pedro's claim to ancient rights and privileges in the different states that made up Aragon, and defended those rights against outside challenge. This *Chronicle* is thus a political treatise and tool of power as much as a history – but, garbed as 'the past', its claims for Pedro's dominion were much the greater.

What can historians do with chronicles? Obviously they provide a great deal of factual information, and helpful subjective description. The history of early medieval politics would be exceedingly difficult to write without the surviving narrative histories. Some chronicles record useful flashes of human passion: a chronicle entry concerning an ecclesiastical synod held in 1234 to discuss the murder of a controversial inquisitor reports that one bishop 'burst out "Master Conrad of Marburg [the inquisitor] deserves to be dug up and burnt just like a heretic!"', a detail that illuminates just how unpopular he had become.[20] At the same time, historians have always been wary of chronicles: information may be distorted, mistaken, fanciful, or deliberately misleading. Chroniclers' use of numbers, when estimating sizes of armies or numbers of deaths for example, are often curiously neat and suspiciously high. Matters of patronage and audience can cause quite large distortions: the anonymous *Life of Edward the Confessor*, completed in 1067, avoids all mention of the Norman Conquest, because the purpose of the work was to honour Edward and his dynasty. Chroniclers' subjective assessments, whilst enlivening, are of course also partisan. Jean de Joinville's vivid portrait of Louis IX's wisdom and holiness was written in the context of the later (successful) campaign to canonize the French monarch, and these sections of his chronicle reflect none of the contemporary criticism of Louis for unworldliness and over-dependence upon the mendicant orders.[21]

So, unsurprisingly, we note that chroniclers are not always 'trustworthy', whatever that phrase may mean. But one should not seek to avoid or eradicate bias in the chronicle evidence. There were many elements in the world surrounding the chronicler that might affect how he (or very occasionally she) wrote, and that 'bias' is a potential source of great importance. It can tell us *about* that world. Rather than discounting the evidence of clearly political chronicles as propaganda, one can analyse how they set about their projects of legitimation, and the underlying assumptions this reveals. For instance, the very idea of a king can change over time: as Sverre Bagge has shown, through a careful reading of the implicit ideals embedded in certain German chronicles, their notion of a good king shifts between the tenth and the twelfth centuries. In the earlier works, a king is a patron, a warlord and someone protected by God as part of his personal charisma; but, in the mid-eleventh century, the chroniclers start to develop a more 'public' notion of kingship. Distinctions are made between the individual person and the office he holds, and the king governs the people on behalf of God.[22] At no point does any one chronicle set out to explain or reflect upon this change – but it is precisely their implicit, taken-for-granted quality that makes them so valuable to an historian. In this kind of analysis the 'facts' and opinions that a chronicle provides are less important than the way in which it provides them: the language that it uses, the imagery it deploys, and the hidden assumptions about political theory that it reveals.

And those assumptions may well be hidden to the chronicle authors themselves – things that they do not consciously know about themselves and their cultural milieu. As the literary historian Steven Justice has demonstrated, the English chroniclers who recorded the so-called 'Peasant Letters' of 1381 did not understand either the nature or content of what they had copied down; and their misconceptions were based upon a wider set of negative assumptions they held about the peasantry. Precisely by noting this blind spot in the sources, one can use the prejudice of a text against itself: having identified the manner in which Knighton and Walsingham, in particular, make assumptions about rebel motives and actions, Justice is able to present a much richer, more nuanced and greatly sympathetic account of the rising – not by eliminating their 'biases' but by using them to illuminate those elements the texts unwittingly let slip.[23] In a parallel fashion, a nuanced understanding of the gender biases of medieval texts, allied with a very close and careful reading of the surviving sources, makes it possible to sketch the underlying role of women as preservers of family memory, orally passing on stories that only intermittently make contact with the written record.[24] It is not, therefore, the case that one must eradicate or overcome the bias of a chronicler (or, indeed, any other medieval source); rather, the ways in which medieval culture, politics and society inflect a particular text provide the historian with an extremely fertile resource for further research.

## Charters

A number of records from ninth-century Brittany survive for us today, including the following charter, issued on 17 June 860, and recorded in the cartulary of the monastery of Redon:

> Notice of the way in which a man called Uuobrian accused another called Uuetenoc about an allod which Uuobrian had sold him a long time before. Uuobrian said that he had not sold him as much land as he [Uuetenoc] was working. Thereupon Uuetenoc raised a court case, gathering his supporters;

these were called Fomus, Iacu, Rethuualart, Drehuuobri. When his charter had been read and his witnesses and sureties had testified, it was revealed that all [the land] that he worked had been purchased from Uuobrian. Then Uuobrian, vanquished as much by the charter as by the witnesses and guarantors, confessed. This was done in Ruffiac church, on the 15th kalends July, Monday, before Machtiern Iarnhitin and Hinuualart and Litoc, the representative of *Princeps* Salomon, and before many noble men [. . . names listed]. Eusorchit [a cleric] then read the charter in public, to the effect that all had been sold to Uuetenoc just as he had said from his own charter.[25]

What is a charter? In broad terms, it is the record of an agreement, whether of the transfer of land or other property from one party to another, the settlement of a dispute, or the bestowal of certain rights.[26] The first two cases are included in the example above: the charter itself records the settlement of a dispute, in this case in a legal setting, and it mentions the existence of an earlier charter between Uuobrian and Uuetenoc recording the original sale of the disputed allod. What was transferred by charter did not necessarily have to be land, however, nor was it necessarily something 'sold' by one person to another. Duke Henry of Sandomierz issued a charter in 1166 to a monastery at Zagosc in Poland, stating that 'I give [the monks] the tavern in Czechów in order [to enable them] to restore the oxen in the said villages . . . No one may presume to inflict any injury on, or demand any service from, the taverner whom [the monks] should establish at Czechów'.[27] Duke Henry was transferring the income and control of the tavern to the monastery, whilst implicitly retaining certain rights of lordship over the taverner (and possibly also a future reassertion of ownership of the property itself); and he was not selling it to the monastery but donating it as a gift. Nor did charters recording the settlement of disputes necessarily have to be produced by courts. A Catalan document from around 990 records that one Ramió, having realized that a certain Julius had been stealing bread and wine from him, decided *not* to take Julius to court, but to make a private agreement, part of which committed Ramió and his descendants to refraining from any future prosecution – a record of this promise being a primary purpose for creating the document.[28] Finally, charters were used not only by private individuals, but at the very highest levels of society: medieval towns and cities petitioned kings and princes for a charter establishing their rights to act independently as civic entities, usually allowing them freedom from certain kinds of taxation, the exercise of legal jurisdiction, and other specific matters. Many English towns 'gained their charter' in the twelfth century, setting them on a course for civic expansion in that and the following century. The most famous charter for the anglophone world is probably the Magna Carta ('Great Charter') issued by King John at Runnymede in 1215, which sets out fundamental rights in English common law, along with sundry other matters such as the removal of all fish-weirs from the Thames and Medway and the king agreeing not to sequester other nobles' timber.

Collections of charters – cartularies – are one of the richest medieval sources for the early middle ages, and indeed beyond. The majority of what survives relates to monasteries, because they had the means and desire to archive such records over long periods of time; in the case of Uuobrian and Uuetenoc, the latter donated the land under dispute to the monastery some five years later, and hence the monks of Redon wished to keep a record of the earlier charter in case of future argument. There is some evidence to suggest that in certain areas of Europe at least, lay people also made archives (albeit often still storing them in monasteries or churches); work on how to trace this kind of documentary practice is still in progress.[29] There is possibly a very slight hint of this in the mention of the earlier charter that Uuetenoc brought to court, in the case from Brittany: clearly someone had kept this document because of its potential future importance.

Charters touch upon elements of the lives and activities of people from many different social levels, and by 1300, as Michael Clanchy has shown, charters were being regularly used for land transfer in England even between peasants.[30] They are hence a hugely valuable kind of document, containing information about people, places, properties and practices – although, in each of these cases, care is needed in exactly how one uses the information a charter presents. To take a very simple example, charters that contain information about land donations – a primary feature in monastic cartularies –

can allow us to map the extent, growth or diminution, value and geographical patterns of monastic landholding. By looking at the people making the donations, historians have discussed patterns of pious giving among social elites. In other words, one can look at who gave what to whom. However, matters may be more complex than this initially makes clear. The nature of donations, and the rights they provided over the land given, could vary, and could indeed be subject to future dispute. It is unlikely, to return to the case of Duke Henry and the Zagosc monks, that the duke intended the monastery to be able to do anything it wanted with the tavern in perpetuity, only that it could have the income to restore its flocks. Beyond that indeterminate point, the matter became hazy: the monastery would likely retain the income unless the duke, or another party, made a future claim – but if it attempted to sell the tavern to a third party, it could find the matter subject to dispute by the duke or his heirs. Whether or not one sees 'dispute' behind every property transfer, it is certainly the case that land donated to monasteries seems to have sometimes been handed back and forth between the family of the donator and the recipients, the same piece of land somehow being 'given' at various points in time. *What* was transferred by charter is not always as obvious as one might first think.

Study of monastic holdings also needs to beware of forgery, something far from unusual when dealing with monastic charters. As documents became more essential in the establishment of rights, monasteries had a habit of producing helpful charters, often 'backdated' several centuries, in defence of their claims. Nor were monks the only culprits: the city of Marseilles, claiming Montpellier as a subject territory in a series of cases heard before the pope in the mid-thirteenth century, conveniently 'discovered' charters dating to 1136, 1152, 1163 and 1198 setting out its rights, all of which are now considered to be forgeries.[31] Another possibility regarding Uuetenoc's 'earlier' charter in the Redon dispute is that this was a forgery produced in order to bolster the case against Uuobrian.

The very nature of 'giving' can also be complex. Anthropological work on gifts has long suggested that an element of reciprocity is usually involved: one gives because one expects to get something back. Or, one gives because one wishes to place the recipient in one's debt; or further, one gives precisely because the recipient is unable to give back (or give as much), and therefore one can show off relative wealth and power. Barbara Rosenwein's work on gifts of land to the monastery of Cluny in the tenth and eleventh centuries has demonstrated how many of these transactions were about other matters than the actual land itself. The same pieces of land can be found being gifted and re-gifted over time, with little clear sense of 'ownership' as one might expect from a modern property market. Instead, Rosenwein suggests, property transactions acted as a kind of 'social glue' in a period arguably marked by the fragmentation of authority. Making gifts was a way of connecting oneself with the monastery, and vice versa.[32] An essential technique in pursuing this kind of analysis has been prosopography: the tracking of individuals across multiple documents, tracing kinship networks between those individuals (and, in Rosenwein's case, mapping the areas of land mentioned in the charters). Work on the people mentioned in charters – not only the primary individuals, but the various witnesses and others – has demonstrated just how much one can extract from seemingly sparse information. The order in which witnesses appear in charter lists, the recurrence or otherwise of witnesses across charters, can be used to suggest something of the social fabric behind the charter, its lines of connection, tension and power.

This is true too of the narrative details that some charters contain. Take the charter concerning Uuobrian and Uuetenoc. Just these short lines provide a glimpse of various important themes. The fact that Uuetenoc, the accused, rather than Uuobrian, the accuser, brought the case to court indicates that one might *choose* to use the law, rather than have it forced upon one; it probably also suggests that he had connections to Salomon, a major source of power in the region. Something of the social setting of the law, and its methods, is also suggested. The case involved the presence of a representative of the prince, and other noble men, but took place in the local church: a combination of secular and ecclesiastical authority. The court heard testimony from witnesses (though whether they were giving evidence on the objective facts, or on the character of the protagonists, is not clear), and heard the contents of an earlier charter – it being this written evidence as much as the oral testimony that brought the verdict in Uuetenoc's favour. Indeed, something the charter indicates is the interpenetration of orality and literacy: the written word carried weight and importance, alongside oral testimony, but the charters also had to be read aloud (as the cleric Eusorchit reads the charter itself, in conclusion to the matter) to be made 'public'. The study of more charters, over a longer period of time, would allow us to map the contours of these areas in greater detail; and we would likely find a shift from more oral to more literate ways of dealing with property and evidence, the development of other kinds of courts and legal jurisdictions that separated ecclesiastical from secular, and other changes in documentary practice. Studies of further disputes and their settlements have similarly allowed historians to track patterns of ritual behaviour, lines of social power, and methods by which individuals negotiated their relative position in society.

In all of these areas, and more, it is good to think of charters as being more than passive reflections and records of past events. Civic charters were important as symbols as much as for the detail they contained: as Brigitte Bedos-Rezak has shown, French towns reproduced their charters in multiple forms, by making beautifully illuminated copies or by pretending that an earlier copy had been lost and petitioning the requisite lord for another duplicate.[33] The ability to create and archive authoritative written materials was in itself a demonstration of power – for monasteries, for royal chanceries, and in the later middle ages, for towns and cities. Charters were little repositories of useful memory, ready to be deployed tactically in future disputes. This was, of course, the very reason that charters were kept. The way in which the record was made, the function of the written record, was therefore active rather than passive: charters *did* things, or, at least, had the potential to do things, if not at the moment of their creation then in the future.[34] As we will see further below, this point can be expanded to all the sources of the period: a document was not a reflection so much as an action.

## Images

The medieval images most familiar to us today are either very large, such as the stained glass in Chartres cathedral, or else really quite small, as is the case with most manuscript illuminations. These are, at both extremes, also rather specialized kinds of images. Chartres was a wondrous creation even in the thirteenth century, intended from its very inception to impress and awe the viewer. Manuscript illuminations were for the most part only seen by the kinds of people who illuminated manuscripts, namely monks, or (in the fourteenth and fifteenth centuries) those who bought them, namely very rich people. These images remain useful, but others are also important, and more truly ubiquitous: the images stamped onto coins or embedded in seals, for example, or the simpler pictures painted onto parish church walls or carved into parish church rood screens. It is true that, from the late fourteenth century, illuminated manuscripts in the form of books of hours reached a wider, secular audience; but these were still largely the possession of social elites, and their relative ubiquity should not be extended into a general sense of 'popular' culture. The religious image that most ordinary people would probably have seen most often was two intersecting lines forming a cross: this simple image has been found carved into bedheads, onto loaves, over lintels and in other quotidian settings.[35] It was an action as much as an image, since 'making the sign of the cross' was something taught to all Christians in childhood.

The analysis of images presents a number of potential pitfalls for the historian, some purely technical, some more interpretative and epistemological.[36] At a technical level, medieval art employed a variety of semiotic devices to communicate meaning, and one must be able to decode these to make sense of an image. The precise way in which someone's fingers are depicted was intended, for example, to tell the viewer what the person was doing: listening, arguing, blessing, preaching, and so forth. Different medieval saints have particular objects associated with them, through which one could identify the figure – St Katherine's wheel, St Michael's sword – and, at a less exalted level, the coats of arms of late medieval noblemen played a similar role. Colour was important, in many different ways, and often contextually within a particular image.[37] Different religious orders, and different kinds of clergy, wore robes of identifying colours (in reality as well as in pictures). The relative positions of people within an image represented their relationships and hierarchy.

These may seem daunting matters; in fact, they are for the most part fairly straightforward technical considerations, and considerable help in decoding details can be gleaned from reference books.[38] What matters as much as reading the language of the picture is thinking – as one must do for any source – about its precise context and function. For example, pictures painted onto church walls are sometimes assumed to have been used to instruct the laity in their faith, possibly as kinds of visual aids to preaching. One can certainly make wonderful use of images of this kind in deepening our sense of the imagery evoked within medieval liturgy and religious instruction. Work on specific churches has, however, suggested that this is not always the case: some thirteenth-century churches in France only had paintings on the walls of the apse, not the nave, the details of which were visible only to the clergy. The laity would have seen the fact of the images, but not the images themselves; their lesson was hence more that of clerical privilege and hierarchy than theological detail.[39] Equally, art that might appear to be private and domestic – for instance Andrea Mantegna's fresco (1465–74) for the marquis of Mantua's private chamber – could in fact be 'public', as something that visitors specifically requested to see, due to its fame.[40] Medieval images could be intended to impress, to inspire, to provide models for good conduct, to be meditated upon, to be laughed at, to signal identity and status, to narrate, to scare. The creators of these images drew upon artistic convention, classical and biblical narrative, specific semiotic codes, the desires of their patrons, the available resources – and, sometimes, what they saw around them.

The search for the latter has often been the object of historical (as opposed to art historical) study. Images can provide a lot of important information about the minutiae of medieval life. Various technical medical practices are illustrated in manuscripts, such as cataract surgery, bloodletting and urine analysis. The tools and methods of particular trades – carpentry, goldsmithery, butchery, brewing – can be seen, corroborating textual and archaeological evidence. Some sense of the visual impact of markets and fairs, civic processions and plays, funerals and sacramental rituals can be drawn from visual materials of various kinds. All of this is extremely valuable. But one must be wary. Past historians had a bad habit of taking details from medieval literature as 'straight' depictions of life at the time, without regard to textual context or the stylistic devices of medieval authors (including irony, satire, anachronism, genre convention and the tropological expectations of narrative). A similar problem can befall those using images. Take, for example, a famous set of images, the book of hours known as *Les Très Riches Heures du Duc de Berry*. Look at the picture illustrating the month of February (figure 2.2).

In the bottom left, we see a simple hut, three seated figures warming themselves at the fire. Look closely at the smaller two: their genitalia are clearly visible, if curiously hairless. Clear circumstantial evidence that medieval people wore nothing under their outer garments (and were prepubescent for many years)? Or a visual joke about bare-arsed peasants and their crudity? Given that many of the calendar illustrations juxtapose courtly finery with peasant simplicity, something of the latter is probably more likely; though what exactly is open to argument.[41]

In recent decades, however, historians using images have been less interested in the pursuit of physical details, and more interested in the ways in which images might relate to how people thought about things. The Mappa Mundi, a world map made in thirteenth-century Hereford, tells us little about the actual world (two of the continents are missing) but quite a lot about how some people *thought* about the world. Looking at the Mappa Mundi, one learns about relative perceptual geographies (England, its place of creation, is curiously large); the boundaries between the known and the unknown or the ordered centre and disordered peripheries (the latter, in the north and east, populated by monstrous races); and the overarching theological framework within which existence is set (Christ at the heart of the world in Jerusalem, and Christ also overarching the world at the top

Figure 2.2   Les Très Riches Heures du Duc de Berry, month of February

of the map). Images of Christ of various kinds, compared across the centuries, indicate a general shift in depiction, from Christ in potent majesty, to Christ as the Man of Sorrows, suffering very bodily torment on the cross. An element of this relates to artistic convention, but in aggregate it clearly suggests a shift in how Jesus was thought about, and which elements in the Christian message were deemed most powerful at different points in time.

Like the other sources discussed in this chapter, images were *active* things. They could work to promote and sustain particular ideologies. This was the case with the many repetitious depictions of Jews as hooknosed, untrustworthy outsiders, physically bearing the marks of their 'Otherness' to a Christian audience.[42] Images of Jews desecrating Hosts, to accompany stories of the same, worked not only to demonize the Jews but also to emphasize Christ's corporeal presence in that sacrament. Late medieval Italian cities were visually saturated spaces that constantly used images in a complex variety of ways. Apart from religious iconography directed towards catechetical ends, a late medieval Italian might be confronted, whilst taking a case to law, with a complex and detailed exposition of 'good' and 'bad' forms of government in the form of a vast fresco – a reminder and warning to both citizens and rulers about the necessity of preserving peace, by force if necessary.[43] In a number of Tuscan cities in the thirteenth and fourteenth centuries, criminals (particularly traitors and unscrupulous merchants) who had been prosecuted *in absentia* and hence eluded the reach of the commune were sometimes punished by *pitture infamanti*: pictures depicting the condemned person were posted up in public places as a kind of visual penalty against their honour.[44] A popular story, appearing in Boccaccio's *Decameron* and elsewhere, of a knight hunting down and eviscerating a naked woman who spurned his advances, was depicted on various late medieval Italian bridal chests that carried the young bride's jewels and clothes into her marriage; a very explicit statement of masculine power and feminine submission.[45] Such images were a form of instruction and also a warning about expected gender roles. One might argue that they 'reflect' social attitudes towards women, but perhaps we should more accurately say that they attempt to construct and police such ideas.

These are all examples of images attempting to wield a fairly direct influence: to carry a particular ideological message. But the functions of images can also be more subtle. Christian art of many different kinds, from wall-paintings to statues to books of hours, worked to evoke emotional and bodily responses in its viewers, playing delicately (or not so delicately) upon their feelings. What one felt and thought when looking at Christ crucified could involve a complex weave of associations between the particular image and other works of art, the narrative frameworks for the image rehearsed in sermons, and, for a monastic audience, the texts one might have read reflecting upon the very experience one was undergoing.[46] Work yet to be done in this regard concerns the more secular spaces of images: the carvings and signs that adorned medieval civic streets, for example, which can be demonstrated to have their own rich and complex resonances, and are imbricated in different discourses of gender, social order, commerce and control.[47] Pictures can work to frame one's emotional and cognitive response to events in the world: the art historian Mitchell Merback has argued, for example, that late medieval Bohemian images of the two thieves at Christ's crucifixion were linked to contemporary practices of criminal punishment, specifically, breaking people on the wheel. But the nature of the link, Merback emphasizes, is not simply referential, the image 'deriving from' the practice. The images worked, rather, to stimulate the imagination, provide a template joining 'sacred history to familiar reality', evoking a kind of affective knowledge of ideas about penitence; a map for seeing, when in the presence of either the holy image – or the broken body of a common criminal.[48]

## Legal Records

'Whoever injures someone with an egg [. . .] should pay ten gold pieces if the plaintiff can prove it.' Thus the law in twelfth-century Castile. The history of law has had a particular importance to medievalists. Frederic W. Maitland, mentioned in chapter one above, was a lawyer and worked on law; and Henry Charles Lea, the great American medievalist of inquisition, wrote that 'the surest basis of investigation for a given period [lies] in an examination of its jurisprudence, which presents without disguise its aspirations and the means regarded as best adapted for their realization'.[49] The attractions of law as an historical source are both its provision of fascinating detail – the glimpse of Iberian egg throwing – and its promise of a larger, more structural *system*, which might allow one to grapple with society as a whole. Legal records are of course not particular to the study of the middle ages.

But the medieval period has, for most European countries, a foundational place in the establishment of modern legal systems; and some of the records produced by law contain the richest details for aspects of medieval life that would otherwise fall outside the viewpoint of loquacious chroniclers and other such sources. Records of law are also the widest and most varied set of sources discussed in this chapter; indeed, one could count all charters as being legal records. But my focus here is primarily on the kinds of texts produced by the attempted prevention, detection and punishment of crime: law codes, depositions, court judgments and so forth.

As Lea suggested, law codes can be seen reflecting a society's aspirations; or, to put it another way, what people worried about and what lay behind those worries. The egg-throwing injunction comes in a section of a law code concerned with honour and violent assault; subsequent items concern 'he who makes up an abusive ballad about another' and 'he who calls someone a leper'.[50] There is a danger here, however, of reading too much purpose and design into medieval law. Law codes often recycled details from older – sometimes much older – records, which means that, just as in modern law, some elements could be misleadingly anachronistic. In the early middle ages, issuing a law code might be seen primarily as a way of indicating that you were the sort of ruler who *could* issue a law code. Much medieval law – including, for example, that set out in the Magna Carta – was not based upon the top-down application of a set of systematic principles, but something more bottom-up and petitionary.[51] Law came about because a particular issue or problem was raised, a ruler dispensed a judgment, and thus law was written. This was true for both kings and popes. Canon law, the law of the Church for all Christendom, was constructed very largely from responses to petitions, and decisions made about particular situations. Codifications of canon law – most famously Gratian's twelfth-century *Decretum* – were attempts to clarify discordant canons, where those past decisions had reached conflicting conclusions. This perhaps makes medieval law slightly less suitable as a tool for diagnosing the whole structure of a notionally unified society, as Lea imagined it; but at the same time it becomes a tremendously powerful source for information about communal fears and hopes, social tensions and the like. It can also, from a certain perspective, tell us something about social structure (a topic to which we shall return in chapter 4): the units and classes into which it imagined society being divided, and the relative rights and status accorded to each. In this sense, what law omits or excludes is often as revealing as what it includes. Certain social ideas are encoded in law, and historians have seen it as particularly revealing in regard to gender. In many European kingdoms women had a limited place within the law, their ability to litigate or appeal being circumscribed because of their 'changeable' nature, as one fourteenth-century English legal text puts it.[52] Medieval concepts of the crime of rape, albeit not unitary or static on the topic, tended to focus on the injury done to the woman's family rather than herself; and an acceptable reparation was marriage to the perpetrator or the bestowal of a dowry.

Law in practice, as opposed to legal theory, provides an even richer source of material for such matters. To continue with the theme of sexual violence, historians can study the court proceedings for further indications of cultural ideas and attitudes. The usual defence against an accusation of rape was to allege that the woman was a 'common woman', sexually available to all. Examining accounts in these cases provides insight into ideas about honour, gender, and sexual double standards. The prosecution of sex crime in late medieval Italy, studied by Guido Ruggiero, demonstrates some of the complexities. The civic authorities used a strongly denunciatory rhetoric in the description of sex crimes – the perpetrator 'dishonouring God' as much as the victim – but their actions did not always follow suit. The rape of single women, in particular, tended to be treated extremely leniently, as a somewhat inevitable and natural fact of social life. Sodomy however, a crime carrying particular associations of civic instability, was punished harshly.[53] Women's involvement in crime as perpetrators can also tell us things about the world in which they lived. They never numbered more than one fifth of those prosecuted, probably indicating a real difference in behaviour, and they were rarely charged with homicide. Women did perpetrate violence, but the pattern differed from that of men: other women were the more frequent victims, and they infrequently used weapons.[54]

The uses of legal records are not, however, limited to the history of crime itself. The growth of social history in the 1950s depended particularly upon the study of legal archives, and the development of techniques for mining them effectively as an historical source. Many such texts provide incidental details about the world in which the deponents lived, and these can be invaluable. Barbara Hanawalt has used coroners' rolls to reconstruct a picture of rural life in medieval England; the canonization records (structured similarly to trial dossiers) of St Louis allowed Sharon Farmer to study attitudes towards the poor in thirteenth-century France; Claude Gauvard has analysed themes such as the social construction of space and the construction of community from records of late medieval French royal pardons; and Emmanuel Le Roy Ladurie wrote a detailed study of one village based upon very rich inquisitorial records from the early fourteenth century.[55] The social setting of the law itself – the way in which people *use* courts, and the cultural work that they undertake when so doing – has also recently come under analysis.[56]

Many of the analyses sketched above depend, to a greater or lesser extent, on the numerical analysis of records. This is a powerful tool to which many such sources are suited. The average record of a penance handed out by a thirteenth-century inquisitor could say no more than 'Coinarc saw Waldensians and heard their preaching. He is to go [on pilgrimage] to [the shrine of] Saint James [of Compostella].'[57] It is hard to do much with a single text of this sort; but given hundreds, one can build up a larger picture of those charged by the inquisitor, the penances given, and the shape of heretical activities. In secular law too, whilst individual cases may be short on detail, the survival of court records over many years encourages an aggregate, statistical approach. But this is not the only way in which the sources can be studied. Trial records often contain narrative information on the crime committed, and one can usefully look not only at the incidental detail contained in such accounts, but at the very shape of the narrative and the way in which it was produced. Those involved in violence will, for obvious reasons, attempt to justify their actions. As Daniel Smail demonstrates for some cases in fourteenth-century Marseilles, such justification drew on social norms and could be implicit as much as explicit. For instance, a man called Julian narrated events leading up to the fight he had with another man called Jacme in such a way as to suggest that he was in a hostile part of town, far from any supporting kin, whereas Jacme lived there and was surrounded by potential supporters (both these facts being false, as subsequent evidence revealed); and that Jacme had earlier that year assaulted one of Julian's kin, thus making Julian's attack on Jacme a matter of feud, and hence legitimate. These details were not glossed with such meanings in the record; they were, rather, embedded within the story that Julian told.[58]

Many court cases were petitionary rather than prosecutary: one or both disputants chose to go to law (or, quite frequently, to appeal an earlier decision to a higher court). A principal way in which such sources have been used is the study of dispute settlement, an area of enquiry much influenced by anthropological theory and extending beyond the formal bounds of law.[59] Sources of law can, in this way, show us something about sociocultural tensions and relations. But a good proportion of records, including the inquisition registers used by Le Roy Ladurie and the civic trials studied by Ruggiero, were the product of top-down prosecution, the application of legal force from above. In these cases, historians are allowed different analytical possibilities, such as the ways in which people resisted (or otherwise) the imposition of legal forms on their lives. James Given's study of medieval inquisition has examined, for example, how people individually attempted to elude the religious authorities, and collectively disrupt their activities, through burning their archives or other acts of violence. The coercionary context of these kinds of trials raises further questions about the ways in which the narratives of the sources were produced, as the inquisitor attempted to apply a particular framework of classification to the witness, and the witness (on occasion) negotiated the experience as best he or she was able.[60]

Talk of inquisition raises a final possibility for the use of legal sources and the law: what they reveal of changing ideas about truth and enquiry. Inquisition (*inquisitio*) is a form of legal procedure, applied particularly to the prosecution of heresy in the thirteenth century but also used as the main legal form in much late medieval secular law, apart from in England. *Inquisitio* allowed judges to proceed directly against suspected crimes on the basis of *fama* (rumour/public knowledge), through an investigatory procedure. In this, it largely replaced earlier legal forms such as *accusatio* which required a specific individual to bring an accusation to the court's attention; and the period when *inquisitio* rose to prominence – the early thirteenth century – also saw the decline of the trial by ordeal, whereby the accused could prove his innocence by being relatively unharmed after holding a red-hot iron or some similar test. As these legal forms shifted, the relationships between God, the community and law were refashioned, and historians are still arguing about how best to interpret these changes. What constituted 'truth' within a legal setting was always to some extent a communal matter – the decision of a jury, or a group of oath-swearers, or bound by social expectations of narrative and memory – but *inquisitio* also brought with it the active use of the archive, as witnesses' statements were checked against others, and records were used to catch out past transgressions and shape the possibility of future ones. In this sense, legal records embodied as much as reflected power. The historian's archive is not innocent: it once did things, to real people.

# 3
# Reading the Middle Ages

The annual migrations of European and American medievalists, though slightly contrasting, follow an essentially similar
pattern. Every spring, a vast number of the Americans, some
3,000 or 4,000 strong, both young and old, flock in haste
from all over the USA to a large town in Michigan – Kalamazoo – home to a state university, a lovely but under-
patronized museum of local history, and some rather nice
bars. There, perched cheek-by-jowl in rooms of almost
monastic simplicity, they hold a congress. This involves a
great, exciting, interwoven babble of discussion, argument,
and gossip, and the obsessive purchasing of books to take
back home to their nests. At the end of four intense days,
they depart as swiftly as they arrived. In the early summer,
across the Atlantic, a very similar phenomenon can be
observed, this time centred on the rural edge of the English
city of Leeds. More languages are spoken at Leeds (Polish,
Dutch, German, a little French and Japanese) in addition to
the native English, and there are only two bars, but otherwise
the behaviour is much the same.

The International Congress on Medieval Studies at
Kalamazoo (begun in 1966) and the International Medieval
Congress at Leeds (begun in 1994), to give them more respect-
fully their proper titles, are not, of course, the only conferences that medievalists organize or attend. Many other annual
and occasional events are held across the world; in the year

in which I am writing these words, one finds them on topics as broad as 'Power' and as specific as 'The Battle of Tinchebray, 1106'. Nor by any means do all medievalists attend Leeds or Kalamazoo: other European countries have their own meetings, medievalists attend cross-chronology conferences, and some prefer to shun the large jamborees completely. But these two annual talk-fests are currently the largest gatherings of medievalist minds. And they share a notable feature in comparison to other historical colloquia: both sprang from and continue to embrace *interdisciplinary* study of the middle ages. Neither is purely a historical or literary conference (or for that matter, archaeological or art historical). Medievalists have grown very used to working across and between apparent disciplinary boundaries.

This does not mean that no such boundaries exist, and I shall explore some points of tension below. But all disciplines are agreed that the middle ages, by dint of the nature and fragmentary survival of the evidence, benefits hugely by approaching it from a range of perspectives. Thus, in discussing medieval history, one must note that it is frequently a kind of history in conversation (both collaborative and argumentative) with other approaches; and, increasingly frequently, that it draws upon cognitive tools developed in other parts of academia. Art history I mentioned in the previous chapter. Archaeology, and some other tools drawn from the social sciences and the study of literature, are discussed below. First, however, we must turn to probably the biggest influence: anthropology.

## Anthropology

The Catalan writer Ramon Muntaner (1264–*c*.1330) begins his vernacular chronicle with an account of not the birth but the conception of King Jaime I of Aragon in 1207. King Pedro II, Muntaner tells us, had grown bored with his wife Maria of Montpellier, and had a roving eye for other courtly ladies. This 'much afflicted and displeased' the nobility and people of Montpellier, and all the more so when Pedro set his sights on another woman from the area. Thus a deception was formulated: the king would be invited to the lady's darkened bedchamber, but his wife substituted in the place of her latest rival. In the week leading up to the ruse, all the priests in the area said masses in praise of the Virgin Mary, and on the Saturday, the people of Montpellier fasted. That night, as the king lay with his woman, the people went to church and prayed; and outside the chamber door, throughout the night, there knelt in prayer 'twenty-four notables and abbots and priors and the bishop's clerks and religious, and the twelve [most honourable] ladies and the twelve damsels, with tapers in their hands', and also two notaries.

> And the king and queen rested together, and the lord king believed he had at his side the lady of whom he was enamoured [. . .] And when it was dawn, all the notables [. . .], each with their lighted taper in their hand, entered the chamber; and the lord king was in his bed with the queen, and wondered [at this intrusion], and sprang up at once on the bed and seized his sword. And all knelt down and said weeping: 'Lord, deign to look and see who it is lies by your side.' And the queen sat up and the lord king recognized her; and they told him all they had disposed. And the lord king said that, since it was so, might it please God to fulfil their intention.

Pedro left Montpellier the next day, but six knights and their wives and damsels stayed with the queen for the following nine months, until Jaime I, conceived that night, was born. The two notaries 'in the presence of the king' wrote 'public letters of the event, writing that same night'.[1]

What does one do with such a tale? A hard-headed historian attempting to reconstruct a narrative of important events might well be tempted simply to ignore it, treat it as meaningless background 'noise', whilst continuing a search for hard facts. After all, the combination of miracles and narrative implausibility makes it hard to take as a true story. Another approach might note it as a mark of characteristically medieval simplicity and credulity. But both tactics would surely leave us a little disappointed: must we either diagnose these medieval people as simpletons, or else abandon all attempts to interpret? It is at this conceptual point that anthropology has come helpfully into play.

One of the earliest, and certainly most influential, uses of anthropological ideas was indeed in a ground-breaking attempt to interpret what previous generations of historians had seen as curious but essentially meaningless beliefs surrounding medieval monarchs. Marc Bloch's *Les rois thaumaturges* (1924; English translation *The Royal Touch*, 1973) dealt with the practice of kings curing scrofula by laying hands on the afflicted, something found from the thirteenth to the eighteenth centuries. In taking such a topic seriously – and indeed arguing that it illuminated extremely important aspects of royal power, image-making and pre-modern authority – Bloch was influenced by the work of the anthropologist Lucien Lévy-Bruhl and the sociologist Emile Durkheim. The former gave him the tools to consider whether a pre-modern society and culture ('primitive' in Lévy-Bruhl's terms) could have a different, but internally coherent, way of thinking and acting from a modern one; its own *mentalité*, to use the Annaliste term. Durkheim's work encouraged Bloch to see the ritual and symbolic elements of sovereignty as important: part of 'collective representations' that informed the very functioning of society itself.[2] Something like the 'royal touch' was, for Bloch, not simply a piece of royal propaganda disseminated from the top down, but part of a collective social idea about hierarchy, intervention and structure. Indeed 'structure' was at the heart of his, and later Annaliste, analyses – and similarly in anthropology. In treating Muntaner's narrative of Jaime I's arrival into this world in a structuralist way, one might note the shared set of values across social hierarchies (all 'the people', as well as the notables and bishops, are engaged in prayer for a successful outcome), whilst also seeing how structural subdivisions of those hierarchies allotted different kinds of roles to different sorts of people, with a concomitant belief that the collective whole, through which society functioned, was more important than any individual role. Even the king, in this sense, was part of the structure, rather than hovering above it: whilst placatory in their confrontation with him, it is clear that the nobles specifically, and the city in general, required Pedro to play an allotted role, and manipulated him to precisely this end. Another structural element – the idea of honour, and its link to both place (Montpellier) and kin (the noble families) – is key to understanding the story.

The structuralist anthropology of Durkheim and other later figures such as Claude Lévi-Strauss, Marcel Mauss and Victor Turner, was hugely influential, particularly on French medievalists. Georges Duby found in Mauss ways of understanding the central role of gift exchange in early medieval economies and politics; something that has continued to provide a fruitful line of enquiry for later medievalists.[3] Inspired by Lévi-Strauss and others, Jacques Le Goff has pursued a variety of symbolic elements in medieval culture – notions of 'wilderness', the meanings of marvels, the importance and interpretation of gesture, the different conceptions of 'time' embodied in ecclesiastical and mercantile cultures.[4] Victor Turner has been influential particularly on studies of medieval religion (about which he himself wrote), particularly in his analysis of rites of passage and what he calls 'liminality' – a borderland condition, marked by elements of role-reversal and fluidity, which engenders both charismatic power and collective cohesion.[5] Liminality has been a useful conceptual tool in understanding the ways in which medieval saints and holy people are produced, either in reality or in narrative. Both Francis of Assisi and Waldes of Lyon, for example, came from rich mercantile backgrounds, and underwent sudden reversals of condition through illness and voluntary impoverishment, leading to accusations of madness as they stepped 'outside' society, only to then be reintegrated as leaders of groups (the Franciscans, and the Waldensian heretics), and emerge as charismatic leaders, facilitating social cohesion. The theory has been further adapted and critiqued in regard to female saints, whose social position was arguably always already 'liminal' by dint of their sex.[6] Peter Brown, an influential historian of late antiquity, has developed analyses of the social function of holy men (and occasionally women) in his period, in an anthropological fashion which has provided further models for discussion.[7] In each case, the anthropology allows one to go beyond noting the fact of religious belief to think more about its social effects, its psychic affects, its narrative conventions – and hence to understand more about the social and cultural work that religion performs.

Another area where anthropological work – principally that by Jack Goody and Walter Ong – has been hugely important is in the study of medieval literacy and orality. For

Goody, societies that were not dominated by literacy and texts (including, he would argue, the early middle ages) are characterized by an 'oral' culture that differs in various ways from literate culture. Orality, Goody suggests, is more fluid, transitory, and labile; whereas literacy fixes things – customs, laws, norms – into static positions, and hence facilitates the *development* of further complexities.[8] As European society undeniably did move from a lesser to a greater degree of literacy over the long medieval period – although the degree to which the early middle ages lacked literacy is debatable – there is an obvious attraction to thinking about what differences the presence or absence of the technology of writing made to societies. Some have seen signs of a cultural cleavage between the literate clerical elite and the oral mass populace, played out in various ways and with various effects (something to which I shall return in the following chapter). The idea of thinking of literacy as more than a skill, as something encoding a number of cultural investments, has prompted further analyses. As mentioned in the opening pages of this book, *litteratus* in the medieval West meant Latin literacy, and moreover the implication of a particular cognitive authority and ability. Literacy was something contested in medieval societies. Two ninth-century Byzantine priests were sent by their emperor to preach Christianity to the Slavs of Moravia. To aid their conversionary task, they developed (for the first time) a written form of Slavic, and translated the Greek bible and some other texts into that language. However, when visiting Venice and Salzburg, despite their efforts to aid the spread of Christianity, the priests were attacked by Carolingian clerics for their translation activities.[9] For the western clergy at that time, there were only three sacred languages: Greek, Hebrew and Latin. Anything else defamed God's word. In practice, Latin had become the language of western Christianity, and hence a foreign language to northern Europe. Moreover, within the Carolingian empire – and then more widely, into the German lands, Poland, Hungary and Scandinavia – Latin became also the language of kingship and secular authority. Literacy was not an inert medium; it was deeply implicated in structures of power. Concomitantly, some historians have discussed oral cultures of resistance, seeking to demonstrate different modes of cultural operation – in memorialization, dispute settlement, feud and so forth – rooted in a cognitively different mode from that dictated by textual culture.

However, the ideas of Goody and Ong also point to some of the potential pitfalls of the use of anthropology. Some historians have doubts about the applicability of theories based upon the observation of, say, mid-twentieth-century Polynesian tribes, to, say, fifteenth-century Waldensian heretics. Moreover, the 'literacy thesis' of Goody has been comprehensively criticized within anthropology for its essentialism and nativism – the assumption of a 'simplicity' to oral cultures, and the inherent teleologism of seeing literacy as a 'development'.[10] More broadly, some older strains of anthropology, based upon a view of 'native' society as 'primitive', have unhappily bolstered views of the middle ages (particularly the early middle ages) as similarly basic – as a kind of historical 'childhood' out of which modern society 'grew up'. But as recent work demonstrates, in both the anthropology of oral cultures and the history of the early middle ages, societies that lack textual records are not simple, but in fact highly complex – only that complexity is less apparent to the historian's or anthropologist's first glance. With specific regard to medieval literacy, historians have more recently argued for the interpenetration of oral and literate modes of culture, noting for example the ability of one literate person to disseminate a text to a much wider circle (hence expanding the practical effect of literacy), whilst also pointing to the particular cultural 'charge' that literacy and texts carried with them in the middle ages.[11] One might note here the presence of both in Ramon Muntaner's world: the importance of the two scribes at the apparent impregnation of Maria of Montpellier – literacy – balanced against the importance of the large and various numbers of personal witnesses also present – orality, of a para-legal nature. (One could further note that whilst Muntaner was producing a vernacular chronicle that stood in relation to other historical texts, he was almost certainly reliant upon oral tradition for his source of this particular story; and the tale itself reverses a much older story told of attempts to replace the lawful wife of King Pippin the Short (751–68) with another woman).

Where historians, particularly Anglophone medievalists, have been most cautious about anthropology is in regard to the latter discipline's search for deep structuring principles in human social formations. Whilst this appealed to Bloch's generation of historians, and many of the French medievalists who came after him, it has been treated much more warily by English, American and German historians who have seen their job as dealing more with specificities than with generalities. However, anthropology itself moved on in the second half of the twentieth century. The 'anthropology (or sociology) of the everyday', associated particularly with Pierre Bourdieu and Michel de Certeau, has provided a further set of analytical tools, 'post-structuralist' in the sense that they do not assume the presence of deep, stable structures to human affairs, but see rather more contingent, fluid and ideological structuring principles that ebb and flow in different situations.[12] Bourdieu presents the notion of *habitus*, the set of embodied practices that encode a social group's ideological principles 'below' the level of overt discussion: in medieval terms, for example, the combination of public behaviour and gossip that constitutes *fama* ('fame' or 'rumour' or 'honour', depending on the situation).[13] Bourdieu encourages one to see the logic of apparently inexplicable or barbarous social events from the historical actor's point of view, within the shared systems of their cultural context. William Miller thus demonstrates the coherence of feuds within medieval Icelandic culture, excavating the complex set of ideas about 'exchange', economic or symbolic, within which feuding made sense.[14]

The best of medieval historiography – Miller being an excellent example – talks back to anthropology, furthering discussion and development of the analytical tools that both disciplines use in their attempts to grapple with human societies. And anthropology is perhaps best understood not simply as a provider of 'models' of behaviour which can be taken to the medieval archive, but as a prompt to new questions, rooted particularly in anthropology's willingness to listen to what 'the Other' has to say, and take it seriously on its own terms. Thus recent medieval work has begun to think about the ideological formation of social space, modes of acculturation, the uses of gift exchange, the social construction of emotions, and other such topics. There are problems with the direct application of anthropological models here, not least because anthropologists can talk *with* the subjects of their analysis – a rather key element in the study of emotions, for example – whereas historians can only read/see/excavate the traces of their subjects. But, given that the starting point for historians is the initial encounter with the evidence – the discovery of Muntaner's tale of Jaime I's conception, for example – anthropology continues to provide essential help in developing the right kinds of questions to ask, and the most productive attitude of sympathetic enquiry in which to ask them.

## Numbers and Statistics

Ramon Muntaner's chronicle posed one kind of problem – how to get inside a story from a world not completely like our own. But other kinds of evidence present different challenges. Take, for example, the Florentine *catasto* of 1427. This was a highly detailed and diligent tax assessment survey of the city and its subject environs, carried out in response to the city's ongoing economic problems caused by war with Milan. A fiscal head of household was noted in the survey, and assessment made of not only property value (assessed by its economic productiveness) but also business investments, and holdings in the city's public debt. The records supply other details too: the number of people in each household, the name of the fiscal head and usually his or her occupation, the location of the household and its holdings and so forth. It is, in other words, a very rich record. And vast: nearly ten thousand entries for the city itself, and more for the *contado* and *distretto* (the countryside around Florence and the areas beyond).

This is not a document that presents a narrative, tells of people's feelings, or proffers words allegedly said by a startled king in his bedchamber. It is more like looking at a modern telephone book: a daunting mass of data, with no obvious immediate use beyond that for which it was created. It is here that other kinds of skills and tools come into use, those drawn from economic history. We should note at the outset two broadly different aspects of economics that medieval historians, among others, have found useful: first, economic theory (such as Marxism), which seeks to explain, often on a grand scale, the course of human events primarily through underlying economic causes; secondly, the tools of serial analysis and statistics. That is, plotting the movement of certain variables over time (often via graphs), and condensing large bodies of data into meaningful and comparative proportions (often via tables). Thus, although one cannot 'read' the *catasto* in any meaningful, linear fashion as one might read a chronicle or a sermon, one can make it speak in all kinds of interesting ways, about not only tax but also neighbourhood, lifecycle, gender, and other matters. We do this not by reading, but by counting.

The tax survey – and others like it, in Italy and elsewhere (although the 1427 *catasto* is probably the richest medieval record of its kind) – can be analysed firstly for proportionate relationships in various ways: social roles, gender, household size, geographical location, and so forth. David Herlihy and Christine Klapisch-Zuber did just this, and more, in their important book *Les Toscans et leurs familles* (1978), and they tackled the huge pile of information the *catasto* contains by creating a database. The various pieces of information gathered by the tax officials were placed in different fields, and one can then search across these fields, singly or in combination, to construct different statistical pictures. Some of this database (relating only to the city) is now on-line, and, treading in Herlihy and Klapisch-Zuber's footsteps, we can attempt to ask questions of it ourselves.[15] Let's think about what size a household was, according to whether one owned or rented the accommodation. At each stage, we ask the database a specific question – how many entries of this kind, of that kind? How many entries mentioning this, but not that? – and then try to consider the contextual variables which need to be taken into account. The on-line database tells us that 4,111 heads of household declared that they owned the house in which they lived, whereas 4,196 said they rented (the remainder – 377, mostly servants or grandparents who for some reason were being treated as the fiscal head for the purposes of the *catasto* – lived in houses where they did not pay rent). Of these, 1,278 of the owner-occupied houses had households of six or more people, whereas only 915 of the renters were as large as this. The disparity grows as one moves to larger household sizes: 636 of the owners had eight or more people in their house, compared to 334 renters. If one looks for very large households – ten or more people – there are still 276 owners in this position, whereas only 111 renters made it into double figures. Given a total number of households of this large size – 402 – the owners thus constituted 68.7 per cent of very large households, against 27.6 per cent of the renters (the small remainder being houses of non-owning, non-rent payers). Of course, these were still a minority within the city: households of ten or more people formed less than 5 per cent of Florence's dwellings, only 6 per cent of owners had these very large households, and only 2 per cent of renters.

One could continue playing with such figures for some time, and they would probably make best sense plotted on a graph for each value of household size, rather than the slightly arbitrary divisions that I've chosen here. The 377 non-renters ought also to be further analysed – although mathematical techniques exist for establishing how much their returns could *potentially* affect the figures given. But in any case, the broad point is made: large households in Florence in 1427 were more likely to be found in properties owned by the occupiers. The important thing to note for *us* – as this is not a book about fifteenth-century Florence or medieval household structures – is that through using certain tools of analysis, a forbiddingly detailed record like the *catasto* can be made to speak. Of course, my brief investigation here is but a beginning: one wants to know *why* household size varied thus – the greater presence of family elders, larger numbers of children, or greater numbers of servants? – and this would involve asking further specific questions of the *catasto* and also looking at other evidence for fifteenth-century Florence such as household diaries or letters.

The *catasto* of 1427 allows us to investigate that city synchronically – that is, take a momentary slice through time – but bringing other evidence into play permits diachronic analysis: asking questions about change over time. Samuel Cohn, for example, has used the 1427 *catasto* in conjunction with seven other sets of taxation records, stretching from 1365 to 1460, to examine ten Tuscan villages, comparing the demographic and economic experiences between the mountains and the plains, how they changed during the period, and paying particular attention to the experience of women (which, he argues, became progressively harder).[16] Nor is it only fiscal records that can be usefully examined in this way: Cohn has also used statistical analysis of Italian wills to study patterns of testamentary culture and how they changed over time, arguing from this data that fourteenth-century plague (but more the return of plague in 1363 than the initial 'Black Death' of 1348–51) affected the manner in which Italians disposed of their property and moveables after death.[17] Other historians have used statistics to analyse matters as varied as the gender of medieval saints, patterns of criminal behaviour, the preaching practices of heretics, the contours of monastic kinship networks, the mortality rate of monks during plague, and so on. If you can count it, you can analyse it statistically.

When using statistical and serial analyses one needs to remember the nature of the evidence base. The *catasto* provides but one set of information, and other sources (where they exist) may add nuance to the picture of Florentine society, and could alter it substantially. Drawing graphs and tables is fantastically useful, as a means of generating usable information from large data sets; but, through its numerical and graphical nature, it can start to look beguilingly 'factual'. For example, any study of wills – a form of evidence often subjected to statistical analysis – must be framed by the fact that only a proportion of medieval wills survive for any single area, and many lower social groups never made wills in the first place. Therefore, claims made about testamentary culture reflect the practices of only *part* of the population – that part visible to us from this kind of evidence. When conducting serial analyses of change over time, the historian needs records that provide the same or very similar data across a number of years. Studies on the economic effects of the Black Death have, for example, used manorial records to look at changes in wages in later fourteenth-century England. Any analysis of wage fluctuation must, first of all, be set alongside price fluctuation to give it real meaning. But prices may fluctuate in non-uniform ways, dependent not only on local labour market conditions, but also on factors affecting national or international trade. Furthermore, in order to look at wages over time, historians necessarily focus on regular and formulaic sources that are easily comparable – seigneurial accounts of cash expenditure, for example. But this ignores irregular records of non-monetary elements, such as gifts; and, indeed, there is some evidence to suggest that in England, whilst cash wages were to some degree kept down in accord with the Statute of Labourers of 1351, landowners found ways of circumventing the legislation (to which they themselves were subject) by providing an additional 'wage' in gifts. In other words, a potentially important part of the economic transaction was invisible to serial analysis of cash wages.[18] A graph or chart or set of statistics is only as good as the evidence from which it is drawn; and that evidence will always have some lacunae, and on occasion may be completely misleading.

To turn now to the other aspect of economics, the fragmentary nature of medieval evidence has made it difficult for historians to use economic theory in regard to the period with any confidence. Analyses of medieval economics have tended to be either extremely micro – the fortunes of a particular monastic estate – or hugely macro – the great patterns of international trade over a long period of time. In each case, what we don't know raises doubts over what is presented; a point that could, of course, be made with regard to every area of history, but to which economic history is particular susceptible, due to its attempt to perceive the workings of systems in their entirety. Simple economic theory posits, for example, that a fall in population (as occurred in the later fourteenth century) should lead to a fall in land value, this in turn to a fall in prices, and at the same time there should be a rise in wages. However, as the great economic historian M. M. Postan pointed out, human behaviour complicates the matter: wage earners were more likely to be attracted into tenant-farming if rents were low, and hence they may disappear (as wage earners, at any rate) from the records. A study of wages may not therefore accurately reflect population levels. And, as already noted, there is a grey area around the notion of 'wage': the records usually allow one to study cash wages, which were certainly a major feature of later medieval society. But other benefits from an employer may have affected the attractiveness or otherwise of an apparent cash wage: not only gifts, payment in kind and barter, but also the provision of food and shelter, and the possibility of connecting oneself politically and socially, as well as economically, to a useful future benefactor such as a large monastery.

This is not to say that economic analysis is not possible – a string of articles on late medieval England in the journal *Economic History Review* (itself founded by medievalists) attest otherwise – but that modern economic theory more often provides the prompt to frame certain questions, than the levers of conceptual machinery that will necessarily provide a solid answer. A particular feature of medieval economic life was that, in some respects, its markets (in the broad sense of the word) worked differently from modern ones. It was not the case, as various historians have shown, that medieval economies were utterly pre-capitalist and paternalist: the apparent division and control of labour by guilds was frequently more an aspiration than a fact, and where it was at its strongest – in the production of wool and cloth in north Italian cities for example – it was part of a pre-modern economy closest to nineteenth- and twentieth-century industrialized capitalism, based on a large wage-labour force often in tension with a small entrepreneurial elite.[19] Nor was the Church's prohibition against usury (lending at interest) quite the disbarment that one might expect: moneylending was common to all cities, and was far from limited to Jewish bankers. In the city of Bruges, a lack of supply of coinage in the fourteenth century meant that much business depended upon loans, and the use of letters of exchange and book transfers – aspects of modern, cashless banking. 'Usury' was defined here as lending at a rate greater than 2p in the pound per week – an annual rate of 43.3 per cent.[20] So parts of medieval society, particularly in the large cities and particularly from the thirteenth century onward, had economic aspects not dissimilar to those of much later ages. But in other respects, medieval cultural expectations about profit, social roles, fair prices and so forth mean that straightforward application of economic 'laws' of supply and demand, or 'rational choice theory', are extremely problematic. Take the staple of bread, often used as a key indicator of price fluctuations and standards of living. Local authorities set various requirements for bread, in weight, content and price, which meant that it did not operate as a normal good within a free market. These regulations had unexpected effects on the profit-margins of medieval bakers, making particular kinds of loaves more profitable at certain times and less profitable at others. Bakers were all independent artisans, but they were not permitted to be entrepreneurs in the sense that, say, a cloth merchant might be. They were servants of the broader community, the common good, and the regulations sought to allow them a 'fair' income, rather than something governed by the ebb and flow of the market.[21]

Marxist perspectives, inasmuch as they are versions of economic theory, have provided two particular elements to medieval history. The first – shared by pretty much every historian of every period of every political stripe – is the insight that people's material circumstances tend to affect their social and cultural productions. Not many medieval historians nowadays then go on to talk about 'class' in a classically Marxist fashion, as coherent groups bound together (whether wittingly or otherwise) by their economic interests.[22] But a looser sense of class has pertained, and is in some areas making something of a comeback. Again, the theory at least prompts one to ask the question – are the differential material circumstances of people in this part of medieval society affecting their ideas, expectations, perceptions, solidarities? – whether or not one feels it supplies the whole answer. The other aspect of Marxism that pertains is the epic 'transition from feudalism to capitalism'. The stark and crude division of the span of western history into feudal and then capitalist societies does not much appeal to most medieval historians, partly because we tend to favour nuance over grand narratives, and partly because, for reasons discussed above regarding Bruges, it does not well represent the complex breadth of medieval experience. However, it is true that medieval economies and societies *in aggregate* are of a rather different kind to modern, capitalist societies; and the question of how, through what processes, and on what timescale that change came about continues to be a topic of interest. Recent work suggests that some elements of capitalist 'modernity' – substantial wage labour and a market-based economy – need to be pushed well back into our period.[23]

## Archaeology and Material Culture

As mentioned in chapter 1, the general consensus among historians today is that medieval people were more literate, and much more familiar with documentary culture, than older stereotypes of the 'Dark Ages' would suggest. Nonetheless, it is also true that for the vast majority of medieval people, listening to a text being read was, if not quite 'rare', then something reserved to particular and limited occasions; and being involved in the creation of a text was an even more specific and unusual action. People throughout the middle ages spent *most* of their time not reading or writing, but doing things that we all still do – eating, excreting, sleeping, tidying and cleaning their domestic space, buying and selling or bartering things – and some things that only a few of us now do: agricultural labour, animal husbandry, brewing beer, going on pilgrimage and so forth. All of these things have left some trace in the documentary record, but the written sources only ever capture a snapshot moment, and necessarily miss out the vast majority of human experience. For earlier periods – the fall of the Roman Empire up till, let us say, 1100 – few kinds of document exist to tell us much about such activities, and almost none that recount them for other than the social elite. However, what does survive is material culture, which bears the fuzzy imprint of daily life in a way that texts do not.

Archaeologists work with things and places rather than texts, and their sense of how to 'read' such materials differs in important aspects from those of historians. There has indeed been a degree of tension between the two disciplines, usually implicit on the historians' side, but more explicit on the other. Archaeology, partly because of the techniques it utilizes and partly through disciplinary choice, tends to see itself as a more 'scientific' subject than history. All kinds of science – biology, DNA analysis, carbon dating, computer modelling, magnetic imaging and the like – are used in the service of archaeology. Its sense of how to investigate a historical theme, and its framework and purposes of investigation, tend to differ from those of historians. The root cause of the disciplinary tensions was historians' tendency to treat archaeology as 'the handmaid of history' – a useful helper, but incapable of independent insight – which led some past archaeologists to declare the independence of the spade, and to claim an objective trustworthiness for the archaeological record, in comparison to all those 'biased' texts beloved by historians. Such polarized viewpoints are today more rare, though some disjunctures remain.

Partly because of these differences, but also because of the innate gap between the material and textual records, the findings of historians and archaeologists can differ markedly, even when treating the very same subject. For example, studies of castles in England by historians, working on the basis of documentary sources, for a long time proposed that castle-building, on the classic motte-and-bailey pattern, was brought to the country by the Normans after the Conquest in 1066. They were defensive structures, part of the process by which a military elite subjugated the native population. Archaeological surveys, however, pointed out that motte-and-bailey castles do not seem to be present in Normandy itself prior to 1066: the Normans thus could not have 'brought them over', and must at best have invented them during the process of conquest. However, the archaeologists have argued, excavation of pre-Conquest sites in England may demonstrate the prior existence of large, circular defensive structures, much like the surviving castles. Castles – depending upon how one defines the term – could be more indigenous than one might think.[24] Furthermore, more recent, interdisciplinary work has argued that the siting and style of castles was very rarely a matter purely of military and defensive capability; they are better understood as structures that communicate lordship – social and political dominance – through symbolic, as much as practical, means.[25] What look reassuringly 'solid' and objective – large stone structures plonked firmly in the landscape – can in fact turn out to be as prey to interpretative complexity as the most ephemeral work of fiction.

It is, of course, not always the case that text and material remains prompt radically opposing interpretations. More normally, the two complement rather than contradict each other. This has very much been the case in the history and buildings archaeology of late medieval civic life, analyses of medieval monasticism and its culture, or, to take an area of particular current interest, the study of death. Late medieval culture produced a particular genre of writing on death – the *ars moriendi* or art of dying well – that focused on the theological aspects of sin and salvation; and, as in most cultures, death had been a theme in medieval literature of all kinds for centuries. Thus the written evidence, in broad terms, points research towards beliefs about death and the afterlife, the desire for salvation and the fear of damnation, and is generally directed 'beyond' this world. Study of the material culture of death – mortuary practices, funerary monuments, grave-goods and the like – adds a different perspective over a longer time frame.[26] Whilst supernatural beliefs obviously continue to have importance, other more social aspects are brought into view. Thus the siting of burials can be read for evidence of social stratification, and grave-goods (the various precious or peculiar objects interred with the deceased) can help us interpret social display and funerary culture.

The combination of history and archaeology has produced a sophisticated analysis of the cultures of death for different periods, and more broadly the complex ways in which the surviving material evidence may be interpreted for markers of cultural identity. For the early middle ages, differences in mortuary practices were long used as badges of different ethnic identities: by looking at how people buried their dead, archaeologists attempted to diagnose to which religious and ethnic groups they belonged. However, recent work has pointed out problems with this, noting for example that from English evidence there is no clear division between unadorned (notionally 'Christian') burials and those containing substantial grave-goods ('pagan'); rather, there is a blurred continuum, with a suspicion that grave-goods came and went in waves, affected by economic and cultural factors.[27] Through the use of both textual and archaeological sources, Bonnie Effros has argued that Merovingian funerary ritual employed elements of Germanic and Roman traditions, and hence diagnosing a 'pure' ethnic identity is not possible. Where variations in funerary practice are found within cemeteries, one should not assume that ethnicity is the only factor: age, gender, and social status may also have affected the ritual elements of a particular burial. And, Effros suggests, funerals are symbolically rich, ideological acts; they do not simply 'reflect' an ethnic identity, but can produce and transform it.[28] In a similar fashion, a very careful analysis of treasure hoards and grave-goods (among other matters) in the sixth- and seventh-century Danube region has complicated previous ascriptions of 'barbarian' and 'Slavic' ethnic groupings. Earlier work, for example, noted differences in brooch design between two areas, and, from this and other evidence, diagnosed the existence of two particular barbarian communities, Lombard and Gepid. However, it has been pointed out, the different styles can be found elsewhere in Europe; and other styles can be found within apparently Lombard and Gepid 'regions'. Similar arguments can be advanced for the alleged 'incomer' group, the Slavs. In fact, argues Florin Curta, rather than imagining 'a great flood of Slavs coming out of the Pripet marshes' to bang up against the edge of the last of the Roman Empire, one might better see 'Slav' identity as something formed within existing communities, in response to the vast building programme initiated by the emperor Justinian on the Danube frontier and in the Balkans.[29]

In this and other areas, particularly for the early middle ages, the richness of archaeological material far surpasses that of the extant texts, and may make us aware of things otherwise completely unsuspected. Some elements of late medieval culture are seen only through objects and never mentioned in texts: a number of remarkable pilgrim badges depicting male and female genitalia have been found in Germany, the Netherlands and elsewhere. These cheap, plebeian objects have no known textual glosses, and we would have no hint of the curious mixture of sacred and profane found here, were it not for the material survivals. They remain open to interpretation.[30] Landscape archaeology can indicate the possibility of deep-seated patterns to human culture and politics: the study of settlement patterns, for example, can be mapped in different ways to agricultural practice, and in turn to soil type. Careful analysis of different kinds of soil, and the necessary demands of making it agriculturally productive, suggest that the very ground upon which we stand may influence all kinds of cultural complexities. For example, a certain clay soil that must be ploughed very swiftly necessitates agricultural collaboration, which leads to closely nucleated settlement patterns, which in turn facilitate collaborative action in more complex areas, and perhaps shape certain kinds of social and political identities.[31]

Archaeological study has also had a great impact on the study of the medieval economy. Take Scandinavia, for which very little written evidence exists prior to 1200. Analysis of physical objects and their movements, however, suggests the existence of some important trading links over very considerable distances: whetstones found hundreds of miles from their source, Norwegian iron discovered in Denmark, and so forth. Coin finds at Scandinavian churches also argue that – as was the case in other, better-documented, parts of Europe – they probably served as venues for markets.[32] Archaeology has in fact substantially altered our understanding of the early medieval economy. For a long time, the debate was framed by a thesis developed by the Belgian scholar Henri Pirenne (1862–1935).[33] Pirenne argued that the rise of an Islamic empire in the seventh century severed the long-distance trading routes of the late antique period, collapsing the early medieval economy from one based on intercity trade across the Mediterranean to one landlocked and limited to agrarian simplicity. However, more recent archaeological work has considerably revised this picture. Numismatics (the study of coins) permits one to trace trade exchange of at least certain kinds: if Arabic coinage from the eighth and ninth centuries is found in southern France and northern Spain, and eighth-century Byzantine coins in Marseilles, then a picture of grand-scale trading links begins to emerge. The movement of certain kinds of prestige pottery (locatable by identifying its kiln or, for later finds, the type of clay used) strongly implies the movement of other kinds of more perishable goods, such as silk, alongside it. Recently, the field of bioarchaeology has been able to examine trace elements in human skeletal remains, indicating diet – and the presence of non-local, and hence traded, foodstuffs. Archaeological survivals of various kinds have suggested the existence of early medieval trading places – markets, one assumes – well beyond the famous (and usually coastal) *emporia*; thus what were previously thought of as inactive backwaters seem to have played a larger role in the economy. The most recent grand synthesis of the material across the early middle ages has essentially reversed

Pirenne's model, arguing that it was precisely the presence of new markets in North Africa and the Middle East that underpinned the growth of the European economy.[34] Thus archaeological insights can completely revise the historical record.

These are examples of where material evidence, and specific archaeological study, have complemented and surpassed text-based history's viewpoint. But archaeology has played another important role: encouraging medieval historians to think, and think differently, about aspects of their study that they tend to take for granted. One is the importance of reflecting upon texts as physical objects in themselves. Part of this has older roots in manuscript codicology – the study of how manuscripts are put together – but text-as-material-culture brings further insights. One can think about texts as objects in relationship to other, non-textual objects: a book of hours, for example, can be studied with regard to not only prayers and liturgical writing, but also other devotional objects such as statues, altar pieces and miniatures, and moreover as a part of what one might call 'domestic treasure' – the various precious objects that are valued both materially and for the sense of status they impart, and that tend to be distributed within kin groups via wills and so forth. Historians usually think firstly about what a manuscript says; archaeologists encourage us to think about what one *does* with a manuscript, which may include many other activities than simply reading it.

Another aspect that archaeologists have (in concert with anthropologists) brought to historical attention is the study of space. There are various particular skills that archaeology provides here, from highly technical issues regarding comparative dating and excavation techniques, the use of aerial photography and electronic mapping to the more basic but essential ability to construct a meaningful topography of an area. For example, a study of non-ecclesiastical and non-palatial structures in medieval Constantinople (modern Istanbul) uses various sources, including texts, to build an initial picture of the possible aspects of civic layout: the variety of possible building-types, and a sense of different 'residential zones' (monumental, coastal, high- and low-status residential, and open land). A very careful and comparative analysis of the building remains and archaeological excavations then permits some working hypotheses about the location, design and extent of domestic and commercial buildings, and an idea of street layouts.[35] Late medieval cities sometimes provide the textual sources to reconstruct topographies, but archaeological surveys are essential, and for much of our period, the only option.

Having provided some tools for mapping space, archaeology also encourages us to think about it in different ways. First, change over time. Continuities and contrasts in building techniques and styles can help here, and the presence of new material features at different points in time point to changing usage of buildings and spaces. Thus the study of Constantinople mentioned above suggests that some late antique elite residential buildings were converted into churches during the early medieval period. Secondly, and perhaps most influentially on recent medieval history, both archaeology and anthropology encourage reflection on the social uses and meanings of space. Archaeological theory thinks of material culture and space as part of ongoing human *processes* – in movement, rather than static, and enmeshed within shifting (and sometimes competing) ideas of society, politics and culture. Roberta Gilchrist's influential study of English nunneries has suggested various ways in which architecture and space were implicated in social and gender distinctions. Features such as moats and courtyards, found in various East Anglian foundations, had more in common with manorial settlements than other monastic topographies, and indicate close connections between the nuns and the lesser gentry. By drawing access maps (abstracted plans of the available routes through a building), Gilchrist demonstrates that male monasteries were considerably more 'permeable' than nunneries: an outsider could more easily get into and move between a variety of monastic rooms, whereas various parts of nunneries were only accessible through limited and extended routes. Women's enclosure was thereby more physically guaranteed than men's. Thus monastic space is fashioned not only through practical necessity, but issues of ideology, power and gender.[36] Recent historical work on space has further emphasized its shifting and contested nature. The English marketplace has been analysed as a site of both horizontal social interaction through trade and gossip, and vertical expressions of power through the enaction of public penances and the display of executed criminals; the locations and social meanings of prostitution in late medieval Prague have been read as being transformed under the influence of different religious ideals.[37] These studies, and others like them, engage most directly with anthropology; but it is largely to archaeology that medieval history owes the original inspiration for discussion of the physical world and its meanings.[38]

## Texts and Cultural Theory

> Its claws have driven through the cloud,
> it climbs up with so great a strength,
> I see it grays so like the day, it will unshroud
> the day which will then take at length
> his lady from this noble man,
> for whom I won a difficult entry.
> I will bring him forth from here if I can:
> his many virtues demand no less of me.[39]

The words are those of a watchman, servant to a lady, prompted by the dawning light to consider waking her and her knightly lover, and bid him leave her bed. They form the opening stanza of a short poem written in the early thirteenth century by Wolfram von Eschenbach, himself a knight and author also of *Parzival*, one of the greatest of medieval Arthurian romances. Such a text has an obvious importance to literary critics, interested in the development and technical analysis of literature; but I want to consider here how one approaches such a piece as a historian – and, more broadly, to explore ways in which historians adopt certain tools from literary analysis.

As with archaeology, there is a close relation between the study of history and literature. Both deal primarily with written texts (though in the case of Wolfram's work, texts almost certainly experienced in oral performance, and possibly also composed that way), both are used to close and careful reading of their materials in order to extract all possible meaning, and both are interested in how one moves from a specific text to the wider world of the period. The disciplines have again had a tendency to squabble. Literary scholars have sometimes been prone to appropriating simplistic histories as context for their textual analyses, whilst simultaneously decrying historians' lack of analytical sophistication. Historians tend towards knee-jerk suspicions about abstract theorizing, and have on occasion read literary texts in a lumpenly literal fashion. Medieval literary texts were self-conscious of their literariness, playing with stylistic conventions of great subtlety, alluding to themes not immediately obvious to a modern reader, and were usually soaked in waves of potential meaning rather than claiming any direct referentiality to life. But this does not mean that historians cannot make any use of them. Some narrative poems do contain information on deeds and events: it would be difficult to write the history of the Albigensian Crusade (1209–29) without the *Chanson de la Croisade* for example, and Scandinavian sagas have been vital, albeit hotly contested, evidence for Iceland and Norway. But more importantly literature (and indeed other notionally 'historical' sources) can be read for attitudes, ideas, patterns of thinking and the like. Wolfram's poem tells us nothing of real events, but it can show us something about cultural mores. The watchman has both a loyalty to his lady, and an admiration for the knight with whom she sleeps; there is tension between her desire for her love and her honour; and, as the sun rises to announce the day, the space of the lady's chamber is slowly shifting from a private realm to a potentially public arena. The poem strongly hints that the lady has a husband whom the knight is cuckolding. One need not assume that the poet and the audience approve or aspire to this situation (although it did of course sometimes occur); what is important is that it dramatizes a set of tensions between individual desires of all kinds, and the demands of community and allegiance. Such a tension is familiar in other literature of the period, such as the love affair between Lancelot and Arthur's queen Guinevere. All of this would make sense to Wolfram's audience, both emotionally and intellectually – and hence it gives an insight into the *shape* of their thought and feelings.

Perhaps most interesting is the theme of gender, not only the lady's femininity but the knight's (and watchman's) masculinity. Later in the poem it is clear that it is also the knight's honour that is at stake, and in the stanza quoted above the watchman says that his own duty is prompted by the knight's very many virtues (*sîn vil manigiu tugent*). Masculinity would here appear to be something public, affective and demanding, and about relations between men and other men as much as between men and women. In the idealization of the poem, it also differs by class: the knight can find masculine fulfilment in his lady love sexually, whilst the watchman must be happy with rendering service, a different kind of manliness. This pattern is found not only in 'chivalric' situations but in other areas also, such as artisanal crafts and university intellectuals.[40] Thus whilst a literary text may not often provide 'fact', it can tell us about ways of talking and writing and hence thinking.

Literary theory has prompted historians to recognize the importance of language more widely, not only in realms of literature but all written sources. Language does not simply reflect the world around us; it mediates that world, in both directions, in that our experience of the world is framed and interpreted by language (or, more broadly, cultural ideas and practices), and in turn we attempt to shape the world, and other people's experiences of it, by using language (culture) to present ideas of how we think it is or should be. A good realm of examples can be found in the language of politics. The ways in which elites explain and justify unequal and hierarchical power structures – the hierarchical but reciprocal 'body politic' for example, found in John of Salisbury's twelfth-century *Policraticus* and in many later texts and images – are not simply 'reflections' of the political realm, nor even of how people thought about it. They are, rather, attempts to shape both the thoughts and the reality, and (in this particular image) to make a particular distribution of power and authority appear *natural* and hence beyond question. Following the work of Quentin Skinner and John Pocock for later periods, historians of medieval politics have begun to think about vocabularies of power, tracing for example the complex and shifting meanings ascribed to the term 'the commons' in later medieval England.[41] Mark Ormrod has recently invited historians of that period to think about the complexities of the basic language itself – the slow and intermittent shift from Latin and French to English in the language of royal government – partly in terms of political constructions of national identity but also in relation to fears of vernacular sedition and heresy, and a series of specific negotiations between king and parliament.[42]

It is worth noting, in regard to the last two examples, that what has been termed 'the linguistic turn' incorporates various *different* ways in which historians have become interested in language. Vocabularies, rhetorics, and the meanings of 'keywords' are one area; the politics of vernacularization, and the link between native language and identity, is another. A third area would be consideration of textual *form* and its cultural contexts. Literary texts can very obviously have certain formal characteristics, in terms of rhyme-schemes, rhythm, themes, and so forth. They carry meaning partly through these embedded structures. But what we think of as 'historical' texts can in some ways be viewed similarly. Historians have long noted the formulaic nature of various records – indeed, this has always been a part of 'diplomatic' (the study of documents, *diploma* in Latin). But literary analysis can encourage an appreciation of records' structural similarities that go beyond the more obvious repetitions. Many sources contain narrative, little works of fiction that mould real events into convenient shapes. Preaching *exempla* are an obvious example, and by looking at an array of such materials, an historian can discern some common structural patterns they share. *Exempla* usually have a four-part structure comprising a setting, a test, success or failure, and damnation or salvation. Stories extolling male clerical chastity tend to fall into a limited number of narrative patterns of self-control or divine intervention, shaped by the slightly conflicting themes of the miraculous and masculine self-governance.[43] Narrative can be found also in less obvious places, such as trial documents (as discussed in chapter 2). Deponents and judges each bring something to the record: the former attempt to persuade the court of something (their innocence, their victimhood, their ignorance), whilst the latter provide a juridical grid of interpretation and categorization. These, in combination with the textual habits of the recording scribes, produce the stories presented in trial records, and such narratives bear the imprint of wider cultural expectations – sometimes differing expectations.[44] Thus an appreciation of the narrative elements in our sources can help us, not by attempting to divide the 'true' from the 'false', but by pointing to the wider framework of images, ideas and assumptions within which someone attempted to have their story accepted as true.

Language, narrative, storytelling are all *social*, embedded in and shaping the world around them, and hence important to the historian as well as the literary critic. Language is not simply a means of communication, it is a social deed. As Michael Toch puts it, 'By the very act of speaking, people act and are acted upon'. He goes on to illustrate the point by exploring verbal encounters between lords and peasants in the world of Wolfram von Eschenbach, high medieval Germany. Some documentary accounts, Toch demonstrates, mimic literary encounters in displaying vast disparities of status and power between lord and serf, the latter no more than a tool of the former. But by the thirteenth century a different kind of speech can be found, the peasantry talking in a collective voice as a legitimate group, capable of negotiation with their lords.[45] One of the insights literary and cultural theory has provided to medieval historians is the degree to which social experience is shaped by language – or, more broadly, cultural expressions structured like languages, such as the regulation of clothing and appearance, the conduct of public rituals, and so forth. An area of particular interest has been gender. Feminist medievalists have long analysed the differential experience of men and women, looking first and foremost to socioeconomic conditions for the low status of female labour, the structure of the household and family and the effects that lifecycle had upon women's power. Pioneers in this field also pointed to the power of ecclesiastical misogyny, and this cultural element has in recent years come to the fore, with added complexity. Theorists point out how unstable language is: a structure, but one untethered to fixed points of reference, and hence prey to shifting meanings and innate tensions. Gender, as a system of relations between people and as a constituent factor in people's self-identity, is thus argued to be less solid and stable than one might assume. It is not simply the case that there are men and there are women, based upon a set of bodily differences, from which a certain set of behaviours arise. The medieval period is a particularly interesting field in which to explore the complexities of gender, because of the way in which other social classifications cut across the binary division of man/woman. Scandinavian sagas, Carol Clover suggests, present one unitary model of dominance and power – what we might assume to be 'masculinity' – but in fact are open to both men and women, if they are sufficiently extraordinary. The late medieval clergy in northern Europe, on the other hand, could be seen as a kind of 'third gender', being denied access to traditionally masculine modes of achieving adulthood (marriage, being head of household, etc.) whilst, by definition, not being feminine.[46]

In these and other areas, cultural theory has encouraged historians to look again at what they assume is 'natural' or taken for granted. A principal aspect has been to see all facets of personal identity as constructed rather than naturally arising. Indeed, the notion of individual identity has been historicized in studies of the middle ages. In what was essentially a dismissive move, the cultural historian Jakob Burckhardt (1818–97) claimed that the medieval period had no sense of individuality, and people always thought of themselves as members of groups; the shift to a more 'modern' notion of selfhood, he argued, came only with the Renaissance.[47] A pioneering generation of medievalists questioned the validity of this, primarily by moving the debate back to the twelfth century.[48] Subsequent work has questioned not only the chronology but the terms of the debate: was an ahistorical abstract entity – 'the individual' – discovered, produced, brought into being in a fixed way at any point? Or is it rather that different kinds of identities – some individual, but in our period more collective – were produced in different circumstances? Thus Caroline Walker Bynum has pointed to the way in which pious self-identity depended upon choosing between a variety of *group* identities in the twelfth century, and the importance of imitation as a way of literally re-making the self: as Hugh of St Victor (1096–1141) wrote of the example of the saints, 'we are imprinted by these things through imitations [. . .] But it should be known that unless wax is first softened, it does not receive the form, so indeed a man is not bent to the form of virtue through the power of another's action unless first through humility he is softened away from the hardness of all pride and contradiction'.[49] This 'softening' sounds very unlike modern conceptions of individuality; and Hugh's programme for achieving a pious identity clearly depends on the example of God and the assistance of 'another's action' – being part of a life that is to some extent regulated. Consideration of different *kinds* of identity and individuality, and the means of their construction, have continued to be the focus of attention. Recent work on chivalry has explored the ways in which the apparent tensions contained in that ideology – between violence and peacekeeping, between the individual knight errant and the Arthurian Round Table companionate model – may be seen as essential elements in producing identity, understood within a specifically medieval context.[50]

It is important to end this chapter with a return to reflection on the *medievalness* of this and other matters. I do not wish to state dogmatically that medieval people were essentially different from modern people, any more than I would want to assume the reverse. The question of sameness or difference – identification or alterity – is an important and continuing debate. A great strength of the kinds of theories touched upon here is that they help us to see that one can relinquish the desire for 'essence' and a single, unequivocal answer to such a question. Identity is contextual, and the experience of that identity fluctuates through the contours of age, class, social setting and the like. The kind of subaltern, submissive identity one might imagine for Wolfram von Eschenbach's watchman – an identity predicated on his subservience to lord and lady – need not be read as the limits of all possible identities such a man might possess. As we know from other evidence, someone of the watchman's class held a superior position to other secular men. If married, he might also enjoy a position of authority as head of his own household. As he aged, other offices could become open to him. And on occasion – as was the case quite frequently in fifteenth- and early sixteenth-century Germany – servants, peasants and serfs gathered the collective strength to deny their subservient identity, and challenge their lords in open rebellion.[51]

# 4
# Debating the Middle Ages

History is a collaborative enterprise – or, to put it another way, an ongoing argument. The argument is conducted, mostly, in polite terms of mutual academic respect, and what lies behind the argument is, usually, differences in evidence, viewpoint, perspective and insight. I have no ambition for this chapter to chart every contour of recent medievalist debate, as this would take a much bigger book. There are many specific areas of discussion, the importance of which have shifted at different points in time. A perennial favourite has been medieval demographic change, with particular attention to the depredations (or otherwise) of the 'Black Death' of the mid-fourteenth century, estimates of which have varied between around 10 per cent and 70 per cent of any given population; current views seem to suggest something around 40 per cent, but emphasize the importance (culturally, politically and economically) of local variation – and, as Samuel Cohn suggests, the major return of plague in the 1360s was perhaps of greater long-term impact than the initial onslaught.[1] Some topics were once heated but are now seen as rather outmoded – the effects (good or bad) of the Norman Conquest of England for example – or have settled into a background consensus which yet awaits major new discussion – the general drift of the 'twelfth-century renaissance' for instance. Other debates grapple with terms largely now viewed as overly schematic, but which nonetheless continue to frame the area, such as whether medieval Iberian society was best characterized by *convivencia* (relatively peaceful co-existence between Christian, Jewish and Islamic populations) or *reconquista* (violent conflict as Christian rulers extended their dominion southward).

Most specific areas of study have, at any given time, a particular interpretative dispute in progress, and it's worth trying to understand the wider historiographical contexts within which these specific arguments are conducted. For example, in an area I know well – medieval heresy – current discussions concern the degree to which heresies had independent existences or were the constructions of orthodox power.[2] This theme preoccupies scholars working on various areas from eleventh-century France to fifteenth-century England, in part because of the continued reverberations of a particular book – R. I. Moore's *The Formation of a Persecuting Society* (1985) – which made historians radically reappraise how they understood the relationship between heresy and orthodox authority. But it is also a product of a wider historiographical tendency among many historians to focus upon the ways in which our sources construct, rather than reflect, the reality around them. Arguments are thus shaped, in part, by the methodologies and ideologies immanent to the general business of doing history. Apart from really rather specific topics, usually concerned with the minutiae of high politics, it is rarely the case that debates or reappraisals are prompted solely by the discovery of previously unknown evidence. It is the case though that existing categories of source material are periodically seen afresh from a new perspective, or brought to bear upon new areas – such as the use of canonization processes for writing social history, or the terse records of notarial practice for cultural histories of identity.[3]

In discussing here some debates within medieval history, I am therefore not claiming to present the most important topics for the field (for these will surely change), nor plotting all the ins and outs of particular areas (too specific a task), but attempting to indicate some general themes within which debates have been, and one suspects will be, conducted. Some historians would emphasize differences in the working methods, and means of debate, between early medieval and late medieval histories; it could be argued for example that the relatively sparse source material pre-1100 encourages more structural analyses and greater use of archaeological data, whilst later work has drawn more upon large-scale serial analysis, and is more focused on those aspects of social history which are difficult to capture in earlier centuries. However, these differences are not absolute, and sometimes loom larger in the eye of the outside beholder than the practitioner. I have therefore chosen to emphasize lines of analysis which have been – or could be – shared across the period as a whole.

# Ritual

You were only a king if other people recognized you as a king. How one engineered recognition could vary: issuing laws and coinage, dispensing justice, building castles – or through violence. The royal status of Raoul, king of the West Franks, had not been acknowledged by Duke William of Auvergne, and so, in 924, the former raised an army against the latter and set off for Aquitaine. The forces met at the Loire, each camped on opposite sides of the river. Messengers passed back and forth all day in negotiation. An agreement was reached: William, on horseback, crossed the river, and then dismounted, to approach Raoul on foot. Raoul embraced William, and kissed him. The matter resolved, the two sides parted.[4]

What's in a kiss? How can such an embrace resolve weighty matters, apparently taking the place of pitched battle between warriors? At least part of the answer rests on the entire sequence of gestures: William crossed the river to Raoul (indicating submission); he did it on horseback (indicating status); he dismounted and approached on foot (indicating submission); Raoul embraced William (indicating status – but for both sides, as William did not adopt a more submissive pose, by kneeling for example); and Raoul bestowed a kiss (indicating status – and again, for both sides, treating William fraternally rather than demanding fealty). William had recognized Raoul's kingship – but Raoul was in fact prevented, then and thereafter, from crossing the Loire into the area of William's ducal authority. In the working out of these complexities we are dealing with a language of gestures, and witnessing the power and delicacy of ritual.

Rituals – whether loosely defined as symbolically meaningful action, or restricted to quasi-'scripted' formal activities – pervade medieval society, up and down the social strata. Royal courts were a constant dance of ritual movements: who sat where, who was positioned higher than whom, who passed what to whom, how a head was inclined, a hand turned, a gift rendered and a counter-gift returned. The liturgy was ritual, enacting daily the transformative miracle of the Eucharist, and (at least in the later middle ages) the no less miraculous production of communal accord through the kiss of peace, exchanged between neighbours at the conclusion of mass. Punishments from Church courts demanded ritual humiliations, usually being beaten around the church and the market whilst barefoot and partially unclad. From the twelfth century if not earlier, towns and cities staged rituals of various kinds: the theatre of royal entries to the town, more or less devout processions deployed in the case of deaths, celebrations, saints' days, and calls for divine intervention, the various rituals of guild artisans and confraternity members. Villages undertook annual rituals of different kinds: leading a plough around a fire at the beginning of the year (in the hope of ensuring a good harvest), the sexually charged games of Hocktide (the women chasing and binding men on one day, the roles reversed the day after), the wild celebrations at Midsummer, the annual 'beating of the bounds' that marked the edge of the parish (the children smacked at each waymarker, to drum the geography into their memories).[5]

It is not only the middle ages, of course, that used ritual, and anthropologists enjoy pointing out to modern audiences the ritual behaviour that enters our own lives, such as football games, formal dinner parties, stag and hen nights, and so forth. But medievalists have a particular concern with ritual, because of the key role it appeared to play in three overlapping areas: the negotiation of political power, the sustenance of hegemonic Christianity, and the renewal of peace and community. In each of these areas one sees ritual activities in operation, sometimes alongside, but often in the stead of, other formalized or legalistic structures. Whilst one suspects that modern life would continue fairly smoothly without football matches, dinner parties or outlets of routine bacchanalia, it is tremendously difficult to imagine how medieval politics and society could have been conducted in the absence of kisses, embraces, prostrations, tears, and the other elements of ritual language.

Ritual has thus been of particular interest to historians of early medieval politics (with some recent interest in later periods also), religion and society, and late medieval civic culture. Their specific concerns do not always coincide, and discussions have tended to run along slightly different lines in each area. Work on early medieval politics has been guided in large part by the available narrative sources, which give a clear emphasis to ritual forms of behaviour in the settlement of disputes (such as between William and Raoul), and which seem to suggest that ritual behaviour formed an essential part of what a later age would call diplomacy, whilst being an intriguingly 'unwritten' code; the 'rules of the game' as Gert Althoff has described it.[6] Study in this area has largely tried to understand how ritual fitted into other forms of behaviour and communication. Historians of Christian religion have a different task: liturgy (the principal repository of ritual forms) was a written code from an early stage, albeit one with substantial local variation. Their interest is in understanding the extent and power (or otherwise) of rituals such as the mass, public penance, blessings, and so forth. To what extent were the vast mass of lay people truly engaged by ritual conducted largely in Latin? How important to Christianity was ritual? Finally, in turning to civic ritual – often large-scale ritual involving a considerable number of participants – historians have been interested in analysing how towns and cities represented themselves to themselves and others; and whether rituals such as Corpus Christi processions worked to develop a sense of communal, corporate cohesion, or whether, on the contrary, they were occasions of hierarchy and tension.

There are many debates within and between these areas. One might argue that liturgy was not, in its regular, repetitive form, 'ritual' at all but only 'ceremony' – a distinction sometimes drawn by anthropologists between dynamic activities that negotiated change or renewal, and empty repetitions of a given script that simply announced the status quo. There is argument also over the use of sources. Unlike anthropologists, medieval historians cannot talk with the objects of their study; we are limited to what a past writer (usually clerical) has chosen to record.[7] To return here to our opening example, the question is not so much whether the meeting between King Raoul and Duke William actually took place, as whether the apparent importance of the ritual elements reflects what all participants felt, or was something that the chronicler (Flodoard, in this case) wanted to emphasize. The ritual may loom larger than it should: Flodoard notes that negotiations took place, and these are surely also important. A rather similar interaction some 170 years later gives a fuller picture: Orderic Vitalis tells us of another two armies facing off, those of Henry I of England and his brother (and attempted usurper) Robert Curthose. Matters were again resolved with a fraternal embrace and a kiss, with no fighting; but it is clear that complex political negotiations dealing with matters well beyond personal status preceded this ritual conclusion, including the treatment of other dependent nobles, the transference of certain lands to Robert, the payment of a large annual fee, and a joint agreement to recover from other nobles certain lands formerly held by their father. It is certainly true that symbolic actions (another way of thinking about ritual) were part of it all: Orderic emphasizes that Robert and Henry stood alone and 'unattended' (i.e. as equals), in a large circle of their respective followers, and 'while all eyes were fixed upon them' concluded their discussion, embraced, kissed, and 'were reconciled'.[8] There was certainly an element of public performance here. But how does one balance the ritual element against the gritty negotiation of landholding and finance?

What, in any case, should historians do with ritual? One tradition has been to 'decode' specific rituals, often through recourse to other kinds of texts and imagery. Such an approach has been extremely helpful in shifting understanding away from the tendency to see medieval people as brutish, illiterate and crude. People waving swords around, throwing themselves to the floor, embracing each other, crying in public – all can be seen as means of symbolic communication, not signs of childish behaviour. In this sense, being sensitive and alert to ritual as meaningful action has greatly enriched our sense of medieval politics and culture. But 'decoding' can be problematic if taken too rigidly. What *does* a kiss mean? It can have several valencies within different kinds of ritual context, and may not, moreover, mean exactly the same thing to all observers of (or even participants in) a specific ritual. Different contemporary observers can, indeed, 'read' rituals in quite different ways. Two chroniclers, Richer and Thietmar, record that after a defeat by Otto II in 978, the French moved the eagle atop the palace of Aix-la-Chapelle, in some kind of ritual message to the Germans – only Richer thought that they turned it to the east as a gesture of menace to their neighbours, whilst Thietmar believed it turned west, peaceably directed to their own kingdom.[9] One might be tempted to see this as an effect of the problematic nature of early medieval chronicles and their sources of information, but consider a much later example: both the Venetian ambassador to London and the Drapers' Company scribe record in matching detail processions made by Londoners on the eves of the feastdays of saints John the Baptist and Peter and Paul (24 and 29 June). The ambassador saw the ritual as a great collective communal rejoicing, uniting the city; the scribe depicts it specifically as 'the Mayor's Watch', a strongly hierarchical procession in honour of the civic oligarch's officers, deployed in that year to keep strict order following certain tensions.[10]

Geoffrey Koziol has suggested that simply decoding a ritual in isolation is not terribly helpful: 'if we place it in a vacuum in order to observe it . . . the experiment kills the ritual by isolating it from the complex set of related symbolic behaviour' with which contemporaries would have been familiar.[11] More important, then, is to understand the wider system that any specific ritual fits into; and to see ritual behaviour as a 'language' of considerable breadth and depth, not simply a brief code-book. Anthropology has indeed encouraged historians to think about ritual as something with almost infinitely extensible boundaries – gestures and other forms of symbolic communication not being limited to specific moments of ritual theatre, but suffusing life in general.[12]

The tale of the conception of King Jaime I of Aragon, told in the previous chapter, is hardly a 'ritual' that one can imagine being repeated; but it could be seen as containing ritual features, not only the obvious liturgical elements of prayer and masses, but also the submissive postures and weeping of those notables who burst into the king's bedchamber. Some historians have indeed argued that medieval emotions – at least those of princes and rulers, and as recorded by chroniclers – were more ritual and strategic displays projected outwards than uncontrollable reactions directed inward.[13]

Another question, then, is, what did ritual *do*? Some of those studying medieval religion have, influenced particularly by the anthropology of Emile Durkheim, seen rituals as functioning to restore society to a balanced state. Acts of peacemaking, liturgical rites, fraternity feasts, civic processions and so forth work, it is argued, to activate feelings of community, either through collective representations of wholeness (Corpus Christi processions), projected symbols of sacrifice (the mass), or, in the case of unruly and carnivalesque celebrations, allowing the community to 'let off steam'.[14] 'Peacemaking', as a wider and often political activity, has been analysed through its ritual forms for a much broader area, stretching back to the realm of early medieval politics, into Scandinavian saga culture, to twelfth-century Italy and late medieval France, to mention but a few of the relevant studies.[15] However, work in these areas, and on civic ritual, has increasingly come to question the functionalist argument. Civic rituals were very frequently hierarchical, setting out the complex arrangements of rank within secular society; and in the case of Corpus Christi processions and plays, there is clear evidence that violent argument about hierarchy could break out on precisely these occasions. Furthermore, a number of large-scale revolts were launched on or around grand annual ritual occasions, such as Corpus Christi or Midsummer: not only the events of 1381, discussed in chapter 2, but also the French *Jacquerie* of 1358 for example. Occasions of collective ritual performance were a good time to launch insurrections, whether national or local, because the community was already geared up for collective mobilization, and the ritual context leant an additional weight of meaning (and on occasion, possible excuse) to the political protest.

If ritual is a language, historians are increasingly seeing it as one through which arguments were conducted: a position proposed, countered, something altered in the process. Ritual can be seen not as a mystical recipe for transforming enmity, but a set of possible (public) positions one can adopt, with a variety of potential outcomes. Moreover, ritual always frames the possibility of breaking the script and rewriting the action. Townspeople at Chambly in France went into the local woods, owned by the monastery of Pontoise, on Mayday 1311; but instead of simply gathering the small amount of greenery that custom permitted, they came in great numbers and stripped all that they could. Part of the motive may have been simple material need, but the ransacking was also a particular symbolic action – an assertion of collective strength by the commune – diverging from the existing customary script of subservience and charity.[16] Ritual can also be misunderstood, accidentally or deliberately. At the court of the east Frankish king Louis the German, at Frankfurt in 873 just after Christmas, Louis's son Charles jumped up and announced that he wanted to renounce the secular world, which, according to the chroniclers who recorded the event, occasioned much disruption and alarm. This may not quite be all it seemed, however: Charles, who had been plotting against his father, could have been attempting to enact a ritual of public penitence, in the hope of repairing tense political relations. Either Charles's ritual went wrong, because enacted in the wrong way or at the wrong time, or the chroniclers deliberately misconstrued it, writing it up as an act of apparent madness in a calculated political move.[17]

Analysis of ritual is hence an ongoing part of medieval studies, and has been the site of some intense debate. Its centrality to certain areas of discussion, and its relatively recent entry into new ones (particularly analyses of late medieval high politics), ensure that it will remain so for some time to come. New currents in anthropology may spur fresh perspectives on existing examples, and a greater degree of comparison across the areas discussed here would undoubtedly prove productive. A medieval kiss is, at any rate, rarely just a kiss; communicative action and ritual performance suffuse our texts.[18]

## Social Structures

'Feudalism' is a familiar word, but one which fragments upon closer inspection. Journalists and others sometimes use it pejoratively as a synonym for 'medieval' – some unfair working practices being 'positively feudal' for example. Adam Smith and Karl Marx labelled pre-modern societies 'feudal', focused principally upon what they saw as the essential economic structure of the period (arguably underestimating the extent of nascent capitalism associated with medieval cities). Even in modern historiographical deployment, its meaning is potentially multiple. Marc Bloch's *Feudal Society* used the term to define medieval society as one built upon vertical interdependencies, and more broadly to characterize the structure and *mentalité* of that society, arguing in fact for the existence of two different 'feudal ages', the first marked by the fall of Rome, the second by the eleventh-century growth of cities. Most influentially, 'feudalism' has been taken to denote either (1) the combination of land-holding, patronage and affective personal relationships understood to constitute the hierarchical bonds between king, lords and knights. The lower party would perform an act of homage, making him the 'vassal' of his superior, whilst the latter might then bestow a grant of land (a 'fief') or office or other favour. The bond thus formed assumed a reciprocity of support, the superior supplying favours and protection, the inferior providing service (usually military) to his lord. Or else, following an essentially Marxist framework, (2) feudalism refers to the relationship between lord and subject peasant, the latter provided with land to work in exchange for labour service and subjection to financial exactions, and being in this sense 'unfree' (though not owned or without any rights, as a slave would be). Anyone born or marrying into an unfree family became subject to the same restrictions, and such 'serfs' were bound to the land, unable lawfully to choose to move elsewhere.

The latter situation has tended to be termed 'manorialism' or 'lordship' in recent years, but its structure of vertical bondage and notional reciprocity invites continued thematic connection with the relationships between noble lords and vassals – this being precisely why Bloch wanted to describe a complete 'feudal' society. Another influential French historian, Georges Duby, argued also that the combination of lords, fiefs, vassals and homage were products of a sharp change in medieval society around the turn of the eleventh century, brought about by the collapse of the Carolingian empire and other socioeconomic factors.[19] For Duby, these interpersonal agreements and affective relations took place in a period of governmental anarchy, and assumed the role that top-down, 'public' government had previous played. The wider implications of this last point – and some very important criticisms of it – will be explored later in this chapter, but here I want to focus on the issue of social structures and identities, for this is a theme which stretches beyond the specific discussion of 'feudalism' in current medieval history, taking in issues of civicness, family, gender, socioeconomic change and much else.

Duby's argument about a 'feudal revolution' in the early eleventh century was in one part based upon the apparent rise in status of the warrior class who were the vassals – and hence muscle – of the lord. There had always been a social elite (an aristocracy) and there had always been warriors, but in some times and places the warriors were more a class of specialized labour (as footsoldiers remained throughout the middle ages). However, knights – *milites* in Latin – were a new social group, and the twelfth and thirteenth centuries saw the further development of their identity and connections with lordship, into the formation of a noble class. Their status rose, and an accompanying ideology developed, based upon Arthurian fantasy and ritualized martial practices such as the tournament. Thus knighthood not only raised the social level of mounted warriors, it also associated it with an ideology of social transcendence, where a knight and a lady were thought to be qualitatively different *kinds* of persons from an ordinary lay man or woman. This was in general the situation reached by the thirteenth century; in the late fourteenth and fifteenth centuries a further transmutation occurred, as the very rich, mercantile elites in cities began to blur with their previously 'noble' superiors. These high bourgeois elites frequently adopted the chivalric symbols and ideology of knighthood, even if they had little or no involvement in actual martial practices.

Lower down the social scale, one can also discern social stratification, most obviously the complex differentiations between 'free' and 'unfree' peasants, but also the new social dynamics brought about by the development and growth of cities. In the twelfth and thirteenth centuries, medieval cities grew considerably: it is likely, for example, that Florence quadrupled its population during the thirteenth century, and at the end of that period it was forced to build new city walls some five miles in circumference. The movement of populations in and out of cities, the specialized industries that cities supported and, above all, the development of ideologies and associational forms connected with mercantile groups, meant that different social strata were produced. At the village level, in western Europe at least, the bureaucratization of royal power depended in part upon the establishment of local officials – bailiffs and reeves in England, *baillis* and *prévots* in France for example – whose social status was thus raised.

The previous paragraph mentions not only different kinds of people, but *ideas* about different kinds of people. Historians have sometimes sought to establish an 'objective' social structure in a period – its bases in law, economics, power relations and so forth – but always have to grapple with sources which more frequently present ideologies of social structure – the division of society into 'those who pray/those who fight/those who labour', the notion of chivalry, the disparagement of lower social classes as seen in the chronicle accounts of 1381. That there were social strata arrayed hierarchically is in no doubt for any period; but how exactly they were arranged, and with what distinctions and implications is a harder – and hence more intriguing – question. For the early middle ages, archaeological evidence provides clear grounds for discerning the division of society into elite and subordinate, on the basis of not only high-status treasure hoards and burials for example, but also the differential arrangement of settlements and types of building. Documentary sources provide further clues – but, in the case of charters, the signs are frustratingly hard to decipher. One can track (as Duby did) the use of different specific terms to describe and differentiate social identities in such documents: *milites, caballarii, vassalli, fideles*, and so forth. But how one interprets these precisely may be dictated by the discursive context: 'vassal' in French vernacular literature of the high middle ages seems, for example, to mean something like 'courageous and loyal warrior' rather than anything specific to do with land-holding and homage. Furthermore, the change in vocabulary may demonstrate a shift in scribal practices – the adoption of a new formulary – rather than any change in society itself.[20]

Legal sources may present glosses on social identities – definitions of unfreedom, for instance, or explanations of duties owed by a particular kind of person – and these can be extremely helpful. The twelfth-century law code the *Usatges of Barcelona*, discussing penalties (a fine, and corporal punishment) levied for assaults, makes various distinctions and comparisons between levels of nobility. A viscount is worth two *comitores*; a *comitor* worth two *vasvassores*; and a *vasvassor* increases in value, at it were, for every knight beyond five that he holds. In another section, we are told that knights can have different ranks, possibly on the basis of whether they themselves have vassals. Most interestingly, the code states that a son of a knight is due the compensation of a knight up till the age of thirty; but if, by that point, he has not been made a knight, he is compensated only as a peasant. Moreover, anyone who 'abandons knighthood while able to serve it' is judged similarly as a peasant. Peasants themselves are noted only as those who hold 'no rank besides being Christian'; the latter in distinction to Jews and 'Saracens' (Muslims).[21] This gives us quite a full picture of social levels, and moreover the complexity of ideas about status, its assumed or achieved elements, the way in which it is worked out relationally, and its intersection with other cultural ideas about masculinity and religious identity. But one must also remember that it is an abstract set of ideas related specifically to a tariff of punishments. Whether, in a different context, Catalonian lords made the same fine distinctions between a *vasvassor* with five knights and one with ten knights is uncertain.

Moralizing ecclesiastical writers provide a different depiction of society, and from the later twelfth century this had particular pretensions towards including all social levels: explanations of the particular sins to which different social groups were prone for example, or *ad status* sermons directed towards specific audiences. These are again helpful, and can in some instances overlap and reinforce distinctions drawn in different sources, but once again are contextual. Alain de Lille wrote, in the late twelfth century, *ad status* sermons directed towards soldiers, advocates, the married, widows, and virgins.[22] These distinctions could certainly be made between lay people, but they clearly are not the only lens through which they were viewed. Taxation assessments – rare in earlier periods, but quite a rich source from the later fourteenth century – provide a more structured and economic basis for perceiving social strata. Detailed civic sources, for example in late medieval Ghent, allow historians to produce a picture of relative economic wealth among merchants, citizens and artisans, suggesting further refinements of socioeconomic structure. Making socioeconomic strata visible, literally visible through the clothing one wore, seems to have become a preoccupation of various late medieval cities and kingdoms, which passed sumptuary regulation often on the basis of income or birth. The modern historian Raymond van Uytven notes some various ways in which one might chart medieval 'public opinion' on rank in the Netherlands, which might or might not correlate to economic position: the place given in processions or other public events, the quality of gifts given by urban governments to their visitors, the varied travel allowances permitted to official delegates, and sumptuary laws.[23]

From all of this, medievalists working across many different times and places have been particularly occupied with certain themes. The issue of nobility – rank as a matter not only of wealth but also *birth* – is one. The mechanisms, meanings and reactions against unfreedom are another. And issues of gender – particularly whether gender cuts across or supports social hierarchies – has provided a third. Let us take them in turn. The *Usatges* state that 'townsmen and burghers' are due the same compensation as knights, and that a bailiff (an office-holder) 'who is a noble, eats wheaten bread daily, and rides a horse' is compensated as a knight.[24] This gives an interesting mix of economic and ideological distinction: the ability to afford a horse and a certain diet, and the idea of being born noble. Nobility makes some difference (a bailiff of non-noble blood was due only half the compensation) but, on the basis of this particular tariff, raises an office-holder only to the same relative height as a city burgher. The idea of noble birth of course underpinned the pinnacle of medieval society, the king and his 'lineage'. That nobility and the potential for kingship were, in some times and places at least, understood to be transmitted through the blood gave a particular importance to noble women, with both positive and negative effects: women's status was in some senses high, but they were also pawns within a high-stakes marriage market.

However, whilst most of later medieval Europe had a nobility, to what degree their interests cohered as a class, and what the actual implications of nobility were, could vary considerably from place to place.[25] English Common Law made no substantial distinction between noble and non-noble; its main point of divide was between the free and the unfree. In the period after 1066, a key division was understandably between incoming Norman nobles and more or less subjugated indigenous people. In later centuries, the nobility as such were very clearly defined by admission to the House of Lords; but other 'gentry' families were also recognized as being above and different from the common folk. By way of contrast, for much of the middle ages Norway had no 'nobility' as such, but a very clearly defined group of *håndgangne menn* – 'men who have gone to the hands of the king' – to whom a different law applied than to others. However, in the fourteenth century, government officialdom separated from the king's immediate followers, and due to the unions made between Scandinavian countries, the king himself was frequently absent from the kingdom. In consequence, a much more 'European' ideology of nobility was imported – above all the importance of bloodline rather than service – but to a much smaller and less influential group.[26] Nobility did mean privilege, but it did not always mean power. Noble families did not, in fact, necessarily survive very long: of sixteen families of the lesser nobility in twelfth-century Osnabrück, only six were still in existence by 1300; similarly, of seventy knightly families given fiefs in Eichstätt in the years 1125–50, only forty made it to 1220.[27] This suggests that 'nobility' had a wider ideological function than simply the sustenance of *particular* people's fortunes. It formed part of the medieval world's image of itself.

Not, however, that that image ever went unchallenged. As we have already seen, the English Rising of 1381 saw calls for universal manumission from serfdom, and criticism of lordship. This was far from the only occasion when such views were voiced: various rebellions across the middle ages demanded an end to unjust lordship (though not always necessarily its cessation), the common ownership of property, and justice for all. What being 'unfree' meant was complicated, again varying by place and time. Historians have argued over different timescales for the enserfment of the common people. For Duby, it was part and parcel of the feudal 'revolution', occurring principally around the eleventh century. Others have suggested that it came about more steadily from the fall of the Roman Empire, with local landed warriors demanding service of those weaker people around them in return for 'protection'. By the thirteenth century, unfree peasants were bound to the land that they worked, subject to regular and arbitrary financial exactions, and required to render labour services to their lord. How harsh or otherwise these conditions were is also disputed; some have noted that bondage did supply some degree of protection in times of economic hardship, but others have argued that the lord's expropriation of the peasants' surplus labour rendered peasant existence perilous in the extreme. When a drastic drop in population levels occurred in the fourteenth century (through famine and then plague) it does seem to have signalled the beginning of the end of serfdom in some areas at least. But for some parts of Europe – notably Bohemia and Poland – the late middle ages saw a so-called age of 'second serfdom', with lords harshly reasserting dominance in the face of fourteenth century change. The processes by which domination was achieved and sustained are key topics of study, and recent comparative work has brought to light the variations in experience across Europe (and, indeed, contrasts elsewhere in the pre-modern world, such as Japan). In Denmark, for instance, the peasantry had not been enserfed as in England, France or Germany, and they mainly worked land held by leasehold for specific, relatively short, terms. It was, however, a tenet of Danish society that one needed a protector within law who was one's social superior. Changes in legal procedures in the thirteenth century paradoxically led to the peasantry becoming more dependent on, and tied to, landlords for legal protection. In northern Italy, in contrast, a similar period saw rural peasants moving from being tied to the land to a kind of 'share cropper' status known as *mezzadria*, whilst in Hungary the peasants remained obligated juridically to their lords in terms of services and dues, but from the thirteenth century were free in person, being able to move their labour elsewhere without restraint.[28] Historians have further discussed the roots of peasant resistance to these issues, arguing in part about patterns of socioeconomic fortune – for example whether, in the immediate aftermath of fourteenth-century plague, different groups were better or worse off – and also about whether peasants possessed something that Marxists would call a 'class consciousness', a sense, that is, of collective predicament and unity. Recent argument here has focused not only on large-scale popular revolt, but also smaller-scale tensions at the level of the village.[29]

The paragraphs above, largely reflecting the past historiography and in part the sources, have tended to assume male knights, burghers and peasants. But what of women? They have sometimes been presented as, in the title of an influential book, a 'fourth estate' in medieval society, outside the normative tripartite structure.[30] But they were of course present at every level, and much work in the last few decades has been concerned with discussing what a recognition of their presence might do to our understanding of medieval social structure. The discussion differs, depending on whether one is looking at ordinary or noble women. In the lower strata of society – the vast majority of the medieval population – historians have investigated women's experience within the household and the workplace, thinking about their relative power and status, and the changes (if any) wrought by socioeconomic shifts over the centuries. Lifecycle has been noted as particularly important in women's lives: young women in northern Europe frequently went into service, which provided a degree of economic independence. Upon marriage, this shifted radically, as although a collaborative model of marriage *might* pertain for many couples, in law and the marketplace, the woman was largely subordinated to the man. Widowhood brought further shifts, either a return and enhancement of independence if economically stable, or else a rather drastic fall into dependence upon others if not so fortunate. Comparisons between different parts of Europe are again apposite, the most important perhaps being a putative distinction between marriage models in northern and southern lands. In England and other parts of northern Europe, couples tended to marry fairly 'late' – in their mid-twenties perhaps, and with little or no age difference between them. In Italy and other southern areas, women tended to marry younger – maybe still in their teens – and to older husbands.[31] For elite women across Europe, something more like the latter model tended to hold sway. Analysis of this social stratum has looked at the power that women wielded within noble households, noting for example the common expectation that ladies would literally hold the fort in a husband's absence, and more broadly the implication of women as both agents and objects in power strategies of various kinds.[32] For all social levels however, a key and continuing area of analysis is how status and gender combined. At one extreme, given the extraordinary travels and encounters experienced by the outspoken late medieval mystic Margery Kempe, one may argue that her socially privileged background (daughter of a very powerful mayor of Bishop's Lynn) likely played a role in facilitating her adventures.[33] At the other, one can note that common elements of medieval misogyny, such as tales of violent and just retribution against sexually active women, were common across all social levels. *The Game of Chess*, a popular medieval text printed by Caxton, tells of how the emperor Octavian taught his sons to swim, joust and pursue other 'knightly' activities; whilst his daughters were to sew and spin 'and all other works belonging to women', in case they were ever impoverished. The section on 'The Queen' concludes with a tale of a regent who relinquished her besieged castle to the king of Hungary, on the promise that he would wed her. He slept with her for one night, then 'on the morn, he made her common to [i.e. raped by] all the Hungarians, and the third day after he did put a staff of wood from the nether part of her through her body unto her throat or mouth'.[34] This she deserved, the text says, for her inconstancy and adultery. Even a queen could be subject to misogynistic horror; because, in the end, she was only a woman.

## Cultural Identities

[The civic leaders in Strasbourg] have set on high in the cathedral a certain boorish image under the organ, which they thus misuse: on the very sacred days of Whitsuntide [. . .] a certain buffoon hides behind that image and, with uncouth gestures and loud voice, belches forth profane and indecorous songs to drown the hymns of those that come in, grinning meanwhile and mocking at them [. . .] Moreover the Bürgermeister has his own place in the Cathedral, where he has been accustomed to talk with others, even when masses are being sung [. . .] Moreover, they commit other irreverencies also in holy places, buying and selling in the church porch [. . .] and bearing fowls or pigs or vessels through the church, even at times of the divine service. . . .[35]

This account of impious and ribald behaviour in Strasbourg's cathedral comes from a letter to a papal *nuncio* written by Peter Schott, a clergyman in the city, in about 1485. The compositional context is complicated, bound up with a particular dispute between certain religious reformers and the ecclesiastical and secular authorities in the city. Schott's picture of lay abuses was thus part of a propaganda battle. It also conflates a specific, annual practice linked to the Whitsun festival – the mocking image – with what is likely a more regular, and highly common, lay appropriation of sacred space for mercantile and social activities.[36] But the image it conjures of a rumbustious, impious, profane laity clashing with the solemn and sacred power of the Church has a much wider resonance. The Russian theorist Mikhail Bakhtin, writing in the early twentieth century, saw episodes such as this as a sign of cultural divergence, an important gap between a monovocal, official, sacred culture and a heteroglossic, popular, 'low' culture of the masses.[37] Looking to other medieval episodes, such as the persistence of folk magic, the veneration of springs and other unofficial shrines, the belief in non-Christian supernatural entities, or occasions when orthodox faith was apparently mocked or subverted, various historians have taken the theme of cultural division as a key interpretation in the study of medieval religion. Jean Delumeau famously argued that the middle ages were 'barely christianized', the elements of apparent orthodox devotion forming a mere veneer over an essentially pagan underbelly.[38] Similar albeit less extreme views have been propounded by other French medievalists, notably Jacques Le Goff and his student Jean-Claude Schmitt: that there were important differences between 'official' and 'folk' (rather than 'pagan') cultures, although the two were not utterly separable, and intertwined in important ways. Nor were these cultural differences only religious: Le Goff has argued for a shift between 'church time' and 'merchant time' in the late medieval period, for example.[39]

Anglophone historiography has tended to push in the opposite direction, for some time explicitly wedded to the image of a medieval 'Age of Faith' and devout credulity, but more recently and subtly insistent on the specifically medieval nature of pre-Reformation Christianity, arguing for its own vitality and depth. Some historians have suggested that there was little or no difference between 'folk' and 'official', or 'popular' and 'elite', religion.[40] The extent to which the clergy were, particularly at the parochial level, deeply connected with the secular community has been increasingly emphasized; late medieval sermons on marriage from Poland, for example, indicate considerable understanding of, and sympathy for, the realities of everyday lay life.[41] Opinion is thus divided. Two aspects to this argument within religious history link the area to wider medievalist debates: the nature and importance of cultural divisions, and the means and effectiveness of acculturation (the successful dissemination and sustenance of a particular, dominant world-view).

We saw earlier some ways in which medieval society was divided by social hierarchy, and how these strata arguably changed over time. The kind of 'division' explored here is not unconnected to those issues, but is at a more profound level: whether various parts of medieval society had fundamentally different world-views, cultural mores, or *mentalités*. A particular division emphasized by narrative sources from quite an early period is that between *litterati* and *illitterati* – literate and illiterate. As we have seen, to be a *litteratus* implied knowledge, learning and wisdom, and was largely synonymous with *clericus*. The *illiterati*, on the other hand, were also the *rustici*, the *simplices*, the *idiotae*.[42] Without sharing the disparaging sense implied by these terms, various modern historians have seen this perceived division as an essential faultline running through the middle ages. Following the work of some influential anthropologists (as discussed in chapter 3), certain historians have argued for elements of fundamental difference between oral and literate cultures, the former recursive and fluid, the latter capable of cumulative knowledge and reflection, and the development of bureaucratic mechanisms of power.[43] Our access to 'oral' or 'popular' culture can come however almost only through written sources, and historians have emphasized how intertwined, within those materials, the spoken and the written become; and moreover, the clear importance that 'oral' cultural elements – such as custom – had within 'official' culture.[44]

There is also the issue of change over time. To return specifically to the religious question, we know for a fact that, in the early centuries of Christian conversion, pre-Christian religious practices, rituals and places persisted within the general populace. This was in large part because 'conversion' initially meant a change of policy by the relevant local ruler, and mechanisms for instructing and acculturating the general populace into the new faith were initially sparse. A principal tactic by early Christian proselytizers was to transform existing pagan sites or temples into Christian ones. It is probable that this did, in fact, fairly swiftly erase pre-Christian theological ideas and religious rituals.[45] But it arguably preserved a deeper continuity of practice and expectation, the use of certain shrines for healing for example, or the performance of particular rituals of protection relating more to a sense of 'good fortune' than Christian eschatology. By the thirteenth century, it is clear that the Church was expending considerable energy on instructing the laity through preaching and a well-endowed parochial system of spiritual care. Thus by the time that Peter Schott was writing his letter about practices in Strasbourg, any sense of 'pagan' survival is surely unhelpful. The lay practices he decries are more like grotesque manuscript marginalia, used to define the ordered central space of the Christian text.[46] More interesting is the issue of *how* local cultures became Christianized – and the degree of variation that persisted within this notional uniformity. The use of ritual practices, visual imagery, preaching and other pedagogic techniques, all played a role. The means by which cultures are produced and re-produced has been pursued in other areas also, such as the development of post-Roman 'barbarian' identities, and the imposition of a 'Carolingian' culture.[47]

Recent writers have tended to argue that what marked medieval Christianity most particularly was its relatively universal character and shared practices, expressed within local variation. Even those elements one might initially see as 'folk-loric' – such as blessing fields or ploughs to ensure a good harvest – can be seen as deeply Christian in that they deployed Christian prayers, often employed the services of a priest, and were performed at times in the ritual calendar that was, whatever its originary rhythms, by the thirteenth century clearly 'Christian' time. Most Christians of whatever status went to mass; most said prayers; most attended confession; most were baptized, and received Extreme Unction on their death beds. The point can be expanded to encompass other aspects of culture: ritual customs such as 'Maying' were practised up and down the social scale, from the village to the royal court. Late medieval vernacular literature was not restricted to the nobility, and reached at least some way down the social scale. Collective activities such as civic processions or legal courts or religious confraternities involved people across many social strata. The cultural idea of 'chivalry', notionally particular to one social class, can be seen in the fourteenth and fifteenth centuries (and indeed beyond) to be something attractive to non-nobles, particularly mercantile elites who adopted or appropriated elements of its symbology in their self-representation. It has been argued that the social theorizing of Parisian theologians – surely the pinnacle of the *litterati* – was deeply informed by their contact, through preaching and the administration of confession, with ordinary lay people.[48] Even medieval heretics and their supporters *shared* large elements of religious imagery and practice, as much as they diverged from the culture of their orthodox neighbours.[49]

However, one might read some of these examples of shared culture in a slightly different way: as evidence for how successful, over time, dominant culture was at acculturating other social groups. If Christianity *became* a shared culture, it did so through the Church's efforts, embodied particularly in the activities of the mendicant orders, some reformist bishops, and a reinvigorated system of parochial care. One must remember, moreover, that even at the end of the middle ages, the bulk of the surviving evidence tells us principally about the higher ranks of society. Recent work on literacy has emphasized the existence of a much higher level than some older historiography had assumed, starting with the Carolingian empire, and noting later particular peaks of vernacular literacy in north Italy, southern France, Scandinavia and large cities throughout Europe. This has, in turn, helped to question hard and fast assumptions of cultural division, and encouraged the use of literary sources as evidence for shared cultural mores across social classes. But one must be wary: much more literacy than previously assumed is not the same thing as *general* literacy. In a similar fashion, evidence for greater overlap between religious practices than previously assumed is not the same as *complete* overlap. In both cases, something may be lost in the move from one paradigm to another. Whilst books of hours, for example, were certainly a very common feature of late medieval lay religiosity, they were a feature still restricted by and large to a limited, mostly civic, elite. As we saw in discussion of the 1381 Rising, medieval chroniclers could see themselves as members of a political and literate elite, and their negative views on the 'rabble' below them could lead to cultural misunderstanding. The evidence of certain inquisitorial trials indicates both the presence of some very unorthodox and arguably 'folkloric' beliefs, and, perhaps more interestingly, the vibrancy of storytelling and gossip among non- or semi-literate groups; the latter being an element of 'oral' culture which only enters the historical record at extraordinary moments.[50]

We must thus be alert to the possibility of cultural difference, and think carefully about the contexts (social, evidential, chronological) within which cultural mores were expressed. Recent work on attitudes towards sex and sexuality in the period have interestingly drawn out strands of similarity and difference, noting the influence of ecclesiastical viewpoints on social concerns with sexual immorality but also indicating ways in which lay ideas could vary, showing greater tolerance for unmarried sexual activity at times of economic prosperity for example, or, in some parts of Italy, largely excluding clerical involvement in marriage ceremonies.[51] Study of medieval preaching and religious art highlights the importance of what literary scholars would call 'reader-response theory', the necessity of thinking not only about the message intended by the author or preacher, but the ways in which such a message was likely to be received, and the importance of mapping the potentially different ways in which it could be understood. Whilst the theological culmination of the mass was the elevation of the Host, it has been argued for instance that for some lay people the moment of making offerings or saying personal prayers could, for *them*, have been the focus of the ritual.[52] More anthropologically inspired research has emphasized the number of potentially competing conceptions of 'sainthood' at play in canonization proceedings, and the varying cultural contexts and interests they indicate.[53] Such contexts and cultures were clearly not hermetically separate from each other – indeed, as Laura Smoller has demonstrated, the expectations of the (literate, clerical) investigators could, over time, shape the ways in which canonization witnesses 'remembered' their testimony for the written record – but they remain different spheres of cultural association.[54] Moreover, for some historians, the process of communication or education between clergy and laity should be seen as an operation of power, the imposition over time of an ecclesiastical hegemony in terms of morality and social order.[55] With this thought, we turn to our last section.

## Power

In the summer of 1306, on the order of King Philip IV, all the Jews in France were arrested. Their property was confiscated, their families rounded up, and they were expelled from the kingdom; a group perhaps some 150,000 strong. Many headed south, to the Iberian peninsula, or east, to Italy. This was, sadly, far from the nadir of Jewish/Christian relations in the middle ages. There was no accompanying popular violence or pogroms, no programme of anti-semitic preaching, as there had been before and would be again. Philip IV's actions do not particularly stand out amid the broader history of hatred. But they arguably do present a remarkable moment in the exercise of royal power, deployed through an extensive and well-organized machinery of governance. Philip's officials were commanded directly by the throne; the plans for the expulsion were drawn up some weeks in advance of the deed, but successfully kept secret; and the seizure of people and goods was achieved with notable uniformity and great swiftness.[56]

But just a few years earlier, another event from Philip's reign gives a very different picture of governance and authority. In 1300 the king had imposed a tax to fund his ongoing campaign in Flanders. As happened throughout the kingdom, a royal official consequently toured the administrative area surrounding Carcassonne to collect the tax. At the town of Foix, in the Pyrenean foothills, he found himself physically barred from entry and the inhabitants unresponsive to threats of royal authority. Moving on to the town of Varilhes he managed to extract some money, and set off back to Carcassonne. En route, however, he was waylaid by the *bayle* (local official) of Foix and some others, who took the money and his belongings, and sent him on his way. Once back at the city, the royal official sent two sergeants to summon the inhabitants of Foix for contempt; but they too were barred from entry, and were then beaten up at another village. In subsequent years the counts of Foix refused royal orders to hand over the perpetrators, or indeed to accede to the tax. Eventually, the French crown gave up trying.[57]

The theme of this section is not the degree of power wielded by Philip IV of France. Rather, the two examples from his reign highlight two poles of possibility across the whole medieval period that play key roles in larger debates, and have implications for the study of power not only at a royal level. The example of the Jewish expulsion underlines the power of bureaucracy, centralized control, and the potential for the arbitrary intercession of the state throughout the realm. That of Foix demonstrates lack of effective authority at every social level, the limited resources of force at royal disposal, and the difficulty of actually collecting taxation. One could multiply the examples from other times and places: the successful expansion of the Carolingian empire, set against its limited ability to control the peripheries of its realm; the centralization of royal justice in Henry III of England's reign, versus his problems in controlling baronial rebellion in the 1250s and 1260s. For a long time, medievalists tended to think about this spectrum of power in terms of the 'strength' or 'weakness' of individual kings – tending, like the chronicle sources which informed their studies, to associate this to some degree with quasi-moral qualities inherent in the particular monarch – and more broadly to place these judgements within a particular narrative of the rise of the state. Once upon a time, it was said, there was the Roman Empire, a strong and efficient state, with a centralized bureaucracy, taxation, standing armies, and a consequent monopoly on order. When it collapsed, Europe was plunged into governmental darkness, where the only authority came from the sword of whichever local warlord fought his way to the top of the heap. Then the Carolingians came along, and provided a new 'empire' that had at least a modicum of centralized governance. But this too fell (or was frittered away), and around the turn of the eleventh century, a period of feudal anarchy ensued, with localized warlords again holding sway. Finally, across the twelfth to fourteenth centuries, strong monarchs, particularly in France and England, developed centralized, bureaucratic states that provided a stable system of governance and law. These in turn fostered parliamentary powers and led to constitutional monarchies. The foundation stones for the modern state had been laid.[58]

In recent years, however, this tale has come under multiple attack. Various faults are noted: the tendency for French and English experiences to be taken as the dominant paradigm for all Europe, the teleological nature of the narrative, the assumption that centralized, top-down authority is obviously 'better' than decentralized and localized power (or indeed that top-down authority has the 'best interests' of those it governs at heart). Most productively, historiography has moved away from debates about the merits or demerits of particular individual rulers, and has started to think instead about the nature and effectiveness of different elements of rule, and how these changed over time. 'Kingship' is increasingly seen by new strands of political history not as a quality inherent in specific individuals, but as a construct of political culture and a structural component within *wider* mechanisms of dominion. Moreover, what we mean when we talk about a 'state' in the medieval period has been much discussed. All are agreed that it was at no point identical to the modern 'nation-state' – although there is much argument as to whether or not some idea of 'nation' did pertain in various European countries (again, notably, England and France). Different requisites for potential statehood have been noted: the tools to raise regular finance, the maintenance of social order, the ability to intervene at will regardless of geographical and customary variations, the degree to which governance operates independently of direct personal engagement by the ruler. A further question is the necessary degree of interrelation between these elements – how does one square a relatively strong system of royal justice and a relatively weak system of centralized taxation, as in thirteenth-century France?

Certain historians have suggested that tax – or more broadly, the ability to raise regular revenue – must lie at the heart of any discussion of medieval statehood. For the early middle ages, a key debate has been over degrees of continuity in governance after the apparent 'fall' of the Roman Empire. In a synthesis of the historiography, Chris Wickham has argued that some areas – most notably north Africa and Byzantium – retained elements of the Roman apparatus of taxation, whereas others – Britain being a key example – did not. The ability to tax depended upon information gathering and record keeping, means of cooperation between localized and centralized officials, and an acceptance of regularized coercion. In those lands where the Roman system was abandoned, it took tremendous effort to build anything comparable afresh – such an effort, in fact, that one did not see it in much of Europe for many centuries. A strong taxation system did not guarantee a 'strong' state with regard to all matters – Byzantium in the early middle ages was not able to bat away external pressures – but it made possible modes of governance to which other kingdoms could not aspire.[59] In a study of later periods, Mark Ormrod has suggested, with regard to finance, that we could helpfully think about different *kinds* of 'state', arguing for a four-fold typology of 'tribute' state, 'domain' state, 'tax' state and 'fiscal' state.

Thus, whilst the Anglo-Saxon and Norman states did use forms of taxation, these were always applied extraordinarily, and basic royal revenue derived instead from demesne lands and regalian rights. For Ormrod, this makes them 'domain' states. In England, the key change comes only in the mid-fourteenth century, with the introduction of permanent forms of indirect taxation (on overseas trade) and a more frequently imposed direct taxation (on moveable property); at this point, the realm moves to being a 'tax state'.[60] The ability to impose tax, of whatever kind, has itself a complex relationship with other kinds of regnal power. It was common in later medieval Europe for a ruler to grant exemptions from certain taxes to particular corporate groups, most often cities, in exchange (explicitly or implicitly) for other forms of political support. Whilst the consequent growth in civic independence could be seen, in the short term, as a diminution of centralized power, it has also been argued that the governmental machineries developed in precisely these urban settings played a key role in later state development. Equally, in some situations rulers could grant an element of financial autonomy to local areas to promote economic activity and trade, whilst retaining taxation rights over the subsequent trading routes – as was the case under the Sforza and Visconti nobles in fifteenth-century Tuscany.[61]

Beyond all this however is a still wider question. As Patrick Wormald has put it, 'Power is the staple of modern historical discourse . . . . Yet, when asked what they *mean* by power, historians can look shifty.'[62] To answer this, one must look beyond the specific machinery – a taxation system, a jurisdictional area, and so forth – to the ways in which such elements were permitted to operate in the first place. And the question can in fact be widened from the issue of royal or governmental power, to encompass the broader realms of medieval society – the power wielded by nobles over commoners, the power wielded by civic elites over city-dwellers, the power wielded by the Church over Christendom, and power at its most local levels, in the villages and parishes and households.

First, violence. It would be wrong to depict medieval society as characterized by constant violence. But it is clear that the possibility of violence – and its intermittent strategic enactment – played a role in the creation and maintenance of political systems at all levels. Whether we are in a world of small-scale minor lordships, or broad, cross-boundary 'empires', the ability to inflict decisive physical force was a common factor in control. Frankish expansion in the eighth century began, at the very least, through military victory, and resistance to the empire, such as the sworn conspiracy of central German landowners in 786 against Charlemagne, could be met with violence both real and symbolic: the ring-leaders were blinded and executed. There are several reasons why Lithuania was brought within late medieval Christendom or Wales under English royal control, but pre-eminent was the use of military force. The potential for, and periodic reality of, horrific violence characterized relations between lords and peasants also. Orderic Vitalis tells us that Count Galceran of Meulan, in 1124, punished peasants who had illegally cut wood from his forests by having their feet amputated. Felix Hemmerli, a mid-fifteenth-century writer in Zurich, recommended that peasant farms be razed to the ground once every fifty years or so, in order to prevent them from becoming 'arrogant'.[63] Such actions were not constant, and as a strategy could backfire – one might argue that it was precisely the harshness of serfdom in fifteenth-century Germany that sparked major peasant rebellions and the sixteenth-century 'Peasants' War' – but the *threat* of violence was ever present. Violence could come from central authority, such as royal justice, from within local hierarchies, such as the lord and his men, and from communal sources, as when people were subjected to humiliating public penances for fornication or adultery. Individuals attempting to maintain 'honour' had recourse to violence – in 1479 one Fritz Schreppler attempted to cut off his wife's nose in the marketplace in Nuremberg, both a physical assault and an act of symbolic meaning, as various similar cases attest.[64] Part of what kept the medieval social order in place at all levels was physical force, and the meanings given to violent action.[65]

Another set of tools, connected in some ways with the above, was the bestowal of patronage and the cultivation of personal charisma. Much work has been done on the former topic, in older work on institutional structures and kingship, and in recent historiographies which take a more anthropological view of power. The process of patronage – bestowing office, lands or favours in return for political support – is familiar across medieval politics, from the creation of the Carolingian empire, to the activities of various Emperors in the German lands, to the consolidation of the Capetian kingdom under Blanche of Castile. Studies of civic oligarchical elites indicate similar systems of patronage and kinship networks at a more local level, and one suspects that further work lower down the social scale would provide yet more. Understanding how patronage operated in part leads us back to issues of social structuration, but also directs us towards interactions of secular with ecclesiastical spheres of power. In the eighth to eleventh centuries in particular, it has been argued, the large degree of secular patronage of the Church (particularly in the form of monastic endowments) demonstrated not only piety on the part of lords, but also political manoeuvrings. In part, the point of patronage was to demonstrate, not only to the donee but others, that one was capable of bestowing it. (This was similarly the case with later medieval guilds: by banding together, more lowly people became capable of acting collectively as patrons, gaining some of the social cachet this implied.[66]) As recipients of patronage, monasteries themselves became political players of major importance – Cluny perhaps being the most famous, but others also such as Bury St Edmunds, Redon and St Bertin. As discussed in chapter 2, medievalists have been reflecting in these areas upon the complex nexus of obligation, expectation, and assumed kinship in the concept of 'the gift'. What nobles received back from monasteries was not simply spiritual sustenance, religious kudos or practical assistance (although all those things surely were in play); they were also binding themselves in ideological ways to the sense of charismatic power embedded in monastic shrines, with a hope that such *fidelitas* might assist their own operations.[67] Religion in a broader sense – the standing implied by adherence to good Christian practices such as charity – pervaded late medieval civic politics also: by the fifteenth century, most oligarchies in each north European city were members of the same guild. Personal charisma, that rather indefinable sense of individual magnetism that has long exercised sociologists and political advisors, was clearly possessed by some secular leaders – William Marshall springs to mind, and Henry V of England – but it perhaps most frequently worked through religious resonances, such as modelling one's behaviour upon the apostles, or other pious exemplars. The succession of charismatic preachers who shook the politics of late medieval Italy – John of Vicenza, Bernardino da Siena, Savonarola – were undoubtedly remarkable men, but also men shaped by a notably similar mould. Making use of such charismatic qualities was another tactic available to medieval rulers, most famously perhaps in the Dauphin Charles's use (and then abandonment) of Joan of Arc.

Linked with charisma, but more programmatic, was the use of symbolic practices and the development of particular ideologies of power – both, again, primarily using religious ideas and imagery. The most famous case here is that of the Capetian monarchs who, Marc Bloch argued, imbued their kingship with sacral elements such as being anointed 'king', investing heavily in holy relics, and claiming a quasi-sacramental power principally through the 'Royal touch'. One might see a parallel tactic in the late medieval use of Arthurian chivalric imagery – another charismatic model – in the pursuit of royal aims, most famously in Edward III's creation of the 'Order of the Garter' in 1348; and it has indeed been argued that the Capetian and Plantagenet monarchs thus developed two contrasting models of kingship, the former 'sacral', the latter 'chivalric'.[68] How 'sacred' imagery became associated with kingship – and whether the two terms are easily compared across the early and later middle ages – has been further debated.[69] Various rituals, as discussed above, clearly performed and reproduced social hierarchies and power. Explicit ideologies of power and hierarchy were also found throughout the middle ages, from texts loosely known as 'mirrors for princes' which proffered advice to rulers, to more abstract treatises on the nature of politics, influenced by Aristotle's *Politics* (a text made available to a western audience through Latin translation in the later thirteenth century). John of Salisbury's image of the medieval polity as a body is perhaps the most famous, and one of the most pervasive, ideological statements of power and reciprocity. Its resonance and persuasive force rested in large part on placing a natural image at the heart of a political ideology, one which could be reproduced visually and which had potential emotional affect at all levels of society. Other strands of ideology similarly worked by associating a right ordering of the universe with God, nature and the experience of history. Gender played a key role here, particularly in the other common image for the polity as a household: just as man ruled woman, so the king ruled people, and so on. Political tensions could be signified in gendered terms, at many levels of society. A thirteenth-century public mural of a tree festooned with disembodied penises, in the Tuscan town of Massa Marittima, associates the incursion of Imperial power with images of sodomy, communal violence and the magical emasculation of men by witches.[70] Another image of potential power – the idea of the 'nation' – has been discussed in recent work on the medieval period, with a particular attention paid to the English case. John Gillingham and Patrick Wormald have argued for a long-held sense of 'Englishness' which could be used as a political resource in certain disputes.[71] This sense of 'nationhood' was not identical to modern nationality (and the kingdom not identical to the nation-state) but the degree of alleged difference has been disputed.

The biggest challenge for medievalists, with regard to 'the nation' and 'the state', is to think about these topics within their medieval setting, rather than as pale foreshadowings of later developments – or, indeed, seeing those later developments (pre-eminently the modern nation-state) as the only necessary, conceivable and meaningful outcome of the medieval period. Matthew Innes has argued strongly that power in early medieval politics was innately interpersonal, and that conceptions of 'statehood' that emphasize only the abstract or impersonal elements of rule fundamentally misunderstand its nature.[72] The development of textual, bureaucratic machineries of government (associated particularly with north Italy, France and England) has been much studied, and historians have argued for their roots in monastic practices of record-keeping, the extension of papal models of government, the propagation of royal chancery techniques, and so forth. But others have also argued against assuming a 'top-down' imposition of 'the state' (for good or ill) and its machineries, suggesting that much of what looks familiar to modern governmentality comes more from the bottom up, from local practices of notarial culture, parochial or village government and conflict resolution.[73] A parallel can be seen here with the other side of the issue, in studies of popular resistance to power, such as the 1381 Rising or smaller and more localized revolts. An older historiography tended to read such events in the light of future forms of popular political resistance, and hence rather despaired of the apparent failure of medieval peasants to forge a collective politics of class identity or coherent programme of political reform. But recent work has looked much more sympathetically upon the ways in which specifically *medieval* ideas of collective justice – some based upon religious models, though some not – informed resistance; and has seen more low-level resistance than previous generations recognized, and also the involvement of non-elite groups in issues thought of primarily in terms of royal politics.[74] Power – and opposition to power – has at all levels become a far more complex topic for medievalists in the last few decades.

# 5
# Making and Remaking the Middle Ages

> When I see men of the present time, hard-pressed by misfortunes, anxiously scanning the deeds of their predecessors for consultation and strength, and unable to get as much as they wish, I conceive it will be a great service to posterity to commit to writing the deeds of the present for the use of the future.
>
> Eadmer, Historia novorum[1]

Around the time I began writing this book, we had some wood delivered in order to make book shelves. As I helped the delivery man unload the timber, he asked me what I did for a living. 'Medieval history', I said. 'Oh', he replied. 'Right. . . . Much call for that, is there?'

Despite his doubtful tone, the question rather pleased me. It implied the possibility of an *artisanal* approach to studying the middle ages – a jobbing medieval historian called in to fix a particular kind of problem, implicitly standing alongside other skilled trades. This might not reflect the experience of real academic careers, but it had a certain allure, partly because of its resonance with the English title of Marc Bloch's great work of historiographical instruction, *The Historian's Craft*. If, however, we are not able to justify our practice in the same terms as a cabinetmaker or silversmith – or indeed as a trade self-evidently important to modern society, such as dustman, surgeon or advertising executive – how does one give account for what we do? *Is* there much call for medieval history, and in what terms, and to what ends? In this final chapter I want to reflect briefly upon the uses of medieval history, the different purposes to which we can make and remake the middle ages, and the continued importance of so doing, not only to other historiographies but also to society more broadly.

For Eadmer (*c*.1060–*c*.1128), the answer was easy. One writes history for posterity – by which he meant, along with many others before and after him, for future rulers. The idea that history provides a 'storehouse of examples', particularly for statecraft, is perhaps its oldest justification. In modified form, it has continued to be invoked in recent times; for instance in 1988 the great medievalist Richard Southern argued that the past that he studied provided us with a 'treasure of unused wealth', particularly from a spiritual perspective.[2] But such an argument has always been problematic for medievalists, because the very formation of 'the middle ages' – the cutting away of the period between the Fall of Rome and the Renaissance – depended upon an act of disavowal. Those early-modern writers and thinkers who encouraged us to think of that millennium as 'medieval' did so by asserting its discontinuity from and essential irrelevance to coming modernity. How can one persuade 'posterity' (whomsoever we now consider to populate that category) that it can make future use of examples drawn from a time instrinsically understood to be irrelevant? Only, it might seem, if the examples are all brutally negative ones; that is, by continuing to assert the difference and inferiority of the period, in a viciously circular argument. Such attitudes continue to inform, in subtle fashion, much of the contemporary world's view, both popular and intellectual: plenty of books addressing 'essential' human characteristics begin with the Greeks and the Romans, and then jump swiftly to the Renaissance or Enlightenment, confident that anything in the middle has little relevance. It also underlies the periodic assertion that we are living in a 'new middle ages', usually diagnosed by a breakdown in centralized authority and degraded forms of culture. Such Cassandra-like prophecies operate through exactly the same process of disavowal: they warn us *against* being like the middle ages, because such a fate would all too clearly signal the collapse of all we hold dear. There is also an occasional manifestation of the apparent reverse of this view, a highly conservative yearning for a new middle ages of deference and accepted social hierarchy. The politics of this aside, it falls prey just as much as negative views to a homogenized and distorted notion of the period.[3]

There is however another strand of medievalism, in European culture in particular, which looks to the period as an important source of origins. Nationalist elements of this were mentioned in chapter one, but there is more here than simply the earlier triumphalist narratives of individual nation-states. Various social and political entities that continue to structure the world today can be traced back to the middle ages. The most well-established area is perhaps political constitutionalism, which in the nineteenth and early twentieth centuries was particularly fond of tracing an unbroken line between modern political mechanisms and medieval precursors, English parliament being the pre-eminent example. Recent work on medieval politics has much more nuanced things to say here, about the nature of 'parliament' in medieval England, the similarities and differences between those parliaments and the contemporary French *parlements* and Iberian *cortes* (Aragon in fact gained an annual parliament earlier than other western European countries), the degree to which medieval politics recognized anything like an abstract constitution, the complex competitions of power involved in the periodic limitations placed upon monarchy, the web of interpersonal relationships and local networks of patronage that affected the implementation of national policies, and so on and so forth. These matters do not fit well with a simplistic desire to give contemporary parliamentary democracy deep foundations – but they have tremendous potential as part of an analysis of how political mechanisms evolve and mutate. In a period and globalized setting in which parliamentary democracy no longer looks quite as stable, all-embracing or self-evidently and automatically desirable to all, an enriched sense of the medieval contexts from which it emerged may once again become more important to modern analysts. A similar argument could be made regarding the idea of 'nationhood' – the roots of which, for most European countries, undoubtedly stretch back to the middle ages, but the sense and effect of which have changed considerably over those centuries (as discussed in the previous chapter).[4]

In thinking about 'origins' or 'roots' and so forth, medievalists can also remind contemporary debates about less well-recognized medieval elements to modern identities. Work on late medieval Spain and Italy has recently suggested that important elements in the creation of modern ideologies of race, and associated prejudice, are located in our period, in ideas about blood lineage and 'purity', and in languages of social exclusion.[5] There is also the concept of Europe itself, a rather obviously unstable identity in the early twenty-first century, but one which, through the shift of various global currents, has begun to rediscover the extent to which it has been unthinkingly built upon a medieval notion of 'Christendom', and indeed a papal Christendom which divided the continent into 'West' and 'East'. In the multicultural and multifaith twenty-first century, medievalists have important work to do in reconsidering the ways in which Catholic Europe was constructed during the medieval centuries, the interface between individual faith and social collectivities negotiated in the process, and the relationships made and broken between political and religious power. Modern discussions about the role of faith (of whatever creed) within society have thus far been founded on a fairly unquestioned narrative of western Christian developments, in which the medieval once again plays the role of a simpler, 'pre-modern', space from which later complexities evolved. A return to religious history of the period is likely to raise considerable questions in these areas, about the supposed unity of the Christian community, the balance of 'top-down' imposition to 'bottom-up' enthusiasm, and the very issue of what 'belief' and 'faith' are, sociologically, philosophically and politically.

The otherness or alterity of the middle ages can also be a powerful intellectual resource, not as a grotesque 'Other' to modernity, but as a reminder that how we are now is not how we have always been – and indeed that any assumed 'we' is the product of particular rather than universal circumstances. The lived contours of human experience are a fertile field here. One might think of the varying shape of medieval households: their understanding of *familia* as something extending beyond blood kin, the period of service undertaken by a large proportion of young medieval people (sometimes into their twenties) particularly in northern Europe, the different and largely less private geographies of space within domestic dwellings, and their accompanying effects on emotional, social and cultural relations. Marriage – sacralized by the Church across the high middle ages – may continue to present a link between medieval and modern, but a medieval perspective can highlight the considerable variations of practice within Europe (as discussed in chapter 4 above). Reflection upon monasticism, chivalric association, guild membership and the like also remind a modern audience that marriage is but one form of emotionally affective association, and was certainly not considered the 'foundation' to medieval society that some have claimed it to be for the modern era. Work on medieval gender and sexuality presents further differences. Expectations of manhood differed in important respects across social strata, and a paradox yet to be fully explored is that most medieval discussions of social roles were written by clerical men disbarred (in theory at least) from adopting lay models of full adult masculinity (combat, procreation and being head of household). Medieval notions of what constituted 'right' and 'wrong' sexual behaviour also do not map neatly onto modern expectations, the most obvious example being *sodomia*. It may not have been until the twelfth century that the sin of Sodom was understood primarily as a sexual sin; and even thereafter *sodomia* could be defined as sexual activity that could not lead to procreation, and thus a category that potentially incorporated such 'unnatural' practices as a woman straddling a man during sex. Most importantly, it was seen as a sin – an act, to which all but the most saintly were in theory liable – rather than a part of a psychological or socio-biological identity. Modern scholarship has much debated whether or not something like a gay identity existed in the medieval period; there is little doubt, regardless of the answer, that such an identity was not identical to modern sexual identities.

In all of the above, I have implicitly been suggesting that medieval history matters if for no other reason than that it is 'good to think with'. The weakness of such an argument is that equally good claims could of course be made for other areas or disciplines. But a further support to the continued importance of medievalism is that not only is it good to think with, it *has* been good to think with – that is, it has been implicated, explicitly or tacitly, in various important intellectual arenas. At the broadest level, this is obviously the case with the medieval-as-anti-modern arguments discussed above; to put it another way, conceptions of modernity rest upon notions of the medieval, and discussions about modernity and indeed postmodernity cannot escape some sense of where they are understood to have come from. Current political arguments – about ethnicity, about Islam and the West, about immigration, about globalization – frequently draw upon received narratives of western 'development' underpinned by notions of medieval-to-modern transitions. Suggestions, for example, that 'the problem' with Islam is that 'it needs a Renaissance and an Enlightenment' construct that religion as following an identical timeline to western Europe, only somehow retrograde by several centuries; and such arguments tacitly rest upon a notion that 'the problem' with medieval Christianity was somehow 'solved' by processes of Reformation and the Enlightenment.[6] In addressing the multiple misconceptions here implied, medievalists have an essential role before them.

Moreover, medieval studies has played a part, not always recognized by its own practitioners, in wider academic debates. Historians' analyses of serfdom, slavery and other socioeconomic factors in medieval Europe were of supreme importance to the Indian 'Subaltern Studies' group, whose work laid the foundations for postcolonial theory. Bruce Holsinger has argued that various French theorists, from Georges Bataille to Jacques Derrida to Pierre Bourdieu, made considerable use of medievalisms and have drawn ideas and language from the period itself.[7] To this particular pantheon, one could add other writers who seek to provide depth to their analyses by drawing upon medieval examples, or exploring developments from the medieval to the modern, such as the anthropologist and political theorist James C. Scott and the philosopher Charles Taylor; and, of course, one may remember the importance of the medieval to the theories of Norbert Elias, Karl Marx and others.[8] These examples are worth listing not simply to cheer up those medievalists who may feel their area is underappreciated; rather, they may prompt us to recognize that medieval history is, whether it wishes it or not, in dialogue with other parts of academic and intellectual endeavour. It can remain a largely passive partner, or choose to be an active player, finding a voice with which to speak back to these other disciplinary perspectives. In order to so do, we could remember that historians are well equipped to analyse change over time, and medievalists, perhaps more than most, are accustomed to thinking of time in *la longue durée*, and of change in profound terms. Our experience of a society that is not modern – nor simply 'anti-modern' – provides a powerful position from which to engage and critique more narrowly focused perspectives.

The question of how to justify doing medieval history – or equally, why one personally wishes to pursue it – begs a further question: what is the medieval history being done? I have discussed in the preceding chapters various and specific ways in which medieval history was, is, and can be done, but the topic is worth some broader reflection in conclusion. Academic medieval history began, we might say, by providing nation-states with narratives of becoming – as both the 'roots' of their later flowering, and the inchoate, pre-modern 'other' to which they gave order and meaning. In the mid-twentieth century, there was a greater focus on the creation of social structures: cities, aristocracies, hierarchical divisions that foreshadowed the wounds of 'class', and would become swept away in 1789 (from a Francophone perspective) or left behind as the first western feet touched Plymouth Rock (from an American viewpoint). In recent decades, there has been a focus on the medieval as the Other of the individual modern subject – the sense of self, of identity, of what an earlier age would call 'human nature' – played out with a greater, devoutly postmodern suspicion of 'now' rather than 'then'; a delirious middle ages of alternative possibilities.

So where now? The last few sentences, my tongue partly in cheek, suggest a shifting *Zeitgeist* underlying and directing our academic endeavours; and if so, our future medievalist projects will presumably bring the idea of nationhood ever further under question, will interrogate the relationship between religion and society from ever more fraught viewpoints, and may look to medieval concepts of the common good and corporate entities as an alternative ground for political action in these globalized, post-democratic times. Less abstractly and fancifully, one can point to plenty of areas where discussion has only just begun, which must surely provide future fertile ground for research: for example the possibilities of properly comparative history, comparative by country within the period (religious experience in pre-Reformation France and England, for example), comparative by time across the period (bureaucracies of power 800–1400 for instance), and perhaps most importantly comparative across the assumed chronological boundaries of the period (local, civic capitalisms 1200–1700 perhaps). New tools may prompt further explorations; one suspects that the time is ripe for computers to once again play a role in historiographical analysis, after the brief initial bubble of enthusiasm in the early 1980s. The possibilities of GIS in regard to historical data, of word-searchable textual analysis, of contextually smart databases, and surely much else, all lie before us.[9] Furthermore, developments elsewhere in historiography will likely have some medievalist impact – most notably the increasing interest in world history. Particularly in the US, where medieval historians are often forced to teach well beyond the time and place of their specialism, the possibilities of much wider historical palettes and perspectives are potentially invigorating. Japanese scholarship has already, for some years, been providing interesting comparanda for western experiences of matters such as medieval historiography, literacy and bureaucracy, dynastic power and identity, and 'feudalism'. The rest of Asia and Africa currently remain largely unexplored from this perspective, but the potential is there.[10] And finally, whilst modern historians often seem reluctant to stray far beyond their given decade, medievalists are used to the challenge of tackling large vistas of time and space, and negotiating the demands of evidence produced by people from very different contexts and cultures. Our core topics may not, at any given moment, seem as self-evidently 'relevant' as, say, another fat book about the Nazis. But our potential ability to work and think comparatively, diachronically, and with a strong sense of the protean nature of human existence, make medievalists particularly suited to framing much larger debates about the nature of history and all it contains. We are, in other words, well equipped for historiography carried out under the shadows of globalization and postmodernity.

One could also pursue the issue of 'where next?' via a methodological emphasis. Medieval history – medieval *studies* one might as well write – has become ever more interdisciplinary. Its practitioners periodically fret about what 'interdisciplinarity' might mean, but in aggregate, work across and between disciplines, and informed by wider debates in the humanities and social sciences, is where the current flows. An essential demand of interdisciplinary study is that one pays attention to, and joins in with, discussion that extends beyond one's particular area of specialization. It encourages us to talk, and just as importantly, to listen. One outcome of an interdisciplinary middle ages therefore may be the greater willingness for medievalists to 'talk back', to other disciplines, to critical theory, to political debate, to the public. Our future medievalisms, one hopes, thus will be situated within wider discussions, feeding dynamically into the large, collective endeavour of the humanities.[11]

If at points medievalism has seemed 'irrelevant' to a wider readership, that is not entirely the fault of that audience, nor the shifting currents of the contemporary *Zeitgeist*, but also the attitudes of a few past practitioners, who at various points were happy to sit upon nineteenth-century laurels and smugly ignore the changing world – and then retreat wistfully into the imagined lands of their period as the climate around them grew less welcoming. 'We should never forget our greatest danger: we began as antiquarians and we could end as antiquarians', as Joseph Strayer remarked in 1971.[12] This may seem pessimistic, but is in fact quite the opposite. Those days are largely gone. Medieval studies today is a place of discussion, debate, passionate argument, prompted and encouraged by the communicative demands of interdisciplinarity, set within an avowedly international frame. Those whose formative academic years are being shaped by such dialectics are well equipped, not only to pursue the ongoing discussion within the discipline, but also to carry the debate further afield, to pastures new.

# Notes

## Chapter 1   Framing the Middle Ages

1   It is possible (if *mapellus* is a variant or mistranscription of *napellus*) that this was a juice made from the plant monkshood (aconite); my thanks to Richard Kieckhefer.

2   Bartolomeo's depositions are edited from the Vatican archives in P. K. Eubel, 'Vom Zaubereiunwesen anfangs des 14. Jahrhunderts', *Historisches Jahrbuch* 18 (1897): 609–25. The case is discussed, and further evidence against the Visconti edited from MS Vat. Lat. 3936, in R. Michel, 'Le procès de Matteo et de Galeazzo Visconti', *Mélanges d'archaéologie et d'histoire de l'École Française de Rome* 29 (1909): 269–327.

3   U. Eco, 'Dreaming of the Middle Ages', in *Travels in Hyperreality* (London, 1987), 69.

4   Quoted in E. Breisach, *Historiography: Ancient, Medieval and Modern* (Chicago, 1983), 207.

5   P. Burke, 'Ranke the Reactionary', *Syracuse Scholar* 9 (1988): 25–30; A. Grafton, *The Footnote: A Curious History* (London, 1997).

6   P. Novick, *That Noble Dream: The Objectivity Question and the American Historical Profession* (Cambridge, 1988), 26–30.

7   M. Innes, 'A Fatal Disjuncture? Medieval History and Medievalism in the UK', in H.-W. Goetz and J. Jarnut, eds, *Mediävistik im 21. Jahrhundert* (Munich, 2003), 73–100; R. N. Soffer, *Discipline and Power: The University, History, and the Making of an English Elite 1870–1930* (Stanford, 1994).

8   C. Carpenter, 'Political and Constitutional History', in R. H. Britnell and A. J. Pollard, eds, *The McFarlane Legacy* (Stroud, 1995), 175–206.

9   H. J. Kaye, *The British Marxist Historians*, 2nd edn (Basingstoke, 1995).

10  Novick, *That Noble Dream*; P. Freedman and G. Spiegel, 'Medievalisms Old and New', *American Historical Review* 103 (1998): 677–704.

11  G. Spiegel, 'History, Historicism, and the Social Logic of the Text in the Middle Ages', *Speculum* 65 (1990): 59–68; P. Zumthor, *Speaking of the Middle Ages*, trans. S. White (Lincoln, NB, 1986).

12  W. R. Keylor, *Academy and Community: The Establishment of the French Historical Profession* (Cambridge, MA, 1975), 43ff.

13  N. F. Cantor, *Inventing the Middle Ages* (Cambridge, 1991), 86ff. Cantor's book must be treated cautiously on this and other topics – see the review by Robert Bartlett, *New York Review of Books* 39.9 (14 May 1992) and subsequent discussion (*NYRB* 39.14) – but it raises important issues nonetheless.

14  S. Berger, M. Donovan and K. Passmore, eds, *Writing National Histories* (London, 1999).

15  E. Power, *The Goodman of Paris* (London, 1928); *Le Menagier de Paris*, ed. G. E. Brereton and J. M. Ferrier (Oxford, 1981).

## Chapter 2   Tracing the Middle Ages

1   *Anonimalle Chronicle, 1333 to 1381*, ed. V. H. Galbraith (Manchester, 1927), 151.

2   C. Dyer, 'The Rising of 1381 in Suffolk', in *Everyday Life in Medieval England* (London, 2000), 221–40; H. Eiden, 'Joint Action Against "Bad" Lordship: The Peasants' Revolt in Essex and Norfolk', *History* 83 (1998), 5–30.

3   J. G. Clark, 'Thomas Walsingham Reconsidered', *Speculum* 77 (2002): 832–60.

4   For example David d'Avray's discussion of editing sermons in his *Medieval Marriage Sermons* (Oxford, 2001).

5   R. H. Bloch, *God's Plagiarist* (Chicago, 1995).

6   R. Brentano, *A New World in a Small Place: Church and Religion in the Diocese of Rieti, 1188–1378* (Berkeley, 1994).

7   There is also a National Library in Florence, which contains some medieval manuscripts, though considerably more limited than its French or English equivalents.

8   R. F. Berkhofer, *Day of Reckoning: Power and Accountability in Medieval France* (Philadelphia, 2004).

9   S. D. Goitein, *A Mediterranean Society* (Berkeley, 1967–93), 6 vols.

10  For a thorough guide, see J. A. Burrow and T. Turville-Peter, eds, *A Book of Middle English* (Oxford, 1991).

11  H. Tsurushima, ed., *Haskins Society Journal, Japan* 1 (2005).

12  *Patrologia Latina* 198, 441–2, quoted in C. Holdsworth, 'Were the Sermons of St Bernard on the Song of Songs ever Preached?', in C. Muessig, ed., *Medieval Monastic Sermons* (Leiden, 1998), 295.

13  Robert Mannyng of Brunne, *Handlyng Synne*, ed. I. Sullens (Binghamton, 1983), 225–31.

14  R. McKitterick, 'Political Ideology in Carolingian Historiography', in Y. Hen and M. Innes, eds, *The Uses of the Past in the Early Middle Ages* (Cambridge, 2000), 162–74.

15  P. E. Dutton, 'Raoul Glaber's "De Divina Quarternitate"', *Mediaeval Studies* 42 (1980): 431–53; E. Ortigues and D. Iogna-Prat, 'Raoul Glaber et l'historiographie clunisienne', *Studi Medievali* 26.2 (1985): 537–72.

16  Rodolphus Glaber, *Historiarum libri quinque*, ed. and trans. J. France (Oxford, 1989), 94–5 (III, i).

17  Dino Compagni, *Chronicle of Florence*, trans. D. E. Bornstein (Philadelphia, 1986).

18  G. M. Spiegel, *Romancing the Past: The Rise of Vernacular Prose Historiography in Thirteenth-Century France* (Berkeley, 1993), 2.

19  *The Chronicle of San Juan de la Peña*, trans. L. H. Nelson (Philadelphia, 1991).

20  *Annales Erfordienses*, Monumenta Germaniae Historica, Scriptores 16, 29.

21  R. W. Southern, 'Aspects of the European Tradition of Historical Writing' I–IV, *Transactions of the Royal Historical Society* [hereafter *TRHS*], 5th series, 20–3 (1970–3); Jean de Joinville, *Life of Saint Louis*, in *Joinville and Villehardouin: Chronicles of the Crusades*, trans. M. R. B. Shaw (London, 1963).

22  S. Bagge, *Kings, Politics and the Right Order of the World in German Historiography c.950–1150* (Leiden, 2002).

23  S. Justice, *Writing and Rebellion: England in 1381* (Princeton, 1994).

24 E. van Houts, *Memory and Gender in Medieval Europe, 900–1200* (Houndmills, 1999).

25 W. Davies, 'People and places in dispute in ninth-century Brittany', in W. Davies and P. Fouracre, eds, *The Settlement of Disputes in Early Medieval Europe* (Cambridge, 1986), 75.

26 A more precise and technical set of definitions for charters, chirographs, and other English documents is given in M. T. Clanchy, *From Memory to Written Record*, 2nd edn (Oxford, 1993), 85–92.

27 P. Górecki, *Economy, Society and Lordship in Medieval Poland, 1100–1250* (New York, 1992), 51.

28 A. J. Kosto, 'Laymen, Clerics and Documentary Practices in the Early Middle Ages', *Speculum* 80 (2005), 44.

29 Kosto, 'Laymen'; W. Brown, 'When Documents are Destroyed or Lost', *Early Medieval Europe* 11 (2002): 337–66.

30 Clanchy, *From Memory*, 46ff.

31 R. C. van Caenegem, *Guide to the Sources of Medieval History* (Amsterdam, 1978), 72.

32 B. Rosenwein, *To Be the Neighbour of St Peter: The Social Meaning of Cluny's Property, 909–1049* (Ithaca, 1989).

33 B. Bedos-Rezak, 'Civic Liturgies and Urban Records in Northern France 1100–1400', in B. A. Hanawalt and K. L. Reyerson, eds, *City and Spectacle in Medieval Europe* (Minneapolis, 1994), 34–55.

34 For one sense of this, see W. Brown, 'Charters as Weapons', *Journal of Medieval History* 28 (2002): 227–48.

35 D. Alexandre-Bidou, 'Une foi en deux ou trois dimensions?', *Annales: Histoire, Sciences Sociales* 53.6 (1998), 1155–90.

36 J.-C. Schmitt, 'Images and the Historian', in A. Bolvig and P. Lindley, eds, *History and Images* (Turnhout, 2003), 19–44; and, more broadly, J. Baschet and J.-C. Schmitt, eds, *L'Image* (Paris, 1996).

37 M. Pastoureau, 'Voir les couleurs du Moyen Age', in *Une histoire symbolique du Moyen Age occidental* (Paris, 2004), 113–33.

38 For example, F. Garnier, *Le langage de l'image au Moyen Age*, 2 vols (Paris, 1982–9).

39 M. Kupfer, *Romanesque Wall Painting in Central France* (New Haven, 1993).

40 E. Welch, *Art and Society in Italy, 1350–1500* (Oxford, 1997), 295–302, figs 152, 153.

41 J. Alexander, '*Labeur* and *Paresse*: Ideological Representations of Medieval Peasant Labour', *Art Bulletin* 72 (1990): 436–52.

42   D. H. Strickland, *Saracens, Demons and Jews* (Princeton, 2003).
43   N. Rubinstein, 'Political Ideas in Sienese Art', *Journal of the Warburg and Courtauld Institutes* 21 (1958): 179–207.
44   S. Y. Edgerton Jr, *Pictures and Punishment* (Ithaca, 1985).
45   D. O. Hughes, 'Representing the Family', *Journal of Interdisciplinary History* 17 (1986), 13–14.
46   S. Lipton, '"The Sweet Lean of His Head"', *Speculum* 80 (2005), 1172–208.
47   M. Camille, 'At the Sign of the Spinning Sow', in Bolvig and Lindley, eds, *History and Images*, 249–76.
48   M. B. Merback, *The Thief, the Cross and the Wheel: Pain and the Spectacle of Punishment in Medieval and Renaissance Europe* (Chicago, 1998), 124–5.
49   H. C. Lea, *A History of Inquisition in the Middle Ages* (New York, 1888), I, iii–iv.
50   *The Code of Cuenca*, trans. J. F. Powers (Philadelphia, 2000), 91.
51   S. Reynolds, *Kingdoms and Communities in Western Europe, 900–1300* (Oxford, 1984), 268–71.
52   P. J. P. Goldberg, ed., *Women in England, 1275–1525* (Manchester, 1995), 239.
53   G. Ruggiero, *The Boundaries of Eros: Sex, Crime and Sexuality in Renaissance Venice* (Oxford, 1985).
54   T. Dean, *Crime in Medieval Europe* (Harlow, 2001), 77–8.
55   B. Hanawalt, *The Ties that Bound: Peasant Families in Medieval England* (Oxford, 1986); S. Farmer, *Surviving Poverty in Medieval Paris* (Ithaca, 2002); C. Gauvard, *De Grace Especial*, 2 vols (Paris, 1991); E. Le Roy Ladurie, *Montaillou* (Paris, 1978).
56   D. L. Smail, *The Consumption of Justice: Emotions, Publicity and Legal Culture in Marseille, 1264–1423* (Ithaca, 2003); A. Musson, ed., *Expectations of the Law in the Middle Ages* (Woodbridge, 2001).
57   J. Duvernoy, ed., *L'inquisition en Quercy* (Castelnaud La Chapelle, 2001), 148.
58   D. L. Smail, 'Common Violence: Vengeance and Inquisition in Fourteenth-Century Marseille', *Past and Present* 151 (1996), 55–7.
59   C. Wickham, *Courts and Conflict in Twelfth-Century Tuscany* (Oxford, 2003); P. Hyams, *Rancor and Reconciliation in Medieval England* (Ithaca, 2003).
60   J. B. Given, *Inquisition and Medieval Society* (Ithaca, 1998); J. H. Arnold, *Inquisition and Power* (Philadelphia, 2001).

## Chapter 3 Reading the Middle Ages

1 Ramon Muntaner, *The Chronicle of Muntaner*, trans. Lady Goodenough, Hakluyt Society, 2nd series 47, 50 (reprint: Nendeln, 1967), I, 10–16 (cap. III–VI).

2 R. C. Rhodes, 'Emile Durkheim and the Historical Thought of Marc Bloch', *Theory and Society* 5 (1978): 45–73; P. Burke, *The French Historical Revolution: The* Annales *School 1929–89* (Cambridge, 1990), 16ff.

3 For example E. Cohen and M. de Jong, eds, *Medieval Transformations: Texts, Power and the Gift in Context* (Leiden, 2001); W. I. Miller, 'Gift, Sale, Payment, Raid: Case Studies in the Negotiation and Classification of Exchange in Medieval Iceland', *Speculum* 61 (1986): 18–50; M. de Jong, *In Samuel's Image: Child Oblation in the Early Middle Ages* (Leiden, 1994).

4 J. Le Goff, *Time, Work and Culture in the Middle Ages* (Chicago, 1980) and *The Medieval Imagination* (Chicago, 1985).

5 V. Turner, *The Ritual Process* (Chicago, 1969).

6 C. Walker Bynum, 'Women's Stories, Women's Symbols', in *Fragmentation and Redemption* (New York, 1991), 27–51.

7 P. Brown, 'The Rise and Function of the Holy Man in Late Antiquity', in *Society and the Holy in Late Antiquity* (London, 1982), 103–52; P. Brown, 'The Christian Holy Man in Late Antiquity', in *Authority and the Sacred* (Cambridge, 1995), 55–78.

8 J. Goody and I. Watt, 'The Consequences of Literacy', in J. Goody, ed., *Literacy in Traditional Societies* (Cambridge, 1968), 27–68; W. Ong, *Orality and Literacy* (London, 1982).

9 J. M. H. Smith, *Europe After Rome: A New Cultural History 500–1000* (Oxford, 2005), 38–9.

10 J. Halverson, 'Goody and the Implosion of the Literacy Thesis', *Man* n.s. 27 (1992): 301–17.

11 B. Stock, *The Implications of Literacy* (Princeton, 1983).

12 P. Bourdieu, *Outline of a Theory of Practice* (Cambridge, 1977); M. de Certeau, *The Practice of Everyday Life* (Berkeley, 1984).

13 T. Fenster and D. L. Smail, eds, *Fama: The Politics of Talk and Reputation in Medieval Europe* (Ithaca, 2003); C. Wickham, 'Gossip and Resistance among the Medieval Peasantry', *Past and Present* 160 (1998): 3–24.

14   W. I. Miller, *Bloodtaking and Peacemaking: Feud, Law and Society in Saga Iceland* (Chicago, 1990).
15   See http://www.stg.brown.edu/projects/catasto/overview.html, accessed August 2006. Note that one must read all the accompanying files, particularly the 'code book', in order to make meaningful use of the database. The source is described in further detail in *Les Toscans et leurs familles*, and more briefly in the English translation: *Tuscans and Their Families* (New Haven, 1985).
16   S. K. Cohn, 'Prosperity in the Countryside', in *Women in the Streets* (Baltimore, 1996), 137–65.
17   S. K. Cohn, *The Cult of Remembrance and the Black Death* (Baltimore, 1992).
18   S. A. C. Penn and C. Dyer, 'Wages and Earnings in Late Medieval England', *Economic History Review* n.s. 43 (1990): 356–76.
19   H. Swanson, 'The Illusion of Economic Structure', *Past and Present* 121 (1988): 29–48; G. Rosser, 'Crafts, Guilds and the Negotiation of Work in the Medieval Town', *Past and Present* 154 (1997): 3–31.
20   J. M. Murray, *Bruges, Cradle of Capitalism 1280–1390* (Cambridge, 2005), 130ff.
21   J. Davis, 'Baking for the Common Good', *Economic History Review* n.s. 57 (2004): 465–502.
22   For a recent picture of a Marxist middle ages, with critical commentary, see S. H. Rigby, 'Historical Materialism: Social Structure and Social Change in the Middle Ages', *Journal of Medieval and Early Modern Studies* 34 (2004): 473–522.
23   C. Dyer, *An Age of Transition? Economy and Society in England in the Later Middle Ages* (Oxford, 2005).
24   B. K. Davison, 'The Origins of the Castle in England', *Archaeological Journal* 124 (1967): 202–11; R. Allen Brown, 'An Historian's Approach to the Origins of the Castle in England', *Archaeological Journal* 126 (1969): 131–48; R. Liddiard, ed., *Anglo-Norman Castles* (Woodbridge, 2003).
25   R. Liddiard, *Castles in Context* (Macclesfield, 2005).
26   R. Gilchrist and B. Sloane, *Requiem: The Medieval Monastic Cemetery in Britain* (London, 2005).
27   V. Thompson, *Death and Dying in Later Anglo-Saxon England* (Woodbridge, 2004), 33–5.
28   B. Effros, *Caring for Body and Soul* (University Park, PA, 2002) and *Merovingian Mortuary Archaeology* (Berkeley, 2003). See also H. Williams, 'Rethinking Early Medieval Mortuary Archaeology', *Early Medieval Europe* 13 (2005): 195–217.

29  F. Curta, *The Making of the Slavs* (Cambridge, 2005).

30  A. M. Koldeweij, 'Lifting the Veil on Pilgrim Badges', in J. Stopford, ed., *Pilgrimage Explored* (York, 1999), 161–88.

31  T. Williamson, *Shaping Medieval Landscapes* (Macclesfield, 2002).

32  P. Sawyer, 'Markets and Fairs in Norway and Sweden between the Eighth and Sixteenth Centuries', in T. Pestell and K. Ulmscheider, eds, *Markets in Early Medieval Europe* (Macclesfield, 2003), 168–74.

33  H. Pirenne, *Mahomet et Charlemagne* (Brussels, 1937).

34  M. McCormick, *Origins of the European Economy* (Cambridge, 2001).

35  K. R. Dark, 'Houses, Streets and Shops in Byzantine Constantinople from the Fifth to the Twelfth Centuries', *Journal of Medieval History* 30 (2004): 83–107.

36  R. Gilchrist and M. Oliva, *Religious Women in Medieval East Anglia* (Norwich, 1993); R. Gilchrist, *Gender and Material Culture* (London, 1994), 163–7.

37  J. Masschaele, 'The Public Space of the Marketplace in Medieval England', *Speculum* 77 (2002): 383–421; D. C. Mengel, 'From Venice to Jerusalem and Beyond: Milíč of Kroměříž and the Topography of Prostitution in Fourteenth-Century Prague', *Speculum* 79 (2004): 407–42.

38  For an early example, see C. Pamela Graves, 'Social Space in the English Medieval Parish Church', *Economy and Society* 18 (1989): 297–322.

39  Edited in A. Flores, *Mediaeval Age* (London, 1963), 141; the translation (by Gillian Barker and Kenneth Gee) slightly amended here, with thanks to Professor David Wells.

40  R. M. Karras, *From Boys to Men* (Philadelphia, 2002).

41  J. Watts, 'The Pressure of the Public on Later Medieval Politics', in L. Clark and C. Carpenter, eds, *Political Culture in Late Medieval Britain* (Woodbridge, 2004), 159–80.

42  W. M. Ormrod, 'The Use of English: Language, Law and Political Culture in Fourteenth-Century England', *Speculum* 78 (2003): 750–87.

43  C. Brémond, J. Le Goff and J.-C. Schmitt, *L'"Exemplum"* (Turnhout, 1982), 111–43; J. H. Arnold, 'The Labour of Continence', in A. Bernau, R. Evans and S. Salih, eds, *Medieval Virginities* (Cardiff, 2003), 102–18.

44  B. Hanawalt, 'Whose Story Was This? Rape Narratives in Medieval English Courts', in *Of Good and Ill Repute: Gender and Social Control in Medieval England* (Oxford, 1998), 124–41.

45 M. Toch, 'Asking the Way and Telling the Law: Speech in Medieval Germany', *Journal of Interdisciplinary History* 16 (1986): 667–82.

46 C. Clover, ' "Regardless of Sex": Men, Women and Power in Early Northern Europe', *Speculum* 68 (1993): 363–87; R. N. Swanson, 'Angels Incarnate?', in D. Hadley, ed., *Masculinity in Medieval Europe* (Harlow, 1999), 160–77.

47 J. Burckhardt, *The Civilisation of the Renaissance in Italy* (London, 1860).

48 R. W. Southern, *The Making of the Middle Ages* (London, 1953); W. Ullmann, *The Individual and Society in the Middle Ages* (Baltimore, 1966); C. Morris, *The Discovery of the Individual 1050–1200* (London, 1972).

49 C. W. Bynum, 'Did the Twelfth Century Discover the Individual?', in *Jesus as Mother* (Berkeley, 1982), 97.

50 R. Kaeuper, *Chivalry and Violence in Medieval Europe* (Oxford, 1999); S. Crane, *The Performance of Self: Ritual, Clothing and Identity During the Hundred Years War* (Philadelphia, 2002).

51 P. Blickle, *The Revolution of 1525* (London, 1991).

## Chapter 4   Debating the Middle Ages

1 S. K. Cohn, *The Black Death Transformed* (London, 2002).

2 M. Zerner, ed., *Inventer l'hérésie?* (Nice, 1998); P. Biller, 'Goodbye to Waldensianism?', *Past and Present* 192 (2006): 3–33; F. Somerset et al., eds, *Lollards and Their Influence in Late Medieval England* (Woodbridge, 2003).

3 Farmer, *Surviving Poverty*; D. L. Smail, *Imaginary Cartographies: Possession and Identity in Late Medieval Marseille* (Ithaca, 2003); C. Beattie, *Medieval Single Women* (Oxford, 2007).

4 *The Annals of Flodoard of Reims, 919–966*, ed. S. Fanning and B. S. Bachrach (Ontario, 2004), 10–11; see G. Koziol, *Begging Pardon and Favor: Ritual and Political Order in Early Medieval France* (Ithaca, 1992), 111.

5 R. Hutton, *The Rise and Fall of Merry England* (Oxford, 1994); R. W. Scribner, 'Ritual and Popular Religion in Catholic Germany', *Journal of Ecclesiastical History* 35 (1984): 47–77.

6 G. Althoff, *Spielregeln der Politik im Mittelalter* (Darmstadt, 1997); G. Althoff, 'The Variability of Rituals in the Middle Ages', in G. Althoff, J. Fried and P. Geary, eds, *Medieval Concepts of the Past* (Cambridge, 2001), 71–87.

7   P. Buc, *The Dangers of Ritual* (Princeton, 2001).

8   *The Ecclesiastical History of Orderic Vitalis*, ed. M. Chibnall (Oxford, 1975), V, 315–21 (bk X, cap. 19).

9   H. Fichtenau, *Living in the Tenth Century* (Chicago, 1991), 32.

10  S. Lindenbaum, 'Ceremony and Oligarchy', in Hanawalt and Reyerson, eds, *City and Spectacle*, 171–88.

11  Koziol, *Begging Pardon and Favour*, 298.

12  T. Asad, *Genealogies of Religion* (Baltimore, 1993).

13  G. Althoff, '*Ira Regis*: Prolegomena to a History of Royal Anger', in B. Rosenwein, ed., *Anger's Past* (Ithaca, 1998), 59–74.

14  C. Phythian-Adams, 'Ceremony and the Citizen', in P. Clark and P. Slack, eds, *Crisis and Order in English Towns 1500–1700* (London, 1972), 57–85; J. Bossy, 'The Mass as a Social Institution 1200–1700', *Past and Present* 100 (1983): 29–61. See also M. James, 'Ritual, Drama and Social Body in the Late Medieval English Town', *Past and Present* 98 (1983): 3–29, although his analysis is more subtle than later critics sometimes credit.

15  Koziol, *Begging Pardon and Favour*; Miller, *Bloodtaking and Oathmaking*; Wickham, *Courts and Conflict*; see also Davies and Fouracre, eds, *Settlement of Disputes*.

16  A. W. Lewis, 'Forest Rights and the Celebration of May', *Mediaeval Studies* 53 (1991): 259–77.

17  S. MacLean, 'Ritual, Misunderstanding and the Contest for Meaning', in B. Weiler and S. MacLean, eds, *Representations of Power in Medieval Germany 800–1500* (Turnhout, 2006), 97–119.

18  K. Petkov, *The Kiss of Peace* (Leiden, 2003); K. M. Phillips, 'The Invisible Man: Body and Ritual in a Fifteenth-Century Noble Household', *Journal of Medieval History* 31 (2005): 143–62.

19  G. Duby, *La société aux XIe et XIIe siècles dans la région Mâconnaise* (Paris, 1953).

20  S. Reynolds, *Fiefs and Vassals* (Oxford, 1994); D. Barthélemy, *La mutation de l'an mil, a-t-elle eu lieu?* (Paris, 1997).

21  *The Usatges of Barcelona*, ed. and trans. D. J. Kagay (Philadelphia, 1991), 65–6 (nos 4–7, 9, 11).

22  Alan de Lille, *The Art of Preaching* (Kalamazoo, 1981); these being only the lay categories, with further sermons for various kinds of *oratores*.

23  R. Van Uytven, 'Showing off One's Rank in the Middle Ages', in W. Blockmans and A. Janse, eds, *Showing Status:*

*Representation of Social Positions in the Late Middle Ages* (Turnhout, 1999), 20.

24  *Usatges*, 67 (nos 8, 10).

25  Joseph Morsel argues provocatively that a concept of 'the nobility' *as a group* only appeared *c.*1400; 'Inventing a Social Category: The Sociogenesis of the Nobility at the End of the Middle Ages', in B. Jussen, ed., *Ordering Medieval Society* (Philadelphia, 2001), 200–40.

26  S. Imsen, 'King Magnus and Liegemen's "Hirðskrå": A Portrait of the Norwegian Nobility in the 1270s', in A. J. Duggan, ed., *Nobles and Nobility in Medieval Europe* (Boydell, 2000), 205–20.

27  R. Bartlett, *The Making of Europe* (London, 1993), 47.

28  M. H. Gelting, 'Legal Reform and the Development of Peasant Dependence in Thirteenth-Century Denmark', in P. Freedman and M. Bourin, eds, *Forms of Servitude in Northern and Central Europe* (Turnhout, 2005), 343–68; J. M. Bak, 'Servitude in the Medieval Kingdom of Hungary', ibid., 387–400; P. Jones, 'From Manor to *mezzadria*', in N. Rubinstein, ed., *Florentine Studies* (London, 1968), 193–241.

29  P. Franklin, 'Politics in Manorial Court Rolls', in Z. Razi and R. Smith, eds, *Medieval Society and the Manor Court* (Oxford, 1996), 162–98; R. B. Goheen, 'Peasant Politics? Village Community and the Crown in Fifteenth-Century England', *American Historical Review* 96 (1991): 42–62.

30  S. Shahar, *The Fourth Estate: A History of Women in the Middle Ages* (London, 1983).

31  R. M. Smith, 'Geographical Diversity in the Resort to Marriage in Late Medieval Europe', in P. J. P. Goldberg, ed., *Women in Medieval English Society* (Stroud, 1997), 16–59.

32  A. J. Duggan, ed., *Queens and Queenship in Medieval Europe* (Woodbridge, 2002); S. J. Johns, *Noblewomen, Aristocracy and Power in the Twelfth-Century Anglo-Norman Realm* (Manchester, 2003).

33  K. Parker, 'Lynn and the Making of a Mystic', in J. H. Arnold and K. J. Lewis, eds, *A Companion to the Book of Margery Kempe* (Cambridge, 2004), 55–74.

34  William Caxton, *The Game of Chess* (London, 1870) (facs. BL King's Library C.10.b.23), second traytye, pars 11.

35  Peter Schott, *Lucubratiunculae* (Strasbourg, 1497), fol. 116; translated in G. G. Coulton, *Life in the Middle Ages* (Cambridge, 1928), I, 242.

36  D. Dymond, 'God's Disputed Acre', *Journal of Ecclesiastical History* 50 (1999): 464–97.

37  M. Bakhtin, *Rabelais and His World* (Bloomington, 1984).

38  J. Delumeau, *Catholicisme entre Luther et Voltaire* (Paris, 1971).

39  Le Goff, *Time, Work and Culture*; J.-C. Schmitt, 'Religion Populaire et Culture Folklorique', *Annales ESC* 31 (1976): 941–53.

40  J. van Engen, 'The Christian Middle Ages as an Historiographical Problem', *American Historical Review* 91 (1986): 519–52; in response, J.-C. Schmitt, 'Religion, Folklore, and Society in the Medieval West', in L. K. Little and B. H. Rosenwein, eds, *Debating the Middle Ages* (Oxford, 1998), 376–87.

41  R. Schnell, 'The Discourse on Marriage in the Middle Ages', *Speculum* 73 (1998): 771–86.

42  H. Grundmann, 'Litteratus-illitteratus', *Archiv für Kulturgeschichte* 40 (1958): 1–65; M. Irvine, *The Making of Textual Culture* (Cambridge, 1994); Clanchy, *From Memory*.

43  D. H. Green, 'Orality and Reading', *Speculum* 65 (1990): 267–80.

44  A. Gurevich, 'Oral and Written Culture of the Middle Ages', *New Literary History* 16 (1984): 51–66; J. M. H. Smith, 'Oral and Written: Saints, Miracles and Relics in Brittany *c.*850–1250', *Speculum* 65 (1990): 309–43; M. Innes, 'Memory, Orality and Literacy in an Early Medieval Society', *Past and Present* 158 (1998): 3–36.

45  R. Fletcher, *The Conversion of Europe* (London, 1997); P. Brown, *The Rise of Western Christendom*, 2nd edn (Oxford, 2003).

46  M. Camille, *Image on the Edge: The Margins of Medieval Art* (London, 1992).

47  R. McKitterick, ed., *Carolingian Culture* (Cambridge, 2003).

48  J. Baldwin, *Masters, Princes and Merchants: The Social Views of Peter the Chanter and His Circle*, 2 vols (Princeton, 1970); P. Biller, *The Measure of Multitude: Population in Medieval Thought* (Oxford, 2001).

49  H. Grundmann, *Religious Movements in the Middle Ages* (Notre Dame, 1995).

50  J.-C. Schmitt, *The Holy Greyhound* (Cambridge, 1983); M. G. Pegg, *The Corruption of Angels: The Great Inquisition of 1245–1246* (Princeton, 2001).

51  J. M. Bennett, 'Writing Fornication', *TRHS*, 6th series 13 (2003): 131–62.

52  V. Reinburg, 'Liturgy and the Laity', *Sixteenth-Century Journal* 23 (1992): 529–32.

53   M. Goodich, 'The Politics of Canonization in the Thirteenth Century', *Church History* 44 (1975): 294–307; A. Kleinberg, *Prophets in Their Own Country: Living Saints and the Making of Sainthood in the Later Middle Ages* (Chicago, 1992).

54   L. A. Smoller, 'Defining the Boundaries of the Natural in Fifteenth-Century Brittany', *Viator* 28 (1997): 333–59.

55   R. Rusconi, *L'ordine dei peccati* (Bologna, 2002); A. Vauchez, ed., *Faire croire* (Rome, 1981).

56   W. C. Jordan, *The French Monarchy and the Jews from Philip Augustus to the Last Capetians* (Philadelphia, 1989).

57   J. B. Given, 'Chasing Phantoms: Philip IV and the Fantastic', in M. Frassetto, ed., *Heresy and the Persecuting Society in the Middle Ages* (Leiden, 2006), 273.

58   J. R. Strayer, *On the Medieval Origins of the Modern State* (Princeton, 1970).

59   C. Wickham, *Framing the Early Middle Ages* (Oxford, 2005), 56–150.

60   R. Bonney and W. M. Ormrod, eds, *Crises, Revolutions and Self-Sustained Growth* (Stamford, 1998).

61   S. R. Epstein, 'Town and Country', *Economic History Review* 46 (1993), 464.

62   P. Wormald, 'Germanic Power Structures', in L. Scales and O. Zimmer, *Power and the Nation in European History* (Cambridge, 2005), 105.

63   P. Freedman, *Images of the Medieval Peasant* (Stanford, 1999), 242, 38.

64   V. Groebner, 'Losing Face, Saving Face: Noses and Honour in the Late Medieval Town', *History Workshop Journal* 40 (1995): 1–15.

65   G. Halsall, ed., *Violence and Society in the Early Medieval West* (Woodbridge, 1998); R. Kaeuper, ed., *Violence in Medieval Society* (Woodbridge, 2000).

66   R. Weissmann, *Ritual Brotherhood in Renaissance Florence* (New York, 1982).

67   M. McLaughlin, *Consorting with Saints: Prayer for the Dead in Early Medieval France* (Ithaca, 1994), 176–7.

68   G. Koziol, 'England, France and the Problem of Sacrality in Twelfth-Century Ritual', in T. Bisson, ed. *Cultures of Power* (Philadelphia, 1995), 124–48; but see also N. Vincent, *The Holy Blood: King Henry III and the Westminster Blood Relic* (Cambridge, 2001), 186–201.

69   J. Nelson, 'Royal Saints and Early Medieval Kingship', *Studies in Church History* 10 (1973): 39–44; G. Klaniczay, *Holy*

*Rulers and Blessed Princesses: Dynastic Cults in Medieval Central Europe* (Cambridge, 2002).

70 G. Ferzoco, *Il murale di Massa Maritima* (Leicester, 2005).

71 J. Gillingham, *The English in the Twelfth Century* (Woodbridge, 2000) and Patrick Wormald, 'Engla Lond: The Making of Allegiance', *Journal of Historical Sociology* 7 (1994): 1–24.

72 M. Innes, *State and Society in the Early Middle Ages* (Cambridge, 2000).

73 Smail, *Imaginary Cartographies*; G. L. Harriss, 'Political Society and the Growth of Government in Late Medieval England', *Past and Present* 138 (1993): 28–57; A. Musson and W. M. Ormrod, *The Evolution of English Justice* (Basingstoke, 1998).

74 S. K. Cohn, *The Lust for Liberty: The Politics of Social Revolt in Europe 1200–1425* (Cambridge, MA, 2006); D. A. Carpenter, 'English Peasants in Politics, 1258–1267', *Past and Present* 136 (1992): 3–42; C. Liddy, 'Urban Conflict in Late Fourteenth-Century England', *English Historical Review* 118 (2003): 1–32.

## Chapter 5 Making and Remaking the Middle Ages

1 Quoted in Southern, 'Aspects of the European Tradition . . . IV', *TRHS*, 5th series, 23 (1973), 252.

2 R. W. Southern, *History and Historians*, ed. R. J. Bartlett (Oxford, 2004), 133.

3 O. G. Oexle, 'The Middle Ages through Modern Eyes', *TRHS*, 6th series, 9 (1999): 121–42.

4 S. Reynolds, 'The Idea of the Nation as a Political Community', in Scales and Zimmer, *Power and the Nation*, 54–66.

5 D. Nirenberg, 'Mass Conversion and Genealogical Mentalities: Jews and Christians in Fifteenth-Century Spain', *Past and Present* 174 (2002): 3–41; S. A. Epstein, *Speaking of Slavery: Color, Ethnicity and Human Bondage in Italy* (Ithaca, 2001).

6 For various perspectives of this kind, see new afterword to F. Fukuyama, *The End of History and the Last Man* (London, 2006); R. Scruton, *The West and the Rest* (London, 2003); S. Huntingdon, *The Clash of Civilisations and the Remaking of the World Order* (New York, 1996).

7 W. C. Jordan, 'Saving Medieval History', in J. van Engen, ed., *The Past and Future of Medieval Studies* (Notre Dame, 1994),

264–5; B. Holsinger, 'Medieval Studies, Postcolonial Studies, and the Genealogies of Critique', *Speculum* 77 (2002): 1195–227; B. Holsinger, *The Premodern Condition* (Chicago, 2005).

8   J. C. Scott, *Domination and the Arts of Resistance* (Yale, 1992); C. Taylor, *Sources of the Self* (Harvard, 1992).

9   For recent developments mainly in literary study, see K. Van Eickels, R. Weichselbaumer and I. Bennewitz, eds, *Mediaevistik und Neue Medien* (Ostfildern, 2004).

10   L. K. Little, 'Cypress Beams, Kufic Script and Cut Stone: Rebuilding the Master Narrative of European History', *Speculum* 79 (2004): 909–28; J. P. Arnason and B. Wittrock, eds, *Eurasian Transformations, Tenth to Thirteenth Centuries* (Leiden, 2004).

11   J. M. Bennett, 'Our Colleagues, Ourselves', in van Engen, ed., *Past and Future*, 245–58.

12   J. R. Strayer, 'The Future of Medieval History', *Medievalia et Humanistica* n.s. 2 (1971): 179–88.

# Further Reading

## Chapter 1   Framing the Middle Ages

On medieval magic and its contexts, see R. Kieckhefer, *Magic in the Middle Ages* (Cambridge, 1989). Overviews of both medieval and medievalist historiography can be found in various general books, notably E. Breisach, *Historiography: Ancient, Medieval and Modern* (Chicago, 1983). Of particular, if highly idiosyncratic, interest is N. Cantor, *Inventing the Middle Ages* (Cambridge, 1991). An excellent introduction to academic and popular medievalisms old and new is given in M. Bull, *Thinking Medieval* (Houndmills, 2005); for US perspectives see J. van Engen, ed., *The Past and Future of Medieval Studies* (Notre Dame, 1994). For one sense of how the academy has changed, see J. Chance, ed., *Women Medievalists and the Academy* (Madison, 2005).

There are many general textbooks: for the early period see M. Innes, *An Introduction to Early Medieval Western Europe* (London, 2007) and J. M. H. Smith, *Europe After Rome: A New Cultural History 500–1000* (Oxford, 2005); for the central middle ages, J. H. Mundy, *Europe in the High Middle Ages* (New York, 1973) and M. Barber, *The Two Cities: Medieval Europe 1050–1320* (London, 1993); and for the late middle ages, the best of a dull bunch is D. Waley, *Later Medieval Europe*, 3rd edn (Harlow, 2001). Two sparkling works on England supply wider thematic dividends: M. T.

Clanchy, *England and its Rulers, 1066–1272*, 3rd edn (Oxford, 2006) and R. Horrox and W. M. Ormrod, eds, *A Social History of England 1200–1500* (2006). P. Linehan and J. Nelson, eds, *The Medieval World* (London, 2003) is a fascinating collection of articles.

## Chapter 2    Tracing the Middle Ages

A selection of sources on the 1381 revolt are collected in R. B. Dobson, ed. and trans., *The Peasants' Revolt of 1381*, 2nd edn (Houndmills, 1983); for European comparators, see S. K. Cohn, ed. and trans., *Popular Protest in Late Medieval Europe* (Manchester, 2004). There are many general source collections and translation editions; one might note in particular those published in the series Oxford Medieval Texts, Manchester Medieval Sources, and Broadview Press's Readings in Medieval Civilizations and Cultures. For particular genres see the series *Typologie des sources du Moyen Age*, some of which are wholly or partly in English, e.g. B. Kienzle, ed., *The Sermon* (Turnhout, 2000). R. C. van Caenegem, *Guide to the Sources of Medieval History* (Amsterdam, 1978) is a bit old-fashioned, but still helpful. On issues of women and medieval sources, see J. T. Rosenthal, ed., *Medieval Women and the Sources of Medieval History* (Athens, GA, 1990).

For English research, E. A. Gooder, *Latin for Local History: An Introduction* (Harlow, 1978) is very useful for manorial records, R. E. Latham, *Revised Medieval Latin Wordlist* (Oxford, 1965) a handy addition to classical Latin dictionaries, and C. Trice Martin, *The Record Interpreter* (Chichester, 1982) an indispensable guide to palaeographic detail.

For a variety of cases and viewpoints, see K. Heidecker, ed., *Charters and the Use of the Written Word in Medieval Society* (Turhout, 2000), and a brilliant analysis of early medieval evidence is G. Koziol, *The Footsteps of Kings: West Frankish Royal Diplomas and Their Stories (840–987)* (forthcoming). F. Curta, 'Merovingian and Carolingian Gift-Giving', *Speculum* 81 (2006): 671–99 provides a helpful survey of approaches to gift exchange; for later periods, see V. Groebner, *Liquid Assets, Dangerous Gifts* (Philadelphia,

2002). For a general introduction to chronicles, see B. Smalley, *Historians of the Middle Ages* (London, 1974); particular studies appear in the ongoing annual yearbook, *The Medieval Chronicle* (Amsterdam, 1999–). Most important for England is A. Gransden, *Historical Writing in England*, 2 vols (London, 1974–82); see also C. Given-Wilson, *Chronicles* (London, 2004). Legal sources have no general introduction as such, but useful issues are raised in M. Goodich, ed., *Voices from the Bench* (Houndmills, 2006), and T. Dean, *Crime in Medieval Europe* (Harlow, 2001) is an excellent guide to the subject area. Two good introductions to medieval art are M. Camille, *Gothic Art* (London, 1996) and V. Sekules, *Medieval Art* (Oxford, 2001).

## Chapter 3   Reading the Middle Ages

P. Burke, *History and Social Theory*, 3rd edn (Cambridge, 2005) provides a guide to anthropological approaches among other things, and P. Monaghan, *Social and Cultural Anthropology: A Very Short Introduction* (Oxford, 2000) gives a quick way into the discipline. Four works particularly influential on medievalists are E. Durkheim, *The Elementary Forms of the Religious Life* (London, 1915), M. Douglas, *Purity and Danger* (London, 1966), V. Turner, *The Ritual Process* (Chicago, 1969), and P. Bourdieu, *Outline of a Theory of Practice* (Cambridge, 1977). Essential for understanding medieval literacy is M. T. Clanchy, *From Memory to Written Record*, 2nd edn (Oxford, 1993).

An excellent guide to statistical analysis is given by P. Hudson, *History by Numbers* (London, 2000), and a clear discussion and critique of economic theories pertaining to the medieval period in J. Hatcher and M. Bailey, *Modelling the Middle Ages* (Oxford, 2001). The early medieval economy is analysed magisterially and controversially in M. McCormick, *Origins of the European Economy* (Cambridge, 2001), a book discussed in *Early Medieval Europe* 12 (2003). Nothing as synoptic exists for the later period, but see D. Wood, *Medieval Economic Thought* (Cambridge, 2002) and R. H. Britnell, *The Commercialization of English Society, 1000–1500* (Cambridge, 1993).

There are various guides to archaeology and its theories, such as P. Bahn, *Archaeology: A Very Short Introduction*, 2nd edn (Oxford, 2000) and I. Hodder, *Archaeological Theory Today* (Cambridge, 2001). Specifically on the medieval period, see C. Gerrard, *Medieval Archaeology* (London, 2003). On castles, addressing the issues raised here, see R. Liddiard, *Castles in Context* (Macclesfield, 2005); for burial practices, G. Halsall, *Early Medieval Cemeteries* (Glasgow, 1995) and the review article by T. Dickenson in *Early Medieval Europe* 11 (2002). Also interesting is R. Gilchrist, *Gender and Archaeology* (London, 1999).

Literary theory plays an influential role in N. Partner, ed., *Writing Medieval History* (London, 2005) and the chapters there by Murray and Beattie offer excellent analyses of medieval gender and sexuality. See also R. M. Karras, *From Boys to Men* (Philadelphia, 2002), R. M. Karras, *Sexuality in Medieval Europe* (London, 2005) and M. Erler and M. Kowaleski, eds, *Gendering the Master Narrative: Women and Power in the Middle Ages* (Ithaca, 2003). An excellent discussion of theoretical issues by an historian of late antiquity is E. A. Clark, *History, Theory, Text: Historians and the Linguistic Turn* (Cambridge, MA, 2004). Joel T. Rosenthal usefully discusses the narrative elements of various sources in *Telling Tales: Sources and Narration in Late Medieval England* (University Park, PA, 2003).

## Chapter 4   Debating the Middle Ages

On ritual, see E. Muir, *Ritual in Early Modern Europe* (Cambridge, 1997) and G. Koziol, *Begging Pardon and Favour* (Ithaca, 1992), particularly pp. 289–324. A critique of the concept for medievalists was launched by P. Buc, *The Dangers of Ritual* (Princeton, 2001), and a trenchant reply given in Koziol, 'The Dangers of Polemic', *Early Medieval Europe* 11 (2002): 367–88. C. Humphrey, *The Politics of Carnival* (Manchester, 2001) presents a concise and insightful discussion of rebellion in the context of ritual.

Various key articles on 'feudalism' are reproduced in L. K. Little and B. H. Rosenwein, eds, *Debating the Middle Ages* (Oxford, 1998); see also S. Reynolds, *Fiefs and Vassals* (Oxford, 1994) and subsequent reviews. An interesting take on social structures from several different perspectives is given by S. Rigby, *English Society in the Later Middle Ages: Class, Status and Gender* (London, 1995). Two key works exploring 'two cultures' models are J. Le Goff, *Time, Work and Culture in the Middle Ages* (Chicago, 1980) and A. Gurevich, *Medieval Popular Culture* (Cambridge, 1988); for a different view, see J. van Engen, 'The Christian Middle Ages as an Historiographical Problem', *American Historical Review* 91 (1986) and E. Duffy, *The Stripping of the Altars* (Yale, 1992). On ordinary lay people's relationship(s) with religion, see J. H. Arnold, *Belief and Unbelief in Medieval Europe* (London, 2005).

Power is a topic much debated, and wonderfully framed by Tim Reuter in the posthumous collection of his essays, *Medieval Polities and Modern Mentalities*, ed. J. L. Nelson (Cambridge, 2006). To pick just a few works of interest, for the early period, see particularly M. Innes, *State and Society in the Early Middle Ages* (Cambridge, 2000) and C. Wickham, *Framing the Early Middle Ages* (Oxford, 2005), and for later periods W. M. Ormrod, *Political Life in Medieval England* (Basingstoke, 1995), D. Nirenberg, *Communities of Violence* (Princeton, 1997) and J. Watts, *Henry VI and the Politics of Kingship* (Cambridge, 1996). The case for and against the medieval 'state' was the focus of keen discussion between R. Rees Davies and Susan Reynolds in *Journal of Historical Sociology* 16 (2003).

## Chapter 5   Making and Remaking the Middle Ages

On modern uses of the medieval, again see M. Bull, *Thinking Medieval* (Houndmills, 2005), and for an area of current debate, B. Holsinger, *Neomedievalism, Neoconservatism, and the War on Terror* (Chicago, 2007). The medievalness of Europe is set out in R. Bartlett, *The Making of Europe* (London, 1993) and J. Le Goff, *The Birth of Europe* (Oxford, 2005), and given a particular modern importance in P. J. Geary, *The Myth of Nations* (Princeton, 2002). The political importance of *la longue durée* for feminism – and implicitly for much else – is strongly argued in J. M. Bennett, *History Matters: Patriarchy and the Challenge of Feminism* (Philadelphia, 2006).

# Index

Adam of Dryburgh, 35
Africa, 7, 10, 77, 112,
 126
Aix-la-Chapelle (France),
 92
Alain de Lille, 99
Althoff, Gert, 90
Andrea Mantegna, 47
*Annales*, 13, 14, 60
 *see also* Bloch, Marc;
 Febvre, Lucien
Anonimalle Chronicle, 24
Anselm of Liège, 36
anthropology, 13, 43, 58–65,
 78, 79, 93, 94
Aragon, 38, 58, 93, 121
archaeology, 48, 58, 72–9,
 88, 97
archives, 7, 19, 20, 26, 28–
 30, 42, 45, 54, 55, 56,
 64, 117, 134
Aristotle, 116
Arthur (King), 31, 79, 80, 85,
 96, 116
Avignon (France), 1, 2, 3, 6,
 7

Bagge, Sverre, 39
Bakhtin, Mikhail, 104
Bartolomeo, priest of Milan,
 1–8, 134
Bataille, Georges, 124
Bedos-Rezak, Brigitte, 45
Bernardino da Siena, 35,
 116
bias, 39, 40, 73
bible, 28, 35, 47, 62
Bishop's Lynn (King's Lynn,
 England), 103
Black Death, 68, 86
Blanche of Castile, French
 regent, 115
Bloch, Marc, 12, 13, 60, 64,
 95, 116, 119
Boccaccio, 50
Bohemia, 101
Bourdieu, Pierre, 64, 124
Brentano, Robert, 28
Brown, Peter, 61
Bruges (Belgium), 70, 71
Burckhardt, Jakob, 84
Bury St Edmunds (England),
 115

Bynum, Caroline Walker, 15, 84
Byzantium, 62, 76, 112

Cairo (Egypt), 29
Cambridge (England), 12, 28, 134
Camden, William, 9
Carcassonne (France), 110
Castile, 51, 115
castles, 73, 88, 103
Catalonia, 98
Cellarius, Christopher, 8
Certeau, Michel de, 64
Chambly (France), 94
Charlemagne, 36, 62, 96, 107, 108, 111, 114, 115
Charles the Simple, king of the Franks, 38
Chartres (France), 46
chivalry, 10, 79, 81, 85, 96, 97, 100, 103, 107, 116, 123
*see also* knights
Christianity, 5, 8, 17, 37, 46, 48–50, 62, 74, 87, 89, 90, 98, 103–15, 122, 124
and clergy, 5, 23, 35, 38, 47, 59, 62, 84, 104, 105, 107, 108, 109
and lay piety, 35, 43, 47, 50, 59, 74, 77, 89, 90, 104–9
and monasteries, 36, 37, 41, 42, 43, 46, 51, 70, 74, 78, 115
and paganism, 5, 74, 105, 106
and papacy, 2–4, 5, 6, 30, 37, 52

and parish churches, 25, 28, 41, 42, 44, 46, 47, 59, 76, 78, 89, 104
and Roman Catholic Church, 5, 10, 18, 70, 106, 108, 113, 115, 123
*see also* Eucharist; heresy; Jesus Christ; saints
cities, 5, 6, 17, 29, 36, 37, 42, 43, 45, 50, 51, 53, 70, 76, 77–8, 90, 92, 93, 95, 96, 97, 99, 100, 107, 108, 113, 115, 125, 126
Clanchy, Michael, 42
class, 13, 14, 37, 71, 81, 85, 96, 100, 102, 107, 118, 125
Clover, Carol, 84
Cluny (France), 37, 44, 115
Cohn, Samuel K., 67, 68, 86
Conrad of Marburg, 38
Constantinople (Istanbul, Turkey), 77, 78
Crusades, 38, 80
Curta, Florin, 75
custom, 24, 62, 94, 107
*see also* law

Dante Alighieri, 3, 7, 8, 28
death, 21, 35, 68, 74, 107
Delumeau, Jean, 104
Denmark, 76, 101
Derrida, Jacques, 124
Dino Compagni, 37
dispute settlement, 41, 45, 55, 63, 88, 90, 91, 93, 118
Duby, Georges, 13, 61, 96, 97, 101
Durkheim, Emile, 60, 61, 93

Eadmer, 119, 120
Eco, Umberto, 4, 134

economy, 13, 15, 64, 65, 66,
    67, 68, 69, 70, 71, 74,
    95, 97, 99, 101, 102,
    109, 113
  and markets, 48, 70, 76,
    77, 78, 102, 114
  and tax, 23, 24, 25, 28,
    65, 66, 67, 68, 110, 112,
    113
  and trade, 10, 68, 69, 76,
    79, 113, 119
  and wages, 68, 69, 70, 71
Edward III, king of England,
    116
Effros, Bonnie, 74
Eichstätt (Germany), 100
Elias, Norbert, 124
emotions, 64, 65, 80, 91,
    93
Engels, Friderich, 14
England, 10, 11–12, 14, 17,
    19, 20, 23, 24, 27, 28,
    29, 31, 35, 38, 42, 48,
    54, 56, 68, 69, 70, 73,
    81, 87, 97, 101, 103,
    111, 112, 113, 116, 117,
    121, 126
Enlightenment, 9, 10, 120,
    124
ethnicity, 74, 75, 124
Eucharist, 89, 90, 93, 109

Farmer, Sharon, 54
Febvre, Lucien, 12
Felix Hemmerli, 114
feud, 55, 63, 64
  see also dispute settlement;
    violence
feudalism, 13, 71, 95–6, 101,
    111, 126
  see also lordship; peasants
Flanders, 17, 110
Flodoard of Reims, 38, 91

Florence (Italy), 13, 17, 28,
    37, 65, 67, 68, 97
Foix (France), 110
forgery, 43
France, 10, 11, 12, 15, 16,
    17, 18, 19, 20, 28, 29,
    31, 36, 37, 47, 54, 76,
    87, 93, 94, 97, 101, 108,
    109, 110, 111, 112, 117,
    126
Frankfurt (Germany), 94
French Revolution of 1789,
    29, 125

Galceran, count of Meulan,
    114
Gauvard, Claude, 54
gender, 15, 40, 50, 51, 53,
    66, 68, 74, 78, 80, 83,
    84, 96, 99, 103, 117,
    123
  and masculinity, 50, 81,
    84, 98, 123
  and sexuality, 15, 18, 53,
    80, 81, 89, 103, 108,
    114, 117, 123
  and women, 15, 24, 27,
    40, 50, 53, 54, 61, 68,
    78, 81, 83, 84, 89, 100,
    102, 103
Geoffrey Chaucer, 25, 28
Germany, 8, 10, 11, 14, 16,
    18, 19, 20, 28, 75, 83,
    85, 101, 114
Ghent (Belgium), 99
gifts, 41, 43–4, 61, 64, 69,
    89, 99, 115
Gilchrist, Roberta, 78
Gillingham, John, 117
Given, James B., 55
Goitein, Shelomov Dov, 29
Goody, Jack, 61
Gratian, 52

Guinevere (Queen), 80
Gurevich, Aron, 13, 14

Hanawalt, Barbara, 15, 54
Haskins, Charles Homer, 14
Henry, duke of Sandomierz,
    41, 43
Henry I, king of England, 91
Henry II, king of England,
    37
Henry III, king of England,
    111
Henry V, king of England,
    116
Henry Knighton, 24, 40
heresy, 4, 5, 13, 15, 54, 56,
    61, 63, 68, 82, 87, 107
Herlihy, David, 66
Hilton, Rodney, 14
Hocktide, 89
Holsinger, Bruce, 124
Holy Roman Empire, 6, 10,
    16, 17
honour, 1, 39, 50, 52, 53, 60,
    64, 80, 81, 92, 114
Hugh of St Victor, 84
Hungary, 20, 62, 102, 103

Iceland, 80
individuality, 84–5, 125
Innes, Matthew, 117, 134
Inquisition, 4, 5, 6, 34, 38,
    54, 55, 108
Islam, 15, 17, 22, 76, 87, 98,
    124
Italy, 1, 6, 11, 17, 19, 20, 28,
    31, 36, 53, 66, 93, 102,
    103, 108, 109, 116, 117,
    122

*Jacquerie* (France, 1358), 93
Jaime I, king of Aragon, 58,
    59, 60, 65, 93

Japan, 20, 33, 34, 57, 101,
    126
Jean de Joinville, 39
Jerusalem, 37, 48
Jesus Christ, 48, 49, 50, 51
    *see also* Christianity;
    Eucharist
Jews, 15, 29, 50, 70, 87, 98,
    109, 110
Joan of Arc, 4, 116
John Gower, 25
John of Gaunt, 23
John of Salisbury, 81, 116
John of Vicenza, 116
John XXII, pope, 2, 4, 6, 8,
    17
John, king of England, 42
Justice, Steven, 40

Kalamazoo (USA), 57, 58
Kantorowicz, Ernst, 16
kingship, 59–60, 88–9,
    111–12
kinship, 39, 44, 68, 77, 115
Klapisch-Zuber, Christine,
    66
knights, 3, 8, 50, 59, 79, 80,
    81, 85, 95, 96, 98, 99,
    102
    *see also* chivalry; lordship
Koziol, Geoffrey, 92

Lancelot, 80
languages
    Latin, 5, 7, 8, 30, 31, 36,
        38, 62, 82, 90, 96, 116
    vernaculars, 8, 30–1, 38,
        62
law, 5, 10, 12, 18, 28, 29,
    31, 37, 41, 42, 45, 50,
    51–6, 62, 63, 79, 82, 88,
    98, 99, 100, 101, 102,
    107, 111

law (cont.)
  see also custom;
    Inquisition;
    sources – legal
Le Goff, Jacques, 13, 61, 105
Le Roy Ladurie, Emmanuel,
  54, 55
Lea, Henry Charles, 15, 51,
  52
Leeds (England), 57, 58
Lévi-Strauss, Claude, 61
Lévy-Bruhl, Lucien, 60
libraries, 26, 27, 28
  see also archives
Life of Edward the Confessor,
  39
literacy, 6, 7, 28, 29, 31, 40,
  42, 45, 61–3, 72, 76,
  105, 106, 108, 111, 117,
  126
Lithuania, 114
Loire (river), 88, 89
London (England), 12, 23,
  92, 134
lordship, 23, 41, 73, 83, 85,
  95, 96, 98, 101, 102,
  114, 115
Louis IX, king of France, 39,
  54
Louis the German, king of
  East Franks, 94
Lucius III, pope, 37
Ludwig of Bavaria, Holy
  Roman Emperor, 6

magic, 2–7, 10, 104
Magna Carta, 42, 52
Maitland, Frederic W., 12,
  51
manors, 26, 29, 30
Mantua (Italy), 47
Mappa Mundi, 48
Margery Kempe, 103

Maria of Montpellier, queen
  of Aragon, 58, 63
marriage, 50, 53, 84, 100,
  102, 103, 105, 109, 123
Marseilles (France), 43, 55,
  76
Marxism, 13, 14, 66, 71, 95,
  124
Mary, Blessed Virgin, 59
Massa Marittima (Italy),
  117
Mauss, Marcel, 61
medicine, 37, 47
medievalism
  and alterity, 4–5, 8, 10, 21,
    35, 59, 63, 65, 72, 84,
    85, 95, 120–7
  and the future, 125–7
  and gender, 15
  and interdisciplinarity,
    57–85, 73, 127
  and modern nationalism,
    16, 17, 121, 125
  and national differences,
    10–15, 18–20, 64
  politics of, 10–12, 22,
    120–7
  and popular culture, 4, 21,
    120–1
  and professionalization of
    history, 8–9
memory, 40, 45, 56, 62, 89
Merback, Mitchell, 51
merchants, 8, 37, 50, 61, 71,
  96, 97, 99, 104, 105,
  107
Midsummer, 89, 93
Migne, Abbé Jacques-Paul,
  26
Milan (Italy), 1, 2, 4, 5, 6, 7,
  17, 65
Miller, William Ian, 64
Monod, Georges, 16

Montpellier (France), 43, 58, 59, 60
Monumenta Germaniae Historica, 12, 26
Moore, Robert Ian, 87
Muratori, Ludovico, 26

nationhood (medieval), 17, 112, 117, 121–2
Nelson, Janet, 15
Netherlands, 75, 99
Norman Conquest (England, 1066), 38, 39, 73, 86, 100
Norway, 76, 80, 100
notaries, 1, 7, 59, 87, 98, 118
numismatics, 76
Nuremberg (Germany), 114

Ong, Walter, 61, 63
Orderic Vitalis, 91, 114
Ormrod, W. Mark, 81, 112, 113
Orvieto (Italy), 28
Oxford (England), 12, 15, 28

palaeography, 31
Paris, 18, 20, 28, 36, 107
Parliament (English), 11, 24, 28, 31, 82, 100, 111, 121
Patrologia Latina, 26, 27
patronage, 19, 39, 95, 114, 115, 121
peasants, 23, 40, 42, 48, 83, 85, 93, 95, 97, 98, 101, 102, 114, 118
*see also* class; feudalism
Peasants' Revolt (England, 1381), 23, 24, 25, 40, 93, 97, 101, 108, 118

Pedro II, king of Aragon, 58, 59
Pedro IV, king of Aragon, 38
penance, 51, 54, 79, 89, 94, 114
Peter Schott, 104, 106
Petrarch, poet, 8, 9
Philip IV, king of France, 109, 110
pilgrimage, 75
Pippin the Short, king of the Franks, 63
Pirenne, Henri, 76, 77
Pisa (Italy), 36
Pithou, Pierre, 8, 9
Pocock, John, 81
Poland, 20, 41, 62, 101, 105
Pollard, Albert Frederick, 12
Pontoise (France), 94
popular culture (medieval), 46, 62–3, 75, 104–9
postmodernism/ poststructuralism, 15, 64, 125
Power, Eileen, 18
Prague (Bohemia), 79
prosopography, 44

Ramon Muntaner, 58, 60, 63, 65
Ranke, Leopold von, 11, 14, 15, 16, 134
Raoul, king of West Franks, 88, 90, 91
Redon (France), 40, 42, 43, 115
Reformation, 11, 29, 105, 124, 126
religion, *see* Christianity
Renaissance, 11, 19, 20, 21, 84, 86, 120, 124
Richard II, king of England, 23

Richer, 92
ritual, 45, 48, 60, 74, 83,
    88–94, 106, 107, 109,
    116
Robert Curthose, 91
Robert Mannyng of Brunne,
    35
Rodolphus Glaber, 36, 37
Roger Wendover, 36
Roman Empire, 9, 10, 17,
    21, 95, 120
Rolls Series, 12, 26, 27
Rosenwein, Barbara, 44
Rubin, Miri, 15
Ruggiero, Guido, 53, 55

St Albans (England), 27, 36
St Bertin (France), 115
St Denis (France), 36
saints, 39, 46, 54, 61, 68, 84,
    89, 92
    *see also* Christianity
Saladin, 37
Salvemini, Gaetano, 13
Salzburg (Austria), 62
Savonarola, 116
Scandinavia, 10, 31, 62, 76,
    80, 84, 93, 100, 108
Scott, James C., 124
Sforza, dukes of Milan, 113
Sicily, 6, 17
Skinner, Quentin, 81
Smail, Daniel Lord, 55
Smith, Adam, 95
Smoller, Laura, 109
sociology, 12, 64
soil, 75–76
sources, 12, 23–56, 63, 65,
    67, 68, 69, 73, 82, 87
    books of hours, 28, 46, 48,
        50, 77, 108
    charters, 29, 34, 36, 40–5,
        52, 97

chronicles, 24, 25, 26, 27,
    36–40, 58, 63, 65, 66,
    97, 111
diaries, 67
ecclesiastical, 29, 30, 34,
    35, 38, 54, 87, 109
legal, 1, 7, 24, 25, 28, 29,
    30, 31, 33, 34, 51–6, 82,
    98
letters, 7, 24, 25, 28, 31,
    33, 34, 40, 59, 67, 70
literary, 7, 25, 27, 31, 79,
    80, 81, 104
manorial, 26, 29, 30, 68
and narrative, 25, 37, 38,
    44, 54–5, 65, 80, 82, 83
sermons, 7, 25, 35, 46, 47,
    51, 54, 68, 82, 98, 99,
    105, 106, 107, 109, 110
visual, 7, 29, 32, 36, 46,
    47, 48, 49, 50, 51, 81,
    83, 117
wills, 29, 34, 68, 77
Southern, Richard, 15, 38,
    120
space, 54, 64, 72, 77–80,
    104, 106, 122, 123, 126
Spain, 5, 17, 20, 51, 76, 87,
    109, 121, 122
Spiegel, Gabrielle, 38
statistics, 25, 54, 66, 68, 69
Statute of Labourers
    (England, 1351), 69
Stockholm (Sweden), 28
Strasbourg (France), 104, 106
Strayer, Joseph, 14, 127
Subaltern Studies, 124
Suger, abbot of St Denis, 36

Taylor, Charles, 124
Thietmar, 92
Thomas Walsingham, 24, 27,
    36, 40

Toch, Michael, 83
torture, 3, 4, 10
Toulouse (France), 1
Tout, Thomas Frederick, 12
Très Riches Heures du Duc
    de Berry, 48
Turgot, Anne-Robert-Jacques,
    9
Turner, Victor, 61

United States of America, 14,
    15, 18, 19, 126
Usatges of Barcelona, 98, 99
usury, 70
Uytven, Raymond van, 99

Venice (Italy), 17, 29, 62, 92
violence, 10, 53, 54, 55, 85,
    88, 96, 109, 113, 114,
    117

Visconti, dukes of Milan, 1,
    3, 4, 5, 6, 7, 17, 113,
    134

Waldes of Lyon, 61
Wales, 114
Wat Tyler, 23
Wickham, Chris, 112
William, duke of Auvergne,
    88, 90, 91
William Caxton, 103
William Langland, 25, 27
William Marshall, 116
William of Newburgh, 37
Wolfram von Eschenbach, 79,
    80, 83, 85
Wormald, Patrick, 113, 117

Zagosc (Poland), 41, 43
Zurich (Switzerland), 114

# RUNNING FOR THE HOUSE

Howard Kleinhendler

ISBN: 1500282588
ISBN 13: 9781500282585
Library of Congress Control Number: 2014911568
CreateSpace Independent Publishing Platform
North Charleston, South Carolina

# PROLOGUE

The burly men shoved and kicked the DEA agent as they marched him blindfolded into a small, dark room deep within the walled compound in Mexico City. The ten-year veteran and father of two had been tortured for eight hours and drifted in and out of consciousness, oblivious to the pain from the wire cuffs jamming into his wrists. A white sheet hung over a cracked plastered wall, and two naked sixty-watt bulbs dangling from the water-stained ceiling lit up the man's bleeding face. The Sony camcorder sat on the edge of a pile of phone books loosely stacked on a rusted metal desk taken from the nearby grade school.

Behind the agent facing the camera stood the short cocaine pusher, barely thirty, his left hand firmly grasping the man's chin. The outcast son of a well-to-do family, he had struck out on his own to get rich quick, enjoying the fleeting success that some of his peers had achieved—free women, fancy cars, and the constant highs of cocaine and heroin. It was time to move up to the next level by taking on the Great Satan and making a name beyond the local neighborhood.

He spoke in halting English with a heavy accent as the man grimaced in pain. "To all you gringos who think you can come to my country and tell me how to live, this is what happens to your stinkin' *vigilantes.*"

He pressed the silver barrel of the Beretta 3032 firmly against the agent's temple and glanced over his shoulder. In the corner of the screenshot, another man could be seen. Lean and tall with cropped hair and a ruddy complexion, he was obviously of Slavic descent.

"Finish it," he whispered gently in Russian.

The chairman closed the laptop and pushed it across the table. The high-resolution screen had shown small clumps of the DEA agent's brain among the blotches of blood that splashed the camera lens.

Belowdecks of the forty-eight-foot Sea Ray Sundancer making its way to Biscayne Bay along the Miami River, three men talked quietly over a bottle of French Riesling while the din of the engines made their sounds inaudible to any machine trying to eavesdrop.

"The Russians are winning the new cold war," said the chairman, a tall elderly man. "It's no longer about aircraft carriers and stealth bombers. That contest is over. Today it's cornering the South American drug trade and manipulating energy and commodity markets from Chicago to London. Washington is watching the wrong game, and when they finally figure it out, we'll be too far behind to catch up."

A second man, dressed in a navy-blue blazer, nodded his head. "That's the problem with our system," sighed the professor. "The Defense establishment needs a bogeyman to justify the flow of large weapons projects, and we're running out of Arabs to kill. You can't get funding for a *Seawolf* attack sub or a *Nimitz*-class carrier to patrol the Caribbean

Sea. As for the markets, the banks use the price gyrations to feed their trading desks."

The judge reached for his glass and spoke up in a deep Southern drawl. "We can go loud and reveal some of the big politicos that are funded by the cartels, or maybe post a few videos, like the one we just watched, to get the soccer moms riled up. That would slow things down."

"That's gossip column stuff," said the chairman as he sipped his wine. "We need to take this into our own hands and eliminate some of the players."

"Yeah, but it's a tough neighborhood, and we don't have the muscle on-site to break through the networks of locals and hired hands," said the judge.

"Remember Botswana?" asked the professor. "We took out the heads of the warring families with a couple of B-52 runs and pinpoint SEAL raids. With no one left standing, Mugabe put his boy in place, and we've had twenty years of control and some decent economic prosperity. Why not run the same play in Mitu?"

The chairman shook his head. "Too many eyes on our backyard and the cartels are spread out and sophisticated. You chop off one head, and three pop up somewhere else. Africa is another planet. It's like taking a shit on the moon. No one cares. We need a new weapon—something silent, deadly, and most of all, anonymous. This way we can pin the carnage on the Russians and get the virus to turn on itself."

The judge lit a cigarette and took a deep puff. "There's nothing sexy on the market that I'm aware of."

The professor had nothing to offer either.

The chairman continued. "That's the point. We need to get into the room with the experimental next-gen stuff and put it to use for our purposes, without the pestering of congressional oversight committees or the risks from sniveling libertarians who confuse treason with whistle-blowing."

"That would set off all kinds of bells," cautioned the professor.

The chairman spoke softly, his voice barely above a whisper. "True. We can't do it, but a congressman on Strategic Forces could."

There was silence, and then smiles all around.

The professor leaned forward to the edge of his chair. "We've got fifteen months until the next midterms. It's gotta be a newbie, detached from any political machine. We can't stack up a bunch of IOUs."

"How can we trust someone outside the family?" asked the judge.

"We find an ideologue," the professor said reassuringly. "Not a Tea Party lunatic, but a naïve lefty who believes in the founding fathers and social justice. I'll spread word that I'm looking to get back into consulting now that my wife has passed."

The chairman headed for the rear stateroom. "He'll have to be carefully vetted by each of us, and we'll need to take out some quality insurance."

The professor and the judge climbed the steep stairs to the deck and signaled the captain to make for shore. The woman with red hair slowed to one-third and gently turned the ship portside while the two men settled into their captain's chairs and silently looked out at the water, taking in the myriad forces around them. They understood power.

Not merely the power of large guns and heavy bombs, but the vastly greater power of a heaving sea surrounded by subtropical air masses that could turn serenity to havoc in short order. It was a sensitivity acquired from a lifetime of service to their country: in combat, in the clandestine services, and in public office. It had prepared them well for their roles in a small group of black ops planners who could read the playing field and make the right moves before the enemy realized what was going on.

Forty minutes later, the ship reached dock at a villa on Williams Island. The three men got into their cars and drove away in different directions. Operation Open Sky had begun.

# 1

The rows of screens flashed crowded lines of symbols and numbers in the trading pit at Joesell & Frank, a Manhattan hedge fund on Park and Fiftieth. Two dozen caffeinated men furiously traded stocks during the market's opening hour, when heavy volume sent prices into violent short-term swings. Over a hundred million would change hands in just under an hour. As the clock hit ten thirty and the frenetic pace started to subside, the phone rang.

"I'll be right there. I just have to take this call," said Berger to his desk chief. John Berger was a senior trader at Joesell when he received a call from his childhood friend, Michael Gordon. Gordon, a New York City trial lawyer specializing in complex defense cases, hadn't called in years. The two had been inseparable growing up on Manhattan's Upper West Side, but had drifted apart as adults.

"Mike, what's up, man? How the hell have you been?" roared Berger, a bald, round man in his late forties who always seemed to be in a good mood.

After a few empty comments, Gordon got to the point. "Joannie, I know this is going to sound crazy, but I'm serious; I'm going to run for Congress."

The line went silent for a minute. Berger had put his hand to the phone and told his secretary to hold his calls. Then he kicked the door of his office shut.

"Mike, let's back up a minute. How are Emily and the kids? You still kicking ass on the basketball court?" Berger struggled to formulate a response to what he suspected was a severe midlife crisis hitting his old pal. Gordon had been the proverbial jock growing up, the star basketball player who was sought after by the popular girls. His parents had the money that gave him a debt-free ride through Penn and then law school. After two years in Thailand with the Peace Corps, he joined a top ten Manhattan firm. His wife, Emily, was a blond bombshell. With life that good, Berger couldn't understand why Gordon wanted to spend time in the crazy house called Congress.

"Listen, John, I'm fed up with the eighty-hour work-weeks, the arguments in front of brain-dead judges who don't give a damn. I'm tired of answering to money-hungry managing partners. It's time to do something meaningful, worthwhile—something that makes a difference."

Gordon's mother had died the previous year. As an only child, Gordon shared an unusually close bond with the warm, gentle retired school librarian and made sure to visit three to four times a year. He sought her advice when logic and deduction failed and unexplainable intuition provided the obvious answer. Although not a spiritual woman, she always stressed her conviction that man must help others if he is to realize his self-worth.

As the years of law practice dragged on, Gordon felt a nagging emptiness. He couldn't be sure if it was a midlife realization of man's mortality or simply reduced testosterone. But he no longer measured accomplishment through the year-end bonus or by the number of trial victories. He needed to do something different—drastically different.

Gordon thought Berger would understand. He, too, had once been a wide-eyed idealist working on the Hill, trying to make a difference. He was senior staff to the Senate Foreign Relations Committee and had worked hard in getting foreign aid to countries that were hurting. He knew the ins and outs of power as only senior staffers understand, for it was they who presented the issues to their masters— the elected officials whose attention span was limited by all the important cocktail parties needing attendance and the constant kissing of ass to donors and special interests. That sideshow stuff tore away at Berger, who felt that important decisions were being made by a bunch of twentysomething kids from Harvard and Berkeley. The House was much worse than the Senate. In Berger's eyes, House members were a traveling circus of incompetents from widely different backgrounds whose egos were large and who did their best work half-drunk, from behind closed committee room doors where only a handful of people knew what really was going on.

Berger switched to speakerphone as he undid his necktie. "So what about starting a business? Plenty of guys start something up and find it fulfilling, you know. Maybe a bar in the Village or something in manufacturing. I know people."

"Stop it, Jonnie. I don't know squat about business. That's why I've been working my ass off for the past twenty years in Manhattan law firms. I can't start a business, and if

I buy a stock, it immediately goes down. No, I'm serious, I want to do this."

"Yeah, but there's no money to be made in the House," clamored Berger. "Maybe a hundred seventysomething minus pension and you need a place in DC. You've got kids. What the hell are you thinking? If you want to get laid, being a House member is not the place. The young Southern girls will charm the hell out of you, but the minute you squeeze their ass, it's lawsuit time and your career is over."

Gordon's tone grew anxious. "I've got to start somewhere, and I'm forty-five years old. I'm not going to run for local school board. The House is still considered entry level in some places; you know the founding fathers stuff about farmers and countrymen who leave their homes and work in the people's house for two years."

Berger laughed. "*Please.* Don't give me that founding fathers bullshit. None of those guys could win a seat in Congress today, even in western Texas. The government they created is inherently dysfunctional. Nothing can get done in the Senate because every dickwad can filibuster until he gets tired of reading phone book numbers on C-SPAN. The House is all about bringing home the pork, like a million bucks for a Confederate war statue in Mississippi or ten million dollars for research into hog breeding. Hell, John Murtha turned a white trash trailer park in western Pennsylvania into a Defense Department manufacturing mecca."

Berger nervously looked at his watch. He hadn't checked his trading screen in over seven minutes. "Have you thought of therapy? I know a great shrink over on Fifth Avenue. She really knows her shit and likes to prescribe nice purple pills that make you feel all kinds of things. It's really good before sex."

"All right, John. I see you're not following me," moaned Gordon. "Give my best to Cathy and the kids."

Berger recognized this tone. "Listen, Mike, do me a favor. Think about this for another week, and if you're still serious, call me back. I'll see what I can do."

"OK, Jonnie, you got it. Cheers."

The week went by slowly. Gordon had two court appearances and traveled to Miami to schmooze a wealthy client who had just lost a bundle to a Ponzi scheme. Instead of calling in the morning, Gordon waited until after the market closed, when Berger's blood pressure would be back to around 130 over 90 and he'd be tallying up his gains for the day. Hopefully it was a good day.

"John Berger's office. How may I direct your call?" The voice belonged to an older woman.

"Is John in? It's Mike Gordon."

"Hold, please."

The wait had been five minutes already, and Gordon was about to hang up when a hurried voice came on.

"Mike, it was a bear of a day—market down two hundred and seventy-five points—and we just got a huge capital call," huffed Berger. "Byron Wolf, two eight two, six nine zero, ninety-nine oh-one. He's in Houston. Talk to him about Congress. He'll steer you the right way."

"Byron who?" said Gordon, not knowing whether Berger was up to some pathetic joke.

"Byron Herbert Wolf, distinguished professor of political science at Rice University, former lead staffer to the Watergate Commission, and top consultant to independent prosecutor Ken Starr's Whitewater investigation. He's the smartest guy I know and can get anyone on the phone, from Bush to Clinton and everyone in between. We were good friends when I was up on the Hill. Tell him I told you to call. He owes me one for getting his granddaughter into Columbia Law. Got to go."

That was it. No more jokes or discouragement, just a name and a number. Byron Wolf. A quick search brought up a *Wikipedia* article that confirmed what Berger had said and then some. Over thirty published articles. The man seemed to know his political shit. Houston was nice this time of year, and Gordon had always wanted a genuine cowboy hat. He picked up the phone.

# 2

**W**alking through Hermann Park to the Rice campus, Gordon stopped to admire the manicured lawns and the towering maples and oaks beginning to turn autumn rust. After passing through security, Gordon was directed to a discreet office on the second floor. A slight old woman with snow-white hair was seated behind an old desk, her reading glasses perched at the end of her nose. Her hands moved nervously, and Gordon couldn't tell if she was knitting or maybe scribbling a note.

Peering up slightly, the woman uttered in complete indifference, "The professor is in the back. He's expecting you."

He left Grandma still fidgeting behind her desk and stepped through a large chocolate-colored wooden door. The room was cavernous, with twelve-foot ceilings, large cathedral-like windows on one side, and floor-to-ceiling bookcases on the other, stacked three layers deep with everything from *War and Peace* to *Huckleberry Finn*. Along what was left of the walls of the room were a myriad of photos of dignitaries: Nixon, Carter, Ford, Brezhnev, Kissinger, Kurt Waldheim, Bill Clinton, W, and Menachem Begin. In the center of the room stood a large round table surrounded by six plush velvet chairs. Papers and books were strewn all about.

Wolf stood beside the bookcase, clutching a hardcover. He was tall and slender, in his mid-seventies, with chiseled features and sunken blue eyes.

"Good morning, Mr. Gordon," Wolf said in an almost musical tone. "Berger told me you're the punctual type. Have a seat, why don't you?"

Gordon hesitated. There was only one chair that didn't have a stack of books piled on it.

Wolf stretched out his arm toward the empty chair. "Go ahead, take it."

Gordon melted into the plush velvet as Wolf handed him *All the President's Men* by Bob Woodward.

"So what was Nixon's mistake?" Wolf asked in a gentle but assertive tone.

Gordon figured he'd roll with it, like motion day in New York City trial court when judges give you twenty seconds to discuss a presentation that spans thirty pages and for which you had planned a fifteen-minute speech. "Um, the president orchestrated a break-in of DNC headquarters and then tried to cover it up," Gordon said hurriedly.

"Berger said you needed a lot of work, but I had no idea how bad it was." Wolf sighed as he turned toward the window. The office looked out on the campus, peppered with students hurrying for their classes. Gordon sat silently as Wolf slipped his hands into his back pockets and continued looking out the window.

"The mistake was not the break-in or the cover-up. It was passing over the career professionals at the FBI and putting in new blood after Hoover's death. This motivated the Deep Throat leak to the press, which dictated the public's perception of Nixon's culpability." Wolf was matter-of-fact, talking with his back to Gordon and staring out at the campus.

Gordon didn't know where Wolf was going and then recalled that Deep Throat turned out to be the FBI's number two man under Hoover who was passed over for the top job when Hoover died.

Wolf turned to face Gordon. "You see, Mr. Gordon, it's not the act that needs attention; it's the public's perception of the act that means everything. Bill Clinton can jerk off with Monica Lewinsky all day. If it's casual White House sex, it's survivable; if it's a breach of national security, it's time to move back to Little Rock. Clinton succeeded in getting the public to perceive the former, so he survived."

Wolf shuffled through a few papers on the table to reveal a telephone. "Betty, get us two cups of coffee—black, no sugar. Would you, dear?"

Wolf cleared off a chair and sat down opposite Gordon. "So how are you going to get people to perceive you as something they want or like?" asked Wolf. "Are you going to hire fancy PR guys and mail a bunch of shiny flyers with pictures of you and your wife hugging your kids? That's what I get from these Texas hillbilly Republicans who have the IQ equivalent of the cattle they tend to but who can get a thirtysomething mother of three to cry over partial-birth abortion. Down here, you wave the flag, tell the people you love Jesus, love low taxes, and want to save the unborn from the radical Left, and you're in."

The white-haired lady, now known as Betty, set the china cups and coffeepot on the table and left.

"But you're from New Jersey," mused Wolf. "You need to deal with real issues like unemployment and health care. Nobody understands the causes of these problems. The masses are programmed by the particular bent of the twenty-four-hour news cycle that they attend to. If it's Fox, then they're buying Republican and Tea Party crap about lower taxes and less government. CNN and MSNBC, more Democratic, want you to hear about entitlements and deficit spending. It's all about the perception and what's driving it. You can't compete with network and cable television on the party-line level. If it's a party-line district, then the election is decided by the mass media and the president's performance. If there are a lot of independents, then you have to localize the issues and go after your opponent on a personal level. You see, the blanks have no moral fiber. They simply go with the flavor of the day. It's not about you tasting that good. It's more about the other guy smelling like shit."

Gordon switched to litigation mode: say something and hope it sticks.

"Well, I live in New Jersey's fifteenth congressional district, and the Republican incumbent, Brett Parker, has been there awhile, so it seems we may have to be on the offensive rather than run a strictly issues campaign."

"Brett Parker has the intellectual acumen of a pregnant seal," snarled Wolf. "But he's the poster boy for the anti-abortion zealots and prides himself on proposing legislation every year to ban modern birth control. Rumor is that his longtime chief of staff, Peggy Tang, not only tells him how to vote but also buys his clothing. He also manages to court big labor by voting way left on minimum wage and card check. The only way to take out Parker is by cutting off his balls. And that's going to be expensive."

Gordon was surprised at how serious Wolf seemed with these remarks. He sounded like a Marine Corps drill sergeant.

"How much money have you raised so far?"

"Ah, none yet. I wanted to sit down with my father and stepmother and talk it over before heading out to fund-raise." Gordon's father had sold his small business years ago and had amassed a comfortable nest egg.

"Mommy isn't going to make this happen," snapped Wolf. "You can't wipe your ass today for less than a million dollars, and it's going to take two or three times that to bloody up Parker."

Gordon made a good living, but he had never asked someone for money before and had no idea how to raise $2 million for a campaign. He didn't like attack ads and believed that people should be elected for their ideas and convictions, not because they dumped on the other side.

"How long you staying in Houston?" asked Wolf.

"Well, I've got a pretrial hearing in Beaumont tomorrow afternoon and was gonna head back home after that."

"Who's the judge?"

"Ware Hudler."

"Oh, you're going to love him. Ware's a real informal type, likes to get to know the lawyers around him. Been on the bench forever," Wolf said. "Why don't you come back on Saturday and join me for some gator hunting? We're going down to Seadrift."

Gator hunting? Gordon couldn't kill a cockroach.

"Ah, I'm already booked on the Friday-night red-eye," mumbled Gordon.

"Nonsense," roared Wolf. "Change the flight. I'll see you at eight a.m. at my place. Let Betty know."

Wolf finished his coffee and started for the door.

"Gotta get to class, Gordon. Nice meeting you."

The meeting seemed surreal. It was only nine fifteen, and Gordon already felt like he'd been there for hours. As he lifted his coffee cup, Betty walked in, holding a note in her hand.

"Here's the professor's address. Don't be late. He'll have extra gear for you. Now, why don't you follow me out?"

Gordon made his way to an empty bench in the campus yard just opposite Wolf's office. He already had a lot to do to prepare for tomorrow's court hearing and didn't have the time to shop for gator hunting clothes. A slender young woman walked by and dropped a notebook at Gordon's feet. Gordon returned it to her without saying anything.

"Thanks, stranger," the woman said in a friendly tone.

"You look kind of stressed out. Is everything OK?"

"You wouldn't happen to know where I could shop for some hunting clothes, would you?" Gordon's voice was soft and fragile, like a lost child asking for directions home.

"Oh, sure," the woman said reassuringly. "It's gator season, and everybody's heading south for the weekend. There's a nice shop just a few blocks west on Holcombe Street. Holloway's. But you're gonna need a permit for the gun."

"I'm not looking for a gun," Gordon said sheepishly. "Just need some socks and maybe a Windbreaker."

"Oh, that's the place," chimed the woman as she walked away.

Gordon checked his phone: only three messages, none too important. He headed over to Holloway's.

# 3

**G**ordon arrived at the courthouse early to put the finishing touches on his presentation for his biggest client, Rohr Pharmaceuticals. He was quite anxious, as the hearing dealt with a variety of important motions, including what witnesses may be called, whether any documents would be excluded from trial, what order the defendant lawyers would present their cases, how experts would be presented, and what they would be allowed to say. It was a huge case involving more than a dozen multinational drug companies accused of fixing the wholesale prices of their prescription medicines. The plaintiffs were seeking more than $1 billion in damages and were represented by a horde of leading Texas plaintiff lawyers.

"The judge is not in today," said the court deputy, his head firmly buried in the local *Beaumont Enterprise*.

"But my records show a one p.m. pretrial conference on the pharmaceutical antitrust multidistrict litigation," exclaimed Gordon.

"It's been moved to the ranch. Three twenty-five Sour Lake Road. They start the roast at six, but you're fine if you get there by eight." The lean Southerner glanced up from his newspaper at Gordon, who was neatly dressed in a gray pinstriped suit and black spit-polished shoes.

"You may want to wear something more comfortable," cautioned the deputy.

"You mean the hearing is informal?"

"I mean the ranch might be a bit dusty and could ruin those nice dress shoes you got on." The deputy chuckled and went back to his newspaper.

Dumbfounded, Gordon shuffled out of the courtroom. Here he was with a litigation bag stuffed with motion papers, prepared to argue at least seven different issues, and now he had to figure out what was wrong with his shoes. He called his secretary.

"Did you get any notice changing the time for today's pretrial in the antitrust MDL?"

"Oh, yes, Mr. Gordon, was meaning to call. We got something late last night. Says the hearing is moved to the Big Dog Ranch, three twenty-five Sour Lake Road, Beaumont, eight p.m. Casual attire."

"Thank you." Gordon's voice didn't hide his annoyance. The stress of the hearing was enough to handle without screwups from his secretary. Luckily, Gordon had packed some casual clothing for the flight home.

He spent the next few hours in the court's attorney lounge reviewing case law and finalizing his argument outlines. According to the GPS on his phone, the ranch was a ninety-minute drive. Gordon always liked to arrive early at court appearances, and planned on getting there by seven thirty. He worried the judge's home would not be large enough to accommodate the nearly two dozen lawyers who were supposed to show up. He would have to elbow his way to the front and fight to be heard.

The drive passed through scenic farmland and herds of cattle lazily grazing in the afternoon sun. He finally reached a road sign pointing to Sour Lake, but the GPS had stopped transmitting data. He was out of cell phone range. He drove until he reached a gas station and pulled in to ask for directions.

"You drive three miles up the road and take your next left, then your first right," explained the attendant, a short, rugged man with a weathered face. "Enjoy the roast."

Gordon was puzzled—first the deputy and now the gas attendant talking about a roast. Was there some comedy show going on nearby? He couldn't imagine it, as the road was deserted and there was nothing but tall prairie grass and vast open space. It was getting dark as Gordon pulled up to a large dusty sign marked "Big Dog Ranch." He drove ahead cautiously. The road was no more than a narrow dirt path more suitable for donkeys than cars. To the right were enormous herds of cattle. To the left, stands of grown corn stretched as far as the eye could see. The smell was overbearing. Between the cow manure and the corn fertilizer, it was hard to breathe. It was a cool evening, but Gordon shut the car windows and blasted the air-conditioning. Finally, Gordon could see what looked like a gate with two lights on either side. A state trooper waved a flashlight, directing Gordon to pull over to the left.

"Pull up behind the pickup and leave your keys in the car and the door unlocked," the trooper said in that matter-of-fact tone that highway cops are known for.

Gordon wasn't too sure about leaving his car unlocked, but this wasn't Lower Manhattan and the guy with the badge and a gun was nearby. He walked through a grassy patch and reached a gated entrance. There was an expanse of land followed by a cobblestone walkway. To the right stood a nineteenth-century center-hall Colonial, freshly painted, with marble columns and manicured Japanese boxwood hedges sprinkled with a rainbow of colors from the azaleas and agapanthus. A huge man with two extremely large Dobermans tugging at him approached. On his arm was an attractive petite Asian woman at least half his age in a black tube dress with an off-white sweater slung over her shoulders.

"Hi, I'm Ware. Glad you could make it."

Gordon was floored. Was this the judge? The guy was humongous, at least six feet seven, 280 pounds, with a full head of silver hair. He was dressed in blue jeans and a worn red plaid hunting shirt under a sky-blue Windbreaker. His knee-high boots were splattered in mud.

"This is Isabelle. Welcome to my home. You can set that heavy bag over there under the punch bowl table. The hog should be ready in about a half hour. After supper, we'll settle down to business."

"A pleasure to make your acquaintance," Isabelle said with a coy smile. She locked eyes with Gordon's. "Hope we can get to know each other a little better."

The dogs were getting aggressive, staring and growling at Gordon.

"Ah, come on now, girls. That's no way to treat a guest," gnarled the judge as he moved off to greet two other lawyers who had just arrived.

Gordon stumbled over to an eight-foot folding table with a large clear bowl filled with red liquid. He took a quick sip and almost choked. The punch was heavily laced with a mixture of 110-proof bourbon and some home-brewed licorice cognac. His nose felt on fire, and all his saliva had dried up. Gordon shoved his heavy litigation bag under the table and moved off to what appeared to be a string of glowing lights.

There were at least two dozen people sitting on floral carpets around a huge fire pit. At one end of the pit, a man was slowly turning a fifteen-foot-long rotisserie that went through what had to be a two hundred-pound pig, which was entirely intact, head, feet, and all. Another man with a full-size paintbrush and bucket was smearing the pig with thick brown brine. A woman carrying several white sacks threw fistfuls of colored powder over the pig. Red, white, and black puffs clung to the sides of the animal as it turned over the roaring fire. The entire area was encircled with tall burning torches. There was no man-made light, just the flames and the glow of a full moon.

Still trying to shake off the punch, Gordon walked over to a canopied structure that looked like a bar. Behind it was a slender man with a moustache dressed in a white serving apron.

"Can I have Diet Coke, please?" Gordon asked, practically begging.

"So sorry, senor," the man said in a heavy Mexican accent. "We only have alcoholic beverages here. Judge Hudler insists that his guests relax, and the best way is with good food and strong alcohol."

"What about a bottle of water?" pleaded Gordon.

"Oh, no bottled water here. The judge thinks all water should be free and doesn't understand why anyone would pay for something you can get from a garden hose. He wants to ban the sale of all bottled water. But there's a hand pump about a hundred yards in that direction that is connected to an underground well. The judge uses it to soften up the feed for some of the younger cattle. Just be careful. Sometimes the water is brown."

Gordon stared in the direction of the pump, seeing only black darkness. He wasn't going to risk getting stampeded by a thirsty bull, only to contract some waterborne disease.

"Got anything cold?" asked Gordon.

"Here you go, amigo. This is the closest thing to water we carry." The man pulled out a frosted bottle of Fat Tire beer and handed it to Gordon.

"It tastes good. I think they make it in Chicago," said the barkeep.

By now, Gordon was desperate. The punch was still ripping away at his throat, and his nose was almost beginning to bleed from the strong combination of smells coming from the cow manure and the spiced up pig. He ripped off the cap and gulped down half the bottle. To his surprise, it was a sweet brew, with only a slight chalky aftertaste. He could live with this.

Gordon settled down on a blue-and-pink carpet just yards from the smoldering hog. To his right was Megan Riley, a smart-looking blonde in her late thirties from Boston's Hyde Park. She represented Schering Plough and was known for her attention to detail. Gordon had spent countless hours with her and other defense lawyers on conference calls and at many of the nearly one hundred depositions taken in the case. She was a bit of the hippie type, never wearing much makeup and always dressed in formfitting pantsuits.

"Megan, what's up? Can you believe this place? Talk about originality. This has gotta be the weirdest court proceeding ever." Gordon was feeling better now, almost giddy. He hadn't eaten since one in the afternoon, and he had just consumed a fair amount of strong alcohol.

"This is a disgrace, Michael." Megan's face was red, and she had that serious look that litigators put on when they want to get their point across to the jury.

"Can you believe what they did to that poor pig? They shoved a spit up its ass until it came out of its mouth and have been roasting the poor thing for hours. It's inhumane."

"Well, that's how they eat down here. They like farm animals. It's something about being close to nature and living off the land." Gordon was trying to be reassuring, but Riley would have none of it.

"If this weren't such a goddamned corrupt place, I'd call the local ASPCA, but for all I know, Hudler's cousin runs it. You know that the town sheriff is his brother? Why do you think there's a trooper working the parking lot?"

From her shoulder bag, Riley took out a long, flat tin can that looked something like sardines.

"I'm sticking to health and principle. I'll have none of this phony prehistoric carnivorous gorging. Care for some tofu chips? They're imported from South Korea."

Gordon shook his head and watched as Riley removed several thin mushroomlike white disks from the can and slowly dropped them into her mouth. She then pulled out a bottle of Poland Spring. Gordon wanted to warn her about the judge's problem with bottled water, but he'd thought better of it, as it would only set Riley off again.

"You know this whole case is a joke, don't you?" mused Riley. "The plaintiff's lead counsel is Vern Walters. Walters and Hudler go back together thirty years, when Hudler was a judge in Jefferson County criminal court and Walters was the county prosecutor. Hudler made headlines when he sentenced a twenty-year-old semiretarded kid to death for driving the getaway car in a botched Seven-Eleven robbery. When Hudler and Walters got tired of electrocuting Mexican gang members, Hudler got a seat on the federal bench, and Walters went into private practice. He's brought dozens of class actions before Hudler, and they all settle before trial at huge numbers. Rumor has it that Ware gets a piece of the pie on the side. Makes sense, doesn't it? It costs money to raise all these cattle."

Before Gordon could fully digest what he had just heard, huge screams rang out from around the fire pit. Judge Hudler had poured two huge buckets of water on the fire, and gray plumes of steam were engulfing the pig. It seemed quite amusing to those sitting closest to the action, as ash and dust covered their faces.

"This is the final touch on the cuisine. They let the pig steam in its juices," Riley said as she finished off the last of her tofu chips. "Oh, look, here comes Walters." Riley leaned forward on her knees to get a good view. A muscular man in a cowboy hat headed toward the pig with two long carving knives.

"He's going to cut off the pig's ass and give it to Ware," joked Riley. "It's some kind of Viking tradition, and supposedly, it's the best part of the pig."

"Have you been here before?" asked Gordon. It seemed like Riley knew an awful lot about this place.

"Oh, sure, this is my fifth roast. My first was about seven years ago on the Rezulin product liability case. You remember, the type two diabetes wonder pill that made your liver stop working, a lovely Warner-Lambert product that spawned five thousand lawsuits around the country. I drank two cups of the punch and passed out on Ware's lap. I'm pretty sure we had sex. All I know is that I woke up the next morning with nothing on except a Mexican guayabera shirt. Since then, though, Hudler makes it a point to mention that he considers me a topflight litigator. It's brought me a lot of business."

Riley stood up as the smoke from the pit reached a scary intensity.

"Want anything from the bar?" she asked.

"Oh, no, I'm fine, thanks." Gordon waved his hands frantically in front of his face to clear the smoke cloud that had floated over from the fire pit.

The judge had taken over the carving from Walters, and the festive atmosphere continued. Waiters walked through the crowd with platters of steamed oysters and clams, spiced rice, and assorted salads with dressings that made the punch taste dull. The hog slowly waned into a thin skeleton as the din of the crowd continued. There was a heated debate between Caleb Flynt, one of the plaintiff's attorneys and former Baptist minister, and Seth Birnbaum, Pfizer's lawyer from New York, about how to deal with what likely would be an all Spanish-speaking jury.

"You can't close to the jury in Spanish. I don't speak Spanish. It gives you an unfair advantage because you can relate to them in their native tongue and appeal to their cultural and emotional bias, while I can't," insisted Birnbaum.

Flynt looked up at the stars. "As the prophet Isaiah said, 'The Spirit of the Sovereign Lord is on me, because the Lord has anointed me to proclaim good news to the poor.' The crimes you drug companies have committed are a sin and an affront to Jesus Christ. I will do the Lord's work any way I see fit."

"Yeah, right. I suppose the Lord also told you to take a third of the recovery and spend it on fancy cars and stately mansions." Birnbaum chuckled as he gulped down some punch.

"'Therefore I will give him a portion among the great, and he will divide the spoils with the strong.' I'm just following the path the Lord has placed before me."

Flynt raised his glass of Portuguese rum.

"Cheers, Mr. Birnbaum."

"Yeah, see you in hell, you redneck lunatic," muttered Birnbaum.

Riley was back with a scotch and a healthy portion of clam.

"Hey, what's going on over there, Megan?" Gordon pointed to a heated conversation between the judge, Walters, and Reed Calhoun, the local Beaumont lawyer the defense hired to join their team to even the playing field in this orgy of good old boys. There was a woman with a steno notebook taking notes.

"Oh, they're working out the pretrial stuff," snorted Megan, who was obviously intoxicated. "The girl with the notebook is a court reporter taking down the judge's rulings."

"But, wait a minute, I've got several important arguments to make. They can't do this without me."

"They sure can," Riley said over an embarrassing burp.

Determined to make his mark on the proceedings for his client, Gordon headed for the judge, who was listening intently to Walters and Calhoun.

"We'll do this just like we did the vitamin case last year. I'll open for an hour and call ten witnesses and my two experts—Wade Philips and Breen Shaw," explained Walters.

"Oh, I like Shaw. He's got a wonderful cottage on the water in Lake Charles. Isabelle and I were there last summer," said the judge.

"Yeah, we took his deposition out there a couple of weeks ago. Fine place," agreed Calhoun.

Gordon was beside himself. The judge had spent a week at the cottage of the plaintiff's expert, and the defense was going along with it.

Gordon pushed Walters aside and stood face-to-face with the judge.

"Your Honor, I'm Michael Gordon for Rohr Pharmaceuticals, and I have a number of pretrial motions I'd like to raise with the court." Gordon's voice was rushed and high-pitched.

The court reporter dropped her pen and froze; her eyes and mouth flung wide open as she stared at Gordon in disbelief. Walters and Calhoun stopped talking and turned toward Gordon. Their steady gaze was the kind that usually preceded a fistfight. As Walters stepped closer, the judge put his arm around Gordon and walked him away from the lawyers.

"You know, Michael, the professor tells me you're thinking about a run for office back East. One of my mentors told me a long time ago that a salmon that swims upstream is more likely to become bear fodder. You know what I mean, son?"

"You've spoken to Professor Wolf?" Gordon asked as the judge's grip tightened around his shoulder.

"Oh, sure. Byron and I are good friends. Tells me that you've got great potential and should make a strong candidate next year. Don't worry none about the little conversation we were having back there. Everything will be squared away before trial—assuming, of course, there isn't a settlement beforehand."

The judge gave Gordon a strong slap on the back and headed over to Megan Riley, who had just passed by with a drink in each hand.

"Megan, my darlin', it's been forever," the judge roared as he placed his hand firmly on her backside.

Gordon looked at his watch. It was 11:00 p.m. and he still had quite a drive back to Houston.

# 4

**G**ordon had barely fallen asleep when the alarm rang. He was still hungover from the raucous at the judge's house, and his head pounded. After gulping down two cups of black coffee and a corn muffin, Gordon made his way to River Oaks, an old-money Houston neighborhood better known for its residents serving time in federal prison for the Enron scam. Gordon pulled into the driveway at 7:45 a.m. He pushed back the seat and closed his eyes, relishing the fifteen minutes he still had before having to ring the professor's doorbell.

*Clack, clack, clack.*

Gordon popped up in his seat to the rapping of Wolf's knuckles on the driver's side window. He quickly glanced at his watch. 7:47 a.m. Wolf was all smiles as he opened the car door.

"Great to see you, Mr. Gordon," roared the professor. "Glad you're on time. Carmine hates it when we're late."

*Carmine?* He didn't know anyone named Carmine. But after last night, Gordon was ready for anything. Carmine was probably some middle-aged cowhand who spent his weekends trapping and slaughtering marine mammal life in order to prove his manhood.

Wolf was a comical sight, dressed in a wild red-and-orange Hawaiian shirt, khaki shorts, knee-high wading boots, and a tan-and-blue fishing hat. His eyes were hidden behind black sunglasses, and what looked like a half-smoked Cuban Cohiba was stuck in the side of his mouth.

"Hello, professor. Great weather, huh?" It was already seventy degrees and not a cloud in the sky.

"So how'd it go with the judge last night?" Wolf asked as he loaded the back of his Ford Explorer with a twelve-gauge shotgun, two snatch hooks, and a six-foot bangstick.

"Oh, it was quite an interesting evening over at the ranch," mused Gordon, who still did not understand what all the gear was for. He pointed to what looked like a long spear. "What's that long stick with the barrel at the end?"

"That's a bangstick," the professor said as he continued to load the car. "You place it right behind the gator's front eye and pull the trigger. A small charge enters the brain and kills the critter. That's, of course, after you shoot him."

Wolf pulled out a long-barreled silver gun that looked like something right out of a Clint Eastwood movie. "Here, Gordon, you hold on to the three fifty-seven. Never know when you might need it."

Gordon felt uncomfortable with the gun. It was heavy, with a six-shot barrel and a tan wooden grip engraved with the words *From Henry.* He promptly stuffed it into the back of his pants, under his shirt.

The drive to Seadrift was serene. The roads were mostly empty, and Wolf seemed adrift, not really acknowledging Gordon's presence. About forty-five minutes into the trip, Wolf snapped to life.

"You know, Michael, while politics is taught as a science, it's really more of an art. It's the art of shallow persuasion. It's all about the twenty to thirty seconds the voter spends in the booth looking at the ballot and pulling the lever. People like to think it's about research and issues. But the decisions by millions are made on the mundane—what a candidate looks like, what the pastor says about him, party affiliation. Will he lower my taxes? Is he going to win? People don't understand government and the compromise it takes to accomplish something in a two-party partisan system. In the old days, you had a monarch who ran the show and cut your head off or burned you at the stake if you got out of line. It permitted extremely effective governance, albeit with the elevated risk of corruption and empowerment of the elite at the expense of the masses, who we refer to today as the middle class. But are we really better off with our open democracy and three-legged form of government that rises and falls on the whims of middle-aged housewives who take their advice from Oprah? I'd say no."

This was the first time Wolf had mentioned Gordon by his first name, and Gordon took it as a sign of acceptance. The professor must have been getting to like him, although he wasn't sure why. Yet the detached tone of Wolf's ranting seemed odd to Gordon. *Why is this guy talking about royal executions?*

Wolf took a sharp turn onto a bumpy dirt path. As the car jolted from side to side, Gordon struggled to stay upright. The .357 bored into the small of his back. Finally, they reached a clearing at the mouth of a narrow lake no more than a hundred feet across. Waiting there was a stout, muscular man in his early sixties, about five feet ten, wearing the same tall wading boots that Wolf had on.

"How've you been, buddy?" Wolf roared as the two embraced.

"Gordon, this is Carmine Bruno, the finest soldier this country has seen since Stonewall Jackson."

"Proud to meet you," Bruno said in a Southern drawl. Gordon cringed as Bruno's grip practically crushed his hand.

Wolf put his hand on Bruno's back and smiled. "You know, Carmine is a direct descendant of Pope Pious VII."

"Oh, is that a fact?" quipped Gordon. "I thought the pope didn't marry."

Wolf chuckled as he turned to open the rear liftgate of the SUV. "Those guys had more women than you or I could count. Carmine, though, is quite proud of his Italian heritage."

Bruno pulled a large sportsman ax out of his waistband and cut the line of the twenty-foot, single-engine flatboat wedged in the mud. The professor threw his gear aboard and made his way into the boat, which dropped deeper into the water under his weight.

Gordon felt squeamish as he took a closer look at the simple craft.

"Is that thing strong enough for us three and an alligator?" Gordon asked, desperately looking to the professor for reassurance.

"Oh, we've done fine with this baby. It just loves sneaking up on those gators," Wolf said as Bruno climbed aboard.

The three traveled for about two hours through a maze of narrow waterways dotted with tall weeds and brush.

Mosquitoes the size of half dollars kept dashing at Gordon's face while he desperately tried to swat them away. Birds chirped loudly in a cacophony of sounds that Gordon had never heard before. Bruno sat in the back of the boat manning the rudder while Wolf kneeled in front trying to spot the gators. Gordon felt as if he were on another planet. There was no sign of mankind anywhere, just the boat and the surrounding nature.

Bruno turned the boat into a shallow marsh and cut the motor. The boat glided for a bit and then came to a stop. Patches of tall grass broke the glass-like surface of the water. Wolf moved backward from his forward perch and gently pointed to his right, toward a small island-like clump of dirty grass in the middle of the clearing. He then tapped Bruno on the shoulder and shook his head toward a disturbance in the grass. Gordon could only see the fluttering of a swarm of flies and the tall grass gently moving about. Bruno and the professor clearly saw something else. Bruno grabbed the snatch hook, which looked like a noose attached to a metal pole, and slowly climbed out of the back of the boat and into the water, barely cracking the surface, while the professor reached for his twelve-gauge.

Bruno gently waded toward the grassy patch when Gordon saw it. Slowly slithering into the water was a huge alligator, at least fifteen feet long with huge bulbous eyes and massive jaws. It was heading straight for the boat. Wolf aimed at the gator's head, but the gun misfired, flinging Wolf overboard into the water. The creature continued toward the boat as Gordon lent his hand to help Wolf. The professor seemed fine and was able to stand in the water, which was no more than four feet deep.

Bruno came up from behind the animal and swung the snatch hook at its long snout, but the gator quickly dodged to the left, avoiding the noose. Water splashed violently as the gator swiped Bruno with its huge tail. Bruno lost his balance and submerged under the water. The gator then lifted out of the water and lunged for the boat with its huge gaping jaws wide open. It crashed down on top of the boat, only inches from Gordon, who scurried back toward the rudder. The gator was now halfway onto the boat, its eyes locked on Gordon's. Gordon pulled the .357 Magnum out of his waistband and pointed it at the gator, which was no more than two feet away, violently thrashing its tail as it tried to slither completely onto the boat. His hands shook violently.

"Shoot the damn thing!" yelled Wolf.

Gordon squeezed the trigger, which set off a loud booming sound. The recoil forced Gordon backward against the raised outboard motor and onto his side. He straightened up to take another shot, but the gator was gone. Everything fell silent as Wolf climbed back into the boat. Then Bruno popped up to the far side with the snatch hook firmly around the gator's jaws. There was a gaping hole in the back of the animal's head as it floated motionless.

"Now that's some mighty fine shooting, boy," Bruno roared as he pushed the gator toward Gordon, who was visibly shaken, his trembling hands still pointing the gun at the dead animal. Bruno gently took the .357 from Gordon's clutch and whispered into his ear. "It's all over now, son."

Wolf rolled a stretch of rope over the animal and tied it to the side of the boat, then moved back to the front, shaking his head at the shotgun and muttering incomprehensibly under his breath.

Bruno started the motor as Gordon settled back into his seat alongside Wolf. The boat listed heavily on its port side due to the weight of the alligator bearing down on the craft. It took three hours to get back to shore. Bruno pulled his pickup truck alongside the edge of the water, and the three men hoisted the lifeless alligator into the bed of the truck.

"Hold on, now. I need to get a picture," said Bruno. He pulled out a Leica manual camera and snapped several poses of Wolf and Gordon in front of the gator—mouth open, mouth closed, tail up, tail down. It was obviously a proud moment for the two old guys. Gordon was just happy to be alive.

"See y'all down by Chico's in about an hour," Bruno said as he pulled away.

Wolf began peeling off his wet clothes. He had a fresh pair of pants and a cotton pullover in the car, and replaced the wading boots with a pair of tan loafers.

"Good thing you stayed put, Gordon. I don't have any more clothing in here. You're gonna love Chico's—best Mexican food north of the border."

"What's Bruno going to do with the alligator?" asked Gordon.

"Oh, he's gonna drop it off at Ray's Bait and Tackle Shop about fifteen minutes down the road. We'll get about four hundred dollars for it."

Wolf turned to Gordon and put his arm around his shoulder.

"You really showed your true self out there today, Michael. You reacted well under stressful circumstances and probably spared me some unpleasant time with a very angry and powerful animal. I'm deeply indebted to you. I'm sure Carmine feels the same way."

"I very much appreciate that, sir." Gordon could barely manage a whisper, as he was still shaken by the prospect of being eaten alive.

"Well, I sure am hungry," said the professor. "You're gonna love Chico's."

# 5

**"W**hat's the *carnitas de pato?"* Gordon asked the waiter, a mild-mannered man with a slight Spanish accent.

"That's a small duck with tacos and tomatillo sauce."

"That's sounds good. I'll have it with a Diet Coke."

Chico's wasn't a cheap sandwich shop, as Gordon had feared. It was an upscale open-air restaurant on the banks of the Gulf of Mexico with a view of the bay that stretched for miles. The oil freighters hovering just below the horizon floated atop the water like marbles on a blue granite floor. Men were dressed in sport jackets and high boots; the women donned designer jeans, cowboy hats, and lots of diamond jewelry.

Wolf must have known three-quarters of the people in the place, which was packed with government officials. Kate Browning, the state treasurer, was in a front booth. Roy Yoder, the Harris County commissioner, was at the bar talking with Congressman Billy Blunt, whose district included large parts of eastern Texas. Wolf worked the crowd on the way to his table like a master of ceremonies, with hugs, kisses, and a slap on the back when appropriate.

When Gordon arrived, Bruno was already seated, digging into a generous portion of *pulpo al carbón*—grilled octopus with onions and peppers. Wolf ordered a bowl of chili, which he swore was the best in Texas.

"Hope you don't mind me having a little something before you guys got here," said Bruno. "I was famished."

Bruno looked a little less menacing when he wasn't dressed completely in black. He wore a French-blue cotton shirt with a white collar and the sleeves rolled up, khaki trousers, and sandals. He could pass for a local real estate agent.

"You sure walloped that gator," said Bruno. "But you should have seen your face. It was whiter than the sheets the KKK boys I grew up with used to wear."

Bruno placed another large chunk of octopus in his mouth.

"You Jewish, Gordon?" Bruno enjoyed needling people. It was a habit he had developed to deal with the boredom and anxiety during travel on long missions with tough odds.

Gordon didn't miss a beat. "My mother is Irish, and my father is originally from England. That makes me Catholic-Protestant. I do have a lot of Jewish friends, though."

Wolf clapped his hands. "Well done, Michael. Bruno isn't the Neanderthal he's making himself out to be. You see, we're trying to get to know you a little better. It's some sort of...What's the word? Ah, psychological profiling. My father was a German SS colonel who was responsible for killing many innocent people, and at one point, I was a member of the Hitler Youth. Bruno is a bastard child of the pope. At first blush, we aren't the typical blue bloods that claim a birthright to this country. But we both are loyal Americans who love our country dearly. And before we decide to help you become the next congressman from New Jersey, we want to make sure you are as loyal and resilient a person as we would expect of one of our own."

Gordon shifted nervously in his seat. He wasn't fond of bigoted Catholics or former Hitler Youth. But he had to win over these guys. "That's quite a history you have, Professor. I think it's a tribute to our democracy that you were able to engage in public service despite your background. I'm sure people understand that, as a young boy, you probably had little choice in that environment."

"Carmine, why don't you tell him a little about yourself?" Wolf said as he licked a spoonful of chili, oblivious to Gordon's last remark.

Bruno gulped down half a glass of a local microbrew with a deep-brown hue and then wiped the foam from his mouth.

"I was drafted by the Marine Corps in 1968. I did three tours in Nam, the last one attached to a SEAL unit tasked with hunting and killing Viet Cong military personnel. We were quite active until the very end of the war, and very successful. I left the military in 1978 to become a special agent with the US Drug Enforcement Agency. My specialty involved Colombian traffickers, and I've spent more time than I'd like to admit on the south side of the Texas border. I retired from the DEA two years ago. Now, I'm just a pensioner, getting fat and soft. I do some consulting work for various government agencies and for folks like the professor."

"Carmine also spent quite some time helping various clandestine intelligence organizations effectively deal with enemies of the state. He has developed a vast network of friends around the world and has some exceptional skills at gathering information. These attributes can be very helpful to a congressional campaign."

"How much is all this going to cost?" asked Gordon. He had started etching out a budget since Wolf had chided him about campaign finances back in his office. But he hadn't thought about outside nonpolitical consultants.

"Cost is not your concern," said Wolf. "What you need is unwavering ambition and the ability to take direction from those who know what they're doing. You see, in real politics, there are no Democrats or Republicans, no neocons or liberals, fiscal hawks, deficit spenders, blah, blah. There are only two types of politicians—winners and losers. We prefer the winners, and we do what it takes to get there. And I mean whatever it takes."

Wolf and Bruno were both staring into Gordon's eyes.

"You got what it takes to win, son?" Bruno asked softly.

Gordon paused a minute and took a sip of his Diet Coke. Leaning back with a boyish grin, he knew what to say. "Hell yes, sir. Hoorah!"

"So let's raise a glass, then," said Wolf. "To prosperity."

"To success," chimed Bruno.

"To victory," roared Gordon.

The rest of the meal went smoothly. Over a dozen people stopped by the table to yuck it up with Wolf. Bruno finally finished devouring whatever the waiter had placed in front of him and slowly polished off his third bottle of beer. A cool evening breeze came in over the Gulf waters, and folks were starting to clear out. Gordon's thoughts turned to getting back to New Jersey and the backlog of work he had to deal with. The near-death experience of this morning was now buried in his psyche, and he felt content, believing that he had met the right people to help steer his campaign. But he still had no idea how he was going to raise the money to go after thirty-year incumbent Brett Parker.

Wolf signaled for the check. "We've got one more stop before we call it quits."

Bruno raised his brow. "The Rabbi?"

"Yes, the Rabbi," said Wolf.

Bruno leaned forward toward the professor. "Are you sure that's necessary?"

Wolf nodded gently.

Gordon was dumbfounded. The last guy he thought these two would want to hang out with was a rabbi. "Don't you think it's a little late to go see a rabbi? It's eleven o'clock at night." Gordon had an early-morning flight and could barely keep his eyes open.

"Oh, this ain't no ordinary rabbi," said Bruno.

"Actually, he's a Catholic priest who presides over one of the largest congregations in Houston," said Wolf. "We call him 'the Rabbi' because he spent years studying in Jerusalem, and he quite often quotes Jewish scripture."

"He actually enjoys company this time of night," said Bruno.

"Whatever," said Gordon. At this point, nothing fazed him—or so he thought.

# 6

The chapel at St. Catherine's the Divine in downtown Houston was deserted. The long rows of empty mahogany pews glowed dimly from their spit-and-polish shine, and a bright spotlight over the altar effused a feeling of holiness. At the end of a narrow hallway beyond the confessional booths, a door was ajar. Gordon followed Wolf into the priest's study.

Father Rudolphus Emerson Murphy was a tall man with a commanding yet welcoming presence. Dressed in complete Roman Catholic vestments with a large gold cross across his chest, he stood to welcome the professor.

"So this is our new recruit?" Murphy asked, pointing Gordon to a chair beside a roaring fire.

"Yes, indeed, Father. He's a wonderful young man who will make us proud," said Wolf. "But if you don't mind, I must be getting on. Good night, Michael."

Gordon couldn't believe that Wolf had just dumped him with this eighty-year-old priest. But there wasn't much time to ponder the issue, as Murphy got right down to business.

"Why do you want to enter public service, son?" Murphy gently took hold of Gordon's right hand.

Gordon felt surprisingly at ease. He wasn't a religious man and hadn't been to church since childhood. Emily never cared for structured religion, and besides, her father was Jewish, which made things complicated. The sexual abuse scandals didn't bode well either. But Murphy seemed sincere and kind. And Gordon was tired, so very tired.

"I want to change the world. We all have a place and time, and while there's no guarantee of success, a man has to make the effort to leave his mark on society. Some are content with the nine-to-five thing and raising a loving family. Others pursue wealth, the vast accumulation of wealth, as if that were itself a worthy cause, an independent accomplishment by which history measures one's status and contribution. I'm bored with that scene. My calling is to set right the wrongs of this country, to call out the corrupt and the selfish, to promote an agenda of social justice and economic prosperity for the weak and the disliked. To me, that's the role of government, and so I'm trying to get involved at the federal level, hopefully to work my way up to the point where I can really have an impact on issues that matter to the John and Jane Smiths of this country."

Murphy, who had been listening intently, leaned forward in his chair to get closer to Gordon. "These are lofty aspirations. But history teaches that government has been terribly inefficient at reaching these goals. On the contrary, strong central government and intrusion has brought us despotic and tyrannical leaders who favored a small class of the wealthy elite, and often subjugated the masses, leaving behind schisms of the desperate and poor, trampled by the state and forced into generations of poverty and submission."

Gordon waved his hand, signaling disagreement. "That was the distant past. Hitler and Stalin would never reach the heights of power in today's Information Age. Free press and the Internet would have exposed them long before sensible people could no longer object. Wealth has been spread out to the distant corners. A kid with a laptop can sell pirated DVDs online and rise to prominence. Even China has given up on ideological communism, instead clinging to a one-party system in great part to efficiently manage its colossal economic machine."

Murphy gazed into Gordon's eyes. "But what if government—pluralistic government—is rife with corruption and the corrupted? What if it has lost the way of its founding fathers and has capitulated to the wild fringes of society, to those who would tear down all the accomplishments of the civil rights movement, on the one hand, and to those who desecrate the sanctity of marriage by legitimizing all male coitus, on the other? Does there come a time when forces outside that government are permitted to take action to keep their country aligned with the greater good?"

"Vigilantism has no place in modern society," snapped Gordon. "It erodes the social fabric by granting power to those who have not earned it through the appointment of the people. Only the people may decide what power has the right to hurt or incarcerate for the benefit of the greater society."

"But if a deranged mother was in the process of trying to drown her child, would you not step in to save that child?"

"I would."

"Even if it meant killing the mother?"

"Yes."

"And who gave you that right?"

"Either God did, or if you're not one to accept divine intervention in manly affairs, then it is the inherent right of self-preservation to assist the victim, a helpless victim, against the purposeful aggression of another."

"Well said, Gordon. Well said." Murphy leaned back in his chair, smiling and clasping his hands together. Looking toward the ceiling, he spoke in a soft undertone. "We are doing God's work here, you know. Sometimes that requires sacrifice, other times it calls for perseverance, and at times it calls for faith—faith in the mission, faith in the cause, faith in the person directing you. Are you capable of that kind of faith, Michael?"

Gordon didn't know exactly what the old man was getting at, but he didn't have the strength to argue. He thought that if Wolf had brought him here, he probably needed to get the guy's approval. Acquiescence usually draws approval.

"Of course," Gordon said convincingly, reaching out to touch Murphy's clasped hands and looking him squarely in the eyes. "Of course, Father."

Murphy lifted a small plastic device from his side pocket. It looked like a wireless doorbell, not much different from what Gordon had on his own front door. Murphy pressed a button, but there was no sound.

"Care for some tea, Michael? Stella makes a wonderful blend."

Murphy drew Gordon's attention to some of the paintings on the wall of the study. There were several landscapes, and others depicting scenes from the Bible. They were both standing in front of a huge oil painting depicting Abraham about to slaughter his son Isaac on the altar when Stella arrived carrying two cups of piping hot tea. She was in a full nun's habit, her shoulders and head covered by the traditional scapular and her face framed by a white linen wimple with only a touch of her jet-black hair emerging from the tightly drawn clothing. She had pronounced features: high cheekbones, a bony chin, and a sharp, pointy nose. Her piercing blue eyes were absorbing, with long black lashes and dark full eyebrows. She practically brushed up against Gordon as she passed to place the tea on the coffee table in front of the fire. Gordon couldn't help but notice her perfume, a strong musk fragrance that filled Gordon's lungs.

"Will there be anything else, Father?" asked Stella. Her voice was kind and feminine. Gordon thought she must be in her early twenties.

"Yes, dear. I'd like you to meet a friend, Michael Gordon."

Gordon was about to stretch out his hand, but Stella curtsied before he could get his hand past his jacket pocket.

"Pleased to meet you, sir." Stella looked up at Gordon as she rose from her bent position. Gordon couldn't help but notice that she had quite a trim figure and stood at about five feet nine.

"Stella's been with me practically from birth, dropped at my doorstep twenty-five years ago, no more than a few weeks old. Her mother was a drug addict who told me she couldn't care for the child. She didn't know who the father might be. So I took her in."

Murphy took her left hand, which bore a slim gold wedding band. "I offered her any choice of college or career, yet she chose the Lord." He looked at the gold ring as he slowly kissed her hand. "She's been like a daughter—the daughter I never could have naturally."

Stella appeared to enjoy the affection. "Hope to see you again, Mr. Gordon."

Gordon smiled faintly and nodded. He wasn't into the kinky nun stuff, but he couldn't help wondering what Stella looked like without all the robes on.

The men sat down to their tea. The conversation lasted for another half hour, drifting from current events to the supernatural. Murphy did most of the talking as Gordon strained to seem attentive. By now, though, his arms felt heavy, and his vision began to blur. The flunitrazepam muscle relaxant in the tea provided a strong sedative but kept the victim conscious to appreciate his surroundings. Gordon slumped in his chair as two young deacons carried him off to a room down the hall from Murphy's study.

It was a small room, with only a four-poster bed, small writing desk, and wooden chair. A sliver of moonlight seeped in from a narrow stained-glass window along the wall opposite the doorway. The men undressed Gordon and placed his neatly folded clothes on the chair. Gordon lay staring up at a cross in the ceiling directly over the bed. He drifted in and out of sleep for about an hour before the heavy wooden door opened. A tall woman wearing a red silk robe entered, her long, flowing black hair falling to her waist. She walked over to the window and stood beside Gordon. Gordon stared at the face, which looked kind against the silhouette that revealed sharp features. Stella removed the robe and gently climbed into bed beside Gordon, pushing his head into the nape of her neck. Gordon relished the scent of her skin as his body began to feel overwhelmed by her naked flesh pressing against his.

They lay together for a while. Gordon hovered in a state of flux, unable to confirm reality from unconsciousness. Stella gently began caressing his chest as her hand slowly made its way between his legs. She rolled on top of him and sat up firmly as the infrared camera in the cross silently recorded.

Murphy picked up the phone. It was 6:00 a.m.

"Good morning, Father. How'd you like our new protégé?" asked Wolf.

"He's been compromised."

"Excellent."

# 7

The house on Cold Brick Road in Bearsville, New York, was remarkably simple. Set back a hundred yards on a rolling five-acre parcel, the two-story stick-frame Colonial was vacant most of the year. Looked after by an unsuspecting neighbor who raised several horses and grew winter wheat, the Crow's Nest was the last place someone would think high-level national security meetings were held. Yet it was this indiscreetness that suited seven people who had spent their lives in secret service to their country as a place to plan, debate, and implement missions vital to America's national security and be exempt from congressional oversight.

The "Committee," as they called themselves, exercised their mandate with a fanatic's passion and a soldier's commitment. They didn't seek recognition or reward and stayed out of the headlines. Success was measured only by results. They were the last line of defense—the actors who stepped forward when all else failed or when government was too paralyzed by petty politics or incompetence to understand. No one felt any remorse for innocent lives lost or collateral damage, as long as the particular mission accomplished its goals. To the members of the committee, the ends always justified the means.

Murphy always arrived early to get the furnace going and to stock the refrigerator with enough beer and wine to permit the discourse to continue unabated by calls for food. There were no telephones in the house, and no cell phones were permitted within fifty miles. That meant leaving the cell phone at home or buried beside a tree somewhere off Highway 87. The members arrived separately, between 6:30 and 7:30 p.m., for meetings that started promptly at 8:00 p.m. in the basement recreation room.

Murphy sat up in a high-back chair as his six colleagues took their places at the oval green velvet table that once enjoyed a prominent spot in the baccarat room at the Bellagio. As vice chairman, Judge Ware Hudler took his seat to Murphy's right. Wolf, the committee secretary, sat to the left. Across from Murphy, at the other head of the table, Colin Short settled in. As deputy NSA director, he brought a political perspective to the meeting, as his job was at the beck and call of the residing president. Phil Gaston, DEA special ops, gently poured a beer while placing a velvet saucer underneath the frosted bottle. Norm Coakley stared patiently at the ceiling. A former SEAL commander, Coakley taught close-combat warfare at Annapolis.

Finally, Sylvia Burton took her seat. The only female to ever serve on the committee, Sylvia had earned her place after forty years with the CIA, many of which were spent in deep cover in the Soviet Bloc. While at Oxford on a Fulbright scholarship, the six-foot green-eyed blonde from Gulfport, Louisiana, courted a KGB colonel stationed in the London embassy, and provided critical intelligence on Soviet coding and communications. Five years into the relationship, the colonel mysteriously reported back to his country. Sylvia thought he had died at Krasnokamensk in eastern Siberia after getting into a drunken brawl with a regular army general at a diplomatic function.

"Welcome, all," said Murphy. "Glad you're looking well. Sylvia, dear, why don't you read off the minutes from our last meeting?"

As the newest member, Sylvia was responsible for taking the meeting minutes. No other records were permitted.

*Meeting September 9, all present, Chairman Murphy presiding.*

*Discussion concerning the movement of nuclear-tipped scud missiles from Diego Garcia to Qalat, just outside Kandahar, concluded with decision to take no action. Fear of forfeiture to unfriendlies outweighs pretext for importation of nuclear-tipped bombing.*

*Report from P. Gaston concerning resurgence of Mexican cartel action in Tijuana region. Field ops noticing sophisticated level of rival gang executions and suspect Russian infiltration. Consider activating Moscow asset for confirmation. Decision adjourned.*

*N. Coakley proposes live testing of new laser technology on Congolese guerrillas as part of covert weapons program. Laser deployed in ordinary handgun capable of precision impact at two thousand yards with force of 50 mm shell. Testing approved by unanimous vote.*

*General discussion concerning Russian political system and Putin's ties to organized crime. W. Hudler proposes NAVSTAT*

*III activation on senior Russian communications to build PR file for appropriate destabilization. C. Short asks for time to get NSA approval. NAVSTAT III activation subject to NSA confirm, unanimously approved.*

*Conversation among members concerning various geopolitical issues affecting national security.*

*Proposal by B. Wolf to recruit subject for Operation Open Sky. Discussion focused on dangers of discovery by vanilla law enforcement or foreign covert branches. Risks include criminal prosecution. Proposal approved by majority: Murphy, Hudler, Wolf, and Burton in favor; Short, Gaston, and Coakley dissent.*

*Meeting adjourned at 10:45 p.m.*

"Thank you," said Murphy.

Wolf lit his pipe and began discussing Gordon. "We've recruited a forty-five-year-old lawyer from New Jersey. Michael Gordon has the looks, the brains, and the love of country to meet our objectives. His paternal lineage dates back to the Massachusetts militia, while his father-in-law was a deep-cover CIA operative. Once he's elected to Congress from NJ-Fifteen, we'll steer him to the Strategic Forces subcommittee, which will provide access to the BITR technology."

Short leaned forward, raising his hand slightly to interrupt Wolf. "I've never heard of that technology at any of our NSA procurement meetings. Where are you getting your facts?"

Wolf continued reassuringly. "The special operations directorate of the air force has been developing a new technology at Oak Ridge. They call it biological identity tracking, or BITR. To put it simply, the movement of ions and conduction of nerve messages within human cells require the correct electromagnetic environment in which to function properly. This very faint field of electromagnetic energy is most forceful at the heart and brain. Every human being emits a unique pattern."

Wolf paused, admiring the undivided attention of his colleagues. "We now have the technology to track these faint fields and assign an identity to every human being on the planet. No more tracking through cell phones or surveillance. If a person is breathing, we can track him down by his electrobiological signature."

"But there's more," said Murphy. "Our engineers at DEA spec ops have developed the ability to scramble the electromagnetic field with targeted bursts of energy waves emitted from satellites or drones. Upsetting the electromagnetic field triggers severe metabolic disturbances, including abnormal cell uptake of electrolytes, such as calcium, needed for heart muscle. We can stop a man's heart or render him brain-dead, and people will think it came from natural causes."

"It doesn't stop with a single man," said Wolf. "We can take out a family or a neighborhood—even a city. It's all invisible, instant, and untraceable."

Burton leaned back in her chair and smiled.

"Where are we in the polls?" asked Gaston.

"We're down about forty, and it's gonna be a tough year for Democrats. But our project plan puts us plus ten on Election Day," said Wolf.

"Forty plus ten is quite a ride," mused Coakley. "This ain't exactly Rhodesia in '79 where we collected the ballot boxes and wrote in the votes later. How much in the bank?"

Wolf snapped impatiently, annoyed by the doubts leveled at him. "We expect to raise five million dollars, almost all soft, since we don't want to tip the other side with FEC filings."

"What kinds of enhancements are envisioned?" asked Short.

"We're looking at a full suite, with zero body count," continued Wolf. "We smash the opponent, Brett Parker, with manipulated COM at die-hard constituents, targeted sexual ads, and good-guy blitzes of staged events for Gordon. We also have ballot box manipulation capabilities at about a quarter of the polling places, if needed."

"I've worked with Parker," said Short. "He didn't come across as someone who could be compromised on sexual misconduct."

"Leave it to us on that," Wolf quipped with a wry smile.

"The boy is promising," roared Hudler. "I spent a little time with him down at the ranch, and he presented as a team player."

"Has his cooperation been ensured?" Burton asked as she lit a cigarette.

"Yes," answered Murphy. "I've personally seen to that."

The meeting carried on for another two hours. When the other members left, Murphy, Wolf, and Hudler stayed behind.

"If the political climate remains as tough as foreseen, we may have to find a way for Parker to exit," Murphy said in a soft tone as he peered at the empty chairs across the table.

"I think our guys can pull this off without that," assured Wolf. "Parker has a big lead, but he's only survived because he hasn't had a real challenge in fifteen years. He has no leadership positions in the House and no ambition beyond his current seat. The RCCC is not even looking at this race and won't take notice until it's too late."

"Yes, but we cannot fail—cannot!" warned Murphy. "Our window of penetration is closing. Once the new search protocol is adopted at all top secret army installations, we're locked out."

"If Parker has to take a fall, then it shouldn't be too difficult to arrange," said Hudler.

"Yes, but we want Gordon to reach a position of stature, and he only gets there if he beats the thirty-year incumbent, not if he crawls in on default," insisted Wolf.

Murphy collected the wine glasses and headed for the kitchen. Hudler followed, while the professor exited through the side entrance.

"The children on the committee may be reticent to take such bold action on the domestic field," said Murphy. "And it appears that our good professor is letting his passion persuade his intellect."

"Nah, the professor has a great track record, and he knows the importance of the mission. Besides, Seaver has been running in stride as of late. Should we take his temperature on this?"

Murphy looked up from rinsing the glasses. "Already have. He assures me success, but I'm skeptical. Perhaps we should prepare a contingency. I do have that authority, don't I?"

Hudler nodded. "Yes, as chairman, you have the ability to achieve an approved mission goal without a new vote and without disclosure to the committee, so long as you have concurrence from the vice chair or the secretary."

Murphy turned off the faucet and faced Hudler. "Well?"

"If he's not within ten by Labor Day, we'll move to Plan B," said Hudler. "We picked up a Russian FSB defector in Sudan a couple of months ago. Says he wants to turn and go back inside for us. We could ask him to pass a little credibility test."

"No," Murphy said as he reached for his coat. "We can't let a stranger clean our laundry. Hans Lange has been looking for work as of late. He'd be useful."

"Ah, good ole Hans." Hudler smiled. "Can't believe the son of a bitch is still breathing."

"Oh, he's breathing quite well, I'm told. Glad he's still on our side."

# 8

**"Y**ou look like shit," Emily said as Gordon walked into the house.

Gordon had barely caught his flight out of Houston and had to rush straight to the office to deal with several urgent matters. He had apologized to Murphy for passing out and thanked him for putting him up for the night.

Emily gave Gordon a peck on the cheek and took his raincoat. "So who'd you hang out with over the weekend?"

"Oh, just a few people that John Berger hooked me up with."

"Berger!" cried Emily. "You spent a weekend in Houston away from the family because that fat slob asked you meet some of his neocon nutjobs?"

Emily considered Berger an insufferable capitalist boor who stood for everything she fought against. Berger, for his part, never treated Emily with much respect, as all liberals were unworthy of any serious attention. Besides, Emily still hadn't forgiven Berger for vomiting all over her $1,000 wedding cake. It was quite a scene when Berger regurgitated the smorgasbord of shellfish, vodka, and cholent. Berger was fond of referring to that wedding as a gathering of the United Nations, for practically every nationality and religion on the planet was well represented. Between

Gordon's Peace Corps buddies and Emily's sorority sisters from Berkeley, the ensemble would have made a sixties crowd at Troubadours feel put off.

Gordon opened the refrigerator, searching for some leftover chicken. "I was there for the conference on the big pharma antitrust case, and I stayed an extra day to meet some professor who says he's going to help me with my campaign."

"So you're really serious about this Congress thing?"

"Yeah, I think I'm gonna go for it."

"I was talking to Momma, and she thinks it's a good idea. Even if you lose, it's a nice line item on the résumé, and you'll make a lot of strong connections."

Ann Singer was a forceful woman. Her husband died two months after landing in Phnom Penh for his second tour with the Twenty-Second Marine Expeditionary Unit. A graduate of Annapolis, Carl Singer had a promising career, cut short by a Khmer Rouge sniper. Ann had raised Emily and her brother Philip on her own, living off her widow's stipend and a $40,000-per-year teaching job at PS 101 in Forest Hills, New York. Although many a suitor called, Ann had refused to pursue romance until the kids were off to college. Growing up without a father was confusing enough.

Emily spent most of her waking hours with the worst of society. As a psychologist at Rikers Island women's prison who wrote her dissertation on recidivist rapists, her clients ran the gamut from social misfits to schizophrenics. She sometimes couldn't trust her own judgment. Although she loved and revered Michael, her lover at night and the father figure she'd never had by day, she could never fully confide in him. Something always made her hold back. Ann was her crutch.

Emily was surprised that Ann went for the whole Congress thing. She had always avoided the limelight and kept a low profile. She personified the good wife, always letting Carl lead the conversation and supporting his opinions, even when she disagreed with them.

But the prospect of entering government brought haunting memories back to Emily. When Carl was away in Nam, there were several visits by two men in dark suits, one of whom was particularly tall and thin. Emily once greeted them at the door, and one of the men waved a badge at her as he walked in. He definitely wasn't the police, as no one had done anything wrong. But Ann quickly ushered them into the study, closing the door behind her. The meetings lasted for hours at a time. Ann wouldn't say a word about them other than that they had some questions about her father and that everything was fine. After about six months, the visits stopped. About a year later, Carl Singer was dead. Emily never connected the events. In those days, kids were taught to mind their own business. But Emily did recall seeing the same man at her father's funeral. Ann's face was stoic and withdrawn, looking down toward the snow-covered ground at Pinelawn Cemetery, when the tall, thin man leaned over to whisper something in her ear. Ann raised her head, and Emily saw a bit of a smirk on her face. It was the only time she had shown any emotion during the funeral.

"Hi, everyone," Ann roared as she walked into the house. "Where's my little king?" Ann poked her head into the living room, looking for her grandson Ryan. Now eleven, Ryan didn't appreciate the lavish attention anymore. But he was a good boy and obediently fell into Ann's arms for that unavoidable Grandma kiss and squeeze of the cheek. Emily and Gordon's other son, Daniel, was out at high school basketball practice and would escape Grandma for now.

"So how was Houston, Michael?" Ann loved Michael and treated him as her own son, complete with the prodding questions and free advice only a mother can perfect.

"Oh, he spent his time with some loser John Berger sent him to meet." Emily sighed.

"Berger," mused Ann. "The guy who threw up at your wedding?"

Emily put a pot of coffee on the stove. "That's the one."

Gordon poured himself a glass of red wine and sat down to a cold helping of chicken breast. "Listen, you guys, Professor Wolf has been a senior policy advisor to both Republican and Democratic presidents, and he has agreed to help me with my congressional campaign. He also introduced me to a leading fundraiser, Carmine Bruno. So, overall, it was a great start to organizing my campaign."

Ann fell into a kitchen chair, visibly shaken. Her hands trembled as she clasped them to her face. Looking down at the table, she spoke in little more than a whisper. "You met with Professor Byron Wolf of Rice University?"

"Yes," said Michael. "You know him?"

Ann closed her eyes. She was obviously in emotional pain.

Emily came over and put her hands on her mother's shoulders. "What's the matter, Momma?"

Ann paused for a minute, trying to compose herself. Then she finally looked up. "Emily, have a seat. About a year before your father was killed, Wolf came to see me. He was with a guy from the FBI, but he did all the talking. He asked about your father's involvement in the Crow's Nest. That was a frat house at Annapolis for Jewish and Catholic men. They kept their meetings secret because the academy didn't like non-Protestants at the time. In fact, they still don't. But it was much worse then. After graduation, every December, your dad used to go up to Cornwall, a small town in Upstate New York, just north of West Point, where the Crows had a club. Actually, it was a small cottage owned by your dad's roommate at the academy. I went a couple of times. It was a quaint little club where the guys and their wives came to catch up and reminisce. There was always a closed meeting for the male members. The other wives and I hung around in the lobby, drinking tea and trading recipes.

"Wolf questioned me for hours about the Crow's Nest—who was at the meetings, what were they discussing, who were they with. He would carry on and on, while the FBI guy just sat quietly and scribbled some notes. When I tried to find out the purpose of these interrogations, Wolf would only say that he worked for a sensitive branch of the government responsible for national security and that he couldn't say anymore, but that Carl wasn't in trouble. He kept on reassuring me that Carl wasn't in trouble, and so I accommodated his questioning.

"At Carl's funeral, there were loads of military officers and politicos. His commanding officer had just paid his respects when Wolf approached me. I couldn't believe that this guy was going to harass me in front of all these people, but he simply walked up and whispered in my ear.

'Your husband was one of our best spies. He died saving his country while behind enemy lines. A sniper didn't cut him down. Foreign agents killed him. But they got to him too late. He had first provided us with intelligence that will save many future generations of Americans. I wanted you to know.' Then he kissed me gently on the cheek. I've never seen or heard from him again."

Emily was dumbfounded. She felt shock at first, learning what had really happened to her father over thirty years ago, then anger that her mother had kept this from her for so long. But Emily kept her emotions to herself.

Emily grabbed Ann's bag and helped her out of the chair. "Why don't we settle you in upstairs, Momma?"

As Ann began climbing the stairs, she turned to Michael. "Wolf only thinks of himself. He pretends to act for the greater good, but it's about his worldview. He'll never care about you. He'll use you like he used Carl and then spit you up. Stay away from him."

Gordon was disbelieving. There was no way Wolf, the son of a Nazi SS colonel, was working for the NSA or even the CIA. Those agencies were very insular, and only blue bloods needed apply. Gordon concluded that Ann was just getting old. The tall guy she had met in her home was not his Professor Wolf. Although, he was intrigued by the notion that his late father-in-law was a spy. He'd try to access his files once he was a member of Congress. Gordon felt even more committed to the cause. Congress was the ticket to the halls of power and access. He had to get in.

Gordon's phone started making funny ringing sounds. He pulled it out to see an icon with a lowercase *f* in a blue square. It was his Facebook account, and it kept buzzing.

He clicked it open. There were more than two hundred friend requests. As of last night, Gordon had only thirty-two friends. The names of the requests were shocking: Rahm Emanuel, Jon Corzine, and Bill Gates. The celebrity list went on to include generals and rock stars.

Then he got a text message from Bruno: *Meet me tomorrow noon at the corner of Flushing Avenue and Waverly. Number 852.*

Gordon cringed. That was downtown Brooklyn, right across from the Brooklyn Navy Yard. Why would anyone want to meet there? It gave Gordon the creeps. But Wolf had told Gordon to leave the fundraising to Bruno. Gordon finished his meal and headed upstairs. He needed some sleep.

# 9

The five-story brick walk-up in downtown Brooklyn was run-down, its lower facade covered with graffiti. A Spanish grocery occupied the retail level, and the remaining floors were littered with boarded windows, some white sheets slung across others, and a few air conditioners hanging precariously along the top floor. Gordon checked the address again, but the battered door at the side of the grocery was marked *852*, the number Bruno had messaged. After waiting ten minutes, he started to pace nervously. Two elderly women sitting outside their apartments across the street spoke loudly in Spanish while pointing at Gordon. He stuck out like a sore thumb, wearing a crisp blue suit, dark sunglasses, and tan Bruno Magli slip-ons.

Gordon was about to send a message to Bruno when a teenage girl approached.

A slinky redhead, about five feet five, in a cream shirt-sleeve blouse and faded blue jeans, she stretched out her hand. "Good morning, Mr. Gordon. I'm Sara Shelby."

The woman's voice was friendly and disarming, a breath of fresh air for Gordon, who was getting increasingly tense. But what was this girl with the adult voice and firm hand-shake doing here?

"Ah, hi," Gordon said sheepishly, staring into the woman's deep-green eyes. Her skin was white as milk, with a splatter of freckles around her nose. She couldn't be more than eighteen, Gordon thought. Not a prostitute, he hoped. He was not in the mood for dealing with a nasty pimp, who was probably staking him out from the Spanish grocery.

"Carmine asked me to bring you upstairs. Right this way, please."

Gordon followed, thinking that she was probably Bruno's daughter or niece.

Shelby was far from it. The only child of an army general whose family's military service dated back to the Revolutionary War, Shelby had found refuge from the constant wanderings and discipline of military life at the Yale School of Drama. Aspiring to a career as a film producer, Shelby had fallen in love with a graduate student, Sean Warner, who also came from a military family, during her sophomore year. The relationship ended abruptly when she discovered photos of Warner with another woman on his Facebook page.

Distraught, Shelby sought an escape and answered a recruiter's call for the Peace Corps. When she got to the interview, there were three CIA officers waiting with the promise of excitement and a choice of foreign assignments. After twelve months of training for the Clandestine Service, including advanced courses in paramilitary techniques and assassination, Shelby was assigned to a contract team in Colombia charged with destabilizing drug cartel operations. Fluent in Spanish and Portuguese, thanks to many years of care by her Spanish grandmother, Shelby's teenage looks and pleasant Midwestern demeanor allowed her entrée to the late-night Bogotá club scene. By the time she left the agency at age twenty-seven, she had been involved in forty-two assassinations, some by her bare hands. It wasn't until her last year at the agency that she learned of Warner's true identity. He had been an NSA special operations recruit sent by her father to break her heart and push her into government service. The Eighty-Second Airborne general wasn't going to let his family line end with a left-wing, peace-loving Hollywood producer.

Gordon climbed five flights of stairs and was led to a wrought-iron door at least four feet wide. Shelby rang the bell, which gave off a loud shriek. The hallway was damp and poorly lit, with only a single bulb hanging from the ceiling. Minutes later, Shelby rang the bell again.

"Is this the right place?" asked Gordon. He was impressed by Shelby's composure and playful smile.

The door opened.

Gordon felt like he had just stepped into the New York Stock Exchange. The room was huge, with at least seven large television screens in the center, hanging in a square pattern to face all directions. Along the walls were rows of computer terminals manned by men and women in all sorts of attire. The man at the far right was wearing a white dress shirt and pressed khaki slacks, while the woman at his side was in torn blue jeans and a tank top. People were hurrying back and forth, and almost everyone seemed to be talking on the phone. No one stopped to look at Gordon as Shelby led him to a small conference room.

"Carmine will be right in, Michael. There's water in the fridge behind you."

Gordon's phone buzzed. It was a message from Bruno: *Welcome.*

Fifteen minutes had passed and still no sign of Bruno, so Gordon decided to look around. He noticed another door to the conference room that led to a long hallway. As Gordon made his way down the hall, he peeked into a small office. Inside, a man in full military uniform sat in front of a huge computer screen with a joystick in his hand. Gordon didn't understand why the army guy was sitting around playing a video game, so he moved in for a closer look. The man was wearing a headset, and the screen displayed the cockpit of an airplane flying over rough terrain.

"Three minutes to target," the military man said as calmly as if he were ordering a latte at the corner Starbucks. Suddenly, three men rushed into the room, whisking past Gordon. Two of the men had gold badges pinned to their belts; the other had a badge around his neck.

"We think Cheese Dog is in building number seven. Let's hit that first with the five-hundred-pound incendiary," said the man with the badge around his neck. The other two DEA officers were busy tapping out messages on what looked like oversized iPhones.

"One minute to target, weapons hot," said the military guy.

The building on the screen began to take focus. It was a single-story cinder-block structure with a red-shingled roof. Next to it were several smaller wooden buildings that looked like camp bunks. There was an open yard with lush green grass and what appeared to be children playing soccer.

"We have positive ID in building seven. You are cleared to engage," ordered the man with the necklace badge.

The military guy moved the joystick back and forth, then pulled a trigger. A rocket emerged on the screen, heading toward the cinder-block building. The screen then filled with a huge fireball as the rocket engulfed the building in flames. Billowing smoke rose as far as the eye could see.

"Let's take out the rest," said the mission leader.

The drone flew back toward the burning building and turned clockwise, now heading alongside the row of wooden huts. A missile was launched, and it exploded in midair, releasing hundreds of small black pellets headed for the ground. The cascade of fireballs moved against the rows of huts like a violent tornado. All that remained of the camp were smoldering holes in the ground. There wasn't a blade of green grass in sight.

Gordon felt a tug on his sleeve. It was Shelby.

"Enjoying the movie, Michael?"

"Well, actually…Um, what just happened in there?" asked Gordon.

"It's national security stuff, but between me and you, I think we just took out a Colombian drug lord and his family and friends," Shelby said, smiling.

"Is that allowed?"

"I think the guys speak to Legal every now and then, but sometimes, you know, we have to make a move before the suits get back to us."

Shelby took Gordon's arm and ushered him back into the conference room.

"You sound like you know your way around here. How long have you been an intern?"

"Oh, I'm more than an intern. I've been with the agency for three years."

Gordon stared in disbelief. Shelby didn't look like a DEA operative, let alone someone who had been working for three years. She had to be barely in college.

"You must be really good to be hired before finishing college."

"Actually, I have a master's degree, Michael, and I'm not as pure and innocent as you think I am." Shelby leaned over to grab a bottle of water from the refrigerator, and as her shirt rode up, a black holster tucked in her pants revealed a Glock 9 mm pistol.

"Gordon, great to see ya," Bruno roared as he barged into the conference room, cell phone plastered to his cheek. "Hey, I'm just finishing up this call, and Sal will be just a minute."

"Sal?" Gordon asked, looking over at Shelby.

"Salvatore Parisi, or as we fondly refer to him, Sally P. But he doesn't like it when we call him that, so keep it to yourself. You definitely don't want to piss him off."

"Oh, great," Gordon muttered, dreading another goon to deal with.

The door swung open and in walked a slender man in his midforties who wasn't more than five feet tall. He was wearing royal-blue cotton pants, an orange shirt, a blue-and-white-striped cotton button-down vest, and worn Pro-Keds canvas sneakers that hadn't been sold in regular stores for at least twenty years.

"So where's the newbie?" asked Sal.

Still on the phone, Bruno pointed over to Gordon.

"Who, this guy in the suit and fancy shoes? Come on, you're kiddin' me," quipped Parisi.

He walked over to Gordon and didn't bother with any formalities.

"Listen, kid, Carmine thinks you're somebody, but as far as first impressions, you've failed miserably."

Gordon's jaw was agape. He couldn't believe that this midget in a clown costume with a squeaky voice had the balls to lecture him about first impressions. He was a comical sight, and Gordon could barely hold back his laughter. It was a good thing he did, though. Sally P. didn't tolerate any belittling.

"Well, it's a pleasure to meet you, sir," Gordon said, leaning over to stretch out his hand toward Parisi.

Parisi ignored him and settled into a chair at the head of the conference table. Bruno quickly finished his call and sat alongside Sal. Shelby took a seat at the other end of the table.

"Why don't you have a seat, Michael?" said Shelby.

Gordon settled down opposite Bruno.

"The way I see it, Brett Parker is the village idiot whose claim to fame is proposing bills on forty-six separate occasions to outlaw birth control. He's won fifteen times because only thirty percent vote in the district, and twenty-five percent of those are senior retirees from Staten Island who wouldn't vote for their own mother if she were running on the Democratic ticket. He doesn't sleep around or do drugs—doesn't even have a Facebook page."

Parisi rubbed his stubby fingers on his chin and continued. "This is going to cost five million dollars, plus special enhancement. We can pull about three million from our 501(c)(4), and run another million through Drew Smith in Birmingham. He's out of jail, right?"

"Yes," said Bruno. "He's been out for six months now."

"OK, let's make sure he doesn't buy his next nickel bag from an undercover cop. We're still gonna need a clean buck in twenties and fifties."

"We're headed to see Pierre this afternoon," said Bruno.

"Good," said Parisi. "He's flush these days and needs our help to move cash and product. Make sure he runs it widespread; this can't be confined to donations from NJ-15. Get the Cubans in Miami, the spics in Harlem, and then the usual fringe players like the NOW gals in SoHo and the Green Energy wonks in Westchester. Who's on point?"

Bruno turned toward Shelby.

Parisi smiled as he made eye contact with her. "I want Ricardo on polling. We'll start with a general and do monthly pinpoints starting in January."

"Ah, Ricardo is in Spain working a few local races until January," said Bruno.

"Well, break him off. This play is straight from Henry—priority one. He wants a twenty-point win. We'll be lucky if we can pull ten. Seaver will head up Enhancements. He'll come online next week when he gets back from Singapore. COM is eyeball and secure fax. No e-mail or phone."

Parisi started for the door as Bruno caught up with him.

"Do we really need to bring Bill Seaver into this?" whispered Bruno.

Parisi stopped walking. "Definitely. Your boy is a nerd in Gucci shoes. He has no chance on his own. We have to tear down Parker. Don't worry, Seaver has improved his techniques since Colombia. There won't be a body count. He's into the latest electronic stuff. Should be interesting."

Gordon found himself alone with Shelby in the conference room, his head spinning from the pace at which things were happening. He also didn't know what to make of Parisi. Over the years, he'd seen his fair share of eccentrics, from multimillionaires who insisted on suing a tenant for being two days late with a $1,500 rent payment to sixty-five-year-old brothers who wouldn't agree to sit in the same room after forty years of partnering in business. But Parisi was in a category all unto himself.

"So what was all that stuff from Parisi in the conference room?" asked Gordon. "I didn't understand too much of it."

"Sally was explaining our operational footprint and getting the project staffed up."

"You mind speaking English?" pleaded Gordon.

"All right, Michael. Parisi explained that Brett Parker is clean and the only way to beat him is by making him look terrible. It's going to take a lot of money. And that won't be enough. We're also gonna need some help from our special operations people."

"I suppose this fellow, Seaver, is the special ops guy?"

Shelby smiled. "Yes, Seaver is a very interesting man. Carmine doesn't like him much. Thinks he's arrogant and a bit eccentric. Seaver works in a small top secret unit within DEA special ops called Enhancements. They use the latest technology and have direct access to NSA and CIA satellite imagery and databases."

Gordon shook his head. "This whole thing seems to be getting out of hand. What happened to good old-fashioned campaigning by knocking on doors, doing debates, and sending out campaign flyers?"

Shelby moved closer to Gordon. "That might work if you want to win a local school board election. You can't defeat a longtime incumbent in a congressional district with seven hundred thousand people by conventional good-guy campaigning. You have no prior political experience or name recognition. This is not going to be about Michael Gordon and where you stand on abortion and deficit reduction. In fact, you are hardly going to open your mouth. There won't be much of a campaign website other than your picture shaking hands with a couple of old ladies and some kids. No position papers. No interviews. People are going to get to know you because prominent community and party leaders are going to endorse you. They are going to vote for you because they are going to come to hate Brett Parker. You can't discuss anything about what we are doing for you with anyone. No one. Not your wife, your kids, or your coworkers. No phone calls or e-mail, either. You heard Sally; this is eyeball and secure fax. That means we meet with you face-to-face, and you will be able to send a fax to a specific number if you need to contact me. Otherwise, we will get in touch with you."

Gordon was about to make a long-winded argument about the founding fathers and the role of open debate in elections. He didn't believe people should be elected by the tactics of special handlers who manipulate television ads to portray a bias that isn't true and that doesn't reflect the issues voters should be thinking about in deciding whom to vote for. But before he could get going, Bruno returned.

"We got to get going. Flight leaves in an hour."

Shelby took Gordon's arm. "Time to meet a sugar daddy."

# 10

The chartered Fokker 27 twin-prop plane had taken off from Teeterboro and smelled like jet fuel. Gordon was stuffed between Shelby and a pile of duffel bags that appeared to be carrying US mail, while Bruno was up front talking with a couple of Haitians. Shelby didn't talk much and stared out the window most of the flight. Gordon found an old *People* magazine in the back of one of the seats.

The plane circled Port-au-Prince several times until the marine traffic controllers cleared it for landing. Gordon could see the rows of military vehicles at the far end of the runway and the makeshift military tents patrolled by heavily armed troops. The plane used most of the runway to land and was met by a black Suburban. Bruno got out first and held open the door for Gordon.

"Don't we have to go through passport control?" Gordon struggled to get his voice above the roaring twin props that were still turning.

"All taken care of," said Bruno, who joined Gordon in the backseat.

The drive through Port-au-Prince was gut-wrenching. Thousands of homeless lined the streets between sprawling tent camps that stretched from the airport to the center of the city. Women in makeshift shelters of blue tarp looked aimlessly at the passing traffic, their children in tattered T-shirts sitting nearby. Smashed and crumbling buildings lined the sloping streets, and huge potholes made the roads treacherous. Crowded tap-tap vehicles meandered along the avenues, with men and women standing on the rear bumpers.

After about forty-five minutes of snarling traffic, the surroundings became more palatable. Homes and businesses were intact. BMWs and Mercedes mixed with old Subarus and Toyota pickups. Designer shops were open for business, and men in slacks and fine cotton shirts were visible at the outdoor cafés, sipping lattes and talking on their phones. Gordon had arrived at Petion-Ville, the upper crust of Port-au-Prince where drug money paid for a distinct separation from the brutal reality of modern Haiti.

The Suburban pulled up to a twelve-foot iron gate door and honked. As the gate opened, three heavily armed guards approached the car, peering through the windows. Inside the gates was a Spanish-like villa set back on a gently sloping incline surrounded by lush shrubbery and a forty-foot horseshoe-shaped swimming pool. As they made their way into the house, Gordon noticed two large generators humming loudly. Haiti was notorious for its power outages, and without backup generators, it was impossible to keep fresh food around for long.

Pierre Lassade gave Bruno a huge hug as he ushered him into a well-appointed living room. Fine silk couches adorned with crafted pillows lined the walls, along with expensive artwork and sculptures. Pictures of Lassade with leading politicians from both Haiti and abroad were set neatly on a mahogany breakfront. And it was cool, a welcome break from the sweltering heat.

They were an odd couple. Bruno had first met Lassade in Spring Valley, New York, twenty-eight years earlier. Bruno was working undercover as part of a joint NYPD/DEA task force trying to infiltrate a Spanish heroin ring based in Washington Heights. He was led to Rockland County by a tipster who said that a lot of the dope was making its way through Haitians from upstate. Bruno and his team busted into the small split-level house to find Lassade in the bathroom trying to flush down thirty small bags of cocaine.

Down at Midtown South, Bruno noticed something refined about Lassade. He wasn't the typical punk who buckled under police pressure or the hardened soul who laughed through sentencing. He was polite and confident, like he knew he was going to beat the rap. A couple of the city undercovers wanted to rough him up, but Bruno held them off. He brought in a box of doughnuts and a couple of large coffees, and the two chatted for hours. Lassade was erudite, fluent in English and French, with a good working knowledge of Spanish and German. They spoke about Haitian history, the Roman Empire, and the struggle of the black man in America.

About midnight, Bruno was ready to break off for home when two FBI agents walked in with a suit from the State Department.

Flashing their credentials, they took custody of Lassade.

"We'll take it from here," said one of the FBI goons.

Bruno turned to one of the NYPD undercovers in dismay. "What the hell was that?"

"You're not gonna believe this, but that pretty milk-chocolate college boy you've been schmoozing for the past four hours is one of Poppa Doc's bastard sons. Looks like they're gonna send him back to Daddy."

Bruno caught up with Lassade in 2003, this time as a cooperator. Lassade was running one of the largest whole-sale drug operations to Europe in the world. With its corrupt leadership and nonexistent police force, coupled with its unique location in the Caribbean, Haiti was the perfect place to store and move drugs from South America. Everyone did business there. Colombia, Nicaragua, Mexico, Venezuela—you name it, they were moving cocaine and heroin freely into Haiti, where it was packaged and smuggled into Miami or shipped off to Europe through Bulgaria.

Together with the CIA, Bruno had developed a working relationship with Lassade, helping him move product and launder money in return for reliable intelligence on leading South American cartel figures. It was a profitable relationship for both sides, as Lassade's information was almost always timely and accurate.

"Pierre, this is Michael Gordon, our new congressional candidate from New Jersey," Bruno said as he ushered Gordon to the center of the room.

Lassade's handshake was firm, and his cologne gave off a fruity scent. As he smiled, Gordon could see three gold inlays, one engraved with a cross. After a few niceties, the conversation turned back to Bruno.

"Carmine, it's been too long. How's the professor and Father Murphy?"

Gordon looked at Shelby, not understanding why Wolf would be mentioned in this setting.

"Oh, they're just fine, working toward the common good. The professor thought you might be able to help us with some campaign financing. Gordon is up against a tough opponent, Brett Parker."

"Oh, yes. Brett Parker. The Catholics like his stance on abortion and birth control, you know. Those are deeply held virtues."

Bruno chuckled as a young Haitian girl walked in with a piping hot urn of green tea and a plate of biscuits. Lassade had at least two wives and four full-time mistresses spanning several continents, but only one child. So much for virtue.

"And who's this lovely flaming redhead?" Lassade asked as he locked eyes with Shelby.

"She's one of ours, Pierre."

"Oh, how young and beautiful they're becoming, ay, Carmine?"

Shelby showed no expression. She wasn't impressed with Lassade, whom she knew as a ruthless killer and one of the biggest money launderers for Carlos Punta, the head of the Nicaraguan cartel.

Lassade carried on about the dearth of foreign aid and the deterioration of Haitian life. "At least when Poppa Doc was in charge, we had stability. You were able to plan and businesses strived. Now, even systematic bribes only get you seventy-five percent certainty. The weak government and the homeless are wild cards that are crippling our economy."

Gordon wanted to say something, but Lassade headed over to Bruno.

"Carmine, why don't we step into my study for a moment?" Lassade took Bruno by the arm and ushered him into a small room off the center corridor.

"You sure this pretty boy can beat Brett Parker?" asked Lassade. "You know I never invest in a loser."

"Not to worry. The Company has put Bill Seaver on this."

Lassade smiled. "How much do you need?"

"We need five bucks from you and your associates, preferably some of it in max donations of twenty-five hundred and five thousand from the natives in Brooklyn and Miami, and from your Manhattan criminal lawyers," said Bruno.

"Whew." Lassade sighed. "That's a lot of green for a white boy from New Jersey."

"This is from Henry, priority one."

Lassade sat down behind a large oak desk. "No wonder Seaver is working this. It'll take a few weeks to put this together."

Bruno spread the curtains and looked out to the pool. "You've got one week. We want the dirty money floating to Prosperity Allegiance USA, our nonreporting federal PAC, and to Confederate Nation, our state PAC in Birmingham. The twenties and fifties will come into Gordon's vanilla campaign account. Shelby will get you the wiring instructions."

"Birmingham?"

"Alabama has no campaign finance laws, so we're able to move a lot of cash with no questions."

Lassade reached for a cigarette. "I'm gonna need some interference from your friends with the customs agents on the Bulgarian border. They've been hiking the bribe prices like crazy and making it very difficult to move product to Western Europe."

"You want protection, or you want to make a point?"

"I want to make a very loud point."

Admiring Lassade's impressive book collection, Bruno picked up a copy of Hemingway's *For Whom the Bell Tolls* and flipped through the first few pages. "I'll get you a package with enough PETN to stir up quite a commotion. Should put the fear of God back in their hearts."

Lassade put out his cigarette and moved closer to Bruno. "And Mr. Punta is going to require a small favor. His kid sister is having a very difficult time getting a green card."

Bruno didn't hesitate. "Done."

"You're a champ, Carmine."

"Don't mention it. Now come say good-bye to Gordon."

# 11

**G**reely's was the only Irish Bar in the La Jolla business district. A bit run-down like the rest of the shops on Prospect Street that were once go-to San Diego tourist destinations, the bar had the best Irish stew on the West Coast. With chunky beef and just the right amount of garlic and Guinness beer, the dish made the painful memories of a difficult life disappear, if only fleetingly.

Bill Seaver didn't have the demeanor of someone who had spent the last thirty years killing people. Hunched over a piping hot bowl of stew in the last corner booth before the kitchen, you would easily mistake the five-foot-nine, 220-pound bearded man with a small diamond stud in his left ear as a retired telephone repairman. He was soft-spoken and nonconfrontational. At Greely's, where he spent most of his weekends, he was known as a peacemaker, often solving disputes among inebriated patrons and even driving a few home in the wee hours of the morning.

Raised by his single mother in Leominster just outside Boston, Seaver had made it to MIT, where he had hoped to become an electrical engineer and work for the NASA shuttle program. Midway through his junior year, he was introduced to Professor Dale Schilling, who was visiting from Stanford and had been experimenting with miniature circuitry that maximized battery power. Schilling was an avid student of Intel's Gordon Moore but didn't think that the future of semiconductor design lay merely in transistor density. He was convinced that Moore's Law couldn't produce effective products without concurrent advances in low-voltage circuitry. What was the point of having a cordless phone that ran out of battery power in two hours?

Seaver shared Schilling's passion for miniaturization, and after graduation, he joined Schilling's staff as a research fellow. The next two years were probably the happiest time Seaver could remember. He developed a strong bond with Schilling, and together, they made broad progress toward low-power design. But Seaver drew more interested in alternative power sources. Nickel cadmium proved clumsy and too heavy to integrate into small devices. Frustrated, Schilling urged Seaver to take a semester of fluid dynamics at the California Institute of Technology. Seaver excelled and began experimenting with biological circuitry. He reasoned that the human body, fueled entirely by organic material, had the most advanced electrical system known to man.

Seaver replaced silicon wafer boards with fetal tissue but kept losing his specimens to decay. Standard formaldehyde retarded conductivity. He volunteered for a local mortuary and learned about various embalming compounds. Still unsatisfied, he shaved his head and spent four months at the Kopan Monastery in Nepal, where Buddhist monks shared secret spices and plant extracts used in food preservation.

Soon, word of Seaver's work spread beyond Schiller's lab and raised concerns with Donald Foster, a Stanford trustee and an elder at First Presbyterian in Palo Alto. Kent Conrad, Stanford's provost, called Schilling into his office one Friday afternoon.

"Dale, I know you like this kid, but he's getting the right-to-lifers all riled up with his fetal wafer boards. Where's he going with this, anyway? Are we trying to build a Frankenstein?"

"No, no." Schilling chuckled, waving his hand at Conrad. "The kid is unconventional, sure, but he has unbelievable passion and is making great progress with the low-voltage stuff."

"Well, is it going to make us money?"

"Not right away. He's still having problems with preserving his specimens, and conductivity with standard copper-based material is consuming a lot of power. But the potential is mind-boggling. The applications run the gamut from minicomputing to cordless phones that are no larger than the palm of your hand. There is also the whole world of military hardware. This technology, once developed, will drop down the size and weight of missile guidance systems hundredfold from today's levels."

Conrad stood up and put his hand on Schilling's shoulder. "Personally, I think the kid is on to something, but the pressure from the board is getting stronger. They don't like this kind of biotechnology. He's gotta stop using the fetal tissue. Get him some mice or chimpanzees. And keep a close watch on him. Word on campus is that he's a bit strange. Did he actually shave his head and spend a winter with a band of Buddhist monks?"

Deeply troubled, Schilling left the office. He knew there was no way Seaver would compromise on his research materials. Schilling struggled with what to do next. He believed in Seaver and wanted him to complete his work at Stanford. But that seemed impossible. After two sleepless nights, Schilling realized there was only one choice.

At 7:30 a.m. on Monday morning, Seaver arrived for work at the lab. After hanging up his coat, he walked into the kitchen to grab a coffee. Sitting at the table was General Greer Davis, head of military weapons development for the US Air Force. Seaver was unimpressed.

"Good morning, General. I'm not in the killing business," Seaver said as he set a pot of coffee to boil.

"This isn't about killing. It's about saving lives by providing our men with the best hardware we can design. You'll have unfettered access to resources far beyond your imagination, and you'll be working with other young, innovative scientists like yourself."

Seaver was tempted. But he felt an allegiance to Schilling.

"Don't worry about Professor Schilling," continued Davis. "He's the one who invited me here. The tight-asses on the board of trustees are about to shut you down. They think you're killing babies for your wafer boards. I'll get you all the fetal tissue you want."

Davis had struck a chord. Above all else, Seaver was drawn to the science. He desperately needed to solve the degradation problem to get to the next level. Seaver headed back toward the lab. "OK, General, I'll give your proposal some thought."

Then three men in long beige trench coats entered, followed by Schilling.

"You should go with these guys," said Schilling. "Stanford isn't ready for your work, and I'd hate to see your future unfairly compromised."

Davis had the final word. "This is simple, son. There's a car waiting outside to take you to a career very few have the opportunity to pursue. Or you can stick around and end up designing thermostats for Honeywell."

Seaver began to realize that he didn't have much choice. Once the government had you in its sights, there was little room for negotiation. You either saluted the flag or were destroyed. Another four young men in light-blue uniforms entered the lab with large metal suitcases. They began packing up Seaver's files.

Schilling gave Seaver a hug. "It's been a pleasure working with you, Bill."

Seaver spent the next three years at Ellsworth Air Force Base in South Dakota. Together with a dozen others, Seaver made strides in miniature circuitry. He pioneered the use of silicon optics to replace copper in semiconductor design and was particularly proud of his work in advanced telecommunications. But the isolation of South Dakota began to wear on Seaver. Ellsworth was teaming with people, but none were compatible. He viewed the local women as Neanderthals who couldn't hold a five-minute intellectual conversation. The military women were too aggressive, perceived by Seaver as a bunch of dykes masquerading as Girl Scouts.

General Davis noticed Seaver's deterioration. Loud outbursts during lab sessions and frequent late arrivals to important meetings were telltale signs of burnout. But

Davis saw enormous potential in Seaver and didn't want to lose him. His good friend Colby Allen was heading up the DEA and needed techies in the Far East. Seaver jumped at the opportunity.

Based in Bangkok, Seaver was assigned to a deep-cover hit team charged with infiltrating and wiping out Asian drug figures. He quickly learned the ins and outs of notorious Patpong Street, where prostitutes and drugs were passed around like candy. Without any field training, Seaver was always second fiddle to a real agent. But that was fine. Seaver knew he was always the smartest guy in the room, and titles never bothered him.

The DEA was a perfect fit for Seaver. Unlike the arrogant FBI that wanted six-foot-tall prep school white kids whose ancestors had sailed the *Mayflower*, the DEA scooped up all types. It was a smorgasbord of people in all shapes and sizes from shitty backgrounds, even those with criminal records and no college degree. But everyone Seaver worked with shared a deep sense of loyalty to the United States and a passion for wiping out the scumbag drug lords who preyed on society's weakest and perverted America's youth.

Seaver spent five years in Thailand and revolutionized the way the agency operated. Instead of the usual drive-by shooting or C4 planted in a target's mailbox, Seaver had developed and used high-tech synthesized biological agents. The operative came in skin contact with a target and left a residue of odorless nerve agent that killed within minutes. Miniature darts were another of Seaver's favorites. A small projectile the size of the tip of a ballpoint pen was fired through a handheld device that looked like a syringe.

The agent placed it under his sleeve, and as he offered his handshake to a target, he fired the small pellet, which painlessly embedded itself. The poison was released within two hours.

General Davis had followed Seaver's career closely and was impressed with his innovative techniques. On his return from Bangkok, Davis had Seaver promoted to DEA liaison to the NSA and placed in their R&D unit. There, Seaver returned to his biocircuitry work, testing various human tissues as hosts for semiconductor design. The NSA guys introduced him to a synthetic compound that preserved his specimens without affecting electrical conductivity. Seaver was elated. He developed miniature listening devices that could be implanted in people and controlled remotely. At Davis's request, Seaver adapted these devices with tiny explosive charges. Once the target had provided the necessary information, he could be readily disposed of.

After a couple of years of spending twelve hours a day thirty floors beneath the Pentagon in white windowless rooms, Seaver wanted to get back into the field. He did a six-week basic training course at Quantico and was assigned to a DEA kill team in Bogotá run by an up-and-coming operative named Carmine Bruno. The two hit it off at first. Bruno liked Seaver's bag of toys that made tracking and killing the bad guys a lot safer for the field agents. For Seaver, it was the first time he actually got to walk around with a gun in his pocket and see up close the faces of the victims his planning and devices killed.

Bruno and Seaver spent three years in Colombia and were responsible for killing over 150 drug operatives. The local police and militias called them Batman and Robin.

But one Sunday evening, Seaver pulled over to a local bodega to grab a sandwich. On his way out, his car burst into flames from a horrible explosion. He was only a minute away from being incinerated.

Bruno got the message and moved his operations to Panama City. But Seaver wouldn't listen to reason. He convinced General Davis to set him up as a military liaison in the US Embassy. From there, Seaver directed dozens of paramilitary attacks against Colombian rebels and suspected drug runners. These weren't the ingenious needle-prick assassinations that Seaver had pioneered and mastered. They were "carpet ops," massive aerial and ground bombings of villages and neighborhoods. The carnage made even seasoned operatives cringe, and reports getting back to Langley spoke of an emboldened rebel force that was gaining recruits. But General Davis believed in Seaver and kept the brass back home at bay.

Seaver finally calmed down once he had run out of targets. Heading back to DC on a Hercules transport for a routine debriefing, he took a call from Jim Stone, acting DEA chief.

"General Davis died this morning from an aneurism," said Stone. "Let's talk next week."

The line went dead, and so did a part of Seaver. Davis was the closest thing he had to a father. Seaver buried his head in his hands and cried.

The next decade was a blur. Seaver did a little consulting work for the Pentagon, but for the most part, he led a bohemian lifestyle out of a one-bedroom apartment in San Francisco's legendary Haight-Ashbury. He mingled with authors and drunks and wrote about two hundred pages of a military novel, but couldn't finish. Broke and bored, he went back to the DEA, which was putting together a political directorate charged with destabilizing foreign governments. Seaver rediscovered his passion for biocircuitry and began developing new listening devices that tapped into the latest satellite technology. The field ops loved his work, but Seaver didn't have much left in his tank. He left after only a year. Fat and complacent, Seaver moved into a small villa in La Jolla. He did an occasional contract for the DEA, but spent most of his time painting and teaching calculus at UC San Diego.

The BMW R1200gs came to a stop in front of Greely's. A couple got off the bike and headed for the back as they slowly removed their helmets. Shelby tied her hair in a bun while Ricardo took a seat across from Seaver.

"We're down forty-four points," Ricardo said, reporting his initial survey results for Gordon's race. "Parker leads in all categories, including registered Democrats. There's nobody above the congressional candidates on the ticket this year, and the national mood is leaning heavy Republican."

Shelby poured herself a glass of water. "Gordon's wife is sleeping with a psychiatrist in LA. She's been seeing him on and off for two years at various professional conferences, but now it's getting serious."

"A messy divorce is not going to go down well in this district," Ricardo said as he flipped through a menu. "Twenty-two percent are Catholic, and twenty-nine percent are seniors over sixty-eight."

Seaver finished up his bowl of stew and reached for his beer. "What are the networks?"

Ricardo ordered shepherd's pie. "There's Time Warner in the northeastern part and Cablevision in the rest. The district spans four zones."

"We can scramble the boxes, I presume."

"Yes, but we're gonna need at least a dozen trucks if we want to cover the whole area."

Seaver turned toward Shelby. "What about vices?"

"Nothing. We searched credit card statements, bank records, E-ZPass, and tax returns for the last five years."

Seaver handed Shelby a thin folder. "Well, then I guess I'm a step ahead of you."

Shelby's eyes lit up as she read through months of credit card statements showing visits to a chiropractor's office in Alexandria. "But these didn't come up on the billings we saw."

"These are his congressional office's credit card bills. I still know some people."

Shelby smiled. She had always admired Seaver's work, having used several of his tiny gadgets on more than one occasion. Chiropractor offices were often fronts for high-end massage parlors where young Asian girls slathered you with oils and lotions until you reached a happy ending. This would be a big break.

Seaver ordered a double espresso. "We're gonna have to escalate this like we did for Lopez in Ecuador." Seaver and Ricardo had managed to get no-name business executive Javier Lopez elected president of Ecuador by destroying the character and reputation of the longtime incumbent, a former general. It was as ruthless as it was brilliant. False rumors of extramarital affairs, close-up photos of embarrassing poses, phony polls claiming the race was far closer than it really was. Lopez went from down twenty points to winning by ten.

Ricardo sipped his beer. "Yeah, but this ain't Ecuador."

"What's the COM protocol?" asked Seaver.

"Eyeball and secure fax," answered Shelby.

"No fax," Seaver said, waving his finger. "We meet monthly until after the primary. No double sites. Three-man max."

Seaver pulled out a small pill bottle, complete with prescription label. Inside was a tiny white disc no larger than a baby aspirin. "This is a carbon-tetrachloride mix. Invades through the sweat glands. Rub this on the wife's palm or forehead. She'll have Stage II breast cancer in three weeks. That should slow down the affair."

Seaver stopped a waiter pushing a cart full of dessert pastries and helped himself to a thin slice of cheesecake. "Vito Menza is DEA domestic special ops. He's going to arrange a town meeting with lots of press. Two Italian women are going to raise havoc over Gordon's proabortion stance. A pregnant teen is going to pull a gun on one of the ladies. Gordon will intervene."

"Nice," cheered Ricardo. "Once that hits the news, I'll be able to start planting some good poll numbers. We've got people at the Newark *Star-Ledger* and the *Philadelphia Inquirer*."

"I want Quinnipiac and Rutgers on board by September," said Seaver.

"Those guys are pretty clean; we may have to hack into their numbers."

"You'll let me know if you need NSA modulation. Who's running the vanilla side of this?"

Shelby finished up her garden salad and reached for the bottle of Perrier. "Stu Lawson. He's on loan to the agency from Langley. Did a nice job on a couple of state races down South last year."

"Who brought him in?"

"Parisi."

"No go. This is too high priority for loaners. Tell Sally we'll use Max Peoples. I'll take care of that. How much in the bank?"

"Two million in PAC split evenly between Birmingham and DC. Another buck fifty in twenties and fifties in Wells Fargo," said Shelby.

Ricardo chuckled. "This ain't happening under ten."

"Well, we've only got five committed," snapped Shelby.

"Calm down, children," Seaver said soothingly. "There will be no shortage of resources. I'm having dinner with Henry tomorrow night. He's on top of this."

Seaver dropped a fifty-dollar bill on the table and headed for the door. "*Nos vemos el próximo mes.*"

# 12

**H**enry Lustig paced back and forth in Seaver's living room while Seaver finished broiling a pan of sea bass and added a little garlic to the roasted asparagus. The two hadn't seen each other in over a decade. But Seaver seemed the same warm mad scientist Lustig had come to know decades earlier.

Lustig had an unusual history. Born in Budapest, he had escaped the Nazis with his partisan parents, who sometimes took him along on German ambushes. On one raid, the young Lustig passed a dead SS captain. Noticing a shiny object on his belt, he bent over the dead man and removed his Luger P08, which he cherished to this day. Relocated to New York's Lower East Side after the war, Lustig enjoyed a comfortable upbringing, thanks to his father's thriving jewelry business. With the help of an influential senator who received substantial support from Lustig's father, Lustig was admitted to Annapolis. But the navy of the 1950s didn't hold much promise for a Hungarian war survivor. The CIA did.

Recruited during his senior year, Lustig was posted to the US Embassy in Budapest as a military attaché. After five years, he had become the agency's station chief, managing fifteen active agents deeply embedded in the

Soviet-controlled Hungarian government. His sources provided a trove of valuable information on Soviet weapons capability and troop strengths and revealed the identities of over a dozen double agents working for the Soviets in Western Europe. Then there was Karine.

Karine Lamy was a French doctor working for the Red Cross in Budapest. Tall and thin with deep-blue eyes and dirty-blond hair, she was the envy of the social circuit. For some reason, she took a liking to Lustig who, at six feet three with rugged features, managed to garner a fair amount of attention to himself from the local ladies. At first, it was strictly business, with Lamy doing most of the talking and complaining about Soviet roadblocks that delayed ambulances en route to emergencies and inferior Russian medical practices that pervaded the Eastern Bloc. Lustig always promised to try to help, although there was little he could do. The relationship slowly turned romantic, and after four months, Lamy moved into Lustig's studio apartment. There, Lustig gave himself to Lamy, both physically and emotionally. He let her inside, sharing his true identity with her. Lamy convinced him to bring more work home, and he made phone calls from hotel rooms while on vacation with her. Soon, some of his double agents fell off the grid without explanation.

Lustig's supervisor gave him the news. Lamy was a Soviet agent. She managed to jump a train for East Germany before the agency could apprehend her. Distraught and emotionally broken, Lustig offered his resignation, but the agency still saw value in his organizational and recruiting skills. He was reassigned to Beirut, where he monitored weapons smugglers and infiltrated several extreme Islamist groups. It was back-office stuff as far as CIA work went.

One day, on a trip to Jerusalem's Old City, he bumped into a Catholic priest while visiting the Church of the Holy Sepulcher. The missionary from Huntsville, Alabama, saw the pain within Lustig. They struck up a conversation, which turned to the meaning of life and God's intervention in man's affairs. Lustig enjoyed the discourse, and soon, the two began studying the Bible. The relationship continued for several years and covered vast areas of study, from the Corinthians to Kabbalah. After graduation from seminary in Rome, Lustig was ordained in Jerusalem and given the name Rudolphus Murphy.

Seaver set down a basket of steaming garlic bread. "Father, would you like some white wine with your fish?"

"Oh, that would be wonderful, William."

The two settled into their meal, hardly talking much. Then Seaver raised his glass.

"It's been a fateful journey. May the last leg serve us proud."

"Well said." Murphy smiled as he gulped down his wine.

"What was it like in the Crow's Nest?" asked Seaver.

"Ah, it was so long ago, and yet it was yesterday," mused Murphy. "We were a serious bunch, a collective of hard souls chastened by the pranks and hazing of the upperclassmen and the WASPs. Yet we found comfort in each other's company and swore to make a difference in the world. Many of us faded away after the mandatory years. Wives, children, and the pursuit of wealth consumed the ideological passions. But a select few carried their commitment beyond the age of bewilderment and high testosterone levels. Many of those have died serving their country. There aren't too many left from my day.

"Carl Singer was one of our best. He had a mole inside the North Korean nuclear program and fed the gooks wrong analyses. He single-handedly set back the program by decades and prevented the Viet Cong from getting a dirty bomb. That would have been terribly messy. But, alas, his trusted secretary did him in. She had a younger sister in Lillehammer who was struggling to raise her twin boys after her husband died. The Russians threatened to kill the kids in a most dreadful way. The secretary capitulated and led Singer into a death trap. He was making a delivery of phony files to his Korean contact at Weil am Rhein when East German agents closed in. But I guess Singer sensed his fate. The file he delivered was coated with cyclosarin. Three of the North's top nuclear scientists who studied the file died within weeks. So did the courier. I'm sure Singer sunk to the bottom of the Rhine with a smile on his face. The body buried under his tombstone on Long Island is a dead Swiss army regular who was killed in a car accident."

"So that's why you're personally caught up with the Gordon operation?" asked Seaver.

Murphy reached for the salt, which he spread generously over his halibut. "Gordon is critically important to Operation Open Sky. It's the committee's top priority right now. Gordon checks all the boxes—psych, physiology, naïveté—and he loves America."

Operation Open Sky had been spoken about for years, but no one ever believed it would make it to the operational stage. The CIA could never get the necessary presidential finding. The DEA was too worried about a failure that could dramatically cut back on its operations. The Pentagon couldn't obtain congressional funding. The committee could technically pull it off, but why now? And why take the risk?

Seaver poured himself some more wine. "Is there a finding?"

"Not exactly," said Murphy. "The deputy director has a finding to destabilize Islamic activity. We bootstrap into that."

"But we're talking about a weapon that can change the balance of power."

Murphy reached for one of Seaver's Cohiba cigars. "William, you know the committee doesn't officially exist. There are no congressional oversight meetings, no detailed budget reports. We are a group of contractors funded by a black box in the Energy Department's nuclear research budget. We function through a presidential finding taken during the last days of World War II, with a mandate to protect the country from foreign elements that pose a risk to national security. We carry out the mandate in a clandestine fashion, mostly through the DEA, which operates with impunity, both domestically and around the world, with no obligation to report to the president or to Congress. The administration has the right to appoint one member to the committee, and it is typically the deputy national security advisor."

Murphy stared into Seaver's eyes. "Sometimes we have to take matters into our own hands when the wheels of government cannot make the decisions required to keep our children safe, even if that means taking control of government assets, albeit temporarily."

Seaver grinned. He understood the work of the committee and was amused by Murphy's Boy Scout allegiance to the cause. He volunteered for the Gordon assignment in part for his personal distaste for right-wing religious zealots like Brett Parker, who Seaver believed had no place in government, and for the opportunity to make it onto the committee. Of its seven members, four were over seventy.

Seaver started clearing the dinner plates while Murphy slowly puffed at the Cuban smoke, enjoying its deep flavor and fine aroma.

"William, we have to get this guy elected by a comfortable margin so he is respected in the caucus and gets the committee assignments we need. You're authorized to do whatever it takes."

"The matter is well in hand and will be successful," Seaver said reassuringly.

Murphy drank some more wine. "You remember how we first met, William?"

"No, not offhand." Seaver wasn't one for reveling in nostalgia.

"Thailand, '83," said Murphy. "You were standing in the gift shop at the Sukhumvit Hotel in Bangkok, trying to find some American toothpaste. I was a young deacon teaching English in a local orphanage to kids who were, for the most part, abandoned by their prostitute mothers. I was there for a meeting with Bishop Trevor Prince and others who were organizing funds for the construction of a new convent."

Seaver slowly nodded his head. "Yes, I remember that night. I was the lookout on the hit."

"Well, you were a polite lookout. You graciously translated a note a young mother had left me when she dropped her newborn off at the church that morning. Dr. Prince fell ill that night. They found him outside the next morning, stark naked and bleeding from his ass."

Seaver laughed. "Those were the early days with chlordiazepoxide poisons. It was supposed to kill much more quickly and appear as an aneurysm. Prince was laundering a lot of drug money."

"The convent never got the funding, you know," said Murphy.

"Yeah, I guess that's too bad."

"No, not really," continued Murphy. "When Prince's fundraising dried up, I was called back and ultimately got my pulpit in Houston."

Seaver handed Murphy a cappuccino. "I presume that was God's will."

"Oh, yes, indeed, William. Nothing happens on this earth without God's direct intervention. I firmly believe in that. One day, I'm sure you'll come to that conclusion yourself."

"I somehow doubt it, Father. My hands are too soaked with blood to be deigned by any great spiritual revelation."

Murphy took Seaver's arm. "Oh, no, William. There are no nonbelievers. There are only blind men who have never seen the light of day. That day will shine for you, just as it did for me when I left Beirut."

Seaver admired the old man's optimism. But God and the teachings of the apostles weren't things that occupied Seaver's mind. He had left his Sunday school readings and organized religion behind when he enrolled at MIT and converted to the faith of scientific fact. He viewed religion as a set of rules based on promises that were impossible to predict or verify. Like many who reach adulthood and succumb to the freedoms of choice and the pull of capitalistic society, Seaver wouldn't bow to a set of rules he couldn't understand. Yet he did recognize that life was not merely a series of coincidences. There certainly was some form of higher power that impacted man's endeavors in some way.

"Oh, I hope so, Father. Maybe I will be saved in the end."

Murphy slowly sipped his espresso. "I'm sure you will."

"By the way," continued Seaver, "have we taken out any insurance on Gordon?"

"Oh, yes. Some of the highest quality. And the dividends are already paying handsomely."

"Good. I'd hate to see all these efforts go to waste should Gordon decide not to stick with the program."

The two men chatted for another hour. As Murphy reached the door, he put his hand on Seaver's shoulder. "I won't be seeing you again until after the election. Keep a close eye on the young helpers. They don't join for the right reasons anymore."

# 13

The playfield around State School 24 in Vladivostok was filled with overgrown weeds and patches of cracked concrete. The children of Ms. Petergorski's ninth-grade class pondered whether to venture out for recess or wander about the halls, perhaps finding some new leak in the boys' room or throwing stones at the ceiling and watching the chipped paint float down. They were a tattered bunch, sons and daughters of dock loaders and farmers, secretaries and factory workers. Yuri was a shy boy, shorter than his peers, with freckles and thick black-rimmed glasses. The youngest of Mikhail and Eta Topkin's seven sons, Yuri shunned sports and free play, instead spending time staring closely at plants and trees, old Russian Volgas in the parking lot, and even the groundkeeper's rusty tractor. These things intrigued him, and he would often strike up conversations with those who understood how machines worked and why plants grew and what purpose they served.

His friends thought him an odd one, an introvert, not likely to succeed at anything more than proletariat work, perhaps a future mail clerk or mechanic. Not the coveted soldier or communist apparatchik who lived the life of privilege and authority. But, then again, fourteen-year-olds can be harsh on their peers, even a little too judgmental.

Yuri loved to read and would spend hours in the school library while others played ball in the yard or boasted about their adolescent trysts with girls. Although detached from the daily norms of student life, Yuri managed good grades with ease. Studies came easily, and ideas flowed through his mind effortlessly. In fact, although he rarely engaged others, school was an outlet from the cramped apartment quarters he shared with his mother and siblings. Yuri's father, a decorated war veteran, had died of cancer when he was three. His mother, a nurse, struggled to meet the needs of her unruly hoard of sons, whose personalities and behavior differed like the vast geography of the Soviet Union.

The students filed out of class to the main schoolyard for twenty minutes of energized hysteria. Sports and conversations shared the same space as snacking youths and circles of giggling girls peering at their admirers. Yuri stumbled out last, having stopped to talk to his biology professor about his conclusion that the evolution of man can be deduced from a tadpole. The conversation was interrupted by the growing commotion in the middle of the yard. A group of boys were busy shoving and yelling at a fellow classmate who had sat in the middle of the soccer field.

Borris Yogislov was a hulking mass. At six feet four, he towered over his classmates. Yet, despite his peaceful, boyish face, he marched to his own beat. "Yogi," as he was called, was busy devouring an enormous ham sandwich. Kids dashed toward him with taunts, but nothing broke his concentration. As the soccer game carried on around him, Yogi seemed to relish his meal while peering up at the sky on an occasional break between bites.

All this intrigued Yuri, as he sensed a certain finesse in Yogi. Maybe it was the way he carefully held his sandwich to avoid spilling crumbs or how he folded his napkin and placed it on his lap. The bravado of sitting in the middle of the field was more bewilderment than mischief. About ten minutes into the afternoon recess, Yuri walked straight over to Yogi, who was now munching on an apple. The frenetic pace of the schoolyard slowed as a crowd gathered to witness what would likely be an ugly confrontation. Yuri approached the giant teen and held out his hand.

"Shake," said Yuri.

The crowd hushed in silence as Yogi finished his last bite of apple.

But instead of the flying teeth and bloody concrete everyone had expected, Yogi stretched out his hand and shook Yuri's. Yuri then sat down beside Yogi in the middle of the yard, not saying a word, but knowing that he had just slain a dragon. The episode proved to the young Russian that diplomacy could be just as powerful as brute force.

The two boys became inseparable for the remainder of their school years. After graduation, they traveled together to the army intake center on their first day of compulsory service. Yuri, the orphan of a decorated veteran, was drafted into Russian military intelligence. This meant a dry and warm office job in Moscow. Yogi, the son of a carpenter, was sent to the paratroopers. The two never saw each other again. A year into his tour, Yogi's helicopter was shot down over Kabul.

After the army, Yuri went to Athens on a student visa to study ancient ruins. This was his first assignment for the KGB. He ran ten undercover agents throughout Southern

Europe, where he installed a sophisticated network of listening devices in many government buildings. He even managed to bug the Vatican. After three years, he was promoted to station chief. Perestroika changed the world, and Yuri returned to Moscow, where he steadily climbed the ladder of the newly formed FSB. He ultimately became director of the industrial espionage directorate.

Charged with stealing business secrets, from the Coca-Cola recipe to the latest clinical Phase II antibiotic at Pfizer, Topkin funneled some of his secrets to the Russian industry for handsome payments. While this was strictly forbidden, Topkin didn't feel threatened. One of his protégés in Athens was now the head of the interior ministry who regularly received generous portions of Topkin's side earnings.

Putin's dominance of Russian politics surprised many of the Old Guard and even the newly minted FSB senior ranks who were used to totalitarian regimes with iron-fisted leaders. Putin achieved the same level of control and repression as his octogenarian predecessors while remaining popular with the West and even wielding influence on world affairs beyond the old Eastern stomping grounds. He mixed capitalism, crime, and PR into state policy and managed to line his pockets and those of his straw men in the private sector while still filling Moscow grocery stores with fresh produce. This opened up a new avenue of state-sponsored initiatives, from international black market smuggling to the drug trade.

Topkin saw enormous revenue potential in South American cocaine smuggling. He knew he couldn't get directly involved in the internecine turf wars, nor could he subcontract out his own crop for export. Instead, he took a page from the Mafia's playbook and began shaking down cartel leaders. At first, it was the classic power play. Kidnappings and drive-by shootings drew some attention, but the big players weren't noticing. That changed when a Special Forces team pulled the head of the Medellin cartel out of a downtown Bogotá restaurant in broad daylight and blew his brains out in front of his wife and three kids. The hit made front-page news and announced to the rest of the leading players that the Russians had indeed arrived.

But the Colombians knew that the Russians weren't like the Americans; they were willing to cut a deal. Soon, 35 percent of all exports were running through Russian intermediaries, who took 5 percent off the top. Topkin took another 2 percent by laundering cash through Russian ghost accounts. The cash flow funded FSB slush funds used for general national interests, from bribing foreign officials to balancing struggling municipal budgets whose local leadership towed the party line.

Topkin's efforts made him a lot of friends in high places. But in Russian government, friends only stick around for as long as you deliver. To make sure Washington didn't get too aggressive, Topkin dispatched none other than his stepdaughter, Carla Eshrova, to keep an ear to the ground and bring any new policy initiatives to Moscow's attention. Enrolled at Georgetown's LLM program in taxation, the tall blond beauty had an excellent deep cover, which Topkin wouldn't hesitate to put into good use when the time came.

Little did he know that Eshrova's time would come sooner than he expected.

# 14

**E**mily Gordon had just returned from seeing her son Ryan off to school and settled down to her morning coffee. Flipping through the local newspaper, she saw a photo of her husband flanked by police brass.

"Did you see this morning's *Trenton Times?*"

Gordon finished knotting his tie. "No, not yet."

"There's a front-page story on how you wrestled a gun away from some freaked-out pregnant teen at the Trenton Rotary Club meeting the other day. Nice picture of you with a state trooper. What made you lunge at that kid? For all you know, she might have shot at you."

Gordon peered over Emily's shoulder to get a glimpse of his photo. "I don't know, really. She was standing right near me, and her hand appeared shaky as she held out the gun, so I just grabbed it."

Emily looked up at Gordon. "You know, I'm proud of you, Michael, and so are the boys. I heard them bragging to their friends about how you are going to be a famous politician and get them box seats to Yankees games."

Gordon chuckled. He loved his boys and hoped they wouldn't be too disappointed if he lost the election. But there was something a little odd about Emily. Her voice was softer than usual, and she appeared tired. There were dark circles under her eyes, and it looked like she'd been crying a lot.

Gordon moved his hand through her hair and down the back of her neck. "Is everything OK, Em?"

Emily dropped her coffee cup and began sobbing uncontrollably. Gordon tried to hug her, but she pulled away and hobbled over to the living room couch. She buried her head in a cushion and balled for a full ten minutes. Gordon quickly called his office to push off his 9:00 a.m. meeting and sat across from her in the Queen Anne chair until she finally sat up.

"So do you plan on telling me what's wrong?"

Emily bit down on her front lip, her voice cracking with emotion. "I've got breast cancer."

Gordon's heart fell into his stomach as he struggled for words.

"It's a small lump, Stage II, and they say it may be treatable through a lumpectomy and radiation, without taking off the whole breast."

Tears started to well up in Gordon's eyes. He tried to say something, but his voice was gone.

"I had this weird rash on my palm, so I went to the dermatologist. He didn't know what it was and said I should have an allergist look at my diet. So I went Dr. Korman, who said I was long overdue for a physical. He felt it right away and sent me for tests. I found out yesterday."

Michael moved over to the couch and pushed Emily's head into his chest. He held her for a while, still unable to find the right words.

Emily got up and straightened her sweater. "You go off to work and let me deal with this. I want you acting strong for the kids, and don't mention a word of this to them or to Momma."

"I love you, Em, no matter what," said Gordon.

"I know." Emily walked Gordon to the door and stood at the threshold until he got into his car.

Gordon spent the rest of the day in a daze. It was as if his meetings and phone calls were all happening in a dream. Finally, at six, as he polished off his third cup of coffee, his phone rang, showing a 661 area code with no name on the caller ID. Gordon normally did not pick up cold calls, but he took this one.

"Hi, Michael, it's Max Peoples. Can you meet me at Bryant Park at six thirty?"

The scratchy, rushed voice seemed to belong to a middle-aged man who had the urgency of a used-car salesman making a pitch on the last day of a sale.

"Max who?" Gordon asked as he tried to focus on what the man was saying.

"Max Peoples. I'm helping with your campaign. The professor asked me to give you a call."

"Oh, all right. What did you say your name was again? I apologize, but it's been a rough day."

"Don't worry about names. I'll see you at six thirty."

"But how will I know what you look like?"

The line had gone dead. Gordon didn't know what to make of the call; for all he knew, it might have been some right-to-life nut who had seen his face in the paper. But Gordon was still numb from this morning, and he needed some fresh air.

It was a chilly November evening as Gordon climbed the stairs from Sixth Avenue toward the first row of benches in the park. He sat down next to a pair of college coeds who were absorbed in a YouTube video on their iPad. Five minutes, then ten minutes passed. He looked at his watch. 6:40 p.m. Maybe this whole thing was a prank.

The girls had left and a medium-sized man in a gray overcoat sat down beside him. In his late fifties, Peoples was a handsome man with a full head of hair and the right touches of gray. He could pass for a reputable investment banker.

"You know what Plato said: 'Those who are too smart to engage in politics are punished by being governed by those who are dumber.'"

Gordon turned toward who he thought was Peoples, but didn't recognize the voice. It was deep and soothing, with a hint of a Southern accent. "Sorry, sir, but do I know you?" asked Gordon. He had wandered back into his stupor as he once again contemplated Emily's condition.

"I'm Max Peoples, Michael, your campaign manager."

"Are you the guy who called my office a while ago? You sure don't sound like him."

"Well, sometimes my cell phone reception is spotty and distorts sounds,"

In fact, Peoples had used a sophisticated voice scrambler and a dummy smart card in his cell phone that flashed a Los Angeles area code. These were just a few of the toys the DEA handed out to its special operatives. And Peoples had been around for a while.

The son of a neurosurgeon and a civil engineer, Peoples had grown up in leafy Richmond, Virginia. During medical school at Johns Hopkins, he bragged about becoming a neurosurgeon like his dad. But on Match Day, when medical students found out where they would perform their critically important medical residency, his matches all came up in psychiatric programs. This was almost unheard of, as his top three choices were neurology, orthopedics, and general surgery. Peoples, however, was unaware that his assignments had been manipulated by the army's Military Intelligence Corps, which was secretly recruiting top talent into its advanced PSYOPs programs.

After arriving at the Walter Reed Medical Center, Peoples was assigned to severe trauma cases and quickly gained the attention of Dr. Werner Fleck. Fleck was a pioneer in modern psychological warfare who took Peoples under his wing. Together, they refined various interrogation methods using a combination of drugs and psychoanalysis. Once in private practice in New York City, Peoples took his work a step further, integrating hypnosis into the regimen. While he had formally left the army, Peoples agreed to serve as a civilian consultant so he could continue his collaboration with Dr. Fleck.

He proved his skills under pressure in 1992, when on loan to the DEA, Peoples was called into a hostage situation in Spanish Harlem. A heroin dealer had locked himself and his two young daughters in their seventh-floor apartment, threatening to kill the girls if anyone tried to arrest him. The man had already thrown his three-month-old toddler out the window, and his mental state was deteriorating rapidly from what authorities perceived was heavy heroin use. After quickly reviewing his rap sheet, Peoples noticed repeated arrests for shoplifting at a variety of electronics stores. Peoples headed up to the apartment and began talking to the man through the door. After ten minutes, Peoples convinced the dealer that he had a brand-new Sony boom box to deliver to him so he could calm his nerves during the police siege. As the door opened, a SWAT sniper blew off the man's forehead.

"So you said you were my campaign manager, but I thought Sara Shelby was handling that," said Gordon.

"Ah, Shelby, yes. She certainly was tasked with handling the early stages, but now she's moved over to running the financial side of things, like raising money and financial reporting. I will be helping you develop your campaign message and schedule your appearances."

Peoples sensed Gordon's deep distress over his wife's poisoning. Shelby had tapped into Emily Gordon's e-mail and noticed that she ordered a certain skin cream online. She commandeered a UPS truck and made the delivery, gently placing the stylus in Emily's hand, which she used to sign for the package. A tiny prick inserted Seaver's concoction.

"Have you worked on other campaigns?" asked Gordon.

"Oh, a few some years back," Peoples answered as he carefully scanned the area for anyone out of place. About thirty yards away, Vito Menza sat on the grass clutching a novel. Seaver never sent anyone to an outdoor meeting without a backup.

"We should start meeting on a weekly basis so we can coordinate the campaign," said Peoples.

"Well, can't we just talk on the phone? I've been really busy lately at the office, and the election is still a year away."

"I know. But telephones are so distant. I'm working out of an office in the Verizon building on Forty-Sixth

Street. Suite twenty-three-oh-eight." Peoples pointed over Gordon's shoulder at the building.

"That can serve as our temporary campaign headquarters."

"How about Tuesday nights? That's Emily's bridge night, so she won't mind me getting in late."

Gordon cringed as he mentioned Emily. The thought of her possible death scared and saddened him at the same time. Who would take care of the boys? How would he cope with their grief? It was consuming.

"You know, it's getting a little chilly out here. Why don't we head over to the office now?" Peoples gently took Gordon by the arm as they headed uptown along Sixth Avenue.

The suite was well-appointed, but small. The reception area led to a narrow corridor that opened to two offices and a six-man conference room. Just past the conference room were a locked utility closet and then a small kitchenette. A two-way mirror embedded in a mural on the conference room wall permitted occupants of the utility closet to view inside.

Peoples fetched a cup of hot chocolate for Gordon, who took it in both hands. They went over some campaign literature that laid out Parker's weaknesses in bold-faced bullet points, and then reviewed several web page screenshots. Gordon liked the photo of him and the kids on the flip side of the piece, although he couldn't remember when it had been taken.

"Is everything all right, Michael?" asked Peoples.

"Not really." Gordon seemed despondent, staring aimlessly into his cup. "Today I found out that my wife Emily has breast cancer. You know, I really want to be there for her. With her problems and my workload at the office, I'm not sure how much time I'm going to have for campaigning over the next few months."

"Oh, not to worry, Michael. That's why I'm here. You don't want to get too visible yet and start talking about your positions. You see, for every person who agrees with you, there are those who won't. So in order to avoid alienating anyone with opposing political views, we keep focused a few narrow consensus issues that most people can agree with."

"Like what?"

"Oh, we'll let Jose Ricardo, our pollster, figure that one out for us. He's polling the district now to see what hot-button issues will get people out to vote. At the same time, we're compiling a list of negatives on Parker so we can get people to hate him."

Over the years, Peoples had found that speaking simply, in stark terms, was very effective. No verbosity or Victorian English. Short sentences with easy-to-understand words achieved the best penetration.

"Is there anything else troubling you, Michael?"

Gordon scratched his head and looked over at the window. "Yeah, there are these dreams I've been having lately."

"Dreams? Tell me about them."

"Well, they're all the same. I find myself in bed in a small dark room. I don't recognize the place at all, and while there are no lights, I seem to be able to see a woman coming close. She has sharp features and long, flowing black hair. She slowly creeps into my bed and starts caressing me. After a while, I look up and see her on top of me.

Above her head, there's this large brown cross hanging from the ceiling. And then I wake up."

"Go on," whispered Peoples.

"That's it. Once I see the cross, I wake up. I've had the same dream a few times over the past two months. It can't be Emily in the dream. She has short blond hair. I just can't figure it out. Oh, and one more thing."

"Yes?" prompted Peoples.

"After the dream, I wake up with a bad headache."

"I see. Have you seen a doctor about this?"

"No, not yet."

"Good. It doesn't sound like anything serious, but if it keeps up, let me know. I'll arrange for a doctor to look at you. You don't want to go to your regular physician and risk having your medical records leaked to the Parker camp."

"Yes, of course not."

"Well, it's been nice meeting you," said Michael. "Same time next week?"

"Yes. See you then."

After Gordon had reached the elevator banks, Shelby emerged from the utility closet. "Seaver is not gonna like the bad dreams."

"Well, what do you expect when you leave the pharmacology to a priest?" said Peoples.

Shelby smiled sheepishly as she finished off Gordon's hot chocolate. "Not to worry, the sultry paramour in Gordon's dreams is pregnant. If he goes wandering for this mystery woman, we'll be able to contain it. The last thing Gordon wants to do to his ailing wife is break her heart."

# 15

They checked in on the second floor of the NYU Langone Medical Center. Emily handed her paperwork to the courteous nurse assistant while Michael stood nervously at her side. He disliked hospitals. The antiseptic smell and the dreary silence punctuated by the occasional loudspeaker announcements made him uneasy.

The Hispanic woman in navy-blue scrubs placed the identity bracelet on Emily's left wrist. "You need to go to the ninth floor to Neuroradiology for an injection of dye. Then come back here. You're scheduled for ten forty-five."

Emily almost burst out crying. It was seven thirty and she was scheduled for a nine o'clock procedure. "But my appointment is for nine o'clock."

"Yes, I see," the nurse said calmly. "But the surgeon is running late."

Michael took Emily's arm. "Come on. Let's head to the ninth floor."

They waited together for thirty minutes until a black technician called out Emily's name.

Michael stood and offered his hand, but Emily pulled away.

"Wait for me out here. I'll handle this." Her voice was cold and detached. Michael sat back down, trying to

"Yeah, it's something like that." Gordon turned back to the files on his desk.

Patel got up to leave. "You know, Michael, I once prosecuted a guy who ran for state office in Virginia. His cousin was a DEA agent who gave him classified information on his opponent's son who was a crack addict. The guy sent his opponent photographs of the kid's drug buys. He won the election but had to resign after we indicted him."

Gordon looked up. "How much time did he get?"

"He was sentenced to only three years, but that didn't matter."

"Oh, why not?"

"Because on his second night in jail, his throat was slashed."

Gordon picked up the phone. "Ah, that happens, Prete. I gotta make this call."

"Suit yourself," Patel said, walking out. "But keep your eyes open. If any of these DEA guys step over the line, you better call it off. I don't want to find you on Staten Island in the trunk of a car."

That night, Gordon couldn't sleep. Fixated on maintaining a sterile environment, Emily had him move to the guest bedroom. He fidgeted in bed for a while and started thinking about Patel's warning. It did seem strange that DEA agents were spending so much time with him. But like Patel had said, they probably wanted to invest in a congressman in hopes of career advancement as payback. That seemed pretty normal to Gordon, who was used to the quid pro quo of his legal practice, attending fundraisers and corporate dinners to impress the general counsel, who might throw some business your way. It was a basic tenet of capitalism. Why not play the same game in politics?

He went downstairs for a snack and noticed the light blinking on the answering machine. He hit the play button.

"Emily, it's John. How are you managing? I'm so happy they saved your breast. The thought of never sucking at your perfectly round nipple almost destroyed me. Can't wait until you're back in LA for the Sigmund Freud event next month. Love ya."

Gordon stumbled over to the couch. So it was true. Emily was having an affair. That explained the cold hellos and impersonal behavior at the hospital. His stomach began to hurt. He stayed on the couch the rest of the night, pondering his next move. After three painful hours, he had come to a conclusion. There was nothing to do now. Emily was sick and needed aggressive treatment to contain the cancer. If this brought her joy, so be it. He wasn't going to say anything. On the way up to the shower, he pushed the erase button on the answering machine. Emily's secret was safe, although a part of him had just died.

# 16

The Rayburn House Office Building was an imposing structure on Independence Avenue, just south of the Capitol. Its marble hallways and tall ceilings with finely carved moldings presented an almost royal ambiance to what was basically a glorified office building for the country's elected representatives. Inside Suite 4338, Peggy Tang was three-hole punching the final draft of Parker's prepared remarks for the morning's hearing by the House Subcommittee on Africa, Global Health, and Human Rights. Parker used the SAGH committee, a permanent subcommittee of Foreign Affairs, to pass a bunch of feel-good legislation against things like human trafficking and forced female circumcision. It was 8:15 a.m., and Parker had just arrived.

"Brett, I kept the speech nice and simple so we get clear coverage on C-SPAN," said Tang. "Last time, the ladies at the Longhorse political club in Whiting said they couldn't understand half the things you said."

Tang slipped the speech into a one-inch binder and reached for the lint brush. Standing at attention and facing forward, Parker stood like a six-year-old getting dressed for Sunday school as Tang wiped the dandruff off his left shoulder, straightened his tie, and buttoned down the right collar tab of his white shirt.

Tang was a surprising choice as Parker's chief of staff. Born in Rockland, Maine, to a lobster fisherman and school librarian, Tang had been raised in a left-leaning Democratic environment. After graduating from Dartmouth, she volunteered with the Red Cross in South Africa during the apartheid riots. She settled in DC as the wife of a congressional staffer and was hired by Parker in his first term, thirty years ago.

"Thanks, Peg. Did Father Daly call? I'm supposed to be attending a church function this Saturday in Hamilton, but I can't make it. Just make something up."

"Ahem," Tang said in a raspy voice as she looked down at Parker's waist.

"Oh, sorry about that." Parker chuckled as he zipped up his fly.

Tang placed the binder in Parker's hand and escorted him to the door. From there, Jill Rankin, Parker's personal aide who went everywhere with him to make sure he got to all of his appointments, took over.

By lunchtime, Parker was through for the day. After a swim at the House gym, he headed off to his Centreville home in suburban Northern Virginia.

A native of Montclair in northern New Jersey, he had attended public high school and Rutgers College, where he majored in sociology. Not particularly motivated to help the poor, he went to work in the family's drugstore, pouring pills into bottles that his mother had labeled. After work, he'd hang around at Mulligan's Bar & Grill, where he'd down Budweisers and talk politics with the local yuppie kids. He married his college sweetheart, Jane Tully, and moved to Burlington, commuting to the family's new drugstore in nearby Mount Holly.

During the 1970's, Central Jersey politics were as eventful as watching the Delaware flow past Camden. Congressional districts were hopelessly gerrymandered, and elections were mere formalities. But whether it was naïveté or blind ambition, Parker thought he could take down the twenty-four-year incumbent, Democratic congressman Clyde Masters. After an unopposed primary on the Republican ticket, he got clobbered in the general election. Undeterred, he tried again and hit pay dirt. Masters got caught up in a bribery scandal, and Parker squeaked by to victory.

While his election to the House at the tender age of twenty-nine was not remarkable, his subsequent fourteen election victories had bewildered many political scientists. He was disliked in the Republican caucus because he didn't faithfully tow the party line, didn't raise any money, and didn't have coattails for anyone below him on the ballot. Yet Parker was genuinely likeable. A stocky man at average height with blue eyes and brown hair, he could rile up an NRA crowd in the morning and joke over cheap wine in the evening at a Carpenters Local 141 meeting. And then there was his fanatic opposition to abortion. While not a particularly religious man, Parker had quickly realized that impassioned voters created buzz and showed up on Election Day. In a district with no more than 30 percent voter participation, those pledged to stop the baby killers had a strong impact.

But the years had begun taking a toll on Parker. Jane was struggling with early onset of Parkinson's, and his two daughters had long ago left for college. With Congress's light schedule and long recesses, Parker was having trouble filling his time. Two years ago, a bicycle accident had led to shoulder surgery and physical therapy at Snow Chiropractors in Alexandria. A favorite to members and their staffers, Dr. Gail Snow was as comfortable at a NOW luncheon as she was cracking backs with her classic torque release technique. Parker began confiding in Snow and admitted to bouts of depression and anxiety. He hadn't had sex in more than five years and found himself getting erect when taking showers with young men at the Gold's Gym where he lifted weights on the weekends.

Snow gently urged Parker to try her pelvic therapy. Administered by a young "technician" in a windowless room at the back of the office, this procedure coaxed many of Snow's clients to extend their treatments. While he lay flat on his back with a small hand towel folded over his eyes, a twenty-five-year-old Russian woman gently massaged Parker's naked thighs and stomach while gently brushing and then stroking his genitals until he climaxed. It did wonders for his pathetic sex life, and because it was Dr. Snow's place, Parker felt safe.

The doorbell rang at Parker's split-level four-bedroom house. Dressed in jeans and a bleached Georgetown sweatshirt, Parker seemed surprised by the well-dressed redhead with clipboard in hand.

"Excuse me, sir. I'm from Dominion Virginia Power, and we're running a cost-saving program. We install a custom thermostat on your air-conditioning unit that sets the temperature to seventy-five degrees during periods of extended electricity use and brownouts. For participating, you get a three-hundred-dollar credit on your utility bill."

"Ah, I'm sorry," Parker muttered, backing away from the doorway, "but my wife isn't home now, and you really need to talk with her. I'll tell her you came by."

As the door closed, Shelby tossed the ladybug just inside the threshold. A state-of-the-art device, the ladybug embedded itself under the wall molding and monitored all sounds and wireless information in the home. Every cell phone call and wireless Internet connection was now open to Seaver and his team. The ladybug, which looked like the insect in shape, size, and color, was able to move around, both on the ground and through the air, and was equipped with a thirty-megapixel camera that beamed out encrypted photos in twenty-four- to 105-millimeter angles. Across the street, in a telephone utility truck, Vito Menza completed the installation of a relay transmitter, positioned just behind an electrical transformer about twenty feet up the utility pole that stood opposite Parker's home. After completing a series of diagnostic exams on the bug, Menza started up the truck and signaled left as he pulled away from the curb—a sign that the tap was successful. Shelby continued up the block, slowly heading toward her rental car parked a half mile away.

Within minutes, Bruno and Parisi had real-time access to Parker's e-mail accounts. He had a private address, a campaign address, and a congressional Blackberry account hosted on a House server. Two techs from Enhancements were downloading all of Parker's e-mail, scrubbing for any malware or other hacking activity. The last thing Seaver wanted was some punk engineer from Serbia watching the DEA spec ops plants that were about to come.

The DEA had recognized early on that the Internet would revolutionize communications. While no one in the '90s could predict the extent of the social media frenzy, the proliferation of communications over unlocked networks was a bonanza for both law enforcement and the intelligence services. The NSA and CIA opted for sophisticated satellite-based eavesdropping technology. This provided a morass of information that was fed into servers stationed throughout the country. Filtering the data was an enormous task that was delegated to advanced supercomputers. The DEA took a different approach.

Instead of picking off bits and bytes as they wandered from one cell phone tower to the next, Parisi's team infiltrated the net at its core—at its backbone data centers. Spec ops broke into IBM's headquarters and spliced the server wiring that was ultimately installed in key Internet hubs from San Jose to Ashburn, Virginia. Because the tap was in the hard wiring, it was impossible to detect the eavesdropping. It was as if someone had unknowingly carried a note in front of a mirror. There'd be no way to know that someone had seen the reflection. Separate teams penetrated the vast data center server rooms and ran redundant cable to underground runs, where they were capped off in small safe houses several miles away. This enabled the DEA to not only read e-mail but also manipulate it. E-mails sent from one IP address could now be readdressed and delivered from the mailbox of another sender. Because e-mail bounced between many servers and multiple data centers, manipulated e-mail could be disassembled and reacquired at remote locations, making it impossible to trace the source of the tampering.

Blackberry technology took a bit longer to crack. The DEA had to wait until RIM updated its server platform before it could run a hardware tap. This time, it had to access the Siemens servers in Bavaria. An undercover managed to slip past security and splice twenty-seven servers that went into RIM's mainframe encryption platform at its Slough data center, outside of London. Running the cable was easy. From nearby rented offices, a three-man team tunneled under the single-story slab, drilled into the server room, and pulled cable through the regular underground duct runs.

Back at 852 Flushing Street in Brooklyn, fondly referred to as the "Brooklyn Office," Parisi and Bruno were closeted in a small conference room with Rory Munster, an NSA Mideast specialist on loan to the agency.

"Parker's headed for Ankara for a human rights conference next month. We'll start sending him e-mail traced from known operatives of Islamic Jihad in Istanbul. It'll hit his AOL account, so it will trigger CIA filters," explained Munster.

"Then we'll set up a meet at the conference between Parker and Fatima Jamil, a leading pro-choice activist with known ties to Hamas. Jamil is working both sides of the street and has been short on cash lately."

"But how do we get the Feds to pay attention?" asked Parisi.

"No problem," said Bruno. "We'll plant a lead at the FBI special ops center in downtown Manhattan. They'll run it up the ladder quickly. Menza will handle it."

"All right," said Parisi. "But this can't get offtrack or even go sideways. Any glitches, and we kill and wipe the event."

Bruno nodded. He understood that there could be a lot of unhappy people if the DEA was caught manipulating FBI computers. While there was an inherent distaste at the DEA for the arrogant G-Men, they were supposed to be on the same side, after all. But deep down, Bruno relished the thought of sending the Nebraska farm boys on a wild-goose chase, albeit in the name of the greater national interest. He had heard bits and pieces of conversations between Parisi and Wolf concerning Operation Open Sky but didn't have a clear take on it. One thing was obvious, though; it was a very big deal that was grabbing the involvement of major players who hadn't worked together in a long time. Ten years ago, Bruno would have spent more time trying to get the details. But at this stage, he was already numb to sensational eyes-only missions where the stakes were high and the objectives were nearly impossible to satisfy. It was all "been there, done that" to Carmine, who only stepped out of retirement to hearken the call of Wolf, his longtime superior and mentor.

Bruno drove his white Chevy Blazer down Flushing Avenue toward Ridgewood, Queens. He stepped out at the corner of Metropolitan Avenue and Fresh Pond Road to use the pay phone just outside the CVS drugstore. He dialed a local number.

"Yeah, Rita, it's Tony. I need you to pick up the dry cleaning on your way home from the bakery tonight. I've got a meeting in the morning."

The voice mail message was left on an answering machine in Stuttgart, Germany. Two hours later, Vito Menza received a text message from a telephone number in Jersey City telling him that the New York Rangers were playing the Vancouver Canucks at Madison Square Garden. He then called a local Manhattan number, which played back the message from Bruno. The next morning at 8:30 a.m., Menza would meet Bruno at a Starbucks in SoHo.

# 17

**F**oley Square was a three-acre green space in the midst of a ring of colossal buildings comprising Manhattan's legal center. To the east sat 60 Centre Street, an imposing building of Roman classic architecture that housed New York's civil courthouse. Just next door was 40 Centre, home of the federal appeals court. To the north, among several tall administrative buildings, was the criminal courts building at 100 Centre Street. To the west stood 26 Federal Plaza, an imposing forty-seven-story rectangle sprouting from the ground, which was home to a myriad of federal agencies, including the FBI's New York field office.

It was a crisp January morning as Vito Menza found his way to a bench in Foley Square, just east of the corner of Worth and Centre Streets. The area was bustling with police and corrections officers, attorneys, and off-duty federal agents. Dressed in a navy parka and wool Yankees cap, Menza calmly pulled out what looked like a Kindle from his knapsack as he sipped his Dunkin' Donuts coffee. Under Menza's cap was a transmitter powered by a battery pack taped to his back. On the Kindle, Menza could see all the frequencies of cell phone users on the twenty-eighth floor of the Federal Building, where the FBI housed its antiterrorist unit. With an unobstructed view from his park bench, Menza focused the transmitter on the third window in from the north side of the floor. The cell phone number on his screen belonged to Special Agent Pete Koznicki, a career agent who had hit a dead-end desk job monitoring Internet traffic and filtering intel from foreign law enforcement, CIA, and DoD for the special field ops teams.

Although it was only eight thirty, Koznicki had already been at his desk for two hours, scouring the latest domestic and international feeds. Nothing on this day seemed too out of the ordinary. Interpol had posted a hit-and-run in Frankfurt; an elderly couple was found stabbed to death in a Vail, Colorado, cottage; two Vegas prostitutes complained of rough treatment by a Saudi sheik passing through for an electronics convention. Suddenly, Koznicki's phone started buzzing. It was an out-of-area caller with no ID. Koznicki picked up.

"Pete here."

But there was only faint static on the other end.

Koznicki thought it was a bad connection and hung up. It might have been a wrong number or maybe a field agent trying to get through. He turned back to his computer.

Menza had successfully planted a computer worm on Koznicki's phone. Within seconds, the worm linked to Koznicki's desktop through his phone's office e-mail account. Menza now had access to the FBI's antiterrorist computer network.

Back at the DEA, Rory Munster began receiving data from Koznicki's desktop. He sent an e-mail from Fatima Jamil's Gmail account, which went by the name of "Samona."

*Worker bees from your hive have left the queen.*

Koznicki was surprised by the contact, as he hadn't worked with Jamil since the immediate aftermath of September 11. He responded under his account name, "Frogman."

*What nectar is the bee carrying?*

Samona: *An elf of the house has been smoking foreign cigars.*

Frogman: *Interesting.*

Samona: *Standard package for tasty bacon?*

Koznicki paused for a moment. He knew that he had only thirty seconds to respond, or Jamil would sign off, thinking that he had lost interest. The reference to foreign cigars meant an Eastern Bloc espionage operation, which pointed to the Russians. An "elf of the house" meant a member of the US House of Representatives. Koznicki was hoping for a Republican, as he had to lead a secret gay life in order to stay with the bureau, and found comfort in the Democratic platform on same-sex marriage. But he needed authorization to agree to a standard pay package. Ten seconds left. There was no time to get the clearance. Five seconds.

Frogman: *Yes.*

Koznicki had barely gotten off the message. He waited. Three minutes, and nothing from Jamil. He began squirming in his chair, fearing he had lost an opportunity to land a huge investigation that would push him up the chain into field ops. Then, finally, the response came.

Samona: *Regards from Paris.*

Koznicki breathed a sigh of relief. It was game on. He had seen several intelligence reports warning that the Russians were targeting US political figures through sexual blackmail, but this was the first hard lead. He still had to run this past supervising agent Jean Dawson, head of the Special Crimes Unit, but he was confident that she would approve the "standard" $50,000 payoff that he had promised Jamil if the information was good.

Two days later, the package arrived by regular mail. Postdated in Paris, Tennessee, the eight-and-a-half-by-eleven-inch manila envelope contained black-and-white photos of Brett Parker getting his "pelvic therapy" from Carla Eshrova, the young tech at Snow's chiropractic office. Koznicki scanned the photo and ran Eshrova through the face-recognition program. Her file came up two minutes later. Born in Ukraine, she was the only daughter of Yuri Topkin, a colonel in the Russian FSB. She had a law degree from Moscow State University and was in the United States on a student visa while enrolled in a tax LLM program at Georgetown.

Koznicki stared at the visa photograph of the attractive blond-haired, blue-eyed coed and felt a sense of disgust that an FSB officer would send his only daughter on a honeytrap mission. But what would they want with Brett Parker, a nobody congressman with no access to sensitive intelligence? Maybe Parker wasn't as stupid as he looked. Koznicki downloaded the file and went to see Dawson.

"You're shitting me." Dawson chuckled as Koznicki finished his three-minute pitch in her office. "You want fifty grand for a hand-job photo from a washed-up Arab bitch who's been off grid for more than ten years?"

"But this is an FSB plant, a colonel's daughter working for Gail Snow," pleaded Koznicki.

Dawson threw the file on her desk. "Who gives a shit? She probably needs rent money or maybe has a coke habit that Papa can't finance on his government salary. We don't have fifty grand to throw at this garbage. And for what? To nail Brett Parker? He's a walking moron who wants to criminalize birth control so we can lock up more dysfunctional black kids and white trash whose welfare mothers can't care for them."

Back at DEA headquarters in Brooklyn, Munster wasn't happy with the conversation. He had activated the microphone on Koznicki's phone when he tracked him heading up to the executive suite on the thirtieth floor. He could now see Koznicki heading back down to twenty-eight. Dawson had basically kicked him out of her office.

Munster headed over to the conference room where Parisi was holding a staff meeting and motioned to him at the door. As Parisi stepped out, Munster conveyed the bad news.

"Dawson wouldn't approve the package."

Parisi rubbed his chin and began to swear.

Seeing the discomfort on his boss's face, Bruno joined the discussion in the corridor.

"Not to worry," said Bruno. "We'll feed this through Norm Hudson, who's chief of rackets at the US Attorney's Office in Alexandria."

"How much dirty traffic have you run through Parker's AOL account?" asked Parisi.

"About fifteen messages over the past thirty days," responded Munster.

"OK, so Parker's been tagged by the CIA," reasoned Parisi.

"And NSA," added Munster. "We've been sending him messages from Hezbollah and Muslim Brotherhood."

"Yeah, but everyone's busy tracking down al-Qaeda. They aren't gonna do anything about Parker for another six months," said Bruno.

"How well do you know Hudson?" asked Parisi.

"The professor and I handed him his first big case, and we've stayed in touch," said Bruno.

"Will he leak when the time comes?"

"I think so."

Parisi bit his lip. "That's not good enough."

"I can get access to Hudson's e-mail traffic in a heartbeat," said Munster. "If he doesn't leak on cue, we'll do it for him."

"But that would end his career," said Bruno.

Parisi simply stared into Bruno's eyes, not caring to waste his breath responding to Bruno's whimpering pity for some pathetic career prosecutor in Northern Virginia.

"Make it happen," Parisi said as he headed back into the conference room.

Munster and Bruno hurried into a side room. Time was short, as both men were concerned that Koznicki would bury the file after getting his head handed to him by Dawson.

Bruno picked up the phone.

"Attorney Hudson's office. How may I direct your call?" came the response from a young secretary.

"Ah, tell him it's Herman from the Yale Club."

"One moment, please."

"Carmine, how the hell have ya been, pal? It's been forever." Hudson was a jovial man who enjoyed hunting and drinking beer—pastimes that he had shared with Bruno on several occasions. Married to a nice Italian girl from

Bayside, Queens, he had nine children and was content working for Uncle Sam at $150K a year.

"Norm, it's great to hear your voice. Look, I'm in a bit of a jam. We've got some fresh intel on a Russian honeytrap out of Gail Snow's place."

"Well, that's no surprise. Half the Hill gets their backs cracked there. She's quite connected. Who's the target?"

"We're not certain, but we think it's Brett Parker."

"You've gotta be kidding me. My wife is one of his biggest fans. Shows up at all his right-to-life functions. Thinks he's some kind of reincarnated saint."

Munster rolled his eyes. Not another dead end. But Bruno pressed on.

"Look, Norm, we think the bureau is working something up on this, and we don't want to step on any toes. This really isn't our turf."

"OK, I'll give it a look. Who's the contact at the bureau?"

"Dawson, out of Manhattan South."

"I know her. Surprised to hear she's still around. Thought she'd been aged out by now."

"No, she's still around."

"You want feedback on this?"

"No, you run with it. Thanks a bunch, Norm."

Two hours later, the phone rang on Koznicki's desk. His shift was about done, and he had already tossed Jamil's photos in the wastebasket under his desk. It was Dawson.

"Send that bullshit intel on Parker to Norm Hudson in EDVA. Seems he's on to something."

That was it. Dawson had hung up before Koznicki could give his response. He dismissed her as another homophobe, but was glad that he didn't have to stiff Jamil. He knew that would be the end of his credibility and that all further leaks would dry up. He retrieved the file and placed it in the special courier out-box. Time to head home to his studio apartment in Alphabet City. He had a date with a young Wall Street investment banker.

# 18

The winter months passed almost uneventfully. Max Peoples had introduced Gordon to all the county chairs in the district and was assured an uncontested spot on the June primary ballot. There was a slight glitch when it came to the visit with Vinny Cara, the Shore County chair. Shore County was a Democratic stronghold, and Cara ran it like the patriarch of an eighteenth-century Sicilian family. The principal of a four-man law firm, Cara delivered the votes for every state position, from freeholder to township committee to local sheriff. In return, his firm represented twenty-six municipalities and sixteen school districts. The fees were fixed, regardless of the workload, and served as a handsome annuity to Cara and his law partners. It was New Jersey politics at its best—legal bribery that even self-absorbed and opportunistic US attorneys like Chris Christie couldn't crack.

Cara wanted a vig for putting up Gordon. Seaver was livid. After debating whether to poison him with a horrific new compound reserved for known terrorists or simply set him up for a thirty-year federal prison term, Seaver approved, at Peoples's urging, a $10,000 cash drop at Cara's yacht club. Peoples recognized the usefulness of men like Cara who reliably delivered results, while Seaver detested political corruption. It was quite a conversation, as Peoples needed to remind Seaver that this entire operation was about as politically corrupt as it got. The payment satisfied Cara, who explained it as Gordon's club membership fee that was needed to prop up the unknown's credentials among party leaders.

Gordon was holding up pretty well and still had no clue that he was being manipulated. Emily's breast cancer had gone into remission after three months of chemo, and she had thrown herself back into work. The affair with the LA psychiatrist had come to an end, albeit not through Emily's devices. To Seaver's surprise, Emily had grown closer to her paramour during her convalescence, as Gordon spent more time away from home, juggling work and politics. It ended when Shelby tapped into the shrink's computer and forwarded pictures of the professor in bed with one of his patients to Emily, who apparently was OK with cheating on her husband but couldn't handle being betrayed herself.

It was Tuesday evening, and Peoples was going over the coming week's events with Gordon. There was a Saturday-afternoon fundraiser at BLT Steak, and he was to speak at the Point Beach Democratic Committee meeting on Monday at seven. Gordon, as usual, simply listened to Peoples's reports and agreed with most of it. At 8:10 p.m., Gordon began checking his watch. He wanted to be home by nine to catch the kids before they went to bed.

"Great going as usual, Max," said Gordon. "I'd better be off now, as the next train leaves at eight twenty-four."

"Ah, there's a brief stop that we need to make first," Peoples said as he reached for his raincoat.

"Stop?" Gordon asked incredulously.

"Yeah, there's a dinner over at the Waldorf—a farewell party for a managing director at JP Morgan. There are a few wealthy donors that I want you to meet."

"Oh, not tonight, Max. We've got more than two hundred K in the bank, and there's plenty of time to meet with donors. I've really got to catch this train."

Gordon reached for the door as Peoples grabbed his shoulder.

"It'll be just a few moments, I promise, Michael. You'll catch the eight fifty-one."

Gordon paused. He knew he owed a lot to Peoples for handling all the daily responsibilities of the campaign. There was no way Gordon could have kept up his law practice without Peoples's help. But he really did want to see the kids, as Ryan was presenting a science experiment that they had worked on together, and he wanted to make sure it was perfect.

"All right." Gordon shrugged. "Let's go."

The main ballroom at the Waldorf was a palatial space that once hosted the cream of society. The balconies were draped in red velvet bunting, and gold-and-pink tapestries lined the walls. Large crystal chandeliers hung from the twenty-foot ceilings, casting a pale-yellow pall upon the guests. But the room was stale, living off the chic and opulence of yesteryear. The oriental carpet was worn, and the decor screamed of the 1960s. Gobbled up by the Hilton chain, the Waldorf had become just another point of reference on a controller's monthly profit-and-loss report.

Peoples quickly ushered Gordon to the head table, where JP Morgan's head of personal banking was working into a two-inch-thick tenderloin.

"This is Mike Gordon, the New Jersey congressional candidate I mentioned the other day at the bank."

The banker slobbered down the large chunk of steak that he had just placed in his mouth and quickly wiped away the steak sauce from his chin. "Oh, yes, a pleasure to meet you, Mr. Gordon. I've heard wonderful things."

Gordon was bored. He'd met dozens of the same stuffy types—moneyed men who believed they could buy political influence with a few of their dollars. He turned toward the tables just beyond the dais and caught the eye of a striking brunette seated next to a Catholic priest. She had sharp, pointed features and long brown hair. Her gown revealed her bare shoulders, and Gordon couldn't help but notice her healthy cleavage. As he moved closer, he seemed to recognize the priest.

Peoples grabbed Gordon's arm and escorted him over to Father Murphy.

"Good evening, Michael," Murphy said as he stood to greet Gordon. "So, we meet again. How's the campaign going?"

Gordon shook Murphy's outstretched hand but couldn't take his eyes off Stella. He thought he knew her from someplace but couldn't remember where.

Murphy could sense Gordon's confusion and didn't waste any time. "So I see you've noticed my daughter Stella. She does seem to attract a fair amount of attention."

Peoples gently elbowed Gordon in the side to break his stare.

"Oh, yes, I'm sorry, Father. It's great to see you again," Gordon said as his face turned red.

"You mentioned that this was your daughter, but—"

"She's my adopted daughter," Murphy interrupted before Gordon could finish his sentence.

As Stella stood up, her loose-fitting gown betrayed a bump at her midsection. She was six months pregnant and carrying it well. Gordon hardly noticed.

"So nice to meet you, Mr. Gordon. I'm Stella Murphy."

Gordon focused on her piercing blue eyes as he struggled to fight his sense of déjà vu. He kept thinking that he knew this woman. While Peoples made some small talk, Gordon's gaze kept returning to Stella's plunging neckline and her half-naked breasts. Peoples prodded him again by squeezing his left shoulder blade.

"Michael's had a rough day and has a train to catch. It's been wonderful seeing you again, Father," said Peoples. "Good night, Ms. Murphy."

Peoples attempted to tear Gordon away, but after taking two steps, he freed himself from Peoples's grip and headed back toward Stella.

"Excuse me, ma'am, but do we know each other?"

"Yes, I believe we met some months ago in my father's study over a cup of tea. I was dressed a bit more conservatively then."

Gordon still couldn't make the connection. The strong drugs he was given that night made the events seem like a dream. He didn't understand what his brain was signaling. He felt a sense of recognition but couldn't match it with a clear recollection of events.

"I enjoyed our last meeting," Stella said softly as she took a step toward him. "I hope we do meet again."

Stella brushed past Gordon as she headed to talk with those seated at another table. Gordon felt her arm touch his, and he inhaled her musk fragrance. The sensations took a deep toll on him as he headed for his train at Penn Station.

Peoples gave Murphy a brief nod as he left the ballroom. The encounter had pushed Gordon's previous sexual contact with Stella to the forefront of his mind, albeit from Gordon's vantage point, he'd only be dreaming about her. Yet this refreshed the attraction that had begun to fade from Gordon's unconscious. She would occupy his attention for the entire forty-five-minute ride home. That night, his thoughts would be consumed with her. Gordon would now be even more aroused the next time he met Stella, which would probably be after she bore his son, the one she was carrying in her womb.

Peoples, the psychiatrist, had plied his trade well. The insurance policy on Gordon's cooperation had just gone up in value.

# 19

"*Rien n'est impossible à un prêt mond,*" Ricardo said as he sipped a cup of fresh lemonade just outside Antonio's Pizza on the Seaside Heights boardwalk.

Seaver walked beside him in a polo shirt, bleached denim shorts, sandals, and white straw hat. Just behind the two was Shelby, in a cotton jumper and flip-flops. With her hair tied back in a bow, she passed for Seaver's daughter. It was a beautiful summer morning on the Jersey Shore, and the boardwalk was full of local folk and New York day-trippers from Brooklyn and Staten Island.

They made their way over to a small bench facing the ocean as Seaver finished off a taco.

"'Nothing is impossible to a willing mind.' I like that," said Seaver. "Where'd you pick that one up?"

"From my philosophy professor at Stanford," said Ricardo. "He had a proud French lineage and would often pop off some smart-sounding proverb."

Shelby rolled her eyes. They only had fifteen minutes to meet, as protocol did not permit open-air meetings for longer, and these guys were waxing poetic.

"Gordon is still in the toilet," said Ricardo. "Down twenty-five. Nobody wants to pay any attention. My guy at the *Star-Ledger* won't return my calls, and the *Inquirer* says they don't give a shit. Even the *Asbury Park Press* told me to go jerk off. We've done some soft mailings, but they aren't getting any traction. People just don't care."

Seaver popped a roasted almond in his mouth. "Sounds like we need to do something to grab their attention."

"Well, we've already staged three events that made the press, but nothing has stuck. The one with the right-to-life bitch that pulled a gun. One where Gordon pulled a couple out of a burning car on the turnpike. That took some doing, by the way. We had to detonate just under the left rear axle of the Honda Odyssey to make sure the car spun onto the right shoulder but did not topple over. We then had an incendiary go off under the hood. Gordon was five car lengths behind, with Peoples behind the wheel. Peoples did the actual extraction, but Gordon got the credit and the press."

"Yeah, I read about that myself," said Seaver. "It made the *LA Times.*"

"And, just last month, he won a million-dollar Powerball ticket and gave the proceeds to the New Jersey chapter of the Red Cross."

"Million-dollar Powerball is soft stuff," mused Seaver. "Those machines are toys."

"Well, we couldn't have another dramatic rescue without raising eyebrows."

Shelby leaned against the back of the bench, facing the boardwalk, making sure her two chaperones were not attracting any attention. Across the way, in front of the Shore Point Arcade, a muscular young man in ripped jeans and a T-shirt was making eyes at her. Locking his gaze, Shelby blew a huge bubble with the two pieces of Bazooka she was chewing that practically covered her face. By the time the bubble popped, the guy was gone.

Leaning over slightly backward, but keeping her eyes forward so as not to lose sight of the perimeter, she chimed into the conversation.

"Going from forty to twenty-five on just good-guy press is not bad. Wait till you see what we do to Parker."

Seaver kept his gaze straight ahead at the middle-aged woman in a two-piece bathing suit wading in the shallow water. He envied her. Indulging in the simplicities of life with her grandchild at her feet, it didn't matter much that she only earned $40,000 a year, the median for these parts, and never wrote a check for more than $1,600 in her life. She had the ability to shut out the world and enjoy the earth. He wondered what it would be like to have a family. He had always been fond of children but had never found the time to settle down. The demands of the job prevented it. He reasoned that it would be better never to have loved than to have loved and lost.

"We're gonna get bloody," said Seaver.

"Ah, from what I understand, mission protocol is no body count," Ricardo said haltingly as he looked over at the back of Shelby's head.

"Who said anything about a body count? All I said was blood." Seaver tossed another few toasted almonds into his mouth. "Paula Geelan is a fat, rich, bored activist in Georgetown who chairs the Brett Parker right-to-life organization. She's not just your average religious freak who preaches that birth control is murder. She wants to criminalize abortion for rape victims.

"Well, what Paula doesn't know is that her seventeen-year-old daughter, Coleen, is getting boned regularly by her high school boyfriend. Last week, we swapped her birth control pills with dummies. In fact, she might be getting pregnant as we speak. I hear she likes to get laid in the morning.

"Coleen is going to have a very bloody and very publicized miscarriage brought on by her attempt to abort her fetus with a twisted wire hanger. She'll be hospitalized, with CNN right outside her doorstep, and no one to blame but our right-to-life poster boy Brett Parker whose preaching Paula wouldn't dare disobey."

Ricardo sat back and smiled. He wasn't surprised that Seaver would victimize a seventeen-year-old kid, but he marveled at the optimism that something like this could be pulled off. He turned back toward Shelby, who had a half-smoked cigarette in her mouth and had drawn her oversize sunglasses down over her eyes. She launched into the details of the plan.

"We come in to the kid's bedroom at three thirty a.m. with aerosol hyaluronidase, which makes sure she stays out. She then gets an injection of a small concoction that Bill has worked up, a compound of ethinyl estradiol and levonorgestrel, with a couple other goodies that quickly dissipate the increased hormonal levels, and she starts bleeding like shit within two hours. We leave a bloody hanger covered in her prints after we insert a catheter up her crack to bust the placenta."

"Sounds a bit risky if the forensics don't add up," said Ricardo. "Look, we have an ongoing investigation out of

EDVA linking Parker to a Russian spy. Why don't we see how that plays?"

Ricardo was searching for some affirmative body language from Seaver or Shelby, yet neither was looking in his direction.

Shelby gently nudged the back of her elbow into Seaver's shoulder. It was time to go.

Seaver stood up and now faced Ricardo for the first time since they had linked up on the boardwalk.

"We're gonna go with a parade of horribles. First, we spread some photos of Parker in his underwear on Twitter and Facebook, à la Tony Weiner. The images will come from his personal phone that we have infiltrated, so he can deny all he wants. Then we leak photos of his massages at Snow Chiropractors to the *New York Post*. We have a solid blackmail over the editor there, so he'll do what we ask. We follow up with a high-profile arrest of Carla Eshrova on immigration charges, and the world learns about Yuri Topkin's daughter. We end with Colleen Geelan recuperating from a dirty abortion at GW Hospital because she was too scared to talk about it with her Brett Parker–fanatic mom."

"This is gonna make the job we did for Lopez look clean," said Ricardo.

Seaver turned toward Shelby, who was waiting by his side.

"I would start this next month and stagger until right after Labor Day," said Ricardo. "This should bring us within ten."

"Good," said Seaver. "We'll do the rest the old-fashioned way. Cheers."

Seaver and Shelby made their way down the boardwalk as Ricardo sat back down on the bench. He would stay there for another hour.

"Don't you love the smell of the ocean spray this time of year?" mused Seaver.

"Yeah, it brings back memories of youth."

Seaver gave Shelby a curious look, as if asking when she had actually left her youth.

"Don't give me the eyes," said Shelby. "People might think we're an item."

"And what would be so bad about that?"

Shelby was taken aback by the comment. "You know that work and play don't mix."

"Yes, you're right." Seaver sighed. "But I would like to have youth again."

"Keep the dream," said Shelby. "Sometimes it's better than the real thing."

Seaver smiled as they continued walking.

They reached the parking lot, and Shelby headed for her motorcycle.

"Rumor has it that Hans Lange attended Father Murphy's Palm Sunday mass," said Shelby.

"Yes, the professor mentioned it. But, not to worry, Henry is a fanatic about backup plans. You heard Ricardo; we'll be within ten by Labor Day."

Seaver continued down the street toward the NJ Transit bus stop. He'd be taking the local back to New York.

# 20

Topkin didn't travel much and had never been to the United States. So it was quite a surprise to find him strolling about the Broome County Fair, where Gordon and local Democratic candidates were sponsoring a political outing.

Gordon smiled brightly as he worked the crowd of more than three hundred who had come out to gorge on hot dogs, hamburgers, and pumpkin pie. On the far side of the fairgrounds, Peoples was lecturing a union official about the campaign's support for card check. Young volunteers handed out *Go for Gordon* bumper stickers while signing up volunteers for phone banking and lawn signs come October.

It didn't take long to spot Topkin. Standing alone beside a picnic table and holding an uneaten hot dog, he looked like a misfit. Dressed in loose-fitting jeans that had too much stitching and a polo shirt that had a short zipper running from the neck like a warm-up suit, Topkin looked like he had just stepped off a cruise liner on a Mediterranean stopover. He had the traditional Russian male look, with a chiseled jaw, ruddy complexion, and cropped sticklike hair.

Peoples gave a slight nod to Menza, who was working one of the barbecues.

"Good morning, comrade," Menza said in Russian.

Topkin didn't look surprised to have been spotted, nor was he concerned. He, too, had a body man on-site. Lying on the grass about twenty yards away was a young couple sitting over a picnic basket. They were two Spetsnaz commandos. Rumor had it that a good one could rip out a man's heart with his bare hands and stuff it in his victim's mouth before the body hit the ground.

Topkin didn't respond to Menza but merely turned away and started walking toward his car. The young couple followed behind as they all climbed into a rented Chevy Impala.

The fair continued unabated. Gordon gave a rousing speech promising to support senior entitlements like Social Security and Medicare while pledging funding to Planned Parenthood. The crowd was enthusiastic, and for the first time in the campaign, Gordon started feeling confident about the race. A recent Monmouth University poll found Parker ahead by only fifteen points.

As the crowd began dwindling and the barbecue pits began to smolder, Peoples approached Menza.

"Topkin wanted to be noticed. Get word to Parisi."

Menza got on his ten-speed Schwinn and started pedaling off down Culver Avenue. At a light, he asked a pedestrian if he could make a quick call on her cell phone. He dialed an 800 number to a Citibank center. After the prompt, he typed a series of numbers and hung up.

Ten minutes later, a woman rushed into Parisi's office with a typed note and a folder.

"Code Red. Labrador appeared," said the woman.

Inside the folder was a full-length photo of Colonel Yuri Topkin.

Bruno was still on his phone when he entered Parisi's office. Parisi tossed over the file.

"Apparently Ivan isn't happy about our treatment of Ms. Eshrova," Parisi said as he melted into a leather chaise beside his desk.

"We need to shut this down ASAP," cautioned Bruno. "The last thing we want is a scorned father, who happens to be a spy, nosing around Gordon's campaign."

"He already knows the campaign is spiked," said Parisi. "Why else would he show at a campaign event?"

"Seaver must have something in mind. He had to have known that grabbing Eshrova would set off a shitstorm," said Bruno.

"Well, if he's got something going, he sure hasn't clued us in," said Parisi. "I'll report this up to Henry, and he can take it from there. As of now, we stick to the mission."

Bruno headed back down the hall. As he entered his office, he found Bill Seaver with his feet up on his desk, puffing on a Marlboro long. Bruno froze for a moment at the spectacle. He hadn't seen Seaver in years.

"Remember that black girl who used to drive Juan Gomez around in Bogotá?" asked Seaver.

Bruno had to think for a minute, but then it came back. Gomez was the muscle for Carlos Plaza, a drug baron who controlled half the mountains outside of Medellin. He drove around in a white Bentley chauffeured by this hot young black girl they called "Spider."

"Yeah, I remember. We called her Spider."

"Two weeks ago, I got a friend request from her on my Facebook page. She now goes by the name Cynthia Brooks, associate professor of criminal justice at Tulane University. She was one of ours."

"So that's how we got the address of Gomez's mistress's house in Cartagena."

"We got a lot more than that. She mapped out dozens of smuggling routes throughout South America and Europe." Seaver took a puff on his cigarette and slowly exhaled. "Eshrova is also one of ours."

Bruno's jaw dropped. *Of course,* he thought. There was no way Seaver would compromise this mission by picking an unnecessary fight with the Russians.

"We recruited her at Moscow University. Now she's headed back to the industrial espionage unit so Daddy can keep a closer eye on her. He wasn't happy about her massage therapy. We should be getting a pretty good handle on what Topkin and his bureaucratic cronies are selling to the black market." Seaver headed toward the lone window in the room and dropped his cigarette butt into Bruno's flowerpot. "Topkin is not interested in our little operation. He showed up in Broome County to confirm that Gordon is being handled. This way, he can tell his boss that daughter Carla didn't slip up on her own. Wasn't too bright to engage at the fair. We did the job for him."

"I wasn't involved with that, Bill. That was Peoples's call," Bruno said as Seaver walked out the door.

"Yes, I assumed you'd say that. It's convenient to blame others."

Seaver left without saying good-bye. He apparently still held a grudge against Bruno from their time in Colombia.

But Bruno was a hardened man and didn't care much about Seaver's feelings. He grabbed his plant and threw it in the wastebasket. Bruno wasn't about to take any chances with Seaver's cigarette butt.

# 21

The man's heaving thrusts grew deeper between Shelby's legs as the handsome body builder she had brought home to her studio apartment in SoHo kept up a steady rhythm. Sex was just another bodily function to Shelby. No fluttering heartbeats or flushed cheeks. After dozens of undercover operations in which she had feigned her identity and her emotions, reality was boring. She couldn't identify sex with intimacy, for she had spent many emotionless nights in bed with strangers to solicit information, gain trust, or commit murder.

Shelby felt no remorse over the dozens of people she had terminated on behalf of her country. One incident, though, did sometimes come back to her as she lay awake at night. It was a couple from Sofia. He was a military attaché assigned to the Bulgarian consulate in Washington. A senior Mafia figure, he organized the transfer of South American cocaine through Varna and other Bulgarian ports. His wife, thirty years his junior, was a former model. They had placed an ad on Craigslist looking for a woman who would do a threesome. Shelby arrived at the Madison Hotel, just blocks from the White House, and headed up to Suite 479. He was already naked, while the wife was wearing scanty black lingerie.

"Here's your money," the man said as he tossed five hundred-dollar bills onto the dresser. "Now strip."

Shelby gently slid out of the strapless red dress she had on and stood in only a pink thong and white five-inch pumps.

The woman had removed her panties and was lying spread eagle on the bed. Shelby went to her and pushed her face between the woman's legs. The man moved behind and peeled off Shelby's panties. They went at it for ten minutes, until the man left to the bathroom to take a call on his cell phone. Shelby crept up along the woman's body, as if to kiss her lips. Then, with a sudden jerk, she snapped the woman's neck and covered the corpse's face with a pillow.

She lay beside the dead woman as the man reappeared. He was short and bald, with a hanging beer belly. He threw himself on her and began kissing her neck. Shelby raised her left leg and removed a three-inch razor from her shoe heel. As he moved up to kiss her lips, she slit his throat. Blood squirted violently as he gasped for air. Shelby watched unamused until he lay motionless. She then tucked the couple under the blanket and took a quick shower. As she left, she noticed how peaceful they looked lying together, dead, propped up on goose down pillows. It was that peaceful image that Shelby remembered.

After getting back to the States from her various tours in South America, Shelby settled into Lower Manhattan and enjoyed the single life. Weekends were spent engrossed in the latest novel or watching a recent release at the corner theater. It was as if she lived on her own private planet.

Men were her preference, but she also enjoyed a woman's touch on occasion. It was mostly younger college or grad school types who hung around the NYU area. She hardly ever dated anyone twice; one-night stands were easy to come by.

Her life was her work. She adored Bruno and viewed him as a father figure. Peoples was a political junky and had interesting perspectives on the news of the day. Menza, though, was a strange bird. He never spoke much and refused to fraternize. He was almost robot-like.

Seaver was very special to Shelby. He had signed the recommendation that transferred her to the Brooklyn field office, and she marveled at his genius and ingenuity. He had saved countless agents' lives, including hers, with the tools he provided them.

On one such occasion, it was a rainy night at the El Caribe, a seedy bar in downtown Mexico City. Shelby was on a straight recon mission: plant a couple of bugs, hook up a transmitter at the back of the old outhouse behind the club, and get out of there. She was at the bar having a drink when a couple of day laborers sat down beside her. They started groping her chest and insisted that she come home with them. She tried to resist, but they became more assertive. One of the men had a revolver tucked in his waistband.

Shelby was in a bind. She had planted the transmitter the night before, but she still had two listening devices to deliver. In perfect Spanish, she told the taller man that she wanted to do him right there in the bar and that she couldn't wait to get back to his place. She led him into the men's room. As he pulled down his pants, Shelby removed what looked like a hairpin from the lined border of her blouse and jabbed it into the man's neck. Within seconds, the man was comatose. Shelby called for the companion and explained that she thought the tall guy had had a brain seizure. The friend made a quick phone call, and within minutes, five burly men in a pickup truck arrived and dragged off their beleaguered colleague. It turned out the pair were soldiers for a Colombian prostitution ring, and had she gone with them, she would have been shipped off to Eastern Europe as a sex slave.

The body builder finally finished and rolled off Shelby. He didn't talk much as he reached for a cigarette.

"Live around here?" asked Shelby.

"No, I'm from Queens, studying art history at NYU," the guy said as he stared blankly at the ceiling.

After two minutes of silence, Shelby tried to keep the conversation going.

"Well, you sure do keep in shape. Where do you work out?"

"There's a New York Health and Racket Club over on Spruce. I do weights there."

More silence.

Shelby could see that the man had the intellect of a snail.

She got up to use the bathroom and asked the guy to lock the door when he left.

The man quickly grabbed Shelby's cell phone and placed it against his own, transferring the tracer program via the Bluetooth connection. He then dressed and quickly left.

Two hours later, a computer printer on the sixth floor of the Lubyanka Building in downtown Moscow spit out a short message from Ivan Kochenko.

*The carrot is planted.*

Topkin was pleased.

# 22

**B**y October, the campaign had reached a feverish intensity. Gordon had taken leave from his law practice and was knocking on doors from 6:00 a.m. until dusk. Republican operatives at the RCCC began receiving disturbing reports from field operators sensing a tilt away from Parker in the electorate. The last RCCC poll in July showed Parker ahead by twenty-five, and there was some discussion about doing another one. But the regional director waved it off, reasoning that Parker had no chance of losing to a newcomer, especially when the generic congressional polling was showing Republicans with 59 percent. The resources were needed elsewhere.

The Republican approach appeared to be working. They were sticking to the reliable and tested game plan of running a low-key campaign, with the local Republican machine mustering the necessary bodies to make the cold calls and door-to-door stops. Gordon's weekly internal polling showed Parker ahead by fifteen points, with hardly a nudge in the past three weeks despite a blitz of direct mail and cable ads. Gordon seemed resigned to a loss, but Peoples constantly reassured him that an upset was in the making. After weeks of exhausted campaigning, Gordon took a night off to sit with his old pal, John Berger.

The decor at the Four Seasons restaurant on Fifty-Second Street was surprisingly simple for an upscale hotel. Gordon was seated at a corner booth, munching on bread-sticks while he perused the menu. John Berger was running late, so he ordered two appetizers. He knew Berger would eat whatever was on the table.

Vito Menza sat at the bar, keeping an eye on Gordon. It was two weeks before the election, and Gordon was being watched around the clock. Dressed in a navy-blue suit, Menza passed for a Wall Street banker. He placed an expensive-looking ballpoint pen containing a sensitive recording device on the bar, pointing it toward Gordon's table.

Berger arrived a half hour late and gave Gordon a bear hug. Catching his breath, he slid into the plush bench seat against the wall and grabbed a glass of water.

"Whew, what a day, Mike. Dow popped two hundred in the morning and closed down thirty-five. You have any idea how good that is for traders like me?"

Gordon nodded in agreement, although he had a very poor understanding of why Berger was allowed to make a living at what he did. To him, there was no rationale for permitting Las Vegas–style gambling in financial markets that dictated the fortunes of millions of American pensioners. The fact that investments were referred to as "bets" disgusted him.

"I'm starved," said Berger. "I'm gonna order a sixteen-inch steak with a bottle of fine red wine."

A petite blond woman approached the table and took their order.

"So how's the campaign?" Berger's words were hard to make out through his mouthful of mussels. "Spend any time with the professor?"

"Oh, we haven't spoken since the alligator hunt last year. We almost got swallowed by a twenty-foot monster that I shot with a .357 Magnum."

"No shit, you shot something? I thought you Peace Corps guys don't do guns."

"Believe me, I didn't know what I was doing. We were on this dinghy rowboat in the middle of nowhere, and the thing climbed aboard and was about to have me for lunch."

"Well, that can certainly be motivating."

"So who's running your campaign?"

"This guy named Max Peoples—a real pro. We meet once a week, and he schedules everything for me."

"Peoples, ay? Never heard of him."

The conversation turned to family and work. Berger's oldest had been accepted to Princeton, and he was complaining about having to spend $60,000 a year to have his kid turn into a frat boy. Gordon spoke of Emily's breast cancer and how the whole ordeal had brought them closer.

Berger was halfway through his steak when Gordon changed the subject.

"You know, John, I never understood why I have all these DEA people helping me. They even took me to Haiti to meet a big donor."

Berger started coughing uncontrollably. Gordon got up to pat his back, but Berger waved him off. His face turned beet red as he reached for a glass of wine and took a large gulp.

After about five minutes of heavy breathing, Berger regained his composure. He had heard of the committee decades ago when he worked in DC, but it was more myth than fact. He recalled seeing a top secret communiqué that talked about recruiting a congressman to gain access to secret government technology. This couldn't be it, thought Berger. That was too long ago.

"You must be kidding, Mike. DEA people are helping with your campaign?"

"Yeah, early on, I went to this run-down joint near the Brooklyn Navy Yard, and even saw some air force guy shoot up a drug lord's house with a drone. The guy was working a joystick like he was playing in an arcade."

Heavily perspiring, Berger wiped his brow with a napkin. His glasses slid down his nose, and he shoved them firmly against his face as he looked around to see if anyone was watching. Menza had left the bar about twenty minutes earlier, and a tall, shapely brunette had taken a seat two booths away.

The ballpoint pen was still facing Gordon's table.

Berger was having trouble catching his breath. This was how he felt when a stock he bought plunged in after-hours trading and he couldn't do anything until it reopened the next day. He quickly collected his thoughts. If this really was the work of the committee, he had better keep his mouth shut while in a closed room, as he was surely being watched or recorded.

"You know, Mike, I could really use some fresh air. Why don't we take a walk?"

"OK, but we haven't had dessert."

"That's all right. I could forgo the extra carbs."

The brunette removed the pen from her table—a sign to Menza, who was standing across the street with a direct view of the booth. It meant Gordon was on the move.

After walking several blocks, Berger pulled Gordon into a Starbucks.

"Listen, Mike, there is no way the DEA is supposed to be helping you run a campaign or letting you watch their war games. Something is up, and I don't know for sure, but you may be bait for a bigger project."

"Bait? For what?"

"For a covert mission that requires someone with unique access to government secret installations."

"But I don't have access to shit. I can't even get into the executive bathroom at my firm."

"You'll have access in Congress. Look, I may be way off, but just watch your back. Once these guys get what they need, they usually throw you off the back of the bus."

"John, I think you've had too much wine. Let me call you a cab."

Gordon put Berger into a cab and watched him drive away.

Menza had caught the whole conversation on his listening device. The report would be on Parisi's desk within the hour.

Gordon continued walking. After a few blocks, he bumped into Shelby.

"Michael, what a surprise!"

"Well, what are you doing here, Sara? You haven't been following me, have you?"

"No, of course not. I thought I'd do a little early holiday shopping and was heading to Bloomingdale's. Want to join me?"

"Sure," said Gordon. Emily was away at a corrections officers' convention, and Gordon wasn't anxious to hang out with his mother-in-law, who was home watching the kids.

Shelby asked about Gordon's dinner with Berger. Gordon didn't believe his conspiracy theory and thought that Berger was drunk. Then he partially recanted.

"You know, I've been through so much this past year, and I want to win this so bad I don't really care how I get there," Gordon said as he headed into Penn Station.

"Well, I'm sure Berger is just letting his imagination run wild. You know, hedge fund guys can lose it sometimes."

"Yeah, that's for sure."

Gordon disappeared into a throng of commuters as Shelby got into a cab.

"Brooklyn Navy Yard, please."

Shelby arrived at the office a little after 9:30 p.m. Parisi was already meeting with Peoples and Bruno in the main conference room.

"I've listened to the tapes and have read the field notes. From the tone of voice and reported demeanor, I don't believe Gordon bought into it," said Peoples.

"I concur," said Shelby.

"I spent an hour with him and didn't see any change in attitude. The risk is if he loses. Then he might start asking some questions."

"He's not going to lose," said Parisi. "Ricardo says we're down ten, and we have a heavy Election Day package that will give us ten to fifteen points."

"So we just let it ride," said Bruno.

"We're already watching Gordon twenty-four/seven," said Parisi. "It's Berger I'm worried about. Put a tap on his phones—home, business, cell—and his e-mail accounts, and let's get round-the-clock eyeballs on the guy. If he pursues this, we'll have to make him go away."

"On it," said Peoples. "Shelby will handle it."

"Oh, Sara, can you stick around a minute?" asked Bruno.

The others filed out of the conference room.

"You know, it's really none of my business who you sleep with, but according to the CIA, the guy you had over last month is a Russian operative named Ivan Kochenko."

"Well, he had a really nice disposition."

"You mean he was good lay."

Shelby smiled.

"You'd better dust your room and see if he didn't leave anything behind."

"Sure thing, boss."

Bruno had high hopes for Shelby. Her remarkable field talent and girlish looks made for a unique combination that was hard to find. But she was an enigma. No friends or immediate family, yet always cheerful and the life of the party. This worried Bruno. He never liked the unpredictable.

Shelby stopped by the technical office and picked up a wand. The infrared detection device would pick up any prints or electronic devices in the house.

A thorough run of her studio apartment revealed nothing conspicuous—some semen stains under her bed and a dead mouse behind the refrigerator, but no listening devices. She picked up her cell phone and turned on the wand to reveal a slew of strange fingerprints.

She plugged a USB line into the phone and ran a diagnostic on her laptop. It showed a Bluetooth download on September 13, the night Kochenko was over. Shelby unscrewed the back of the phone and completely dismantled it. She threw half the pieces down the incinerator chute and tossed the rest into the East River. Kochenko hadn't gotten much. It was a dumbphone with no Internet access or text capability. Anyone monitoring her would have heard about her pizza orders and nail appointments. Those routines would have to change.

Seaver was surprised to hear about the tap on Shelby's phone. Apparently, Topkin was still pissed off. But that would have to wait. Seaver had an election to win.

# 23

The warehouse in Secaucus was cavernous and nondescript. Nestled in the industrial part of town next to garages and machine shops, the building's steady stream of trucks on this particular Sunday morning went unnoticed. Trucks with insignia from UPS, FedEx, Jersey Central Power & Light, Verizon, NJ Water, and Cablevision were there, having been taken from parking lots all over the country within the past several days. All the vehicles were outfitted with state-of-the-art jamming devices that could overwhelm cable tower and satellite transmissions, substituting those signals with programming devised by Ricardo and his staff.

Past the line of trucks, Peoples was finishing off his briefing to a dozen special ops recruited from foreign stations. They were military saboteurs charged with surreptitiously disrupting electrical power to various Republican towns and polling stations. They carried small laser devices that would cause an electrical transformer to overload and explode. A smaller team had already infiltrated the Oyster Creek Nuclear Generating Station in Lacey Township with a computer worm that would cause a vast electrical surge. While the surge itself would not be harmful, it would be blamed as the cause of the transformer explosions.

Twenty-four hours after activation, the worm program would erase itself, leaving no trace.

At 11:00 a.m., the team convened in the back office, behind several dozen cartons of knitting yarn. Seaver wore denim overalls and a conductor's cap with the letters *LIRR* emblazoned on the front. It was a gift from the father of a drug addict who Seaver had rescued in Colombia. Bruno was the first to report.

"The trucks are outfitted and ready to go. We're gonna hit twelve locations in Broome and Shore Counties in triangulation patterns. We go live Monday night at eight p.m., and we'll broadcast in tic-tac-toe spurts for three hours. The programming will be scattered and targeted to likely voters and heads of households. We're using a high frequency at eight-point-six gigahertz, and the signal is modulated to cut off if it senses a recording device. So TiVo and the like will not be able to record. By Tuesday morning, the trucks will be back in their lots."

"The lights start going out at three a.m. in six adult communities in Broome County," said Peoples. "We're talking seventeen thousand Republican voters with no power. The forecast is for thirty-five degrees Monday night, so these people are gonna wake up cold. They vote at their respective clubhouses, but without power, the clubhouses are not allowed to open. And even if some of the right-wing zealots force the doors open, the electronic polling machines won't work. By the time Broome County chair Claire McFarland realizes what's happened, it will be too late to get provisional ballots out to the communities."

"We've delivered sixty-five tampered machines to Republican towns in Broome and Myrtle Counties," explained Shelby. "Each polling machine has the candidates switched, so every vote for Parker will be registered as a vote for Gordon. We expect to pick up eleven thousand votes. We've also got volunteer challengers at every polling station. Most are vanilla volunteers, but we've embedded fifteen agents at strategic locations to make a fuss and slow down the lines."

"With a thirty percent expected turnout, I'd say a hundred and fifty thousand people vote," said Ricardo. "With our efforts, Gordon should win by five percent."

"Thank you all," said Seaver. "It's been a job well done thus far. Let's go out with a bang. We're now on autopilot. Set your watches—eleven fifteen, mark."

The group dispersed. There'd be no more communication between the team members. Everything was a go. Seaver departed for Beijing right after the Sunday-morning meeting. Shelby would fly to Rome on Tuesday at 2:00 p.m. Menza would head for Caracas on Wednesday morning. And Bruno would leave for Mumbai on Thursday. They would all be away for at least sixty days in case anyone got wind of the fact that the election had been manipulated. Ricardo, however, would stay behind to handle any cleanup, then leave for Madrid on Friday morning, and Peoples would remain in town to help Gordon after the election.

The plan began on schedule with the TV jamming.

Ed and Mary Brill had been voting Republican for the past forty-five years. A retired airline pilot, Ed didn't know much about Brett Parker and didn't really care for his extreme stance on birth control, but voting for a Democrat was blasphemy. At 8:15 p.m. on Monday evening, the eve of Election Day, he flipped on the Fox News channel. Mary settled in beside him on the couch with a warm glass of milk. Then the commercial came on.

It was a grainy black-and-white picture of Parker blowing his nose in the bathroom. He then opened up the tissue and swallowed all the snot that had come out. A voice-over gave the message: "Brett Parker is a dirty man that cannot be trusted." The picture then zoomed in for a close-up of Parker's smiling face, covered in slime.

Mary spilled her cup of milk all over the couch, and Ed grabbed his mouth, trying to hold back his vomit. They both lunged off the couch, thrusting themselves closer to the television.

The spot ended with Parker reaching for another tissue.

The tag line was last: "This message paid for by Pathways Political Action Committee."

Dumbfounded, Ed pulled the TV plug out of the wall and turned to his wife. "I'm not voting for that slob."

"Me neither."

Then the phone rang. It was Irene Petulla from next door.

"Did you see all the mucus Parker was swallowing? The guy is a freak."

"I know. I spilled milk all over the new couch. Ed is livid."

"Well, send the cleaning bill to Parker's campaign office on Rosewood Drive."

"Oh, that's a fine idea. Thanks, Irene."

Two minutes later, in Shore County, a Democratic stronghold, a Verizon truck heading south on the Garden State Parkway pulled up in front of a Cablevision tower and switched on the electronics. The commercial beamed in on all cable channels.

It opened with a close-up of Coleen Geelan in her hospital bed, with IV drips hooked to both arms and an oxygen line in her nose. "I wanted to have an abortion right after I got pregnant, but my mother listened to Brett Parker, who said it was murder. So I stuck myself with a hanger and killed my baby."

The picture turned to Geelan in a pool of blood, lying unconscious on her bed.

A deep female voice provided the narrative: "Colleen was in eleventh grade and made a mistake. She wanted to set her life straight, but Brett Parker set her on a path to lifelong pain and depression. She'll never be able to get pregnant again. Stop Parker before this happens to your child."

Angela Torres couldn't stop shaking. A single mother of four, she didn't care much for politics and hardly voted. But Colleen Geelan had struck a chord deep within her. She quickly ran to the kitchen and started flipping through her mail to find the sample ballot. She'd be heading for the polls tomorrow morning.

At 2:40 a.m., the dials on the main power control board at Oyster Creek started vacillating erratically. Joe Thurgood was on the night shift. An electrical engineer with thirty years on the job, he didn't get flustered easily. At first, he ignored the indicators, thinking it was probably a bird flying into an electrical wire. Then the alarms started going off.

The temperature at the core of Reactor No. 1 was one hundred degrees above critical. The output levels indicated

650 megawatts, fifteen megawatts above maximum capacity. The electrical surge blew out the light bulbs on the main floor, and Thurgood could smell smoke coming from several of the consoles in the control room. He quickly ran to the panel on the wall just beside the door and pulled the red lever. The system began to shut down as the backup generators kicked in and the emergency lighting came on.

Using lasers that were effective at two thousand yards, Peoples's team started throughout Broome County at 2:50 a.m. The transformers exploded loudly, lighting up the Jersey sky like fireworks. Affluent neighborhoods along the Jersey Shore and adult communities farther inland began going dark. By 4:30 a.m., thirty thousand customers were without power.

Scores of emergency personnel rushed to Oyster Creek as the governor considered issuing a mandatory evacuation. Right after the kill switch was thrown, however, the reactor temperature decreased dramatically, and the energy surge subsided. Tests for radioactive leaks were negative.

The Fountain View adult community in Whiting was blacked out. There was no power when residents started lining up outside the clubhouse to vote. It was 6:00 a.m., and there were already forty people in line. Scooter Dibbs, the community president, was helpless. The clubhouse doors remained locked, the voting machines inoperative. Jim Reynolds was furious. At ninety-five, he had never missed voting in an election.

"Scooter, I can't miss a vote," said Reynolds. "I've never missed a vote. Do you want that sissy-boy Democrat, Gordon, to get elected?"

"Look, Jim, we have a call into the electric company, and they said they'd be sending someone out. But the power surge at the nuclear facility blew out dozens of transformers, and the crews are spread thin. Why don't you go home, and when the power is back, I'll call you."

"I ain't budging until I vote," Reynolds said in a determined voice as he navigated his motorized wheelchair back in line.

In Shore County, the turnout was heavy. Polling stations were running out of ballot slips, but Gordon's challengers had brought extra booklets. Cynthia Turley stood in line with her mother, Jeanette.

"You see that commercial with the poor girl all wired up in the hospital, Mom?"

"I sure did, honey. I never voted for a candidate that supported abortion. The sisters at Our Lady of Mercy taught me long ago that it was a sin to vote that way. But at my age, I'm not too worried about sins anymore. I'm voting for Gordon."

In District 19 in Taberville, a Republican area, election officials couldn't get two voting machines to work. Shelby's team had short-circuited the wafer boards the night before. Voters had to settle for the one machine that was operable. Lines stretched out the building and into the parking lot. Many voters simply left.

By 6:00 p.m., power had been restored to half of the adult communities in Broome County. But many people had not come back to vote. After waiting in line for eight hours, Joe Reynolds headed home for a nap and didn't get up in time to make the polls. He died in his sleep that night.

Jose Ricardo monitored the police bands and didn't pick up any chatter to suggest suspected coordinated action against polling stations. By 8:30 p.m., results started to reach Parker's campaign office in Toms River.

Peggy Tang couldn't believe what her computer screen was saying. Voter turnout in heavy Republican areas was less than 20 percent. Returns from polling stations that typically voted 80 percent Republican were coming in at 40 percent. By 9:00 p.m., CNN had Parker up by only three points.

Parker was not paying any attention to the returns. He was working the room at the Hyatt, yucking it up with Claire McFarland and other Republican officials. Tang interrupted his conversation with New Jersey State Senator Pratt Cryan and pulled him aside.

"Ninety percent of precincts in Broome and Myrtle Counties have reported, and we're up only three points."

At first, Parker didn't understand what Tang was saying. He was light-headed from three Heinekens and hadn't paid attention to county returns for over twenty years.

"So that means we still have Shore County to go, right?" said Parker.

"But we've never won Shore County," Tang said, her voice cracking.

It took another twenty minutes to sink in, but Parker slowly began to realize that he might have lost the election. The usual jovial atmosphere in the main ballroom turned to hushed conversation as people circled around Tang's computer to monitor the results. Shore County was breaking heavily for Gordon. With 45 percent of precincts reporting, Gordon was up by two points.

At 10:35 p.m., the unthinkable happened. CNN projected Gordon as the winner.

Several people tried to console Tang, who began sobbing uncontrollably.

Parker had excused himself to the men's room, where he locked himself in a bathroom stall. He felt as if a pro boxer had just punched him in the stomach. He was breathing heavily and wanted to cry, yet no tears were flowing. His stomach began to spasm. He dropped to his knees and threw up in the toilet.

The scene was quite different at Wily's Waterfront Bar & Grill in Belmar. Supporters were smothering Gordon with hugs and kisses as "We Are the Champions" blasted over the din of the packed crowd. Vinny Cara wouldn't take his arm off Gordon's shoulder as he paraded him around the room.

"Toby, come here, babe," shouted Cara. "Come drink to our new congressman."

Toby Foster, the county sheriff, dutifully complied and gave Gordon a huge hug.

"You've done the unthinkable. You've sent that lunatic back to the asylum where he belongs. I love you."

State assemblywoman Sheri Haltman's sentiments were even more direct. "Michael, what you have done tonight is superhuman. I want to bear your next child."

Cara erupted in laughter as he dragged Gordon over to Mitch Winters, the Myrtle County Democratic chair.

Gordon was floating on air and couldn't stop smiling. Emily also seemed happy, surrounded by women trying to get a better idea of what Michael was like as a husband. But Emily's face had withered from the chemotherapy, and her fair complexion had turned pale and blotchy. She wasn't the same person anymore.

Gordon tried to find Shelby and Peoples, but the swell of the crowd had limited the line of sight to ten feet. The press had also arrived, and Michael made several statements along the same lines as his stump speeches. Not missing a beat, he promised to investigate the mishap at Oyster Creek and take steps to bring more green energy to the district.

Peoples stood outside in the parking lot, sipping a strong martini and savoring the moment. Although it was only a four-point win, it was enough to avoid a cloud on the results from the power outages to the adult community polling stations. He reached for the Cohiba in his inside suit pocket and walked toward his car. But the onset of reality soon dampened his elation. Peoples understood that the hard part was just beginning.

# 24

"You went to a fucking county fair in broad daylight? Are you mad?"

Topkin squirmed in his seat, staring at his clasped hands that were resting on his lap. Olga Yogislov was not someone you talked back to.

"What, you're worried about that stepdaughter of yours, the one your bitch brought along when you took her into your house? To hell with her. She's a whore. I don't know what she's doing in the company. If it weren't for the fact that my brother adored you, I'd be delivering your testicles to my favorite Thai restaurant for tonight's soup."

Olga didn't mince words. As head of the Operations Directorate, she was the most powerful person in the FSB. Her husband was Putin's general counsel. Unlike the classical female operative, Olga was not pleasant, both in demeanor and appearance. At six feet two and wider than a Lada wagon, she had chin-length black hair and a large hooked nose. There was about a quarter-inch space between her two front teeth, which were stained from heavy tobacco use. Her ass was huge and shook ferociously as she moved about her office in her white polka-dot dress.

But Olga was an operational genius. She had served three years as a communications officer with a tank division, then managed a post of Russian special ops in Afghanistan. A trained mechanical engineer, she designed advanced armor for Russian attack helicopters that proved immune to Taliban small-arms fire. With the development of the Stinger missile, she engineered jamming devices that could delay targeting long enough for the Mi-24 to effectively engage in evasive maneuvering.

After the war, the KGB put her in charge of interrogations. Twelve captives died while in her custody, ten of whom had confessed to details of their foreign operations. One woman was so terrorized by Olga's tactics that she had choked on her own tongue. Once she had tired of torturing people, Olga started handling deep-cover agents—moles who had been placed abroad ten to twenty years earlier. She proved to be brilliant at infiltrating foreign businesses, delivering the intelligence that started the Russian high-tech industry. Five years ago, when she was promoted, Topkin took over her position as head of the industrial espionage directorate.

"You guys with the tiny pricks are all the same. You have to prove that you're somebody." Olga spit into her ashtray in disgust.

The reference to Topkin's penis size brought forth a most unpleasant memory from tenth grade. Topkin was over at Yogi's house on a Saturday afternoon when Yogi left with his mother to do some shopping. Meanwhile, Topkin had elected to stay in the basement, where he was working on a science project. Olga, a high school senior, marched into the rec room and kicked away the circuit board Topkin was trying to wire. She pulled him up by his shirt and demanded a kiss.

Topkin was overwhelmed by her sheer strength, and with closed eyes, he puckered up his lips. Olga drove her tongue deep into Topkin's mouth. They made out for twenty minutes standing up, with Olga firmly grasping at his shirt. When she finally let go, she sat down beside him and shoved her hand into his pants. To her surprise, there was frightfully little to grab. Luckily, before she could do any more harm, Yogi returned home.

Topkin didn't go back to Yogi's house until the following year, when Olga had left for the army.

"OK, so now that I've given you my thoughts, why don't you tell me what you were doing in New Jersey?" Olga plopped down behind her desk and lit a cigarette.

"Bill Seaver has just gotten some no-name lawyer from New Jersey elected to the US Congress."

"So?"

"So, Seaver's been off grid for three years and hasn't done a political job in ten. If they brought him back, then there's something very big brewing. I think the new congressman, Michael Gordon, is some sort of CIA plant to get access to Soviet agents in the US."

Olga leaned over her desk and smiled at Topkin. "Yuri, you're such a devious little man. But I can tell you that Seaver doesn't work for the CIA. And the CIA doesn't rig federal elections. So your theory is worth shit. You went to New Jersey because you were pissed off that your stepdaughter Carla Eshrova, who didn't even take your last name, got her ass tossed out of the country. You wanted to show the Americans that you are a smart man. Well, listen carefully. The next time you head to New Jersey, it better be on a one-way ticket. Because if you come back, you'll be put in a four-foot cage and shipped off to Siberia."

"Understood, Madame Comrade."

"Cut the comrade shit. Now get out of my face."

Topkin hurried out the door.

Olga buzzed her secretary, who came right in with her steno pad.

"Message to New York consulate: Tell the Farm that Ivan is not happy about pussycat bust. Very embarrassing. Gordon NJ-15 may have to drink some vodka."

While Olga didn't know anything about Operation Open Sky, she recognized that Seaver's involvement with Gordon was a substantial escalation in the committee's operations. Her message explained that people were watching Gordon, and she expected a piece of any intelligence that could hurt her country's interests.

The secretary swiftly returned to her desk to type up the message, which would be hand-delivered by courier.

Olga leaned back in her large executive chair. With her eyes closed, she could taste Topkin's minty breath from the day she had kissed him in the basement. She reminded herself of how good innocence felt.

Two days later, Olga got word from New York: *The Farm has no data on NJ-15 and no intention of spiking the vodka.*

Olga put down the cable. The Americans' speedy denial made Topkin's theory more plausible. She reached for the phone but suddenly felt a shortness of breath and a tingling in her left arm. She settled back in her chair and closed her eyes. It was time she made that appointment with the cardiologist.

She buzzed her secretary.

"Message to Topkin: Your balls just got a size bigger. Surveillance on Gordon NJ-15 authorized."

# 25

"It must be fifty degrees in here," Sylvia Burton complained as she took her seat opposite Murphy.

"Sorry about that, Sylvia. It took a while to get the furnace going," said Murphy.

The committee members were settling in to their January meeting. Wolf sipped at his hot cocoa, while Coakley lit up a pipe.

After the formalities and a reading of the minutes from the last meeting, Murphy got down to business. "As you know, Byron was successful in helping Michal Gordon win a congressional seat. I'll let him discuss the details."

Wolf was all smiles. "In what I can call one of the most triumphant missions of my career, our team steered Michael Gordon to victory over fifteen-term incumbent Brett Parker, who is now an outpatient at the Ross Center for Anxiety and Disorders in Washington, DC. While the margin of victory was a little below our expectations, the results were enough to land him an assignment on the Armed Services Committee. I am informed by reliable sources that the chair, Rob Coleman, will be assigning our protégé to the Strategic Forces subcommittee, which is exactly where we want him.

"His chief of staff is Cindy Collins, one of our top young agents. He will be under our supervision whenever he's in

Washington. Seaver and his team have just returned from overseas and are ready to engage covert activities when necessary."

"The word on the Hill is that Tang is calling for an investigation," said Short. "Says she has evidence of tampering with Parker's cell phone."

"That's going away," said Wolf. "Hank Thompson, Republican from Louisiana, just hired her as chief of staff. She's agreed to bury the hatchet to take the new job."

"Was the basket cleaned at Oyster Creek?" asked Gaston.

"Yes," said Wolf.

"We have a guy on the inside at the Department of Energy. So far, the investigation is focusing on a faulty valve that allowed the reactor to climb above critical. There's no trace of the worm, and no one is even looking for one."

"What about the Russians?" asked Coakley.

"My sense is that Topkin has been ordered to stand down," said Murphy. "He suspects that Gordon is CIA and part of a counterterrorism operation. We may leak some more in that direction to keep him off the scent."

"We now enter the critical phase of the operation," continued Wolf. "As we have previously discussed, the special operations directorate of the air force has been developing biological identity-tracking technology at Oak Ridge. It's time to get our hands on the technology and convert it into a weapon."

"So where does Gordon fit in?" asked Coakley.

"The specs and prototypes are being held at NORAD in the Cheyenne Mountains," said Wolf. "It's all in room MM-two-thirty-six, fourteen floors beneath ground level, and watched under twenty-four-hour guard. The only people with access besides the science team are four-star equivalents."

"And select members of the Strategic Forces committee," said Murphy. "Somebody has to pay for this stuff."

"The plan is to have Gordon and Collins visit the site to view the technology firsthand," said Wolf.

"Collins will photograph the hard-copy specs with a tiny digital camera surgically embedded in her left forearm and download electronic files with a tiny drive in her left earring. The camera has no metal parts and can take infrared and three-dimensional photographs. It's like taking an X-ray but being able to see all the layers between skin and bone. It's made entirely of organic material, which the metal scanners can't pick up. The drive is based on electromagnetic technology. Place it next to the computer's CPU, and all stored data is uploaded wirelessly. She'll also carry a strong aerosol toxin in the two sapphire baguettes on her diamond wedding ring. It's a liquid solution that vaporizes upon mixture. A very small amount can immobilize a person for ten minutes and leave him with no memory of the event."

"What about cameras?" asked Short.

"From what we know, there are no cameras in the lab," said Wolf.

"I take it we have to steal the stuff because the brass won't let us in the sand box?" asked Hudler.

"That's correct, Judge," said Murphy. "The armed services don't share their top secret experimental technology with civilian law enforcement and certainly not with this committee, which officially does not exist. Further, DoD is only interested in tracking people. They haven't developed the ability to kill with the technology. Besides, they'd never get the funding for that. Once we get the technology, we'll turn it into the most powerful weapon on the planet, and we'll be able to keep it from snooping congressional committees and leaky private contractors."

"What do we do with the specs once we have them?" asked Gaston.

"We already have advanced electronic delivery systems," said Murphy. "Our understanding is that the technology is compatible with our current hardware, with just minor adjustments. Once the systems are in place, we'll have remarkable reach to dispose of enemies of the state, anonymously and without fear of reprisal."

"We'll also be able to knock out domestically," said Burton. "That means we can shape a government, or even a presidency."

The room fell silent. After several minutes, Murphy spoke up.

"The purpose of Operation Open Sky is to deliver to this committee—and by extension, to this country—the ability to take life when the security of the nation requires it. I don't expect any abuse of that capability. However, you are correct. We could shape elections or the current cast of characters who preside over our government or our industries. Hopefully, it won't have to come to that. This capability has to be used sparingly and only as a last resort. Otherwise, we risk ultimate detection, and defensive measures will be developed."

"What, like electromagnetic vests?" asked Gaston.

"I'm sure the boys who developed BITR can work up a solution," said Murphy. "The capability brings us unprecedented detection with nonintrusive kill power. If used correctly, it should remain a covert weapon for some time. You see, we don't have to kill through the heart or brain every time. We could, for example, track a man like Jose Estrada, the largest Peruvian exporter of heroin, to his Turks and Caicos home. We know from our satellite surveillance that he typically takes his lunch at one p.m. on the porch overlooking the ocean and has suckerfish on Tuesdays and Fridays. Once he has a mouthful of that bony fish, we flip the switch, and his heart goes berserk. The cause of death is asphyxiation from suckerfish.

"Further, the kill won't always have to come from the sky. As you know, we have remarkable wireless infiltration capabilities. Once we have the correct modulations for upsetting the EM field, we will be able to miniaturize the hardware to something much more portable."

"When is the operation going down?" asked Hudler.

"Before the end of next month," said Murphy. "Sorry I can't be more precise. But by March, the entire lab has been slated to move to Lawrence Livermore, and their security package would pick up our camera and drive. They strip you naked, run you through a full-body scanner, and then give you a glorified hospital gown and paper slippers to wear while you're in the top secret part of the facility."

"What if Gordon doesn't go along?" asked Coakley.

"He won't know what's happening," said Wolf.

"We also have other means of persuasion," said Murphy. "My daughter Stella recently gave birth to a baby boy. She named him Michael Gordon Murphy. If the necessity arises, we will have Stella reintroduce herself and come out with the story of their one-night stand. The owner's photos from that event are remarkably clear. Gordon will want to protect his career."

"What do we do with Gordon once Open Sky is online?" asked Short.

Murphy paused while looking over at Wolf, who feared the response. He knew that keeping Gordon around was dangerous. It was only a matter of time until he became savvy enough to realize that the DEA teams that had helped him win his congressional seat had also broken just about every election law in the book. Gordon knew the faces of the operatives and even the location of the Brooklyn field office. He could cause a lot of damage.

"I have big plans for Gordon," Murphy said reassuringly. "I don't think his wife, Emily, is going to survive the metastasis of her breast cancer once it hits her lungs. At that time, I have a feeling that Gordon might take a deeper interest in Stella. Stella will make an excellent partner who will prod Gordon to seek higher office."

Short and Gaston stared at each other, while Coakley nervously shook his pipe to remove some stuck tobacco.

Burton leaned forward. "This is becoming personal, isn't it, Henry?"

Murphy stared directly into Burton's eyes. "This became personal the day I joined the CIA."

The meeting continued for another forty-five minutes as the conversation moved on to other issues. In uncharacteristic fashion, Murphy was the first to leave.

"I think Gordon has to be put down. He's a walking time bomb," Coakley said as he headed out the door with Gaston.

"But we've got a lot invested in him, and the upside potential is huge," said Gaston. "As long as we keep a close watch on him, I would let things ride for a while. Ciao."

Gaston slid into his Nissan Altima as Coakley continued to his Dodge Ram.

Sylvia Burton was the last to leave the house. She stood outside for a while, breathing in the subzero mountain air.

"Don't stay out too long," cautioned Hudler. "The cold can suddenly bite you."

"Oh, there's no way I'm getting cold under this fur coat." Burton smiled as she waved to the judge. She had more than just a coat to ward off the cold. The thought of the power her committee would soon possess kept her quite warm inside.

# 26

**"Y**ou look different," Seaver said as Shelby walked into Jane's Diner in Burnet, Texas. It was a bright morning in this sleepy town outside of Austin where Seaver had been living since January. After a Priority One mission like Gordon's campaign, operatives had to completely change their appearance and live in their assigned safe houses for six months.

Shelby had cut her hair short and dyed it black. She wore a diamond stud in her nose and heavy glasses. Seaver was unrecognizable. Having shaved his beard and his head, he looked like a taller version of Don Rickles.

"You've improved, I must say," said Shelby.

"How's it going in Cleveland?" asked Seaver.

"It sucks. I volunteer for the local public library, and the highlight of my day is watching reruns of *Family Guy*."

"Middle America suits you."

"Not really. I miss SoHo, but I can't go back there. I'll probably take a place in West Harlem. From now on, I'm only dating black guys. The Russians don't have any of those."

Seaver poured some syrup over his pancakes as Shelby sipped black coffee.

"I hear Gordon's on Strategic Forces," said Shelby.

"Yeah, they're sending him into NORAD to steal some top secret technology."

"But he couldn't steal a cookie from his mother's kitchen." Shelby chuckled.

"He's got Cindy Collins with him."

Shelby took another sip of coffee and looked out the window. Collins had graduated from CIA training with Shelby, then was sent to Lebanon as an agricultural expert assigned to the US mission in Beirut. Their romance had been brief, yet passionate.

It was somewhat of an accident, actually. Shelby had just taken off her towel and headed into the women's shower room at the gym. She flung back the curtain of one the stalls, only to find Collins there, lathering her hair with the water off. Her body glistened in the bright shower light. Momentarily mesmerized, Shelby stared at the glorious curves that were chiseled out of a taught, muscular physique. Collins stretched out her hand and invited Shelby in. The next two weeks were wonderful. Then, one night, Collins called it off. She said it would jeopardize their careers. It was the last time Shelby had ever let herself love another person.

"I hear Ricardo has left the company," said Shelby.

"Went into his family's construction business," said Seaver. "I guess he doesn't think he could ever pull off another caper like the Gordon campaign."

"It all came together perfectly," said Shelby.

"Yeah, too bad it may have to end soon."

"What do you mean?"

"Once Open Sky is operational, Gordon is extra baggage."

"No, there must be some way to keep him online."

Shelby had grown fond of Gordon. She liked his Boy Scout belief that public service was the best way to help the less fortunate and right the wrongs of a selfish capitalistic society. But she knew that naïve approach never lasted. The realities of Washington horse trading quickly tamed and perverted even the best intentioned.

"There's one angle that Henry may pursue," said Seaver.

"Oh?"

"Stella."

"I see. But what's with that cheating slut, Emily?"

"We spiked her food on several occasions with heavy doses of estrogen. The cancer spread to her lungs. She's got less than a year left."

"How's Gordon taking it?"

"He doesn't know yet. She's been keeping it to herself. Peoples thinks he'll get depressed for a while and then throw himself into his work."

"So you brought me all the way out to this hinterland of Southern Neanderthals to give me the latest on Gordon's personal life?"

"You mean I'm that ugly?"

"I'm afraid so."

"Wolf wants you back online. You're to pick the Berger tail. We've waived protocol." Seaver handed Shelby a small navy-blue gym bag. "Your apartment keys and new identification are all there. We got you a one-bedroom walk-up at Amsterdam Avenue and One Hundred and Forty Third Street. Berger works in Manhattan and lives in Scarsdale. You're to monitor all his COM lines and keep eyes on him. We have reason to believe that he's close to a nervous breakdown."

Shelby grabbed the gym bag and got up to leave.

"One more thing," said Seaver. "If Berger becomes a liability, you're the one who's gonna pull the plug."

"Understood."

The shadow on Berger was tedious and boring. Shelby liked hunting bad guys, not hanging around weekend soccer games or spending hours in traffic on the Cross County Parkway trailing Berger's Mercedes. The guy was a workaholic—in by 7:00 a.m. and out by 6:00 p.m., then off to Smiley's for a drink with the rest of the coked-up gang of traders. By the time he got home, his wife, Cathy, was usually in bed, curled up with a book.

One night, as Shelby was about to head for home, she picked up some static on Berger's cell phone. Looking up, she noticed a Verizon truck pull up slowly in front of the house. She took down the plate and punched in the numbers. The plate was phony. Then a young man walked toward the truck from behind Berger's house. Shelby got a few quick photos as the truck pulled away.

Later that night, she examined the pictures under high resolution, but she had managed to catch only the side of the young man's face. After a full forensic workup, the boys at the lab came back with the news. The guy getting into the truck was a Russian diplomat stationed in New York.

Bruno didn't like it. "Why are the Russians tailing Berger?"

Peoples put away his cigar. "They sense something's up with Gordon. That's why Topkin showed up last year."

"Let's up the surveillance and see what the Russians are looking for." Shelby seemed amused, having at last found some intrigue in Berger's life.

Bruno paced back and forth nervously. "We can't do that without tipping off the FBI. They have eyes on every Russian diplomat. They'd be on to us in a week."

"So we make like nothing has happened and maybe plant a few misdirections when convenient."

Bruno liked Peoples's idea. The Russians didn't know that the DEA was on to Berger, and if the need arose, their bugs could be shut down by the DEA technology already planted in Berger's COMs. Any further escalation would just send the Russians in another direction. It was better to know where they were looking.

"OK, let's pull back on the Berger surveillance," said Bruno. "No direct eyes, just COM monitoring from home base. We need to step back and figure out what Ivan really wants."

Shelby was all smiles. Not from being spared the drudgery of following Gordon, but by having one up on the Russians. It further distanced her misstep with Kochenko to the back of her mind.

# 27

Collins paced nervously in her Georgetown apartment. There was some swelling around the embedded camera in her right forearm. Although the camera had been surgically implanted weeks ago and the incision had fully healed, something was causing irritation. She pulled off her wool sweater and slipped on a white cotton blouse. Maybe it was a reaction to her wool softener. She had reviewed the operational plan in her mind more than a dozen times. It had to go off flawlessly. The flight to Petersen was leaving in two hours and Gordon had not returned her latest text. He was driving down from New Jersey himself, and she worried about him making it on time.

Collins got to the airport forty-five minutes before departure, and Gordon was still nowhere in sight. Her calls and texts continued to go unanswered. Then she felt a tap on her shoulder. "Do you have any Advil?" asked Gordon. "I hear the high altitude can mess up your head."

Collins breathed a sigh of relief and reached into her leather shoulder bag. "It's right here, Michael. I even have some Fioricet if it gets real bad." Collins was almost as worried about getting Gordon in and out of the inspection without any commotion as she was about her mission.

Luckily, there would be others in the group. Gordon usually behaved well with others around.

The flight from DC was bumpy and had to circle over Denver in a holding pattern for almost an hour due to bad weather. Once on the ground, a military escort lead the way to the base while Collins, again, went over the mission step-by-step from the back of the black SUV.

The twelve-foot reinforced steel doors at the entrance to Building 17 conveyed the significance of its contents. After passing through three checkpoints, the congressional delegation made its way to Room MM-236. Joining Gordon were Kent Millhouse, a Republican from Missouri who chaired the Strategic Forces subcommittee, and the Phil Nelson, commander of special projects at Petersen Air Force Base, where NORAD was housed. Collins barely managed to squeeze into the small elevator.

Collins was an all-American beauty, her high cheekbones, flowing brown hair, and bright-green eyes wrapped together in a thirty-four–twenty-four–thirty-four body. It made her a sight for sore eyes of the soldiers who guarded this dungeon-like area of the facility. As the elevator descended, Gordon covered his ears to cope with the pressure buildup. The elevator continued on its downward trek for nearly two minutes, and it felt like they had dropped far more than just fourteen floors.

Room MM-236 was larger than Collins had expected. A huge picture window stretched twenty feet across the north side, which permitted the guards stationed just outside the door to look in at all times. The ceilings were twelve feet high, and there were two cameras inside the room, which fed back to central security. Wolf's intelligence had been off.

Collins noticed five twenty-inch computer screens tethered to individual Dell CPUs, each one embossed with bright-red top secret stamps. They all had the same desktop wallpaper and appeared to be connected to a network. In the corner of the room, however, there was a frail man working on a laptop with only an electric cord attached. That had to be the system backup with all the critical electronic data.

Gordon examined the rows of monitors that lined the walls and shook hands with some of the technicians. There were at least a dozen uniformed civil engineers and technicians in the room. Collins casually made her way toward the main file cabinet where the plans were stored. She opened the drawer and inserted her left arm. Appearing to be leaning on her side and fixing her shoe, she began clutching her fist in rapid succession. Each time, the camera shutter under the mole in her arm took a photo. Collins had managed to shoot two dozen pages of schematics before Gordon came over.

"Cindy, you've got to see this. They've got a mockup of a very real-looking human dummy, and they're gonna give us a demo of the electromagnctic field detectors."

"Ah, why don't you head over there without me? I'd like to spend a little more time looking around."

While attention was focused on the demonstration at the far corner of the room, Collins moved toward the man on the laptop. His cubicle was pushed against the wall, and his eyes never left his screen. Collins stumbled at the foot of the man's desk.

"Excuse me, ma'am, but this area is restricted. Please join your colleagues."

The man betrayed no emotion and didn't have the common courtesy to assist Collins. But Collins hadn't banked on anyone's kindness.

As she stood up, she leaned over the man's shoulder and placed her ring finger under his nose. Before he could push her aside, the toxin had begun taking effect. The man froze in place, then leaned forward slightly, with his hands by his side. Collins's body shielded the man from view of the guards, although she wasn't sure about the cameras. She would have to risk it.

She put her arm around the back of the man's chair, appearing to have a conversation. She then turned her head to the left, facing the rest of the room, and dropped her right ear to within six inches of the laptop. The download would take about a minute. After about twenty seconds, the guards began to notice Collins's awkward position, but took no action. They simply stared at her. She threw off her shoe and rubbed her hand up and down her foot and calf as if she were suffering from a cramp. That gave her another twenty seconds. The guards, however, were getting more aroused, and one pointed in her direction. The earring continued to gently vibrate as it proceeded with the download. Collins grabbed a piece of paper from the desk and appeared to be examining it while still maintaining the awkward position.

The second guard picked up a red telephone and started dialing.

The buzzing finally stopped. Collins slowly straightened up and made her way over to the demonstration. Seated to the far right with her hands clasped behind her head, Collins positioned her left forearm at a good angle on the device the air force colonel was using to detect the EM field around a dummy. Collins kept clutching her fist as the camera silently snapped away. The guards continued to monitor her strange behavior.

After the demo, Gordon and Millhouse schmoozed with the other scientists for another twenty minutes as Collins walked from desk to desk photographing whatever was in plain sight. As they left the main room, a marine guard who had just arrived approached Collins.

"Can you please hold out your left arm, ma'am?"

A second marine moved behind Collins.

"Sure, Officer. Is anything wrong?" Collins held out her hand, palm up.

The marine did not respond.

He forcefully pressed his thumb just below Collins's palm and moved it up along her arm to the crease at her elbow. He repeated the motion twice more.

Collins froze. *Did these guys see the camera?*

The mole on her forearm was natural, and the camera was embedded deep under her skin, which made it difficult to detect, even with a delicate touch. The swelling from a day earlier was hardly noticeable. But if the guard flipped her hand over and started the process on the front of her forearm, he might sense something. Collins racked her brain for a plan, but she feared that any resistance would increase suspicion.

The marine let go of her arm. "There you go, ma'am. That should relieve some of the pressure in your arm and stop the hand spasms. My dad is a chiropractor."

Collins breathed a sigh of relief. "Why, thank you, Corporal. I'll make sure to see someone about this."

"Good day, ma'am."

# 28

The waves splashed gently against the silky sand on Mogadishu's Lido Beach. It was a stark contrast to the crime and starvation several miles inland, where warring factions fought for territory and power. Bereft of any state authority, organized crime and international terror groups set up operations with impunity. They ranged from al-Qaeda to Hezbollah to Chechnyan rebels. If you had the muscle and ruthlessness, you found a stable home in this coastal city.

Neo Dembo lay on the hot sand, tended by two of his eleven wives. One rubbed tanning oil on his chest while the other placed a chilled hand towel on his forehead. Dembo had no particular political beliefs, nor was he a member of any of the leading terrorist organizations. He had but one love—money. Russian money, to be precise. And he earned lots of it.

Born in Nairobi to peasant farmers, he was conscripted at eighteen and sent to Afghanistan as a mercenary to help the Taliban. While trying to blow up a key bridge near Kandahar, he was captured by Soviet Special Forces and immediately transferred to Moscow. His Russian interrogators were keenly interested in how a lowly African mercenary could have obtained advanced training in explosives and demolition. He repeatedly explained that he had worked for a heavy construction company where he helped with civil demolition. They didn't buy his story, but it was true. Dembo was brilliant, devouring texts and manuals at an uncanny rate. After six years in Soviet jails, the Russians made him a proposition.

The privatization of Russian's oil industry had given rise to vast wealth in the hands of the few who managed to satisfy those in political power. Putin's rise cemented this incestuous relationship, and billionaires' mansions popped up around Russia as Putin's offshore accounts swelled. To maintain this steady influx of wealth, high oil prices were necessary. Dembo received twelve months of training in sophisticated explosives technology before being sent off to wreak havoc on Africa's oil pipelines.

Dembo excelled. Not only could he blow up pipelines, but he could do it with precision timing as well. This allowed Russian energy traders at London's Portland House to place large bets on oil futures that paid off extremely well after the oil pipelines had been damaged and prices spiked. But lately, with Europe in financial ruin and America not far behind, Dembo's Russian handlers were wary of maintaining artificially high oil prices, which ran the risk of plunging the industrialized world into deep recession. The bombing assignments dwindled, thus Dembo grew restless and low on cash.

The falloff in bombing assignments didn't deter Dembo. His vast network of contacts throughout Africa proved useful to drug smugglers. In just sixteen months, he had established a sophisticated network of pipelines and overland routes that moved cocaine and heroin from ports at Cotonou in the west to Djibouti in the east. The transit route was very profitable, with no shortage of clients.

Dembo was on holiday at Lido. An attractive man and physically fit, having just passed a physical at Havana Hospital, he had brought his pack of wives to the seashore for some relaxation. He had received word that Topkin wanted to see him in Moscow. Dembo surmised that the FSB had some use for his drug circuit.

Bruno paced anxiously in Room 4D at the Brooklyn Office. Major Denton White had a satellite fix on Dembo on the beach, and the main screen filled with the image of his oiled black chest glistening in the sun. The NAVSTAT III had just been launched with BITR, and White was waiting for the authorization. The NSA message came scrawling over the small screen on the right side of the console: *Engage BITR.*

The men in the room watched as Dembo's breathing grew heavy and his face contorted from violent spasms. He quickly sat up, clutching his chest. But the technology was too much for him. His eyes rolled back in his head as he took his last breath and fell dead on his side. The whole episode had lasted twenty-nine seconds.

Bruno left the room and picked up a phone.

"The chicken has roasted."

The other end of the line went dead. Murphy was on his way to the study to have a drink.

# 29

C afé Pushkin was an upscale eatery on Tversky Boulevard in Moscow. Set in eighteenth-century Bavarian decor, with mahogany-paneled walls and bookcases filled with old texts between round maple-wood tables and straight spindle-back chairs, it conveyed a sense of privacy with old-world charm. Topkin settled in for a bowl of hot beet soup and aged ham. He savored fine food and rarely indulged in the pleasures of his rank. No summer holidays to the Caspian Sea or to the West. No trysts with upscale escorts whose pimps regularly bartered for protection with their girls' services. He was a modern Lenin communist who believed in social equality and Mother Russia.

The corruption and the decadence tore away at him. Thirtysomethings driving the latest Mercedes and hopping from one nightclub to the next until dawn were repugnant to his sense of Soviet living. But he knew that political power was tied to Russia's newfound wealth, and he was adept at identifying and satisfying those on the rise.

Ivan Kochenko joined Topkin for dinner on this chilly spring evening. A former commando, Kochenko was Topkin's first deputy and confidante.

"So how was the little red-haired bitch?" Kochenko bit into a spicy pepper, cringing at the sharp taste.

"Not much. She's no competition for our local women. She came faster than a lit match and hardly showed any emotion. A wet noodle."

"Anything turn up on our tap of her phone?"

"Not really. She didn't use it much, and she had a separate smartphone for e-mail. Shortly after we tagged her, she went missing for two months. We think she went into hiding somewhere in Europe and didn't turn back up until a couple of months ago."

"Seems a little strange, no?"

"If she was on Seaver's team and fell off grid after Election Day, then we know she was in on the Gordon campaign and the absence makes sense. You typically send agents to sleep for a while after a big operation like that. We stepped up our surveillance of her a couple of weeks ago. She's been tailing a stockbroker named John Berger, Gordon's childhood friend. We started watching him as well."

"I still don't understand what the CIA wants with a member of the House," said Topkin. "They could just bribe or blackmail any number of sitting members. Why go to the trouble of sending in a new one?"

Kochenko took a sip of black tea. "I don't think this was a CIA job."

"Then who?"

"I can't say, but CIA makes no sense. They have nothing to gain from getting Gordon elected."

Topkin circled his glass of wine under his nose, savoring the aroma. "Neo Dembo won't be visiting us next week."

"Oh?"

"He dropped dead on a beach in Mogadishu. Heart failure. He was only fifty-five. I had high hopes for using his smuggling network."

"Seems unlikely he would crap out on the beach," Kochenko said, skeptical of the cause of death. "It must have been a hit using some type of conventional poison or maybe a radioactive isotope."

"Olga has authorized surveillance on Gordon," said Topkin. "I want you to put a team on him and continue to keep an eye on your red-haired bitch. Seaver is bound to make a move soon, and I want to be there for the show."

Topkin lifted his glass. "*Na zda-ró-vye!*"

# 30

**M**urphy looked regal in his priestly vestments that cloaked him in an aura of holiness. He rose from the presider's chair to the lectern as the last of the pews were filled. The nave was full of life, and the bright lights of chandeliers and rows of candles brought the Roman reliefs and paintings along the walls to life.

It was Good Friday at St. Catherine's the Divine. Unlike many other churches, Murphy held mass at 11:30 p.m. so he could perform communion after midnight. His parishioners didn't seem to mind, as there were over a thousand in attendance. People of all faiths came to hear Murphy talk about death and resurrection. There were Catholics and Protestants, Jews and Muslims.

Sitting two rows in from the far left rear of the church, Dill Seaver fidgeted with his tie. Unaccustomed to formal dress, he squirmed somewhat in his ill-fitted gray suit that he'd rented for the occasion. On the other side of the hall sat Hans Lange. He hadn't missed Murphy's Good Friday sermon in more than ten years.

Looking out at the throng of young and old, white and black, straight and gay, Murphy dove right into the subject of the day—the meaning of life and death.

"There are those among us who fear death. But this fear is only of the unknown. We don't fear the sting of a polio vaccine or the chill of a winter day. Death is but a beginning, a transfer of energy from the perishable to the everlasting. There was no death in Jerusalem on this day millennia ago. There was merely a beginning.

"Imagine yourselves in a dream. You see and touch the characters. You smell the surroundings and hear the voices. When you wake up, it is all a distant memory. That is death. It's waking up from a dream, releasing the trivial and mundane. It's dropping the daily obsessions of financial obligation, career advancement, amassing greater wealth, and collecting more objects identified through lust and desire. You are free from those shackles and have only the thoughts and teachings of the Creator on your mind.

"So why do we cling to life? What fuels the great desire to eat and drink, to sleep and work? We do so because we are filled with emotion. We love. It's the love of our fellow man, of our wives and children that justifies our continued existence on this materialistic planet. It is the good deeds among neighbors and friends. It is the offer of a helping hand for nothing in return. These charities and good giving define us, uplift us, and satisfy us.

"But what of those with evil in their hearts? What is there to do with the men and women who hate and destroy, with the enemies of mankind who threaten our way of life and our happiness? To them, we warn that your lives are ready for the taking. You cannot remain among the loving children of a God who hates fraud and deceit.

"We have sworn to a system of due process, of trial and punishment. We test our theories of retribution against the sensitivities of the prudent. A man may sit on death row for eighteen years, hoping aimlessly for a reprieve, only to meet his death that was long overdue. That is a terrible evil that we tolerate for the purpose of avoiding mistake.

"I propose, however, a keener manner of justice. When there is no doubt as to one's culpability and certainty abounds over the correctness of the means and methods upon which to remove the evildoer from our midst, then there shall be no delay. For justice delayed is indeed justice denied. There is legitimacy in bringing death closer to those who have abandoned their right to life."

The congregation was riveted to Murphy's every word. Sister Mary Rossetti, the abbess of Our Sisters of Brigantine Convent, shook back and forth in her chair with her head buried in her hands. Many women were crying as men stared down at their laps or steadfastly at the altar.

The whole scene amused Seaver. He respected Murphy and believed him to be sincere, but he didn't buy into any one definition of death. According to Seaver, death was an unknown that was better left that way. You didn't need all the answers to survive. But Murphy's philosophy was clear to those who really understood what he was saying. To Seaver, Murphy was justifying the covert activities he and others at his direction carried out for the welfare of the state. There was no purpose for public trials of drug lords and their facilitators. There was no point in hauling al-Qaeda before tribunals and going through the motions to get those animals to talk or even acknowledge your right to exist. In Henry's world, these people deserved to die and should be put down at the earliest moment.

The service carried on for another hour. As people paraded up to bid Murphy good-bye, Seaver slipped past the confessionals and down the corridor to Murphy's study. After all, Seaver hadn't come for the religious service. He had a 2:00 a.m. meeting with the chairman.

"William, it's so good to see you again," said Murphy. "I noticed you in the back. Glad you decided to share in our religious celebration."

Seaver helped himself to some brandy by the fireplace. "Sounded more like a funeral to me. Can I get you something, Henry?"

"Yes, please. I'll have a scotch."

"So now what?" Seaver asked as the two settled into their chairs and their alcohol.

"We didn't get ten points," said Murphy.

"I know. We were lucky to squeak by. The district was loaded with stubborn seniors that don't read political mail and get all their news from Fox News."

"We took some huge risks."

Seaver gulped down the brandy. "Yes, we did. Failure was not an option."

"Well put."

"I don't know if you've heard, but Professor Wolf has fallen ill. An aneurism," Murphy said, putting down his scotch. "He was in the middle of a lecture and started ranting Nazi slogans in German. Then he collapsed. Doctors haven't been able to restore brain function."

"Sorry to hear that. He was a good man."

Murphy smiled. "So that leaves us with a seat on the committee."

"I don't like Upstate New York," said Seaver.

"I'm sure you'll get used to it. We've got a lot to accomplish, William. The Russians are becoming the largest organized crime syndicate the world has known. Putin and his cronies control half the South American drug trade and are moving into Southeast Asia and Indochina. All this money is finding its way to secret accounts in Luxembourg and the Cayman Islands. We need to act swiftly, before our intervention efforts prove futile."

"But wouldn't we prefer Ivan to be chasing cash than to be pedaling nukes to Arab crazies?"

"The Russians are bored with the whole Arab-Israeli thing. No one's buying Migs and T-72s. Today's wars are all about Fajr-5s and interceptor missiles. I hear Putin attends a Passover Seder.

"The big threat now is all this hard cash accumulating to a small group who can use it to manipulate markets and spread crime syndicates to our shores. It's economic and social warfare. In a way, it's far more destabilizing than the old nuclear standoff."

"What do you have in mind?" asked Seaver.

"We need to start taking out a few of Putin's top people. Not him. He stays. He brings stability and predictability. But the oligarchs and some of the leading FSB guys have to start falling off grid so we slow this whole thing down."

"Where do I fit in?" asked Seaver.

"You're heading up a new black ops unit. It's entirely off grid, based on the Jersey Shore. You'll have NSA direct access, and DEA spec ops will support you when necessary. You'll pick your team. In six months, I want Putin so scared that he's wearing adult diapers so he won't shit his underwear."

"Looking forward to it," said Seaver.

"I knew you would, William."

# 31

It was a heated debate at the monthly Strategic Forces subcommittee meeting. Gordon was taking the lead.

"US-Sino relations are the province of the Senate in the first place," he insisted.

Gloria Landis was challenging the committee's mandate to fund superweapon projects aimed at destabilizing China. Gordon pushed the view that the House's role was to give the army the tools it needed for any mission, while foreign policy was better left to the Senate, which was responsible for ratifying treaties.

The conversation carried on for a while, until Gordon got a message from his aide.

"Urgent phone call from your son Ryan."

Gordon left the room to take the call.

"Mom's not breathing. They took her to the hospital. Grandma is crying."

"OK, don't worry. I'll be heading home right away. Love you."

Gordon knew the end was near. The cancer had spread to Emily's lungs and was inoperable. She'd been on oxygen and painkillers for the past six weeks. The hardest part was dealing with the kids. It ate away at Gordon.

He took the next train home. By the time he reached the house, it was over. Emily had died en route to the hospital. Ann Singer was in the living room, making funeral arrangements. She was remarkably composed for someone who had just lost her only child. Gordon tried to console his sons, who seemed withdrawn. When the crying finally stopped, they went back to their Xbox games. That night, Gordon couldn't sleep. He buried his head in Emily's nightgown and cried.

The funeral was well attended. Local and state politicians paid their respects, and two social workers helped the kids cope. Ann agreed to move in full-time, urging everyone to get back to his or her routine. After a week, Gordon was back in DC.

He threw himself into work. Getting up at six and at work by seven, he often wouldn't leave his office at the Rayburn Building until 11:00 p.m. One morning, on his way back from a conference, he ran into an old friend.

"Mike, I've got to talk to you. It's urgent." Berger was panting as he struggled to meet Gordon on the stairs of the Capitol.

"John, get ahold of yourself. I've got a lunch meeting with Senator Lane and then a committee meeting. I can see you at five."

"No, it can't wait. I just need fifteen minutes. Please, Mike, it's important."

Gordon looked at his watch, then over at Collins, who was at his side.

She nodded and left to call the senator's aide to explain that Gordon would be running late.

They headed to Gordon's office. Once inside, Berger locked the door behind him as Gordon made his way to his desk.

"They've been following me for three months, Mike."

"Who's been following you?"

"I don't know, but I see a guy across from my driveway in the morning and sometimes a woman as I leave my office in the afternoon. There are clicks after I hang up my cell phone. My garbage looks like it's been rifled through by a pack of hungry wolves."

"What's the woman look like?"

"Midsize, black hair—I'd say about thirty."

"Maybe you're just under a lot of stress," said Gordon.

"No, I'm certain. This started right after we had dinner together before the election."

"So what do you want me to do?"

"Tell them to stop, or I'm going to the police."

"But I don't know who you're talking about."

Berger shook Gordon's arm. "Come on, Mike. Wake up. Do you think you got elected because of your charm? You think saving a couple on the Parkway and Parker sending Twitter photos of himself was all coincidence? You think the blackouts at the polling stations happened by chance?"

"What are you saying?"

"I'm saying that you are being manipulated into something much larger than just a congressional seat, and I don't care if that's what you want, but those guys have to leave me out of it." Berger was practically in tears. He was scared and didn't know how to defend himself against an enemy that he couldn't see and couldn't identify.

"OK, John. I'll do what I can. Now, just calm down."

"Thanks, Mike. I appreciate it."

Gordon buzzed in his secretary.

"Am I still on for lunch?"

"Yes, at the Sequoia."

"Tell Collins I'll meet her there."

Gordon shrugged off Berger's hysterics. He really didn't care how he had gotten his seat. Emily's passing was difficult, but he'd been getting over it and had even agreed to attend a Fourth of July dinner in New York. Max Peoples had invited him, and Gordon missed Peoples.

Within the hour, the conversation had been transcribed from the DEA tap on Berger's cell phone, and a full report of Berger's visit was on Bruno's desk by 3:00 p.m. Parisi had left the agency after Gordon's election, and Bruno had come back full-time to head the office. Word had it that Murphy was disappointed with the four-point margin of victory and skeptical of some of the tactics. After the Gordon's election and Wolf's death, Bruno was too restless to stomach retirement.

After a brief discussion with Peoples, Bruno decided to quell the Berger incident. He called off the active surveillance but continued to monitor Berger's telephone and e-mail.

That night, Bruno met with Shelby for dinner.

"You look nice in short black hair."

"Please, I hate it. Makes me look like Wynona Ryder. I'd much prefer my natural flaming red."

"Well, you may have your wish. You're coming off Berger and going back on Gordon. I expect he would want you looking the way he remembers."

"Oh, that's a relief. The Berger tail was unbearably boring. The man doesn't do anything besides work. He doesn't even have sex. Then again, if you saw his wife, you wouldn't blame him."

"Yeah, I guess money can't buy everything," Bruno said as the waitress appeared at his side. "Oh, I'll have the seared salmon and a bottle of white wine."

"And you, ma'am?"

"I'll have the same—but I'll share his wine," Shelby said with a slight grin, then turned back to Bruno. "Lightening up after all these years, Carmine?"

"Yeah, trying to keep the cholesterol down."

Midway through the meal, Max Peoples joined them.

"Gordon's coming to the University Club for the July Fourth banquet. We'll talk about reuniting the campaign team for the midterm election." Looking over at Shelby, Peoples continued. "We'd like you to come on board."

"Oh, I wouldn't miss it for the world. But it should be a much softer affair."

"Yes, for sure," said Peoples. "Gordon's making the right moves in the district. The unions are getting behind him, and he's opened a field office in Wrightstown, right near four large senior communities. The constituency services are up and running, and the office is getting two hundred calls a week."

"Stella Murphy is going to the University Club event," said Bruno. "We expect the two to hit it off."

Peoples looked through the menu. "I've already arranged for a room at the club. We're gonna spike his drink with a mix of chloral hydrate and sildenafil citrate. That will numb his senses and get him aroused. Stella will also be wearing a new perfume we designed that raises testosterone levels."

Shelby bit into a breadstick. "My, aren't we getting creative? A Mickey laced with Viagra. But will he remember what happened?"

"Yes, it's a gradual time-release formula," said Peoples. "He will feel naturally attracted to her, and that will build until he won't be able to resist."

A waiter arrived with the chardonnay and poured three glasses.

"Henry wants Gordon for a son-in-law," Bruno said, reaching for his glass. "With Wolf gone, that's about the only reason he's still alive."

"I'll drink to that," said Shelby.

The three raised their glasses.

# 32

Olga Yogislov paced back and forth nervously. She had been waiting for Topkin in his office for more than fifteen minutes. Topkin finally made it to the other side of the desk and took a seat.

"Uri Topolov, head of Yukos Oil—dead. Mikhail Demitriev, head of Volga Shipping—dead. Sonya Alibayev, wife of Defense Minister Tolstayevski—dead." Olga was practically shrieking. "Tell me, you little worm, is this all a coincidence of bad luck?"

Topkin hesitated before answering. Olga had been appointed interior minister when a mysterious car accident killed Putin's former appointee. Topkin was now the number-two man in the FSB and wanted to keep his job. He couldn't let Olga believe for one minute that this rash of unfortunate events was in some way an intelligence failure. Such a revelation would certainly earn him a one-way trip to a Siberian gulag in Karsnoyarsk.

"We are investigating, Madame Comrade," Topkin said diplomatically.

Yogislov grabbed a delicate glass vase from the desk and violently threw it on the floor. The glass shattered just to the left of Topkin. "I don't want an investigation. I want answers. My ass is on the line as well. If I get squeezed for this, your head will be an ornament on my Christmas tree this year. Am I clear?"

"Oh, yes, ma'am." Topkin shuddered. "Just give me a little time."

Yogislov barged out of the room, slamming the door behind her.

Topkin had no idea how to find out what had been causing these freak deaths. Getting help from the other side was out of the question, as Topkin was still relatively unknown outside the FSB and hardly traveled abroad. His prior work in the industrial directorate didn't merit much attention. Anyway, as a product of the former Soviet Union, his natural instinct was to disbelieve anything coming from the West.

Topkin saw no connection in the recent spate of deaths. One had died of heart failure and the next from a brain aneurism. Another had choked at a restaurant. Just bad luck, he surmised.

Topkin quickly called in Kochenko. Maybe he could figure out what was going on.

Kochenko gingerly stepped over the broken glass. "Having some domestic trouble?"

Topkin opened a drawer in his desk and removed a bottle of vodka. His hands were visibly shaking as he poured himself a drink. "Hardly. What have you learned about Gordon?"

"We followed Berger to a meeting he had with Gordon in Washington, DC. First they talked outside, and then they went into his office. We had a tap on his cell phone. The conversation was intriguing." Kochenko played back Berger's hysterical rant about being followed and how Gordon was a pawn in some larger scheme.

"We've known for some time that Gordon was being handled," Topkin said, clearly concerned. "But we could never figure out what the CIA would want with a congressman."

"This isn't CIA," said Kochenko.

"Well, who else would be interested?"

"DEA."

"What are you talking about, Ivan? The DEA chases cocaine in South America."

Kochenko lit a cigarette. "So do we. We make a lot of money off the drug trade. We grow and ship our own product, and we launder money for our competitors. Just look at the recent victims. They were all involved in the drug trade."

"So?"

"Well, when you start putting the pieces together, they point to the DEA. Shelby works for the DEA. She left the CIA three years ago. Seaver is a freelancer but has a long history with the DEA. Dembo dropped dead just as we started looking into his trafficking routes. Then our people start dying."

Topkin poured himself another vodka. "So they have some kind of new weapon. But what do they need a congressman for?"

"Gordon is on the Strategic Forces committee. He has access to the latest experimental weaponry."

"Still, why do they need a congressman? They also have access to this data," Topkin said, raising his voice. His patience was fleeting.

Kochenko thought for a minute as Topkin paced around the room.

"Maybe it's a black ops unit outside normal government channels that can't get their hands on Pentagon secrets or that doesn't want any congressional oversight?"

Topkin turned and smiled. *That must be it,* he thought. But he still didn't have proof.

"What did they do with Dembo's body?" Topkin asked, moving toward the window.

"It's buried in his home village outside of Nairobi."

"Bring it to me."

Kochenko practically swallowed his cigarette. He'd need an army to massacre the entire village before they would allow an exhumation. But Kochenko recognized the look on Topkin's face, and "no" was not an answer.

"Done," said Kochenko.

"If, as I suspect, there are no traces of poison, then we know the Americans have something." Topkin gulped down his vodka and looked over at Kochenko, who was putting out his cigarette. "Are you still here?"

# 33

The cemetery in Magadi was on the outskirts of town, at the foot of a large hill. There was a small hut at the entrance in which an elderly man was watching television on a nine-inch black-and-white set with several feet of patched wiring serving as a makeshift antenna. Dembo was a folk legend to this poor village southeast of Nairobi. He had broken the chains of poverty and oppression to live a better life, but could still don traditional tribal dress and dance through the night to the beat of drums and the puffs of scented air.

It was 3:00 a.m. Kochenko and his pilot landed the Cessna 172 a mile away from the village and bicycled to the cemetery. Kochenko kicked open the watchman's door and put a .32-caliber bullet right above the man's left eye. He carried him out over his shoulder like a sack of rice and headed to the center of the burial ground where Dembo's grave lay marked with a simple wooden cross and the words *Kenya's brilliant son, Neo Dembo.*

It didn't take long to dig up the three-foot-deep grave. Partially draped in a cotton cloth, the corpse had already begun to decompose. Dembo's face was eaten away, and a large tape worm hung from his nose. His stomach had been ripped open by maggots, which were feasting on his exposed intestines. The smell was horrific.

Kochenko and the pilot transferred Dembo into a plastic body bag and threw the caretaker into the grave. After about ten minutes of shoveling, the grave looked undisturbed. They hoisted Dembo onto one of the bikes and hightailed it back to the Cessna. Once on board, they took off for a small landing strip just over the border in Tanzania. There, a Russian Antonov 26 transport plane waited to take them back to Moscow. Stamped *Grade A Pork*, Dembo was concealed in a meat locker for the remainder of the journey.

Twelve hours later, Kochenko and his package arrived at a nondescript butcher shop on Ulitsa Street. The shop carried the usual Russian diet of pork and lamb chops, with occasional scraps of beef. Behind the walk-in freezer at the back of the store, a trapdoor led to a narrow staircase. There, Dr. Ina Zukov, FSB chief pathologist, was ready to carve up what remained of Neo Dembo.

"This guy smells like shit," Zukov said, beginning her Y-shaped incision from just below Dembo's neck down to his abdomen.

Kochenko had smeared strong vapor rub under his nose and offered some to Zukov.

"No thanks, Ivan. Smells are clues. I learn a lot from how a body stinks." Zukov carved up the body like an artist chiseling away at a slab of clay. She slowly removed the internal organs, some of which were decayed. "Ah, wonderful! The liver is still intact," Zukov confirmed, placing it in a glass jarful of a clear liquid.

A young nurse whisked it away for testing as Zukov began recording her notes.

"Two-meter black male, approximately one hundred and fifteen kilos at time of death. Body decayed after two weeks of burial, but liver and left kidney still in situ. Trauma shown to the left forehead, probably from a fall. Scars from old bullet wounds to left forearm, right thigh, and upper back. No obvious skeletal trauma. Liver and partial left kidney sent for analysis. Cause of death appears to be cardiac arrest. Awaiting pending toxicology for further analysis."

Zukov turned to her assistant. "OK, Irena, you can pack him up and put him on ice," she said, stripping the plastic gloves from her hands.

"So what do you think?" asked Kochenko.

"You heard my report," Zukov said as she reached for her coat.

Kochenko grabbed her arm. "I know what the report says. I asked what you think."

"Well, for that, you'll have to buy me a drink."

The two climbed the stairs out of the musty basement and took a cab across town to Mika's, a tony bar just blocks from the Kremlin.

Zukov smiled as she sipped her Bloody Mary. "Well, Ivan, seems you've become important these days. Word is you're Topkin's right-hand man."

"I've been working on some decent cases lately—can't complain," Kochenko said, puffing on a cigarette. "So what killed Dembo?"

"Why is this nigger so important to you?" Zukov took Kochenko's cigarette and placed it in her mouth.

"Look, I'm not going to sleep with you, if that's what you want."

"Oh, so forward of you, Ivan. I hadn't even lifted my skirt to give you a peak of my new couture."

Kochenko laughed. Everyone knew Zukov was a horny slut. At forty-five, she still looked pretty good, and Kochenko would indulge her if he had the time. But Topkin was obsessed with Dembo and wanted answers fast.

"I'm gonna have to take a rain check, Ina."

"Oh, so disappointing of you. I thought we bonded over the stench at the butcher shop."

"So what was it?" Kochenko insisted as he moved within an inch of Zukov.

Zukov puffed a cloud of smoke into his face and gulped down the rest of her drink. "I can't say for sure, but your protégé was poisoned. From the large dark spots on the liver and relative good condition of the kidney, I'd say it was a chemically induced poison—either ricin or VX—that worked very quickly. Body is too beat up to find an entry point, and I couldn't detect any. But it wasn't an aerosol. The nose passage was not inflamed. Somebody probably stuck your boy with a pellet the size of a pinhead. I'll know for sure once the pathology comes back. We rushed it. We'll have an answer in the morning." Zukov got up to leave.

"Thank you, Ina."

"Oh, I'll be expecting you this weekend. Then you can thank me more forcefully."

It was 7:30 a.m. when Rory Munster came rushing into Bruno's office.

"The Russians have tampered with Dembo's grave. The transmitter in the grave marker signaled two feet of movement three days ago. Thermal satellite images show the body buried there is a five-foot-three, seventy-year-old male. Dembo was over six feet and only fifty-five."

"What's an autopsy going to show?" asked Bruno.

"We had an agent insert some metabolized ricin directly into the liver just before the burial, which will show up on autopsy. But because it was introduced postmortem, its readings may raise suspicion."

"Where did the Russians take the body?"

"Satellite photos show a Russian unmarked transport taking off from a dirt field in northern Tanzania three days ago. The trail leads to a landing strip in Novgorod and then a three-car convoy to a Moscow suburb, which stopped in front of a butcher shop."

"So they're using off-grid FSB pathology," said Bruno. "That means their results will be inconclusive, and Topkin will still keep trying to kick the tires. It's time to have a sit-down with Seaver. He started this mess, and he's going to have to clean it up."

"I thought Seaver was out on special assignment," said Munster.

"Yeah, he's always got some special thing going on. Now that he's on the committee, I'm sure he's got Henry thinking about a whole host of outrageous and risky assignments. But we can't have BITR compromised. So, whatever he's up to, he's gonna have to break off and deal with this." Bruno grabbed his jacket and turned to head for the door. "Burn the file on Dembo. I don't want this going any further."

Munster gave an informal salute, acknowledging the instruction.

After Bruno had left, Munster returned to his desk and began typing an e-mail: *Bear hunt continues. Handing off to Jersey Boy.*

Colin Short had just left a deputies' meeting with CIA and DoD. He picked up his phone and saw Munster's message. Munster had been directed to keep Short on notice with anything concerning Gordon. BITR, and Topkin's interest in it, fell within that scope of reporting.

Short tapped in a short reply: *Good. Keep it coming.*

Now that Seaver's team was taking over, Short's ass was covered.

Zukov's toxicology report came back the next day. Topkin threw the file on his desk, cursing in disgust at Kochenko.

"'Ricin in the blood, but anomalies render final cause of death uncertain without further testing of vital organs, such as pancreas.' Where is the damn pancreas?"

Kochenko looked down at the floor. "We brought back everything that we found."

"Ivan, you know I think highly of you, but this is a failure. We must get to the bottom of these mysterious deaths, or Yogislov is going to hang my ass out to dry."

"So let's do this the old-fashioned way," said Kochenko.

"What do you have in mind?"

"The Americans have good technology, but they can't control their libido. Let's set a honeytrap."

"Ah, ridiculous," said Topkin. "Seaver's too old for this stuff and probably can't even get it up without Viagra."

"Gordon's not too old."

Topkin turned and stared at Kochenko. "Who do you have in mind?"

"Santos."

"I want both of you on the next plane to Montreal. We'll set up the paperwork there and bring you into the New York consulate. Don't screw up. The guy is a sitting congressman. It could get messy very quickly. All we want is evidence of new capability. We'll steal the technology another day." Topkin made a beeline for the door as Kochenko stood up to leave. "We may also have to send these cowboys a message they clearly understand. The ambassador of the US Embassy here drives a red Ford Mustang. It's time for him to have an unfortunate brake failure."

"I'll get Carla on it," said Kochenko.

Topkin smiled as he headed off.

# 34

Stella stared at Gordon's face as the morning light shone in from the large casement window in Gordon's Manasquan, New Jersey, living room. Their courtship had brought them very close over the past several months. Gordon couldn't get enough of her beautiful body and spent many evenings dining with her in DC's finest restaurants. They were becoming an item in the Washington power circuit, where they had caught the eye of Brandy Sutton, a top lobbyist on K Street and the widow of a Texas oil billionaire with close ties to the speaker. Getting on her good side was a fast track to becoming chairman of a House subcommittee.

While Stella had successfully seduced Gordon, she had also found a place in his home. The kids loved her. Ryan and Daniel let her into their private worlds of sports and girlfriends, and treated Mike Jr. as one of their own. Even Ann admired her grace and polished personality. Stella knew exactly how to provide comfort without trying to stamp out Emily's place in the kids' hearts. The only question on people's minds was *when*. When was Michael going to propose?

Gordon wasn't there yet. He was very attracted to Stella, but something didn't feel right. Every couple of months, he would get strange flashbacks of lying in a dark room, staring up at a cross. He could see the contours of a naked woman beside him but couldn't make out the face. Then the headaches would start. After a brief stint, he'd be back to normal. Before the election, Peoples had talked him out of seeing a doctor, so Gordon had let it go for the good of his campaign. But now it was happening more regularly as he spent more and more time with Stella. As long as he had this problem, he couldn't propose to Stella. So he just kicked the can down the road. Stella knew not to push. The status quo wasn't bad.

It was a crisp Saturday morning in December. Congress had just broken for its Christmas recess, and Gordon had come home to spend some quality time with the kids and reflect on his first year in office. It had been a good year. He'd found his stride on Capitol Hill, working on interesting assignments for the Strategic Forces subcommittee. In addition to the thirty people on his payroll, he had just opened a second field office in the district. The *Star-Ledger* reported his approval rating at 52 percent, and the Republican Party was still in shambles from his surprise upset.

Stella headed off to the kitchen to prepare breakfast, leaving Mike Jr. to watch morning cartoons from his playpen. Daniel was on a ski trip with his friends, and Ryan was sleeping late, after having had a friend spend the night. Gordon was just finishing up with the *New York Times* when the phone rang.

"Can you get that, honey?" shouted Stella.

Gordon picked up the phone without checking the caller ID.

"Michael, is that you?"

It was a female voice that Gordon faintly recognized, but couldn't place. And it sounded distressed.

"Michael, this is Cathy Berger. Sorry to bother you on the weekend, but I need to meet with you." Her voice quivered, and it sounded like she was crying.

Gordon was taken aback. He couldn't remember the last time he'd spoken with Cathy Berger. "Cathy, how are you? What's wrong?"

"It's John. I can't talk over the phone. Can you meet me at the Friday's in Newark Station at noon today? It's important."

"OK, I'll be there."

The line went dead and then Gordon heard a second click just after he thought Cathy had hung up. *Must have been someone at her place on the extension,* he thought.

Gordon told Stella that he had to leave for an unexpected meeting in the city. Emily would have read him the riot act. But Stella simply smiled and asked when he thought he'd be home. She was so easygoing and forgiving. It gave Gordon a sense of security that he had never felt before.

The weekend traffic was light, and Gordon made it to the restaurant in good time. Cathy was seated in a corner booth, wearing oversize sunglasses, faded blue jeans, and a red turtleneck. Barely recognizing her, Gordon wasn't quite sure if she was the right person when she looked up and asked him to sit down.

"John has lost his mind, Michael."

"What? That can't be. I saw him a couple of months ago in DC, and he looked fine."

"He wasn't fine. Ever since you took office, he's been rambling about some kind of secret organization that's been using you. He thinks he's being followed. It gets worse by the day. Last night, he crawled into a ball in the corner of our bedroom and hasn't gotten up since. He even wet his pants."

"Why don't you call a doctor?"

"He won't let me. Says he'll commit suicide if they take him to a psych ward." Cathy grabbed Gordon's hand and looked him in the eyes. "Can you please help, Michael?"

Gordon wanted to help but didn't know how. He wasn't a psychiatrist. But Max Peoples was. He'd get Peoples on the case. "Sure, I'll help. I know just the right doctor. But it may take a few days."

"OK, but please rush it," Berger said, her voice cracking with emotion.

"I'll do my best. Is John going to be around this week?"

"Oh, yes. He's off until after New Year's. I wouldn't dare take him out to Vail in this condition. So we're staying home."

"Can I get you something, Cathy?"

"Oh, no thanks. I've got to get back. Thanks so much, Michael."

Cathy got up to leave and kissed Gordon on his left cheek. He pulled out his phone and dialed Peoples's number. It went straight to voice mail.

"Max, it's Michael. How've you been? Listen, I need a favor for a friend of mine. It's pretty urgent. Call me back when you can."

That evening, Peoples returned the call from Room 4D at the DEA Brooklyn Office, with Bruno and Shelby listening in as well.

"Hey, Michael. It's Max. How can I help your friend?"

"Thanks for getting back in touch, Max. It's my buddy John Berger. I met his wife earlier today, and it seems the guy is having some sort of breakdown. He won't leave his house or see a doctor. Could you pay him a visit and get him some medication?"

Gordon sounded distracted, and Peoples could hear the television in the background.

"Sure thing, Michael. Where do I go?"

Gordon gave Peoples the address and hung up.

Bruno looked worried. Berger had friends in powerful places and could start talking to the police—or worse, the press. He didn't understand the sudden deterioration in Berger, as he had pulled the surveillance months ago. What Bruno didn't know was that Kochenko had a team tailing Berger and had infiltrated all his COM sites.

"This doesn't sound right, Max," Bruno said, rubbing his hands over his head. "You'd better head over there with Shelby and get this under control. Check his phones and computers. We may not be the only ones who have an interest in him."

Peoples pulled up to the Scarsdale residence in a white BMW at 3:10 a.m. Shelby scanned the perimeter of the home with a sensor device that traced any relay transmissions. The sweep was clean. Infrared heat scanners picked up two people in the house, both upstairs in the rear bedroom. One was in the northwest corner of the room and the other about twenty feet away. Berger was probably in the bathroom while his wife slept. Shelby snaked a thin retractable scope that had a small lens at its tip along the back siding of the home. As she peaked into the bathroom, she could see a naked

Berger sprawled out in the empty Jacuzzi. He appeared to be sleeping.

Peoples picked the front door lock and made his way upstairs, while Shelby stayed outside. He quietly entered the bedroom, where Cathy was fast asleep. He headed toward the bathroom. Berger appeared practically comatose, with a wry smile frozen across his face. His pulse showed a slow heart rate, and he smelled of alcohol. An empty Johnny Walker Blue bottle lay a few feet away. Peoples gave Berger an injection of haloperidol for what appeared to be Berger's paranoid schizophrenia and a second injection of a strong antidepressant. The combination would bring Berger back to his senses for a while.

Shelby had now entered the house and was searching for any listening devices with the wand she had used in her apartment. Nothing had been identified. She found Berger's phone in his study and tethered it to her modified smartphone. The diagnostic program picked up a sophisticated tap that Shelby had not recognized. She took the phone with her. She did the same sweep on Berger's laptop, but it came up clean.

Back at the DEA, Munster hooked up Berger's phone to a stand-alone desktop computer that looked twenty years old. In fact, it had no Internet capability. Lines of computer code flashed on the screen in bright-green letters against a dull-green backdrop reminiscent of the old Microsoft DOS machines. After twenty minutes, Munster had some news.

"This is an old KGB program that the FSB uses today. It's so out-of-date that modern antimalware software doesn't recognize it."

"So some former Stasi geek is hacking into Berger?" asked Shelby.

"Not quite." Munster chuckled.

"To get this old stuff to work on a cell phone, it had to be upgraded for speed and capacity. It's like a souped-up 1965 Ford Mustang that can do zero to sixty in five seconds."

"So this is FSB," said Bruno.

"Definitely," said Munster.

"I'm going to Murphy. He's got to put this Russian angle to bed."

# 35

The beachfront home on Cotton Drive in Long Beach Island was extravagant—three thousand square feet of wood and glass right on the New Jersey shoreline, with twenty miles of unobstructed ocean view. Seaver enjoyed the scenery for the first couple of months. But after a while, he longed for his old La Jolla digs and the Irish stew that only Jane Doyle, the chef at Greely's, could perfect. The ocean looked gray and cold at night, and Seaver was having trouble sleeping of late.

The knock at the door startled him. It was after 10:00 p.m., and the town was normally deserted by then. Many of the neighboring houses were investment properties that were occupied in the summer months but vacant on this blustery December night. It was just after Christmas, and the town's police force was operating on a skeleton crew. Sensing trouble, Seaver pulled a 9 mm Glock from the desk drawer in his study and tucked it in his waistband below his gray Yankees sweatshirt.

As he edged toward the door, the knob turned. Seaver reached for his pistol and moved closer. The door swung open, and a large man filled the entrance. Dressed in a black overcoat and gray Borsalino hat, the man headed straight for Seaver.

"You can take your hand off that pissant nine millimeter, William. If I wanted to hurt you, you'd be dead already," Murphy said calmly.

Seaver breathed a sigh of relief. Henry was actually a pleasant sight on this dreary, lonely evening, but it was unlike him to arrive unannounced. Something important must have been in the works.

"Well, are you just going to stand there, or are you going to pour me a brandy? It's miserable out there, you know."

Seaver took Murphy's hat and coat and ushered him into the living room, where a warm fire was going. He headed into the kitchen, dropping the gun into the breadbasket, and returned with two brandies and a small bowl of assorted nuts.

Murphy settled into the large Queen Anne chair opposite the fireplace, and Seaver took the sofa about six feet away.

Henry sipped his brandy while staring into the fiery-red coals. Minutes passed without a word. Not knowing what to make of things, Seaver finally spoke up.

"So, Henry, you're not here to scold me for missing Christmas mass, are you? You know I'm derelict when it comes to paying homage to Jesus."

Henry smiled as he put down his drink on the end table to his right. "You know, William, some people think I'm obsessed with the Russians. I keep talking about the accomplishments Putin and his gang have made around the globe in organized crime and the lucrative drug trade, but no one else seems to take them seriously anymore."

Seaver's jaw dropped. Henry was pontificating, but why come all this way to the Jersey Shore on this night? True,

Henry usually came to New York after Christmas to speak with whatever bishop or cardinal occupied St. Patrick's Cathedral, but Cardinal Dolan was supposed to be out of town by now, making the rounds in Upstate New York and Connecticut.

"It's not the Cold War anymore. It's not about intercontinental ballistic missiles. Now it's about generating cash, manipulating equity and commodity markets, and hacking into people's electronic transmissions. You see, we are almost a bunch of robots. Yes, we're carbon-based living organisms, but our ideas and our knowledge are all stored on magnetic disks and transferred over naked airwaves where anyone with the right tools can intercept and listen." Murphy downed his brandy and asked Seaver to bring the bottle to the coffee table.

"So that's why I became fixated on BITR and risked a lot to get Gordon elected. Now we have an edge heretofore unknown to mankind. And we've only begun. In several years, we'll be able to infiltrate a person's brain and affect his brain patterns—yes, controlled thought unbeknownst to the victim." Murphy stared blankly at the blazing fire, his eyes glossy.

Seaver was concerned. Murphy sounded apocalyptic, which usually meant there was bad news right around the corner.

"Topkin is a small thinker—two-dimensional all the way. Fifty percent of the time he is consumed with who in the FSB is seeking to undermine him. The rest of the time he's reacting to a situation he did not create and can hardly control. He suspects that something is afoot with Gordon, but he's nowhere near it."

Seaver had been following Topkin's rise within the FSB, but the recent spate of deaths among senior-level Russian cohorts was not caused by the United States. BITR had only been used once, on Dembo. The recent deaths of these Russians were a mixture of natural causes, murder by organized crime, and bad luck.

"Keep your eyes on the technology, William. That is the new spinning sword that guards the path to the tree of life." Murphy downed his fourth brandy and carried on about religion and man's ineptness at handling the choices God put before him.

It was almost midnight when Seaver suggested that Murphy turn in to the upstairs guest room.

"William, pour me a glass of water, would you, please?"

As Seaver headed for the kitchen, Murphy removed a square orange pill from his inside jacket pocket. He stared at it for a while, until Seaver approached with the water.

"Thank you, William," Murphy said in a hushed tone. "Why don't you head upstairs? I'll be up in a while."

Seaver let out a big yawn as he stretched his burly arms above his head and then behind his back. "Sure. See you in the morning, Henry."

Murphy didn't respond. He just stared at the glass of water sitting on the coffee table.

Murphy tossed the orange pill into his mouth and flipped his head back as he gulped down some water. He drifted off into a deep slumber as his eyes gently rolled upward into their sockets. The orange coating contained a strong dose of meprobamate. By the time the cyanide kicked in, Murphy couldn't feel a thing.

At 4:00 a.m., Seaver's bladder made its usual calling. Seaver noticed the light on downstairs and decided to have a little more of the leftover pastrami he had in the refrigerator. Nearing the living room, he recognized the smell— the smell he remembered from many nights of his early days in the back streets of Bangkok As he faced Murphy, the frozen features and contorted mouth cast a comical expression. He looked as if he had swallowed a mouse. But the white foam at the corner of his lips and the faint smell of bitter almonds told another story.

Seaver sat himself down on the couch and just stared at his old friend. He wondered why Murphy would cap himself like that. Everything seemed fine.

He walked over to the closet and looked through Murphy's coat. There was an old appointment card for Dr. Sherman Cantor at Memorial Sloan Kettering in New York. Seaver looked up Cantor online. He was the chief oncologist, specializing in lung and liver disease. Now it was all coming together. Murphy must have been terminal

It took two hours for the cleanup crew to arrive. Three men from DEA special ops cocooned the body in clear wrap like it was a side of beef and zipped it into a black body bag that had a heavy metal ball at its end. About an hour later, a small motorized inflatable boat pulled ashore just outside Seaver's house. Murphy was carried into the boat, which came about and sped away. He would be transferred to a submarine and then ejected somewhere into the mid-Atlantic.

His Houston congregation would be given the news on Sunday with a brief announcement: "Father Murphy, upon deep reflection over this holiday season, decided to spend a year in the Amazon helping indigenous tribes find the voice of the Lord."

Seaver felt extremely lonely.

# 36

The snowfall in Bearsville exceeded twelve inches, and the roads were nearly impassable. Yet the committee managed to get together on the moonless winter night. It was a special meeting to welcome a new member and select the next chairman. The green conference table was covered in red velvet, and each of the seated cohorts had before him or her a fine crystal glass filled with red cabernet.

Bruno stared across the table at Seaver. As vice chairman and acting chair, Judge Hudler had picked Murphy's replacement. He was fond of Bruno, who possessed his common Southerner's love of flag and country.

Seaver refused to make eye contact with Bruno. In Seaver's mind, Bruno was a washed-up quitter who would likely be working in the hardware section of a Home Depot in Greenville if it weren't for Wolf. But yet, here he sat across the table in the Crow's Nest.

Hudler rapped on his glass, and the meeting came to order.

"Gentlemen and lady, let me introduce you to our newest member, Carmine Bruno. Carmine is well known to us from his long years of service in Special Forces and as a DEA contractor. I'm sure he will carry on his fine tradition of service and devotion to his country as a member of our little group here."

Bruno stood for a moment and held up his wine glass, which he gestured toward Hudler.

"Now we must elect a new chairman," Hudler said, and he glanced around the room, making eye contact with everyone. "It is quite a burden sitting at the head of this table, and our brother Father Murphy guided us well during his long tenure. As vice chairman, I am the first to nominate a successor, and I hereby nominate—"

"Judge, sorry to interrupt, but there's something I'd like to share with all of you before we continue with the nominating process," Sylvia Burton said, standing up. In her delicate hand with perfectly polished red nails was a four-by-six-inch cream envelope with the words *To My Brothers* handwritten on front. She passed it to Hudler, who immediately recognized the writing. "Henry found out he was dying six months ago. The cirrhosis was devouring his liver. He gave me this note to share with you at the first meeting after his death."

Hudler, who had been on the verge of nominating himself, was livid at the interruption. He held up the envelope and flung it across the table at Burton. "Since he gave it to you, why don't you share it with us, dear?"

Burton turned it over and cracked open the navy-blue wax seal that bore the insignia of a pagan coat of arms. She pulled out a single folded sheet of paper with writing on one side.

*I have walked into the valley of death and can no longer share in the struggles of the living. During my life of service, both to country and to God, I have seen many perils befall those who sought the path of the wise and yearned to live in freedom and dignity. The Devil, however, has changed his clothes. He no longer travels conspicuously among the nations. He speaks in bits and bytes, and shuffles power through wealth and influence, having abandoned the battlefields of tanks and howitzers.*

*There is one man in this room to whom I entrust the welfare of my daughter and my grandson. Good luck to you, William Seaver, my everlasting friend.*

Burton sat down and started crying. Hudler leaned back in his chair and stared blankly at the overhead lights. The others looked down at their drinks.

After two minutes of silence, Coakley stood up and raised his glass toward Seaver. Slowly, one by one, the remaining members did the same. Finally, Seaver got up and raised his glass as well.

The meeting was adjourned.

# 37

The squeal of screeching tires was deafening as the Lexus 460 sedan took a wide turn onto the northbound ramp of FDR Drive at Sixty-Second Street. John Berger had just rammed his car through the security gates of the UN building on First Avenue, taking down the receiving tent where dignitaries arrived. Three NYPD cruisers and a police helicopter were in hot pursuit. Berger floored the gas pedal as he weaved through the thin late-night traffic, trying to make his way to the George Washington Bridge. His left shoulder was in burning pain from two gunshots that UN security guards had managed to squeeze off during the mayhem. He was losing a lot of blood.

Berger's sensations were beginning to dim. A deafening thud blew out his left eardrum as he slammed into the side of a BMW and narrowly missed driving into a steel beam dividing the road at the approach to the bridge. Then a police cruiser pulled alongside his car and was about to bump him off the ramp when Berger deftly slammed on the brakes. The cruiser careened past his windshield and into oncoming traffic across the divider. Berger could now hear ringing in his ear, and his left arm was immobile. The pain had subsided to numbness.

He managed to make it onto the bridge, where a line of police vehicles was arranged in a horizontal formation to block his passage. With traffic stalled, people got out of their cars, holding up their cell phones as if to film a passing motorcade. Berger pulled to within twenty feet of the blockade and swerved his car around in a one-eighty. Heavily armed police officers began closing in on him as he abandoned the car and made for the railing alongside the bridge's pedestrian walk. He climbed onto the flat-topped handrail and, with his back to the water, faced the oncoming police.

A dozen police officers surrounded Berger, with their guns aimed at his head. But Berger seemed calm, almost giddy. It was as if his job had been done.

"Step down from the rail, and put your hands above your head," shouted a police sergeant, who motioned for two officers on his left to begin moving in.

Berger merely stood on the railing, staring at the glowing beacons of light. The swirling amalgam of blue, red, and yellow looked like a field of blazing tulips, and Berger enjoyed the sweet and sour smells seeping into his nostrils from the Hudson River two hundred feet below.

The semicircle of officers surrounding Berger grew closer and more crowded. Berger could see them slowly stepping forward. Out of the corner of his eye, he caught sight of an officer on his far right removing his bulletproof vest and donning a life vest with a rope attached to its back. Another officer standing directly behind him tethered the rope to his vest.

"I repeat, step down from the railing, and move forward with your hands up."

But Berger could not make out the words. He was just about to slip into shock from severe blood loss. He gazed up at the clear February sky. There was a full moon, which seemed to be smiling at him. About to lunge for him, the police officer with the rope was only three feet from Berger's right arm when he fell back toward the water. The officer raced to the railing, only to catch the white spray of Berger's splash into the Hudson.

"Shit, this is terrible!" Bruno exclaimed as he paced nervously in Room 4D at the Brooklyn Office.

Max Peoples was twirling a pen around his index finger and thumb as Rory Munster listened to the CNN reporter on the fifty-four-inch TV at the far end of the room: *"We now know that the assailant's name was John Berger, a trader at Manhattan hedge fund Joessel and Frank. According to a spokesman for the firm, Berger was let go two weeks ago for poor performance and had recently checked out of the psych ward at Westchester Medical Center. We'll bring you more news as this amazing story develops. Back to you, Anderson."*

Berger's rampage had made the international press and remained front-page news two days after the incident.

"You were supposed to contain this guy, Max. What happened?" Bruno's high-pitched voice was insufferable.

"We thought we had arrested his severe anxiety in December when we moved on him in his house," Peoples said in a hushed voice. "Apparently the cocktail I gave him had a negative reaction, and he was knocked out for two days. I didn't realize at the time that, in addition to having ingested a fair amount of alcohol, he had also taken two sleeping pills. His wife insisted that he had tried to kill himself, so they put him in the psych ward for evaluation. He was out after five days, but the experience shook him up badly. He started making crazy trades and lost two million in one week. His desk chief found out about the psychotic episode and had him fired. He's been in a tailspin since."

"So where does this go?" asked Bruno.

"Vito Menza is the DEA liaison to the fire department team that pulled Berger out of the river," said Munster. "Berger had a handwritten note in his left breast pocket, but the blood from his gunshot wounds and the water damage made it illegible. It wasn't even worth sending to the FBI lab for reconstruction."

"It's gonna get worse once they find out that Berger had worked on the Hill and was close with Michael Gordon," said Peoples. "The wife already put that out there in her interview with police. Gordon is expected at the funeral next week. The medical examiner is set to release the body tomorrow."

Sitting at the end of the table, Munster put down his cup of coffee. "The autopsy didn't show much, according to Menza. He had a one-point-five blood alcohol level, along with traces of Lexapro, an antidepressant."

"This may not even be our fault," said Seaver, who had just walked into the conference room with Hans Lange.

"Carmine, you remember Hans, don't you?" Seaver said as he sat down.

Bruno was dumbfounded. He hadn't expected Seaver to show up unannounced at the Brooklyn Office during the night, and certainly not accompanied by Lange, who Bruno detested, not merely for his German heritage but also because of his sniveling ass-kissing of Henry.

"Oh, sure, Hans, good to see you again," Bruno said haltingly as he shook Lange's hand.

"The Russians had a hack on Berger's phone, which Menza managed to recover from the bashed-up Lexus," said Seaver. "He carefully replaced the real phone with a backup we were gonna swap out. Unfortunately, Berger exited stage right before we could pull another infiltration. But Ivan had a close string on Berger, and they have a somewhat less delicate way of showing their interest than is called for.

"So, you see, this has become quite an international matter, but in the end, it does come down to our core mission of drug interdiction. The Russians think we have a new weapon that can interrupt their lucrative drug trade. We don't want them to know we have it. Thus the next step becomes obvious. They try to steal it. That's why I invited Hans to our little gathering this evening." Seaver paused, looking around the room at the somber group. "Carmine, what do you think happens once the world learns why John Berger rammed into the UN and then threw himself off a bridge?"

"They crack Berger's wife, who talks about his obsession with Gordon's election."

"Good, keep going," Seaver said with a half smile on his face.

"Then they start looking at the election and maybe dig up Parker's former bitch, Peggy Tang, who filed a complaint with the FEC."

"And then it's only a matter of time until the FBI starts carting away our computers," said Munster.

Everyone knew where the conversation was headed.

"I'll do it," Peoples said amid a blank stare. "He's my responsibility."

"Sorry, Max, but you don't do wet work," said Seaver. "Besides, it would violate the Hippocratic oath. After all, you did counsel him over his ailing wife."

"But he deserves better than to get canned by this slimy shit," Bruno said, looking over at Lange.

Lange showed no reaction to Bruno's slur. It was as if he didn't understand English. But Lange was fluent in English and seven other languages. He actually enjoyed Bruno's emotional outbreak because it was a sign of weakness. Hans loved to find a man's weakness.

"No, Lange isn't here to kill Gordon," said Seaver. "We're gonna let the Russians do that. Hans is going to tie up the loose ends once Gordon is down. The Russians have sent Topkin's number two, Ivan Kochenko, and a Brazilian operative, Janaina Santos, to recruit Gordon to their side. Santos is a former model whose dark looks and killer body are very difficult to resist. We think Gordon will go for her. His relationship with Stella Murphy has hit a soft patch."

"How good is the intel?" asked Bruno.

Seaver stood to button his coat. "Straight from Carla Eshrova. She botched a sabotage of our ambassador's car. Instead of cutting the brake lines, she snipped a transmission belt. The car wouldn't shift into drive. She was about to be booted out of the Operations Directorate when Daddy stepped in and pulled her into his bureau."

"So what's the play?" asked Bruno.

"We are keeping this on a need-to-know basis," said Seaver. "It's priority one, with limited COMs. I am taking lead. Go teams will be briefed at the edge of the operation's window and not before. He's a sitting congressman that we put into office. It's got to come off perfectly. No fingerprints."

Seaver started toward the door. Bruno reached for his arm and pulled Seaver into an adjoining room.

"There must be another way to clean this up without wasting Gordon. We have a lot invested in the guy." Bruno locked eyes with Seaver, but his sky-blue eyes showed no emotion.

"There's no choice, Carmine. Henry wanted to take him out right after the mission. He knows too much and can finger a lot of our people. The longer we wait, the more popular and powerful he gets. Our window is closing. Berger just pushed up the timetable."

Bruno stepped back and bowed his head. He knew Seaver was right.

"Keep Shelby out of this," said Seaver. "She's damaged goods. Like Henry once told me, they don't join for the right reasons anymore."

"Understood."

Hans Lange brushed by Bruno on his way out, knocking him slightly to the side.

"Don't you think it's time you headed back home and rejoined your KKK friends?" Lange said mockingly.

Ever the skeptic when it came to Lange, Bruno held back his response. He wasn't convinced the guy had American interests at heart. But one thing was certain about this German shit: nobody could kill better than him.

# 38

**"B**unning James Consulting. How may I direct your call?" the sixty-year-old secretary said in a matter-of-fact tone.

Bunning James was a leading Washington lobbying firm that specialized in government defense contracts. It represented the gamut of special interests, both public and private, from Boeing and Lockheed Martin to the governments of South Korea and the Czech Republic.

"It's Cindy Collins from Congressman Gordon's office," said the secretary. "Can you take the call?"

"Oh, yes. Patch her through," Janaina Santos said, picking up the receiver. "Ms. Collins, thank you for returning my call. As I explained last night at Congressman Milhouse's fundraiser, we're very interested in working with Mr. Gordon on the Brazilian port initiative. Our client would be amenable to servicing American ships at Niterói. We have a deepwater facility already in place for container ships, and we can satisfy the navy's security requirements in short order. The richness of nearby Rio de Janeiro will provide exceptional resources for fleet operations."

"Well, I'm sure the congressman would be happy to meet with you to discuss this further," said Collins. "He's quite tied up for the next couple of weeks, but we could schedule something next month, say around noon?"

Santos didn't want to wait that long. She had met Gordon only briefly the previous evening at the opulent Georgetown residence of Brandy Sutton, a leading Democratic power broker. The two made eye contact, and Gordon wasn't shy about dropping his eyes to the plunging neckline of the sheer white blouse she had on under her black Dior blazer. Santos had her shoulder-length brown hair up in a bun, and her long neck and smooth mocha skin drew a fair share of attention from the male guests. She was a natural beauty and wore little makeup other than shiny lip gloss, which complemented her glossy brown eyes. A slender woman at five foot six, her draw was her simple yet perfect features and gentle smile.

"Will he be attending the honorary ceremony for the retiring commander of the *Enterprise* aircraft carrier in Newport News this Saturday?" asked Santos. "We could perhaps break away for a bit to discuss the Niterói project."

"Well, let me check. I'll just be a moment." Collins moved into the private bathroom of Gordon's congressional suite and typed out an entry on her Christian Singles profile under the name of Jocelyn Young.

*Just got a raise. Looking for lunch with someone who loves his country, guacamole, and Jesus Christ.*

Collins then opened up the profile of James Cortland. Listed as age thirty-five, he was a "lover of nature looking for a compassionate relationship, marriage, and service of the Lord."

A minute passed, then two minutes. Collins was about to sign off when Cortland's profile updated.

*James Cortland added a skill: Fly-fishing.*

Collins went back to her desk, where the phone receiver was still lying facedown.

"Yes, Ms. Santos, the congressman will be able to see you after the ceremony. Can I set up a late lunch at Circle Forty-Two, say two thirty?"

"That would be wonderful, thank you," Santos said, then hung up.

Collins added the lunch date to Gordon's calendar and quickly headed for the door. She had twenty minutes to arrive at a park bench on the waterfront in Alexandria, Virginia. She hailed a cab and made it to within five blocks of the destination before getting out. She had four minutes and had to approach inconspicuously.

Waiting on the bench was a muscular man with a brown beard and heavy glasses, his nose buried in a recent edition of the *Washington Post*. He was wearing a blue hooded sweatshirt under a down vest, with a Washington Capitals cap.

The well-dressed Collins, in three-inch heels and a charcoal-gray pantsuit, made a pass by before sitting down next to Menza, whose disguise caused her to do a double take. Feigning a conversation on her cell phone and not making eye contact with Menza, Collins relayed the details of the planned meeting.

"So, Gail, I can't make it to Newport News on the twentieth. My enterprise server is expected to be down that weekend, and I have to help with the maintenance. I should be able to get together with you and Dad at Circle Forty-Two, say two thirty?" She carried on the phony dialogue for another five minutes before ending the supposed call. "Thanks, sis. Love you."

Collins then spent another minute looking through her purse, as if trying to find something, then got up and left.

Menza stayed another half hour, gently turning the pages of the Sports section. An onlooker never would have guessed that sensitive information had just passed between two undercover agents.

The next morning, Seaver was having breakfast at a rest stop off I-95 in Delaware. Sipping on a mug of black coffee, he smiled as Rory Munster approached.

"Why don't you try the French toast? Mine is really good."

Munster seemed a little nervous. He was a former Green Beret who hadn't been in the field in over five years. After earning a graduate degree in engineering at Carnegie Mellon, he spent most of his time as an NSA analyst. In fact, he had only come over to the DEA last year on loan so Gaston could have an eye on the playing field. But Munster was the only member of Seaver's team whom Gordon had never met.

A waitress approached the table with a pot of hot coffee.

"Can I get you anything?" the young woman asked as she filled Munster's cup.

"I'll have the French toast," said Munster.

"Ivan is making contact on the twentieth at a Newport News restaurant called Circle Forty-Two," Seaver said, pouring more syrup onto his plate. "I want COM on Gordon and Santos. Keep in mind Santos will surely have a shadow. You have to be invisible."

"Any redline protocols?"

"None," said Seaver. "This is strictly eyes and ears. No one makes a move. I don't care if the bitch has a razor to his throat. We can't spook Ivan. He has to get comfortable."

"Time?"

"Two thirty." Seaver causally looked around the diner. There were only three other tables being served. No one seemed to be paying him any attention. "Don't be surprised if you see Hans Lange somewhere along the way. He's playing safety and has operational authority. In the end, we are going to let others do our business for us. I know that isn't usually our way, but there's no choice. Remember, you are not to move in under any circumstances. If the temperature gets too hot, abort."

The men spent the next twenty minutes finishing their breakfast, talking about sports, and putting together a bid for a construction project in Maryland. Seaver paid the check in cash and walked to the parking lot.

"I know Henry would have wanted it this way," Seaver said as he headed for his Chevy Impala. "Let's not let him down."

# 39

**"S**o why aren't we handling Gordon's reelection?" Shelby asked, pacing nervously in Peoples's office on West Forty-Sixth Street.

"Something has come up back at the DEA. They want this handled by vanilla political pros, not field ops." Peoples headed over to the kitchenette for a cup of coffee. Turning around to grab the milk from the refrigerator, he found himself an inch away from Shelby.

"Why am I being pushed aside?"

Peoples took a step back. He'd seen this many times before—young people with a lot of talent who get passed over for promotion or who are judged by a single mistake instead of an overall record. But in this case, Seaver was right. Shelby had been compromised by a high-level Russian agent who she slept with after a causal social outing. It was a huge lack of judgment.

"Look, Sara, the Gordon project has become less important now that we have access to the technology we were looking for." Peoples himself wasn't fully informed about BITR or how far Seaver had progressed with it. He did know that whatever the committee had wanted from Gordon, they already had.

"So they're going to kill him," Shelby said as she retreated from the break room and gathered her jacket and rucksack.

"Look, no one said anything like that." Peoples followed her to the door.

"Good-bye, Max." On the verge of tears, Shelby avoided eye contact.

Peoples walked to the conference room and picked up the phone to dial Bruno, but then put it down. He thought back to an episode from long ago when he was a young resident at Walter Reed.

It was a dreary winter morning, and Peoples was making the rounds in the general psych ward. The place was filled with the usual crowd: a few who had attempted suicide, young girls with eating disorders, schizophrenics, PTSDs, and one bipolar with severe hallucinations who swore every day that he spoke with God. All were military personnel or family with an occasional sitting politician. Upon leaving the ward, Peoples noticed two heavily armed guards rolling a gurney to the elevators. Curious, he followed them up to the fifth floor and into a restricted area marked secure offices. Surprisingly, the two guards thought that Peoples was assigned to the patient, and let him follow along without checking his credentials, which did not carry a security clearance. Proceeding down a long corridor into a section of the hospital previously unbeknownst to Peoples, they came upon patient rooms locked behind heavy steel doors with six-inch square mesh-reinforced windows. He peeked into a few, and each one had a uniformed armed guard sitting at the foot of the patient's bed.

The gurney was wheeled into the last room at the end of the corridor, where two doctors and a nurse were waiting. The nurse pulled the sheet off the patient, who was completely naked. They moved the young woman onto a bare steel bed with a slim mattress and strapped down her arms and legs. Another long strap was tightened across her chest, under her armpits. The woman was heavily sedated but had just opened her eyes.

"Where am I?" the woman said in a weak voice. She tried sitting up, but the straps prevented her from doing so.

One of the doctors filled a large syringe with a clear liquid and injected the drug into the woman's arm. Within minutes, the woman started to convulse. After vomiting, she thrashed about violently, trying to loosen her restraints. Then she lifted up her head and opened her eyes wide, as if she had just received an electric shock. She muttered something incomprehensible, then slammed her body back against the bed. She didn't move again.

The second doctor took her wrist in his hand and looked at the digital clock on the wall. "Time of death, nine thirty-four a.m."

The nurse recorded the information and then pulled a sheet over the woman's face.

Everyone left but the two guards, who took up position outside the room, with the heavy steel door closed.

The next morning, Peoples mentioned the incident to his supervising physician, Werner Fleck, while in the hospital's parking lot.

"Oh, sorry you had to see that, Max. It was an unfortunate but necessary procedure," Fleck said as he searched his jacket pocket for his car keys.

"What do you mean by that, Professor?" asked Peoples, who was determined to press for an explanation.

"Benzodiazepine with a touch of ethosuximide. The combination produces deep sedation but can cause vomiting." Fleck slipped behind the steering wheel and rolled down the window. "It's sort of a long story, but the short version is that the woman you saw yesterday was the widow of an army sergeant who had volunteered for duty in Los Alamos, where the air force was testing a new neutron device. Within six months of the tests, the twenty-six-year-old soldier died of radioactive poisoning. The wife was told that the cause of death was sudden heart failure due to a genetic disorder, but she didn't believe the coroner's report the army had provided. She threatened to go to the press with a story of how the army had used her husband as a human guinea pig. Unfortunately, she herself suddenly became very depressed and was committed for psychiatric evaluation. That was about three years ago. As you can see, her treatment failed."

Without another word, Fleck started the engine and drove off.

Peoples went back to his regular duties and kept quiet. He later learned that the army sergeant and his wife were both orphans who had no next of kin. The army had neatly wiped their existence from the face of the earth.

Six months later, Fleck called Peoples into his office.

"You passed, Max. It's on to the next level."

Peoples had no idea what Fleck was talking about. He still had a year left in his residency and hadn't taken any exams recently.

"Remember that young woman who we put to sleep about half a year ago? Husband died working for the army?"

"Yes."

"You didn't observe that by accident. You were being recruited. By keeping quiet and accepting the judgment of your superiors, you showed an exceptional quality that is hard to find these days."

"Oh, what's that?"

"Loyalty." Fleck stood up and approached Peoples. "Welcome to my world."

Peoples looked at Fleck's smiling face, then down at his outstretched hand. He had about two seconds to decide. He was either going to leave behind his dream of practicing medicine and head for the nearest FBI office or agree to hush over the murder of an innocent young woman who wouldn't let go of her husband, the only relative she had left. Three seconds, then four had passed. Fleck's smile began to fade, and he was about to pull his hand away. Peoples grabbed it.

Peoples went on to work closely with Fleck in developing advanced treatments for the mentally ill. Those efforts helped Peoples treat thousands over the years, both in public and private practice. It gave the lives of those two orphans meaning beyond anything either of them would have likely achieved had they both lived to a hundred.

Peoples stared at the phone. One word to Bruno, and Shelby's career was over. But her career was probably over anyway. The best she could hope for was a post in Sub-Saharan Africa, chasing tribal lords and their doped-up lieutenants. It was an entry-level gig that Shelby didn't have the energy for anymore. She could move over to a day job at the NSA reading satellite images and writing reports.

But that wouldn't work. After spending seven years in the field killing people, you couldn't get a rush from the bean counters in the back room. You began to unravel. Falling in love and having a family wasn't in the cards either. She couldn't acclimate to the role of doting wife and responsible mother. Those before her had tried and had consistently failed.

Shelby was a danger to the organization. She was a wounded tiger, seething with pain and anger. She had to be dealt with and contained, or she could cause untold damage to the committee. Peoples continued staring at the phone as he lit a cigar. He walked over to the window and looked down at the throngs of pedestrians below, each scampering off to a meeting or some other appointment. These were the ones Peoples had devoted his life to protect.

Peoples was once again going to look the other way. This time it might undermine his career, but at fifty-eight and tired of the chase, Peoples didn't mind much. On the contrary, it was a fitting close to that morning on the fifth floor of Walter Reed when an orphan in the prime of her life was murdered to protect the work of others striving for the greater good. Shelby would have to find her own way of dealing with her demons. Peoples wasn't going to decide for her.

# 40

Topkin looked straight ahead, avoiding eye contact with anyone nearby, as he passed through passport control at Kennedy Airport. Dressed in a navy business suit and carrying designer luggage, he looked like an accountant running late for a meeting with an IRS examiner.

"Purpose of visit," the immigration officer asked as she ran Topkin's passport through the computer.

"Business," Topkin answered curtly. He had a script prepared about the tourism business he was there to promote, but there were no more questions from the Asian woman with the gun on her belt.

Topkin slid in next to Kochenko in the back of a black Lincoln Town Car as the driver loaded his luggage into the trunk. The stress of the trip finally catching up to him, Topkin leaned back against the cool leather seats and closed his eyes.

"Everything is so big and overdone in this country. Is there no limit to spending money?" Topkin despised America and its arrogance.

"Ah, we have a development," Kochenko said nervously.

"Not now, Ivan. I need to close my eyes for a bit. Do you have the Nets tickets?"

"Yes."

"Good. We'll talk after the game."

Topkin checked into his room at the Waldorf, enjoyed a steak dinner, and almost lost his voice while cheering the Nets on to victory from his seat four rows behind the visiting team's bench. For a communist, he seemed to enjoy capitalism quite nicely.

Joined by Santos back at the hotel, Topkin got down to business as promised, albeit with a bottle of Dom Pérignon. "Are we prepared for Saturday?"

"Everything is ready. I'm having lunch with Gordon at a restaurant in Newport News, Virginia, after he attends a military function nearby. We have cameras and listening devices planted in the lights, the walls, and even the floor. I have already reserved a table in a rear booth, but no matter where they seat us, we have cameras and sound."

"Good," Topkin said, sipping his champagne. "What's the backup?"

"We have two operators attending at another table in case there's trouble," said Santos. "A man and wife."

"Unwise," Topkin said as he stood up.

"The fewer on-site, the better. Keep the backup close by, but not inside. Who's cleaning up after the party?"

"We have a crew ready to infiltrate on Saturday night. They will collect all the devices," said Kochenko.

"So what did you want to tell me before, Ivan?"

"Last night I got a text message from Shelby," Kochenko said, pulling out his phone.

"And Shelby is who, again?"

"She's the DEA operative I slept with six months ago. We bugged her phone but got nothing."

"Ah, yes, I remember now. I believe you described her as somewhat inadequate." Topkin smiled at Santos, who had a worried look on her face. Seemingly amused, Topkin turned back to Kochenko. "Well, are you going to share this text with us?"

"*Long time. Home this weekend. Want to come over?*"

"I seem to recall that there is a slang term for this type of message," Topkin said as he sat back down on the couch, reaching for a cigarette.

"Booty call," said Santos. "She wants to have sex."

"So why is this a problem?"

"It's the same weekend as our Gordon operation," replied Kochenko.

"And you don't believe in coincidence?"

"It may be the work of the CIA," said Santos.

"I learned a long time ago that it's better to engage the enemy. At least you know where he is. Respond to Shelby. Tell her that you will be at her apartment on Sunday night at ten. Let's see what she wants." Satisfied, Topkin escorted his two agents to the door.

An hour later, there was a knock.

"Carla, darling, come in," Topkin said as he held out his arms to hug his stepdaughter.

"Was there any trouble getting past customs?"

"No, not at all. The drive from Mexico was exhausting, but the border patrol seemed only too happy to look at a pretty face after all the Mexican women they have to deal with."

"Come sit down and have some champagne."

The two chatted for a while, but it was getting late.

"So where are you staying?"

"I'm a few blocks away at the Intercontinental."

"Oh, good. Maybe we can have dinner this week. I'm here until Sunday evening. Has Ivan briefed you on the Gordon operation?"

"Yes, I'll be running backup with another agent posing as husband and wife."

"Excellent. This is good experience for you. Before long, you'll be back in the field full-time."

Eshrova kissed Topkin good night. He disgusted her. She'd never forgiven him for the way he had treated her mother. The drunken tirades and the beatings were etched in her memory. She was a young girl and felt so helpless as she watched her mother's suffering. She was going to take revenge.

It was just after 1:00 a.m. Eshrova didn't return to her hotel. Instead, she stopped at a bar on Second Avenue. It was pretty busy for a Wednesday evening. She went downstairs to the ladies' room and into the third bathroom stall. She sat down and searched the inside of the stall door. In the lower left corner, a message was scrawled: *Josh and Judy, 1972.*

She hung around for another few minutes and then got into a cab.

"Nineteen seventy-two Tenth Avenue," said Eshrova. The code was simple enough: 1972 was the house number; the letter *J* was tenth in the alphabet, which was the street; and two *J*s, as in Josh and Judy, meant the second floor.

She arrived at the three-story walk-up and rang the bell. It took a minute for the door to buzz, and she made her way up the dimly lit narrow staircase. The apartment door was slightly ajar. She stepped in and closed the door.

Seaver was seated in the living room. The curtains were drawn, and the only light came from two distant table lamps.

"Nice to see you, Carla," said Seaver. "Can I pour you a drink?"

There was a bottle of scotch on the coffee table with two crystal glasses.

Eshrova sat down across from Seaver, threw off her jacket, and poured herself a drink.

"They've got the place bugged from every angle," Eshrova said, gulping down the scotch. "Not sure if they're going to make a move right there or try to get him in a more intimate setting."

"Are you on the team?" asked Seaver.

"I'm backup with some goon from the Washington embassy. We're a loving Chechnyan couple on vacation from Boston."

"After it goes down, you stay with the program. I only need to know where and when they plan on making their move against Gordon. Then you disappear."

"It's a new life in the States with protection, right?"

"That's the deal. You have my word." Seaver wasn't sure he could trust Eshrova, but so far, she had delivered good information without getting anything in return.

"I want my mother brought out as well."

Seaver cringed, then slowly put down his drink. "That wasn't part of the deal," he said, his voice betraying his irritation.

"Well, it is now." Eshrova put on her coat and threw her long blond hair back over the collar.

Seaver was caught off guard by the request. Topkin would sweep Eshrova's disappearance under the rug, and no one of any importance would care. Her mother was a different story. She was a respected Moscow lawyer who had been in a long sexual affair with Olga Yogislov's husband, Putin's general counsel. If she disappeared, it would result in a manhunt.

Eshrova fixed her gaze on Seaver, who had followed her to the door.

Seaver met her eyes and gave a reassuring smile. "We'll take care of it."

Eshrova turned and left without saying good-bye.

Seaver headed for the window and watched as Eshrova hailed a cab. No one approached her. Seaver waited for any tailing cars. There were none.

He sat back down and poured himself another drink as Hans Lange, who'd been in the bedroom listening, came into the room. Lange lifted up Eshrova's drink and held it to his nose. There were traces of her Chanel perfume.

"Looks like you're gonna be pretty busy," said Seaver.

Lange smiled and licked the remaining touch of scotch from the bottom of Eshrova's glass.

# 41

The mood at Berger's house was depressing, yet calm. Family and old friends had come by after the funeral to talk with Cathy and the kids, to reminisce about old times, and to remember John Berger. The chatter was all about his trading losses.

"Of course he had to jump," said Kent Carson, a neighbor who worked for Goldman Sachs. "Once you're canned for trading losses, it's over. And it's not just the money. It's the high. It's like a heroin addict who shoots up twice a day having to spend the winter at McMurdo in the South Pole with nothing but tuna fish sandwiches."

"But why did he crash into the UN?" asked Jenny Long, whose daughter had gone to school with Berger's children.

Carson took a sip from his bottle of Heineken. "He probably wanted to send a message that the world is all screwed up, or something like that. You can't be sure what's behind the desperate acts of a man on a suicide mission."

Gordon was crushed by Berger's death. He believed he was responsible or somehow could have prevented it. Cathy was gracious, giving him a warm smile at the cemetery when he passed by after shoveling dirt onto Berger's grave. Her daughter was another story.

Katie Berger was an overweight sixteen-year-old under-achiever who adored her father. Gordon approached her in the den just off the kitchen.

"Katie, I'm sorry for your loss," Gordon said, putting his hand on her shoulder.

But Katie pulled away violently. "Don't touch me. Don't you ever touch me," she said in a trembling voice. "He's dead because of you and your dumb politics."

She turned and started sobbing. Gordon tried to console her, but she waved him off and ran up the stairs.

"Anything wrong, dear?" said Stella, who had just walked over and placed her hand on Gordon's back.

"Looks like Katie is taking this very hard," Gordon said as his voice started to crack.

"I know. Kids react differently to these things. But she'll recover. Just like our kids have."

Gordon felt somewhat reassured, but hearing Stella refer to his sons as "our kids" was unsettling.

"Hey, Michael, long time. It's me, Debbie Gross. I lived on West Ninety-Second Street." Gross took Gordon by the arm and led him away from Stella.

Gordon stared at the woman for a while, not connecting the face to the name, which he vaguely remembered.

"You dated my cousin Denise in tenth grade, remember? Denise Weinstein?"

"Ah, yes, Denise Weinstein," Gordon said with a smile. "I remember her. What's she up to these days?"

"Divorced with three kids, living in LA. Husband ran off with the Filipino maid."

"And how 'bout yourself? You're looking good." Gordon was trying to free himself from Gross's clutches.

"Oh, thanks," Gross said, blushing.

"I'm a VP at Morgan Stanley in the city. Client Wealth Services. I help rich WASPs buy homes in the Hamptons and fund their mistresses' lives."

Gordon found Gross amusing. She was a heavy woman at five feet two, with dark hair, flushed cheeks, and bright blue eyes. Dressed in a hot-pink sweater and black tweed skirt, she struck a comical figure. But her warm and forward personality generated a feeling of trust. She was the kind of person who got you to let your guard down.

"So, not to be nosy or anything, but are you dating yet?"

"Well, I'm in a relationship." Gordon looked around to be sure Stella was out of earshot.

"You don't mean you're still with that tall nun that everybody is talking about?" Gross pursed her lips and squinted her eyes as if she had just swallowed an ounce of concentrated lemon juice.

Gordon was hurt by the comment.

"What's everybody saying?" Gordon asked quietly as he leaned closer to Gross.

"Well, you know, it's not like she's a bad person or any-thing, but the word is she may be some mob boss's love child."

"What?" Gordon said incredulously. "That's impossible."

"Her father was a priest, right?" Gross was talking louder than Gordon preferred. "So how is it that a Catholic priest has a daughter who's a nun and then gets a grandson to boot? Sounds fishy to me. Maybe Pop was taking care of her for someone."

"I met her father. She was adopted."

"OK, suit yourself. But if you want to meet a woman who's not headed for eternal damnation for divorcing Jesus, let me know. I have some very eligible friends."

Gordon watched as Gross headed back into the crowd. She had a point. Breaking sacred vows was a sign of weakness and poor judgment.

The next morning, Gordon got a call from Collins.

"Michael, it's Cindy. Gina Russo won't be able to join you on your Virginia trip tomorrow. I need her at the office to work on the joint striker jet proposal from Northrop."

"Is Anna available?"

"No, she's back in Ohio for the weekend. It shouldn't be much. The event starts at eleven thirty, and all you have to do is smile and shake hands. You're not slated to speak. Chairman Coleman will be there as well."

Gordon was reluctant to attend any official function without an aide by his side. "You know I hate doing these events alone. Do you think I can take a pass? I am still shaken up from Berger's death."

Collins's heart skipped a beat. If Gordon didn't show up, it might tip off the Russians and complicate Seavor's plans.

"Ah, I don't think that would be a good idea," Collins said gently. "I'm pretty sure Coleman expects you."

"OK," said Gordon. He didn't want to disappoint his committee chairman. "E-mail me the itinerary again, please."

"And don't forget you have a lunch date with the Bunnings's lobbyist, Santos, at two thirty."

"Right," said Gordon. "Make sure it's in the e-mail."

Collins slowly put down the receiver. She was beginning to have second thoughts about letting Gordon attend the event alone. She was thinking of accompanying him herself. But then how could she skip the lunch with Santos? It would be too obvious. She would stick with the game plan.

It was Friday afternoon, and most of Washington had left for the weekend. Collins walked the two blocks from the Rayburn building to the DCCC's headquarters and up to the second floor. It was a large open space with cubicles manned by young political science majors trying to get Democrats elected and reelected to Congress. Tony Romano, chief of the Northeast Division, was out on his honeymoon. Collins picked up his phone.

"MassMutual Insurance. How may I direct your call?" It was a male's voice, about forty.

"I'd like to take a loan on my policy," said Collins.

"OK, ma'am. Can I have your policy number, please?"

Collins ticked off a six-digit number, followed by a PIN.

"Oh, sorry, ma'am, our computers are down. Please call back in two hours."

Munster took off his headset. The final operations check had just been confirmed. He was heading back into the field.

# 42

The villa in Sochi overlooking the Black Sea was stately in its architecture and decor. Italian frescos were pasted about the entrance, and a double spiral staircase snaked its way up to the second floor, which led to an open-air veranda with nothing but blue water comprising the view.

Olga Yogislov had just arrived. Wearing a cashmere pullover and wool slacks, Yogislov enjoyed the brisk fifty-degree temperature. Security Council Secretary Viktor Borodin, the Russian equivalent of the national security advisor, had urgently summoned her.

"Olga, my friend, nice to see you. Why are you so overdressed?"

Borodin, a huge figure at six feet four and well over three hundred pounds, was stark naked except for a black thong. His obese midriff bulged over his crotch, and he had large breasts hanging off his chest. His cottage cheese buttocks wobbled like two large blobs of baker's dough, pockmarked by an assortment of red pimples and white pustules. A retired nuclear submarine captain, Borodin had led several ambitious clandestine missions off the coast of Virginia and was very well respected for his military mind. Snooping from behind a desk, however, was another matter. He was ordered to take the Security Council job after the Kursk disaster. He delegated the electronic eavesdropping stuff to underlings and focused on new weapons development. The son of a Russian tank commander, he still believed in conventional warfare and open-field massacres by men and machines.

"Good to see you, Captain," said Yogislov. The skimpy attire didn't faze her. She knew guys like Borodin didn't notice the cold unless it was below freezing, and showing up naked was Borodin's way of asserting his dominance. If you felt uncomfortable, then that's how you were intended to feel.

"This little shit Topkin is running around the States managing some covert operation to recruit a congressman who sits on a sensitive defense subcommittee."

"I was not aware of the details, Captain," Yogislov said nervously. "I know Colonel Topkin has been investigating what he believes to be some kind of new weapon the Americans have developed."

"Well, what has Topkin's wife been saying? Your husband is still fucking her, no?"

"They see each other now and then, but it's strictly social. They don't discuss business." Yogislov still wasn't intimidated. Almost every senior-level Russian official had at least one mistress. Borodin was no exception himself.

"I see. Well, I didn't summon you out here to examine my balls. A few weeks ago, a red-haired woman walked into the back of a grocery store in Brighton Beach, Brooklyn. She sat down across from Vladimir Kutzow, a sleeper agent we had planted in New York fifteen years ago. He wasn't activated yet. She told him to give me a message."

"She mentioned you by name?"

"She identified me as Comrade Captain Viktor Mikhailovitch Borodin and told Kutzow to let me know that she has information that will change the balance of power and return Russia to its rightful position as coequal to the American imperialist regime."

"Did she leave a name or number?"

"Nothing. The whole encounter was under a minute. Kutzow didn't even have a chance to respond. He sat there silently, quaking in his boots, waiting for the FBI to rush the store. Weeks have gone by, and nothing. No visitors. No intel chatter from the Americans that we could discern. It was very professional. She never looked up at the security camera in the store, and she wore dark sunglasses, a heavy overcoat to hide her figure, and a kerchief over her hair."

"So she doesn't know if we took her seriously. She may make contact again," said Yogislov, who was intrigued by the whole affair. The woman had to have been privy to sensitive Russian intelligence to identify a deep plant. "Could she be FBI?"

"No," Borodin said, rubbing his chin. "We have a senior mole in the bureau who checked. They are not on to Kutzow."

"So that means it's someone on the inside." Yogislov swiveled her head around but didn't notice any muscular men in dark suits moving in on her. Apparently, Borodin did not suspect her of treason.

Borodin stood up. "Or maybe a CIA defector. We have to get to the bottom of this, Olga. First, we need to know if other sleeper plants have been compromised. Second, maybe there is some hot information—possibly a weapon—that this woman wants to share with us. Find this woman. No FSB. You will run this out of my office in the Kremlin with contractors the council has on retainer for sensitive missions that can't be traced back. And find out what Topkin is up to. We may be looking for the same thing."

A heavyset woman in a maid's outfit came onto the veranda, holding open a cotton robe that Borodin placed over his shoulders. He was headed to the sea for an afternoon swim. The maid followed behind with a stack of clean towels.

Borodin turned and headed down the stairs to the beach as if Yogislov had disappeared into thin air. This was a good sign. Kindness and chitchat indicated you were on your way out.

Yogislov walked down the long driveway to the street and spotted a black Mercedes across the road. The car flashed its headlights and approached. The back door swung open, and a middle-aged man turned around from the front passenger seat to face Yogislov as she got into the car.

"Comrade Borodin asked that we ensure you make it back to Moscow safely," said the man.

It took forty minutes to get to the private airstrip, where Yogislov was directed to board a Gulfstream IV for the flight back to Moscow. She was the only passenger. It was definitely an improvement from the jump seat of an Antonov cargo plane, which was how Yogislov usually got around on official business.

Yogislov leaned back into the Italian-crafted leather seat and opened the bottle of Smirnoff that was on the table in front of her. She savored the moment. If she caught up with this mysterious redhead, she'd get pushed up the ladder, deeper into Putin's circle, which meant wealth, job security, and privilege. If she failed, she'd probably be sent to Siberia. The stakes were high when you reached this level of play within Russian intelligence. She might as well enjoy what she could for the moment.

# 43

The Coca-Cola truck pulled around back to the service entrance at Circle 42. Munster got out, clipboard in hand, and headed for the kitchen entrance. Menza stayed behind with the engine off.

"Good afternoon. Can I speak to the manager, please?" asked Munster, who was dressed in a deliveryman's uniform, complete with red cap and striped shirt.

"*El gerente no está aquí*," said the teenager washing dishes.

Munster's Spanish was spotty, but he understood that the manager was not in.

"*Quien está a cargo?*" asked Munster.

The man pointed to a short Mexican flipping over a large chunk of salmon on the grill.

"Excuse me, please, but I need to take an inventory of your supplies."

The man glanced at Munster, then waved him through without saying a word.

Munster looked into the main seating area from the service window in the kitchen. The place was practically empty, which was not unusual for the middle of the afternoon. It was 2:25 p.m.

He headed to the cellar to count the cases of Coca-Cola products. The architectural drawings Munster had reviewed showed that the cellar ran underneath the entire seating area. There were only a couple of fluorescent work lights hanging from chains off the low ceiling. The place had a musty smell, and it was littered with boxes and supplies.

Munster pulled out a small square device that looked like an old Sony Walkman, plugged in his earpiece, and waited. At 2:32 p.m., Munster heard two pings. A lookout stationed a block away had just spotted Santos entering the restaurant. Another five minutes. One ping. Gordon was in.

Santos rose from the table. "So nice to see you again, Congressman." She looked fabulous in a Kate Spade dress with a bright floral design. The fabric clung to her perfect figure, which did nothing to disguise the fact that she was braless.

Gordon shook her hand and made eye contact. Her face was absorbing. The more you looked at it, the prettier it became. Her smile could cut through the bow of a Yankee-class attack sub.

After about five minutes of small talk, Menza walked into the kitchen. In fluent Spanish, he told the dishwasher that he had to run another errand and would be back for his friend shortly.

On his way to the truck, he tapped out a series of dashes and dots, which identified the location of Gordon's table. Munster moved underneath the spot and turned on his listening device. The sound was crystal clear.

The conversation dragged on for a while over politics, American history, and the bison meat loaf they both had ordered. As Munster's device was also able to record body temperatures, he could see Gordon's temperature increasing, together with his heart rate. He was definitely turned on.

"You know, Congressman, the Brazilian government is very anxious to step up its military cooperation with the United States. We think the navy could use deepwater access at Niterói, which is a natural launching pad to Southern Europe and West Africa. The sailors will love nearby Rio de Janeiro, with its culture and nightlife, not to mention the attractive young women."

"Why don't you call me Michael?" said Gordon. Unable to mask his strong attraction to her, he couldn't help but stare at the firm nipples protruding from Santos's dress.

Santos sensed his desire and decided to make her move. She slipped off her shoe and softly rubbed her foot against Gordon's inner calf.

"I have a cottage in Rio overlooking the beach. I'd love to show it to you if you had the time to come down. I've spoken directly with General Jose Rodriguez, President Rouseff's military advisor, and he would love to meet with you and discuss the potential for enhanced military cooperation."

Santos stared into Gordon's eyes, her foot still slowly rocking back and forth under the table, gently rubbing against Gordon's calf with each extension.

"How soon could you set up a meeting with Rodriguez?" asked Gordon.

"The general will be at a sporting event in Rio on Saturday the tenth. Why don't you come a few days earlier and I can show you around?"

"I'm looking forward to it."

The meal continued for another hour. The two grew progressively more comfortable as the conversation turned to their personal backgrounds. Santos stuck her fork into Gordon's plate, stabbing a piece of broccoli that he had pushed aside and putting it in her mouth. She told him about her strict father who refused to allow any child to leave the table until all the food had been eaten. Gordon recounted his childhood in Manhattan and his work in the Peace Corps.

Gordon's attraction to Santos deepened by the minute. Santos reached for Gordon's hand several times, entangling her fingers with his and then letting go. After dessert and cappuccino, the two finally got up to leave. It was 4:00 p.m.

Gordon edged up close to Santos and kissed her on the cheek. "Please call my office and set up the trip to Rio. I'll get in Thursday evening and stay until Sunday. That should give us some time to see the sights together."

"That would be wonderful."

Gordon headed up the block to a taxi stand, while Santos disappeared around the opposite corner. Two blocks from the restaurant, she climbed into a white Toyota Sienna, where Kochenko was already waiting for her in the backseat. Eshrova and a security man from the Washington embassy were up front.

No one spoke for the first hour on the drive back to DC. They stopped at several rest stops, spreading out in a sweep to see if anyone was following them. It was all clear. Finally, Santos spoke up.

"He's all in for the weekend of the tenth in Rio. We're going to need a cottage, where I invited him to stay as I show him around. We'll also need a meet and greet with Jose Rodriguez and a complete presentation on a proposed naval facility at Niterói."

"Shouldn't be a problem," said Kochenko. "Rodriguez has been on our payroll for over a decade, and we already have a workup of the proposed naval facility."

"I have just the cottage in mind," said Santos. "We'll be able to compromise him there."

The van finally pulled onto I-395 just outside the Capitol, and Eshrova asked to get out at the Amtrak station.

"Where are you going, Carla?" asked Santos. "Are there any trains running this late?"

"There's an eleven p.m. Acela back to New York. Told my father I would try to meet him before he went back home."

Eshrova collected her things and turned to grab the door handle, but Santos was already standing there with the door open. She walked Eshrova several steps toward the station and stopped. Grabbing her by both arms, Santos looked directly into Eshrova's eyes.

"This is a very sensitive operation. Normally, someone as junior as you wouldn't be in the same building as the operations team, let alone the same vehicle. If this gets too difficult, let me know, and I will take care of it."

Eshrova knew where this was heading. Santos had to demonstrate her macho credentials. It was like a pissing contest, but without the right genitalia.

"Why, thank you, Janaina. That's very sweet of you. But I'm completely ready for this."

"I hope you are," Santos said as she dug her nails into Eshrova's biceps.

"If you spoil this, I will shit on your grave, no matter who your daddy is."

Eshrova didn't back down. She moved a step closer to Santos, pushing her mouth within an inch of Santos's face.

"*Vete a la mierda*," said Eshrova. Then she wrenched herself from Santos's grip and marched for the station entrance.

Santos smiled as she climbed back into the SUV.

"What was that all about?" asked Kochenko.

"Oh, nothing really," said Santos. "I explained to little Carla that this wasn't a game that Daddy could clean up."

"Did she take to it?"

"She told me to fuck off."

# 44

Kochenko felt uneasy as he approached Shelby's walk-up apartment at 143rd Street and Amsterdam Avenue. It was a bevy of activity on this cool Sunday evening. A crack dealer was doing brisk business on one corner while three young black girls approached slowing cars offering cheap tricks. A group of heavily tattooed gang members congregated at the middle of the block, planning their next prank.

Kochenko had turned down backup, not wanting to risk tipping off Shelby. He still thought she had missed the bug he planted on her dumbphone. It was ten fifteen. He looked around for a while and didn't notice anyone out of place. He headed up to the third floor. Shelby answered the door and invited him in. Dressed in only a black satin bra and six-strap garter belt, she didn't have to explain the purpose of her invitation.

"Care for a drink?" Shelby asked as she turned toward the living room, the whitish-pink of her naked buttocks appearing to glow from the fluorescent light in the hallway.

Not much of a conversationalist, Kochenko declined the drink and followed Shelby.

Shelby pushed him down on the couch and sat on his lap while she gently slid off his pants. He leaned back on the couch and groaned several times. As he began throbbing, Shelby abruptly pulled away. She turned him around and pushed down on the small of his back. His ass rose up directly in Shelby's face, who was behind him in a crouched position, while his arms and head hung over the back of the couch.

She licked the small of his back and glided down his body with her mouth. Kochenko continued to moan, oblivious to the six-inch syringe Shelby had removed from under the couch. Shelby moved her tongue around Kochenko's anus thrusting it in and out. Then she carefully inserted the syringe and squeezed the plunger.

It took fifteen seconds for Kochenko to realize he'd been drugged, but it was too late. Shelby had injected him with a high dose of gamma hydroxybutyric acid. Kochenko slid back onto the couch and passed out.

Shelby retrieved another syringe, this one shorter and thicker than the first. She inserted it just below his left butt cheek, into the back of his thigh. The embedded beacon device was just one and a half millimeters in diameter and could be tracked for five hundred miles. It also contained an enhanced synthetic botulinal toxin. Unfortunately for Kochenko, there was no way to remove the device without releasing the poison. Kochenko was a dead man walking.

Shelby waited an hour, then placed a call on the landline. Minutes later, two large black guys arrived. Shelby gave them each a hundred-dollar bill and told them to dump Kochenko on a bench in St. Nicholas Park, just blocks away. They were bouncers at a local club Shelby attended. She told them she needed their help paying back an old lover who had burned her. They were happy to oblige.

Four hours later, Kochenko came to. It took him a few minutes to get his bearings. He felt his pockets; his wallet and cell phone were gone. He tried to stand, but his head pounded. There was a sizable lump just above his forehead—the finishing touch Shelby had delivered with the back of .32-caliber revolver.

Kochenko managed to sit up when a patrol car stopped.

"Are you OK, buddy?" asked the officer in the driver's seat.

Kochenko was wobbly but convinced the officer he was just sleeping off a hangover.

He walked a few blocks and managed to flag down a taxi.

Later that morning, he returned to the apartment at 143rd Street, carrying a mini-Uzi under his jacket. He knocked on the door, but there was no answer. He turned the knob and, surprisingly, found the door unlocked. The place looked different in the daylight. There were pictures of a handsome middle-aged black man with his wife and children lined up on the credenza behind the couch. Loose mail on the kitchen table was addressed to the Honorable Reverend John Black. The closet was full of men's suits and women's dresses. The reality of the situation hit Kochenko like a ton of bricks. Shelby had used someone else's apartment.

Kochenko was in a bind. He was already late with his report to Topkin, and he couldn't admit that Shelby had drugged him and tossed him on a park bench. His wallet had only ten dollars, and the cell phone was a prepaid from Boost Mobile that he had just purchased with cash. At least he hadn't compromised sensitive information.

Kochenko's message to Topkin from the Russian consulate on Ninety-First Street was terse.

"Picked the corn and tasted for flavor. Not suitable for gourmet production."

Topkin was surprised. He thought there would have been more to Shelby's contact. The response was swift.

"Try another sample."

Kochenko had no idea where to find Shelby. He had tried texting her, but the number he had previously used was now out of service. He could continue lying, but that would be found out soon enough. There was no choice but to stall for time. It was possible that Shelby had been victimized by someone else and was in trouble. He couldn't be sure. He had no memory of the events from when he was bent over the couch to when he woke up on a park bench.

Shelby slept in late that morning in her apartment in Jersey City. She held a small tracking device showing Kochenko in a fourth-story office in the Russian consulate. The plan had been executed flawlessly. No one in the vicinity of the apartment last night would be able to provide an accurate description of Shelby. She wore a black wig and heavy glasses wherever she went. Even the club bouncers knew her only as Cindy Rice.

After several hours, Kochenko left the embassy. He had to get back to Moscow to plan the Gordon recruitment in Rio. The tenderness from the injections, which would normally be very painful, had worn off by the time he got his bearings. Shelby really was very good.

Kochenko stepped out onto the street to hail a cab. To his left, he noticed a tall man in sunglasses approaching.

He turned away, not wanting to let on that he sensed a tail, but it didn't matter. The man walked up beside him as a silver BMW pulled up along the curb. The man was matter-of-fact.

"Get in, please, Comrade Kochenko." The man opened the door and gently pushed Kochenko from behind.

"You look like shit, Kochenko. What have you been up to?" Olga Yogislov smiled as Kochenko slid in.

"Oh, I had a late evening with a friend," Kochenko said softly.

"Well, enough with chasing women. We have a lot of work to do."

Kochenko was puzzled. It was unusual for an interior minister to make direct contact with a field agent. Contact was strictly limited to the operations team.

The car headed into Central Park, making its way downtown.

"You work directly for me now, Ivan," Yogislov said, looking out the car window. "You will still maintain your position with Topkin and pursue the Gordon mission. No one is to know about our contact. But I want direct reports on any developments concerning this weapon you are searching for."

"Understood," said Kochenko. "How will I contact you?"

"You won't. I'll find you."

The car came to a stop at Grand Central Station. Yogislov got out and headed for the Metro North train to Westport. There was an old female acquaintance there she wanted to visit. The car continued to the Lower East Side and dropped Kochenko off on Canal Street. He walked three blocks to his apartment. Still extremely fatigued from the doping, Kochenko headed inside and collapsed on his bed. He slept until the next morning, when he felt a tug at his sleeve. It was 7:00 a.m.

"What the hell is going on?" Santos said in an irritated voice. "We were supposed to meet last night. You don't show and don't communicate. I tried your cell, and I got some Chinese guy in the back of a dry cleaners in Queens."

Kochenko sat up and looked at Santos.

"What happened to your head?" she asked.

"It's a long story, nothing serious," Kochenko said, letting out a yawn. "I got mugged last night. They hit me from behind and grabbed my phone and wallet."

Santos's face contorted in a quizzical look. She doubted the story. Kochenko was a six-foot former Special Forces commando. It would take a lot of skill to surprise and subdue him. "Whatever," Santos said as she headed for the kitchen to put on a pot of coffee. Kochenko was a major in the FSB and her superior by rank. She had no right to interrogate him.

"So how'd it go with Shelby?" Santos asked, clasping her coffee mug with both hands.

"She didn't show."

"No shit. What happened?"

"I can't be sure. I got to her place, waited about a half hour, but no one answered and she wouldn't return any texts. The lights were off inside."

"She probably got called on an assignment," Santos said, relieved. She had an eye for Kochenko. "You know those horny bitches are never reliable."

"So how are you getting back to Moscow?" asked Kochenko.

"We're not," said Santos. "I would have told you last night had you shown up. Topkin has delegated operational authority to our team. As ranking officer, that means you. This is your baby, Ivan."

"So what's your plan?"

"We go out for dinner, hit a bar, then he comes over to my place, where I fuck his brains out on camera."

"And what if he refuses?"

Santos let out a sarcastic laugh. "Refuses what?"

"He refuses to go back to your apartment. He refuses to have sex. He passes out from the excitement. Then what?"

"No worries. This isn't my first time."

"Well, to be safe, we have to have eyes on him whenever he's close to you. Take him to the beach and sit next to him with your tits hanging out. Let's get enough so if you manage to get him between your legs, it will be icing on the cake."

"Understood," Santos said in a subdued tone. If Kochenko had personal feelings for her, he certainly wasn't showing any.

"We leave for Rio three days before zero hour," said Kochenko. "We'll meet again there. No contact until then. We can't let this leak."

Santos headed for the door. As she stepped out, she looked back at Kochenko, hoping for a friendly glance or wave. But he had already disappeared into another room.

Yogislov stuck out like a sore thumb among the commuters on the Metro North line. She made her way to the stately

Tudor in Westport, where she was welcomed by an elderly woman. They had tea and talked about old times.

Olga put down the teacup. "We're going to need your niece's help in Rio. I hope this doesn't put you in an awkward position."

The old woman smiled. "At my age, I don't even know what an awkward moment is anymore. I'll do my best."

Olga reached for the woman's hand. "I know you will."

# 45

I t was just after 8:00 p.m. on a warm Wednesday evening, and the pews at St. Catherine the Divine in Houston were empty. A new pastor had been dispatched from the archdiocese to replace Murphy, but he didn't have the presence and wherewithal of his predecessor. Attendance had dropped 50 percent, and for the first time in more than twenty-five years, the church had to close its soup kitchen from lack of funds.

Hans Lange stumbled into the church and made his way to the confessionals. Dressed in khakis and a blue shirt with a navy dinner jacket, Lange passed for one of the many downtrodden energy traders that frequented the neighborhood. He looked around casually. An elderly woman had just closed her prayer book and tucked her beads into her purse.

"Good night, sir," the woman said curtly as she brushed past Lange.

Lange had mixed views on religion. He had been raised in the Protestant Evangelical church, but in his later years, he gravitated to the Roman Catholic traditions. An engineer by trade, he stumbled into the espionage field when one of his supervisors at Daimler-Benz asked him to design a headlight that could explode on impact. Working with a demolition consultant, Lange engineered several proto-types. The final one gave off a tremendous forward shock wave that could obliterate an oncoming four-ton vehicle, while leaving its car intact. Ultimately, it was sold to the US Army for inclusion on VIP armored cars. During the aftermath of Operation Desert Storm, an army general was caught in an ambush outside the Green Zone. A Range Rover had blocked the only path out of a dead-end street, and the general's car was being raked by small-arms fire. The general's driver activated the headlight and drove straight ahead at high speed. The explosion lifted the Rover six feet in the air. When it landed, it was in eleven pieces, and the general was able to drive through to safety.

When he got back to Washington, the general, head of military intelligence, insisted on meeting the car's designer. The two hit it off, and Lange started his new life as a DoD contractor. He was sent to Fallujah to hunt and destroy al-Qaeda operatives and was quite successful. A slight man, standing at five feet four with a diminutive stature, Lange was a master of disguise and a champion marksman. Those two skills, together with his demolition expertise, produced dozens of daring missions behind enemy lines.

The development of accurate and more sophisticated drones lessened the need for Lange's services. There was no point in sending a guy behind enemy lines dressed as an Arab sheep merchant to kill a tribal leader when you could blow up the leader and fifty of his close friends with one five hundred-pound bomb from a drone. Lange tried R&D for a while but found it boring. Then he met Murphy.

The Colombian drug cartels were getting more brazen and exponentially more violent. Washington feared the country would fall into anarchy and destabilize its neighbors. Murphy had dispatched several kill teams to take out the leading drug family members. It was a messy business, as there was no etiquette among the Colombian criminals. If they caught an American, they beat the shit out of him for information and then murdered him in a sadistic and perverse way. Henry wasn't happy with his teams' progress. There weren't enough kills, and those that had been made didn't put a dent in the drug trade. He wanted something that would put the fear of Jesus back into these Colombian motherfuckers' hearts. He needed shock and awe.

Enter Hans Lange. He was ordered to build powerful bombs that would leave substantial collateral damage. But the explosives had to be compact so agents could carry enough with them out in the field to get the mission done. Lange developed compact explosives that had enormous firepower. Murphy was impressed and introduced Lange to the work of the committee. Lange ultimately became close personal friends with Murphy. When Murphy died, Lange wanted out of government service, but no one would accept his letter of resignation. He moved to Basel, Switzerland, and remained on the payroll doing assorted contract work, mostly assassinations.

The confessional had a dim light. After checking that the other two were empty, Lange slipped into the cramped phone booth–like wooden box and closed the door. A narrow slide opened.

"Forgive me, Father, for I have sinned," said Lange.

"'For the living know that they shall die: but the dead know not anything, neither have they any more a reward; for the memory of them is forgotten.'" Seaver was reading a passage from Ecclesiastes that Murphy often used in his sermons.

"I am prepared for that day," said Lange.

"Gordon gets to Rio on the evening of the eighth. Santos has a cottage in the Vila Do Ambro section, just off Grande Street, number sixteen. We think Santos plans on seducing him there on the ninth after an evening out." Seaver's voice was barely audible.

"How many shadows?" asked Lange.

"We expect Kochenko and Eshrova. There might be a tech team as well."

"Our side?"

"Just you, my old friend. The heat is building. There's a *New York Times* reporter asking lots of questions about Gordon's campaign. So far, no one's said much, but it won't last.

"There's a package underneath your seat. It's the only prototype. Range is fifty yards, line of sight. Protocol has been entered. All you do is get close and push the button."

"Any prisoners?" asked Lange.

"No," Seaver said as he closed the panel.

Lange crossed himself and slowly stepped out of the booth. The box contained what looked like a small, thin recording device. But inside was a weapon that would kill without leaving any trace. He gently placed the device in his jacket pocket and strolled out into the warm night air. He marveled at how different the world had become. Once, it was the secure feeling from the grasp of cold steel of an automatic pistol. Now, all he felt against his chest were the contours of a miniature device that killed silently with the push of a button. Lange wasn't even sure you could call it murder anymore.

# 46

It was a chilly Sunday in March as Gordon and the kids pulled up to the Short Hills Mall. Daniel headed for J. Crew to pick up the necessary look for upcoming spring break. Ryan was anxious to get to the Apple store to check out the newest iPad, while Gordon was going to the sale at Brooks Brothers. Stella hoped to get a few minutes in Bloomingdale's.

After two hours, they all settled in the food court and ordered from California Pizza Kitchen.

Stella watched as the kids wolfed down their pizzas and milk shakes. Gordon was in the thick of it, enjoying the downtime and connecting with his two sons.

"Isn't this wonderful, Michael?" Stella said as she took his hand. "We don't need lavish vacations and fancy gadgets to enjoy family. It's spending time together that matters."

Stella looked into Michael's eyes, but she could sense a distance between them. They hadn't had sex in weeks, and he was spending more time than usual away in Washington. She didn't think he had another woman, but wasn't sure. In any case, she had reached the tipping point.

"Michael, do you think we'll get married one day?"

Almost choking on his pizza, Gordon glanced at the boys to see if they'd overheard. Luckily, they were engrossed in heated debate about the prospects of Duke making the Final Four.

"Now's not the time or place," Gordon said, his voice tense and agitated.

Stella read the signs well. Gordon didn't want to deal with it. But Stella knew better. A couple either progressed in a relationship or it declined. There was no standing still.

"OK if we go to the arcade, Mom—I mean, Stella?" said Ryan.

"Sure, darling."

"When did he start calling you Mom?" asked Gordon.

"He does it now and then. It makes him feel more normal."

"Well, I think I'm going to head over to Lacoste. Maybe I can find something for my trip to Rio de Janeiro this week."

"Rio?" asked Stella. "You never mentioned that before."

"Yeah, it's a business trip to see some military leaders down there about a naval base. It's being arranged by this lobbyist from Washington."

"So you guys are going to the beach by yourselves?" asked Stella, who found it unusual that Gordon would wait until the last minute to tell her about a foreign trip.

"Well, not exactly. The lobbyist is a woman from Brazil who said she would show me around town a bit. Nothing to worry about, dear. She's no competition for you."

Sensing the deceit in his voice, Stella tugged on Gordon's shirt as he stood to get up. "Don't go yet."

Gordon sat back down, annoyed at being told what to do.

"How important is your congressional career, Michael?"

"It's everything to me, you know that."

"So you wouldn't want it coming apart by scandal or indiscretion."

"Of course not. What are you talking about?" Gordon was getting worried. Stella had never talked this way before.

"You see, I have the ability to end your career. It's not a threat, just a fact. There are things I know that you don't. So you need to decide, Michael. Do you want your career?"

Gordon was shaken up. Stella looked as if she were possessed. Her eyes stared blankly ahead while she talked in a steely and detached tone utterly void of emotion or inflection.

"Look, I don't think making threats is a way to approach marriage. I'm just not ready yet. I'm still getting over Emily's death and—"

"What if I told you that Emily was murdered?"

Gordon banged his hand on the table. "What? You're crazy, Stella. You're talking crazy. Maybe we ought to go home, where you can lie down. I think you're having some kind of breakdown."

This was the last thing Gordon needed. Things were going well politically, and he was looking forward to his trip with Santos. Now he might have to cancel if he had to check Stella into a psych ward.

But Stella was far from crazy. At her father's request, she had broken her sacred vows to give her virginity to Gordon. He explained that she was serving God by acting for her country. On that fateful night, she swore that she would never give herself to another man. Her devotion to Gordon wasn't simply for love or companionship. It took on the characteristics of blind faith, with the zealotry and sacrifice only religion can inspire.

Stella was hardly a shrinking violet despite her genteel personality. She was full of ambition, although she resigned to see that ambition fulfilled through others. She was fine with living vicariously through Gordon's accomplishments. But if he wouldn't commit to her, she would have to satisfy that ambition another way.

"I'm fine, Michael," Stella said, smiling at Gordon. "This isn't about my mental health. It's about us. I need to know whether we are going to be together forever."

Michael moved his chair back and away from Stella. His face betrayed an underlying disgust for her aggressive approach. Stella got the message.

"To be honest, I don't know, Stella. I just don't know. Call me when you're done. I'm heading over to the Nike store."

Stella watched as Michael faded into the crowd.

Her father had guided her on what to do next. It was last November, just after Thanksgiving. She had gone to Westport, Connecticut, to visit her aunt. Susan Wall was Murphy's only sibling. Married to a successful cardiologist, she raised two children and spent her days attending social clubs and volunteering for local charitable causes. Henry was close to Susan and made a point of visiting every year.

Susan, however, was a Russian sleeper agent, recruited by Yogislov while on vacation in Budapest to visit her family's old neighborhood.

It was Friday evening in the library. Henry had asked Stella to stay up for a while and sit with him by the fireplace. He told her of his illness and, for the first time, his work on the committee. They talked for hours. Stella cried for a while, but Murphy consoled her. He explained that he was going to a better place and was anxious to see his father again.

"Remember all the things I taught you, Stella. You may be called upon to act. Don't hesitate. Then all your sacrifices will be glorified in the eyes of the Lord."

The rest of the afternoon in the mall was uneventful. Stella prepared dinner and helped Michael pack for his trip. Gordon thought the episode was behind him, but he felt more anxious about leading on Stella. He would have to tell her the truth after his trip. He had no intention of marrying her.

"Where will you be staying, Michael?"

"Oh, we haven't firmed up a place yet, probably a hotel in town. The ones along the beach are too pricey for a congressional expense account."

Stella knew this was a lie. The Capitol Police and the State Department had to approve all foreign travel of congressional members. Hotels would be booked far in advance, with security provided, if necessary.

Stella kissed Michael good night and went downstairs. She said she wanted tea for a cold she felt coming on. She climbed up on a kitchen stool and reached for a wide flowerpot on top of the cabinets. She removed a heavy object wrapped in a blue cloth. Stella examined the Luger, checking the trigger mechanism. It was Murphy's gun, the one he had taken off a dead Nazi on a partisan raid two generations ago. The cold steel felt good in her hands. She put the barrel up to her eye and stared into the narrow blackness. It was the picture of death.

# 47

The atmosphere at Fosobox on Rua Siquera was electric. Looking down from the upper-level bar to the young mixed crowd of tourists and locals dancing furiously to the beat of the heavy metal music, Gordon couldn't help but wonder how long it had been. The last time he was at a hip nightclub, he had been in college. Back then, it was tight jeans, cropped short hair, and women wearing slinky tops. Now it was heavy tattoos, thongs, and sex anywhere, anytime.

He spent the day taking in the sights with Santos. It started with a morning tour of downtown, then lunch in an open-air café, and on to the cable cars for a ride to Sugarloaf Mountain and its breathtaking panoramic views. He had checked in to the Copacabana Marriott but was looking forward to the possibility of a nightcap at Santos's cottage by the beach.

"Dance?" Santos asked with a smile. She had opened a few more buttons of her red blouse, shamelessly exposing her bra. There was sweat on her face and chest, which made her skin glisten against the light.

Gordon took off his sport jacket and rolled up his sleeves. "Let's do it," he said in an awkward tone. He hadn't courted a woman in a long time. With Stella, it was different. She had pursued him. Santos was another breed. She knew how to make a man want her, and Gordon had bitten down hard on the bait.

The club had a simple feel. Metal beams held up a tin roof surrounded by bare drywall painted black and sky blue. Mirrored globes circled slowly overhead, splashing rays of light in all directions. The hardwood floor moved slightly with the undulation of the dancers.

Santos's body swayed like creamy chocolate. Her hips and long arms shook in opposite directions as she closed her eyes and became one with the music. Gordon did his best to move about in some organized manner, but he didn't have much. A step to the side, two steps forward, then back, tucking his arms at his sides at a ninety-degree angle and twisting his wrists. His eyes were glued on Santos. Her movements revealed not just an amazing body but also a feminine allure that filled the admirer's mind and wreaked havoc on the libido.

Kochenko and Eshrova had blended in perfectly. Eshrova's long blond hair appeared to sprout from a Stetson hat that covered most of her head. Her low-cut jeans and crop top revealed a toned abdomen and pierced naval. She moved well with the music, as did Kochenko, whose red bandana harbored a sophisticated camera that silently took eleven frames per second. From his vantage point several feet away, Kochenko got good close-ups of Santos and Gordon as they embraced for the slow dance that had just come on.

Santos placed her right hand on Gordon's back and pulled him against her body, placing her lips against his, only to pull back when he appeared to capitulate. Gordon blushed when his erection grazed Santos's crotch, his heart racing. He slipped his hand inside the back of Santos's skirt and gripped the hard muscles of her bare buttocks. She groaned as he squeezed, then let go and rubbed softly. Gordon was young again, feeling his body in a way he had long forgotten. He was her prisoner.

Kochenko had moved off to the side to adjust his bandana when he noticed a glint of red from the corner of his eye. On the other side of the floor, a woman with a red ponytail was dancing effortlessly with a black businessman in gray slacks and a black silk shirt. Shelby looked right at Kochenko, then averted her gaze, focusing on her dance partner. She had tracked him to Kennedy Airport three days earlier, only to lose the beacon. It took just minutes to find his flight in the Homeland Security database. It wasn't about getting even. It was about messing with his brain before she watched him die.

Kochenko motioned to Eshrova, who was still on the dance floor.

He pushed his body up against hers and turned her around to face Shelby. "See that redhead dancing with the black guy near the DJ?" Kochenko whispered in Eshrova's ear.

Eshrova looked but didn't see any redhead. "No," she said.

Kochenko let go of Eshrova and turned around, but there was nothing. He scanned the crowd for several more minutes. Shelby was gone.

Kochenko had started making his way to the exit when Santos approached.

"We're going to my place. You'd better leave now and take the back roads so you get there before me."

"That won't be necessary. I've got enough footage, and your place is set up with electronic eyes at every angle. No need to risk detection."

Santos wanted to protest the sudden change in plans. Kochenko was supposed to be at the cottage to back up the stationary cameras with his own shots. But before she could get the words out, Kochenko had left the club. He was obsessed with finding Shelby.

Santos leaned on Gordon's shoulder in the cab, and the two held hands for the twenty-minute ride to her cottage. The three-bedroom, two-story home was shielded behind six-foot-tall solid metal fencing that kept out the realities of the overcrowded neighborhood that stretched inland from the beach. Gordon helped Santos pull back the heavy gate at the entrance and marveled at the fifty-foot pool to the side of the main door. It was hot and humid, even at midnight, and the water looked tempting.

"Why don't you sit by the pool, Michael? I'll be right out."

Gordon looked around. There was only a dim glow around the pool area, but the underwater spotlights lit up the deep-blue water. Gordon relaxed on a lounge chair, looking up at the dazzling night sky.

Santos emerged from the house barefoot, in a long-sleeve chiffon coverup. Gordon followed the contour of her legs to the bulges of her pronounced hips. Her curves were mesmerizing. She walked to the diving board and crossed her hands in front of her chest, reaching for her waist. The coverup slowly came off, and Santos's full figure was finally on display. Gordon's heart skipped a beat.

Santos dove into the water and swam to the edge of the pool where Gordon was standing. She didn't have to say a word. Her large eyes staring up at him were all Gordon needed. He quickly undressed and jumped in to join her. The two embraced along the far wall of the pool. Santos wrapped her legs around Gordon's waist as the two passionately kissed. His mouth slowly explored her neck and chest, then fastened to her hard nipples.

Santos threw her head back and enjoyed the sensation. Gordon moved up to again kiss her lips. But Santos suddenly pulled back. She had seen something in the second-floor window overlooking the pool. It was a man pointing a small, thin electronic device. There was a red dot flashing at its tip. She shuddered, not recognizing the angular white face peering out of her bedroom.

She tried to untangle herself from Gordon, but he had her in a bear hug. She could feel his entire body shake, first slowly and then violently. It was if a large electric shock had hit him. His breath became shallow, and he coughed uncontrollably.

"Michael, what's wrong?"

There was no answer. Gordon's grip loosened around Santos's shoulders, and he fell backward into the water. His eyes froze open in an empty gaze as he slowly sunk to the bottom of the pool.

Santos stared at his lifeless body in disbelief. She had no idea how he could have died so suddenly. She started for the pool ladder, but then froze at the sound of a loud pop echoing from the house.

The man in the window fell forward, his contorted face pressing against the glass. A streak of blood trickled from his nose.

Santos got out of the water and hurried for her front door. She was just steps away when the door flung open. A tall red-haired woman appeared, wearing sunglasses, a blue jacket, and a white silk scarf. She shot at point-blank range.

Santos fell backward onto the ground. The 9 mm Parabellum hollow point had entered her left eye and exploded into her temporal lobe. All that was left from the side of her face were bone fragments.

The tall woman calmly walked out the front gate and down the street toward the crowded low-income cottages.

Minutes later, Kochenko arrived at the house. He peered into the courtyard and saw Santos's lifeless naked body sprawled on the ground. He made his way into the house and found the dead man on the second floor. He searched his pockets and the surrounding area. But the man had nothing on him except some cash and several keys.

Kochenko looked out the window and into the pool. He could see a large figure at the bottom. Using a skimming pole, he managed to drag Gordon's body to the shallow end. He recognized the face.

He ran down the street, but it was dark and deserted. Whoever had done this had gotten away. On his way back to his car, he noticed something along the gate of Santos's house. It looked like a furry animal. Kochenko pulled out his revolver and lifted up the hairy mass with its barrel. It was a red wig.

# 48

The two were shoulder deep in the Black Sea, riding the relatively calm surf. It was mild for this time of year, and the summer tourists were beginning to crowd the shops and bars. Far in the distance, the loyal maid stood ready with towels and robes.

"That was quite a mess in Rio," said Borodin. "Did you locate the woman?"

"Yes, I met with her at her aunt's house in Westport, Connecticut, before the operation," said Yogislov. "She's the daughter of a former high-ranking CIA officer who recently died. I briefed her on the mission and got her into Rio. She was supposed to bring back the weapon."

"And?"

"She gave us a small device that we're still analyzing. It appears to be some type of experimental laser that was inoperable."

"Did it kill Gordon?"

"We don't think so. The Americans picked up his body, and the story they fed to the press is that he died of natural causes—a heart attack. The Rio authorities were denied access to the body, which the Americans flew out within a day."

"You are suspect?"

"Well, it's possible. Santos was exceptionally beautiful, and Gordon had a few drinks at the club. But he was only in his forties and seemed fit. It's odd that he would collapse in a calm setting after a pleasant evening of dancing."

Borodin squeezed his nostrils and blew a string of snot into the sea. "These Americans are weak shits. He probably overdosed on Viagra."

"Who was the dead guy on the second floor?"

Yogislov shook her head. "We don't know. He had no identification, and his fingerprints were burned off. They buried him in a potter's field just outside Rio."

"What does Topkin's lapdog Kochenko say?"

"Not much. Topkin had him suspended for screwing up the mission. Two agents were knocking at his apartment door to bring him into custody when they heard a loud shot. After prying the door open, they found him with his brains blown out."

Seaver took off the headphones and motioned to the officer in front of the computer screen. "You can call off the satellite feed now. Those two are headed back to shore."

The NAVSTAT III pivoted away from its focus on the Black Sea. Seaver took Shelby's arm and led her to Room 4D in the Brooklyn Office.

"So it appears that our Russian friends think they have something," said Shelby.

"Nah, my guess is they'll figure out that this isn't the weapon they were looking for," said Seaver. "The Russians have their own advanced laser. But at least no one will guess that we pulled the trigger on Gordon from here."

Shelby poured herself some coffee. "What are we going to do with Stella Murphy?"

"We'll keep an eye on her," said Seaver. "Now that she's gained the Russians' confidence, we may want her back on our side. Henry spent a lot of time training her, and she has good instincts. Surprised she was able to pull off the Rio hit on such short notice and with such precision."

Shelby placed both hands on the warm coffee mug. "Too bad about Lange. He was good at his job."

Seaver shook his head. "Hans was too unpredictable. Without Henry, he was a lost soul, and it was only a matter of time before he became a problem. The Germans are hard to predict. At first, they seem cooperative and helpful, and the next thing you know, they've got a gun to your head and to your kid's head. That's why I couldn't trust him with a BITR prototype."

"Seems a fitting end," said Shelby. "I wonder if he realized that he was shot by Stella with Henry's Luger."

"We'll never know," said Seaver.

"So what now?"

"You take some time off." Seaver passed her a package stuffed with cash, passports, and a plane ticket to Dubai.

"Dubai? You're kidding. What the hell I am I supposed to do there?"

"That's the point, my dear."

THE END

# AUTHOR BIOGRAPHY

**H**oward Kleinhendler is a lawyer whose esteemed twenty-year career at his New York practice has spanned cases from civil disputes to securities fraud to white collar crime.

Having made numerous appearances over the years on CBS News, Fox Business News, and Bloomberg Television regarding his legal expertise, Kleinhendler also served as the 2010 Democratic Nominee for Congress in New Jersey's fourth congressional district.

Kleinhendler currently lives with his wife in New Jersey. They have five children.

Made in the USA
Charleston, SC
17 March 2015